The Encyclopedia of
Canadian Organized Crime

The Encyclopedia of Canadian Organized Crime

From Captain Kidd to Mom Boucher

Peter Edwards and Michel Auger

M&S

Library and Archives Canada Cataloguing in Publication
Edwards, Peter, 1956 –
    The encyclopedia of Canadian organized crime : from Captain Kidd to Mom Boucher / Peter Edwards and Michel Auger.

ISBN 0-7710-3044-4

    1. Organized crime–Canada–Encyclopedias. I. Auger, Michel, 1944- II. Title.

HV6453.C3E39 2004   364.1'06'0971   C2004-903767-6

We acknowledge the financial support of the Government of Canada through the Book Publishing Industry Development Program and that of the Government of Ontario through the Ontario Media Development Corporation's Ontario Book Initiative. We further acknowledge the support of the Canada Council for the Arts and the Ontario Arts Council for our publishing program.

Typeset in Minion by M&S, Toronto
Printed and bound in Canada

This book is printed on 50% post-consumer waste recycled paper.

McClelland & Stewart Ltd.
The Canadian Publishers
481 University Avenue
Toronto, Ontario
M5G 2E9
www.mcclelland.com

1 2 3 4 5   08 07 06 05 04

To Barbara, Sarah, and James; and Winona and Ken Edwards, with love
— PETER EDWARDS

To my daughter Guylaine, for your understanding
— MICHEL AUGER

——————●——————

"What is the Mafia?"
— Montreal godfather Vincenzo "Vic the Egg" Cotroni

ACKNOWLEDGEMENTS

We would like to thank our agent, Daphne Hart of the Helen Heller Agency, for her cheerful professionalism, editor Pat Kennedy for her care and patience, copy editor Heather Sangster for her attention to detail, and Paul Cherry for fact-checking support. Peter Edwards would also like to thank Pauline and Amund Hanson for helping him explore the tunnels of Moose Jaw and the south Saskatchewan caves of The Sundance Kid and other outlaws.

INTRODUCTION

Organized crime is a slippery subject, involving slippery people, and evades an exact definition. In drawing up this list of organized criminals and groups, we have been strongly influenced by new anti-gang laws, which define a criminal organization as a group of three or more people whose main activities include committing crimes for some benefit. We realize that sometimes there's a fine line between terrorism and organized crime, as with the attacks by the Hells Angels on the justice system in Quebec in the late 1990s and early 2000s. Other times, criminals are clearly habitual offenders, but it's a generous stretch to call them organized. For the purposes of this book, we have largely focused on criminal activities in which profit was the main motive, as opposed to passion, perversion, mental illness, or politics. We were also interested in criminal activity that was ongoing and which involved planning. Finally, we looked for some specific code of conduct: one existed on the pirate ships of Peter Easton in the early seventeenth century and they can still be found today amongst modern-day biker gangs and Mafia groups.

Also, it should be clear that this is a book about crime and criminals, not ethnic groups. There's diversity in crime as well as in mainstream Canadian life, and organized criminals make up just a minuscule fraction of any ethnic group mentioned here. For instance, crime analysts have estimated that 0.02 per cent of the Italian-heritage community is involved in Mafia activity in Canada.

We often wondered, Why do some criminals enjoy longevity, while others don't? One common thread shared by the successful organized criminals described in these pages is a vital link to transportation routes. To be effective for any length of time, groups have to be able to move goods and people, whether they're taking illegal drugs to market or moving themselves – speedily – out of harm's way. Such access to transportation routes was standard amongst the seventeenth-century pirates of the Atlantic coast, the coureurs de bois of pre-Confederation, the bootlegging gangs that followed crews building the Canadian Pacific Railway, criminals like the Sundance Kid on the Outlaw Trail of southern Saskatchewan at the turn of the twentieth century, the bootleggers of Prohibition, and, today, the cocaine cartels and the Hells Angels, with their acute interest in the shipping ports of Vancouver, Montreal, and Halifax.

But perhaps the most important central thread connecting the groups described in these pages is control of officials – either through corruption or intimidation. They all need to compromise officials in ostensibly legitimate jobs in order to function for any length of time. This was as true in the days of the early seventeenth-century pirates as it is today. Harry Longabaugh (The Sundance Kid) and his associates benefited from the assistance of a corrupt former North-West Mounted Police officer, who helped them hide out in the gullies around Big Beaver in southern Saskatchewan. Montreal mobsters Vincenzo "Vic the Egg" Cotroni and Willie Obront were called "The Untouchables" by crusading police officer Pacifique "Pax" Plante because of their excellent political connections. Maurice "Mom" Boucher of the Hells Angels took a far more brutal route to attain the same ends, using murder and the threat of violence to try to intimidate members of the judicial, legislative, and journalistic communities.

In a sense, the major criminals described in these pages weren't really "outlaws" at all, since they needed a strong, ongoing connection to the legitimate world to survive, much like a leech or a parasite is dependent upon its host. Many tried to use their loot to buy respectability and a place in the legitimate world, and more than a few succeeded. Eric Cobham, a particularly vicious sea dog who prowled Canada's Atlantic coast in the seventeenth century, purchased a title in the French gentry and became a magistrate, while fellow pirates Peter "The Pirate Admiral" Easton and Henry Mainwaring each bought pardons, retiring in luxury with the titles of marquis and knight, respectively. While Captain Kidd was immeasurably less violent, and didn't even consider himself a criminal, his life ended on the gallows, as he had fallen from grace in political circles.

Organized crime is nothing new in Canada, and it was thriving 250 years before Confederation. It fuelled the adventures of fur-trading pioneers like Pierre-Esprit Radisson and Sieur des Groseilliers, known to Canadian schoolchildren as "Radishes and Gooseberries," and the much-romanticized coureurs de bois, who operated outside the law in New France for a century before their fur-trading operation was finally made legal in 1700. The money they generated supported legitimate businesses and, in effect, propped up the economy of the early colony.

Organized crime is also present when you look at such Canadian institutions as the Hudson's Bay Company and the Canadian Pacific Railway. Indeed, bootleggers seized control of the entire town of Michipicoten, a former Hudson's Bay Company post on the north shore of Lake Superior in the fall of 1884, using it as their headquarters for selling booze to men working on the railway. Such activities brought to mind the saying "Steal a dollar and they throw you in jail. Steal a million and they make you king."

Even the Hells Angels biker gang isn't comfortable with a totally outlaw image. They obviously crave a certain legitimacy, which explains the controversial public handshake between a biker and former Toronto mayor Mel Lastman in January 2002; Maurice "Mom" Boucher posing for a photo with an unwitting Quebec Premier Robert Bourassa; or a group of Angels posing for photos with Montreal Canadiens' goalie Jose Theodore or with Pat Burns, back when Burns coached the Toronto Maple Leafs of the National Hockey League. At times, the Angels' actions look like a sad effort to push themselves into "respectable" society.

While we've drawn up a fairly long list in this overview of names in Canadian organized crime, we don't pretend it's complete. Some readers may wonder how Woody the Biker Lion or Pearl Hart made the list and others didn't. We admit that a few entries appear here more for quirkiness than for their organizational skills. In general, however, we were biased toward highly structured groups, which explains why there's more on the Hells Angels and the Mafia than the more loosely-knit Jamaican posses and Vietnamese street gangs. Barring a sudden change in human nature, there will undoubtedly be plenty more additions for future editions.

Acapulco Conference: Southern Summit – Gambling was the topic when Meyer Lansky, the top money-mover of the American Mob, chaired a meeting in Acapulco in February 1970. Among those present were mobsters from Montreal, Toronto, and Hamilton, including Vic and Frank "Santos" Cotroni and Paolo Violi. Attendees wanted to know how to cash in on casinos, which were soon to be legalized by the Quebec government.

The criminals met several times at the villa of former Montrealer Leo Bercovitch, a millionaire who'd made his fortune in various legal and illegal businesses in Canada before settling permanently in Mexico. Accompanying them at restaurants and on the beach was Montreal criminal lawyer Raymond Daoust. At first,

Meyer Lansky poolside in Acapulco

Daoust vigorously denied his attendance, until photos surfaced that showed him sunning himself with the gangsters on the beach.

See also: **Frank "Santos" Cotroni, Vincenzo "Vic the Egg" Cotroni, Paolo Violi.**

Frank "Santos" Cotroni (far left) and Raymond Daoust (far right) in Acapulco

Agueci, Alberto: Horrific Example – Agueci is best remembered as a chilling example of why you shouldn't threaten a Mafia don.

Immediately after he immigrated from Salemi, Sicily, in the early 1950s, Agueci worked as a road labourer in Windsor, Ontario. However, it wasn't long before he graduated to being part owner of a Toronto bakery, and he was considered a threatening presence in Toronto gambling clubs.

When not baking or gambling, he was often in New York, meeting mobsters and plotting how to move drugs. In the late 1950s, he met up with Joe "Cago" Valachi at Maggie's Bar on Lexington Avenue in New York City, when Valachi was on the run from American authorities for narcotics dealing. Valachi instantly and rightly assumed that Agueci was under the wing of Buffalo don Stefano Magaddino. "He is with Steve Magaddino as Steve's family takes in Toronto and Montreal," Valachi recalled in his memoirs, *The Valachi Papers*. Soon, Agueci was helping his new associate, Valachi, hide out in Toronto.

In March 1960, a lieutenant in the Magaddino family approached Agueci and asked him to run large quantities of heroin from his birthplace,

Vito Agueci

Salemi, to the United States through Toronto. A month later, Magaddino himself reputedly gave Agueci the go-ahead and assured him that he would look out for him, should any member of La Cosa Nostra, the American Mob, try to interfere. "Go ahead with this narcotics business, but be very careful who you trust in your organization" was the way Magaddino put it, according to Agueci's brother Vito.

Under the direction of his brother Alberto, Vito Agueci went to Sicily to buy fifteen kilograms of heroin at $3,300 a kilogram. By September 1960, Vito had made four trips to Sicily, buying a total of forty-five kilograms. Also that month, Magaddino fulfilled his promise of guarding Agueci's new turf, punishing an interloper by refusing him payment of $100,000 for five kilograms of heroin that the man handed over to Magaddino. In doing so, Magaddino self-righteously lived up to his promise, and robbed the man at the same time.

It was around this time, Vito Agueci later told federal narcotics agents in New York City, that Alberto became a full member of La Cosa

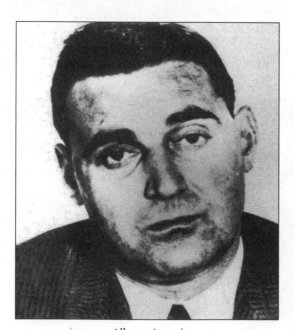

Alberto Agueci

Nostra. As Vito reported, in a meeting at the Fort Erie, Ontario, racetrack, a Buffalo mobster explained the organization's code "about not talking, leaving other members' wives alone, always operating in secret, and taking orders as they come."

Shortly afterwards, Hamilton mobster "Johnny Pops" Papalia, an Agueci associate, vanished after his near-fatal beating of gambler Max Bluestein at the Town Tavern in Toronto, a block east of where the Eaton Centre now stands. The attack brought enormous publicity and police attention to the underworld, with *Toronto Star* columnist Pierre Berton leading the charge.

In order to take the heat off the Mob, Alberto Agueci reportedly ordered Papalia to surrender. However, police had already learned a lot of damaging information about Papalia's operations in Guelph, Windsor, Hamilton, and Toronto. They found that he was involved in counterfeiting, and were particularly curious to learn that numerous Italian Canadians had made return trips to Italy at Agueci's expense.

Soon, Italian police, the French Sûreté, the RCMP, and American investigators joined forces in the case, which wove in with work done internationally on the famed French Connection pipeline of heroin through Marseilles into New York City.

Alberto and Vito were charged as two Canadian connections, along with Papalia, Rocco Scopelliti, also of Toronto, and eight Americans, including Agueci's old friend Joe Valachi. "The first thing Albert says to me is, 'Joe, I'm sorry you got involved in this,'" Valachi recalled. In his memoirs, *The Valachi Papers*, Valachi described how Alberto Agueci simply couldn't handle life behind bars, and quickly turned against his boss, Magaddino, who made no effort to help out with his legal fees.

"I tried to help him, but some guys just can't take being in the can, and I could see right away Albert Agueci wasn't going to last long," Valachi remembered. "All he talked about was getting out on bail. He kept telling me his wife was raising the money to get him out and how he was going to declare himself [inform] if Steve Magaddino didn't get his brother out too,

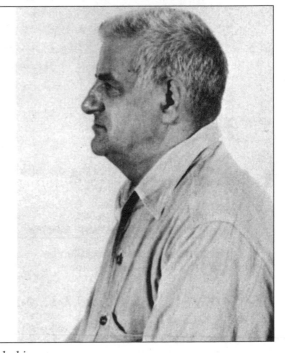

Joe Valachi

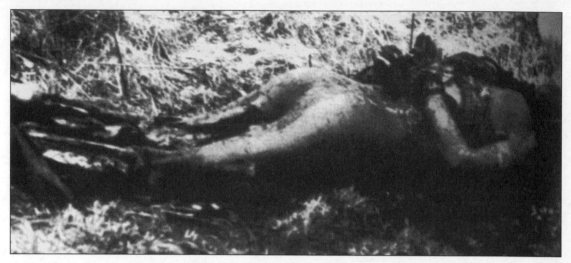

Alberto Agueci's mutilated body was found in a field

meaning he would tell everybody that Steve, his boss, was in on the deal, which he was."

Such talk of informing was suicidal, and Valachi said he warned Agueci about "sending out too many messages," as this would only draw Magaddino's wrath. "But Albert is stubborn," Valachi said.

Agueci again demanded Magaddino's aid in raising his $20,000 bail, and Magaddino, annoyed at his impertinence, again refused.

In order to raise bail money, Agueci's wife, Vita, was forced to sell the family bungalow on Armitage Avenue in Scarborough, Ontario, at a loss and borrow from friends. Then she and their two children moved into a cramped two-room flat in downtown Toronto with friends.

Once freed, Agueci immediately jumped bail on October 8, 1961, hired a taxi, and drove from New York City to Lewiston, New York, where he confronted Magaddino in person with a demand for aid. Again, the Buffalo boss refused.

Police suspected something particularly ugly was going to happen when a wiretap in Buffalo picked up two Magaddino soldiers joyfully talking of taking Agueci to a place called "Mary's farm" to work him over.

"Well, it ain't but a couple of weeks and we hear on the radio that they found Albert's body in some field," Valachi recalled. "He was burned

up. They got a print off a finger and that's how they identified him."

Agueci's death was a horrific one, as some thirty pounds of flesh were carved from his legs before he died. Tortured for three days until he was mercifully strangled, his death sent out an unforgettable message to others in the under-world: You don't threaten the boss.

See also: **Max Bluestein, Stefano Magaddino, French Connection, John "Johnny Pops" Papalia, Joe "Cago" Valachi.**

AK Kannan: Homegrown Street Gang – The AK Kannan street gang was started in Toronto in 1992 by Jothiravi Sittampalam, shortly after he arrived in Canada from Sri Lanka. His street name is Kannan, meaning "god." He survived at least two ambushes on his car, once when he was leaving a Brampton courthouse.

Police believe the AK Kannan and rival VVT gangs have close ties to terrorist groups such as the Tamil Tigers and their Sri Lankan rivals, the People's Liberation Organization of Tamil Eelam.

In Toronto, gang members often hang out at all-night doughnut shops as they battle for more control of the drug trade and extortion and robbery money.

Police in Vancouver say gang members are involved in robberies, weapons offences, assault,

and extortion, while Montreal gang members have been active in home invasion, drug trafficking, and document forgery.
See also: VVT.

Alberti, Michele – *See* **Girolomo Commisso.**

The Alliance: Unholy Union – This union of independent drug traffickers, Montreal bar owners, and members of the Rock Machine motorcycle gang was forged in 1995 to fight off the Hells Angels, who were trying to muscle into the city's downtown drug trade. They often wore rings with ALVALM – for the Alliance motto *À la vie, à la mort,* which roughly translates as "In life and in death."
See also: **Giovanni Cazzetta, Dark Circle, Hells Angels, Nomads, Rock Machine.**

Amodeo, Gaetano – *See* **Nicolo "Nick" Rizzuto, Gerlando Sciascia.**

Anti-Gang Legislation: Gangs Banged – Tough new laws to target mobsters were passed by Parliament in 2001, as the biker wars in Quebec between the Hells Angels and Rock Machine stirred up public pressure for police to be given more teeth to fight organized crime.

Under the anti-gang laws, it's a crime to commit a serious offence for the benefit of, at "the direction of," or "in association" with a criminal organization. The law defines a criminal organization as a group of three or more people whose main activities include committing crimes for some benefit.

The anti-gang law survived its first legal challenge in February 2004 when Madam Justice Michelle Fuerst of the Ontario Superior Court of Justice ruled that the law isn't vague or overly broad. She made her ruling while dismissing a constitutional challenge to the law brought by Steven "Tiger" Lindsay and Raymond Bonner, two alleged members of the Hells Angels accused of extorting $75,000 from a Barrie, Ontario, businessman.

The new law means anyone convicted on an offence faces up to fourteen additional years in prison for carrying out a crime in association with a criminal organization.

Apollos: Angels' Landing Site – The Apollos motorcycle club was the big biker presence in Saskatchewan, until the Hells Angels set up shop in Regina on New Year's Eve 2001.

It was a peaceful takeover, as the Hells Angels moved into the 8th Avenue clubhouse of the Apollos, who then became inactive. The clubhouse was surrounded by a high barbed-wire fence, and a sign noted it was under twenty-four-hour surveillance.
See also: **Hells Angels.**

Arcuri, Giacinto: Acquitted Grandfather – In the late fall of 2002, a jury in Newmarket, north of Toronto, simply could not believe that the frail-looking senior citizen wearing an eye patch could have bound and murdered his burly long-time friend Enio Mora, who was godfather to one of Arcuri's grandchildren.

Mora's body was found September 11, 1996, stuffed into the trunk of his gold Cadillac parked on rural Teston Road near Weston Road in Vaughan, north of Toronto. The 260-pound mobster had been shot in the head four times and his artificial leg was detached and lying near his head, and his pants had been yanked down.

Less than forty-eight hours after the discovery of Mora's body, a special five-member York Region police surveillance team began watching and photographing Arcuri outside his North York home. Over several weeks, police followed Arcuri as he drove around Toronto. Three months after the murder, Arcuri, seventy-two, was charged with second-degree murder.

However, when the case finally reached court in the fall of 2002, the five-foot-five grandfather looked anything but threatening and walked to the witness stand with a severe limp. Arcuri, a retired fish salesman and paver, spoke in court through a Sicilian interpreter, even though he had lived in Canada since 1942. He told the court that he was simply trying to help his old friend Mora on the final day of the mobster's life. He met Mora in a York Region real-estate office. Mora had lost a leg in a gun incident, and wanted a treadmill just like the one Arcuri used to try to recover from a 1994 heart attack. Hours after they spoke, Mora's half-naked body was found in the trunk of his Cadillac.

Arcuri looked feeble and a little confused as he told the story, complaining, "I always had pain in my leg, my arm, and my back."

He said he had known Mora, forty-seven, for about twenty years and considered him a close friend. Police said Mora, a self-employed contractor, was a major local underworld figure, whose associates included major Mob bosses "Johnny Pops" Papalia of Hamilton and Paul Volpe of Toronto, both of whom had also been murdered.

Handling Arcuri's defence was lawyer Joe Bloomenfeld, who had an affable, rumpled, avuncular manner in court and experience defending a string of underworld notables, including boxer Eddie Melo, who would become yet another murder victim.

Arcuri said that he owned land with a group of people, including Mora, restaurateur Nicola Galifi, and "a Chinese person," but he dismissed the idea that anything had soured in their business relationship.

Arcuri said he couldn't explain how a shirt with his DNA and Mora's blood had been found at a roadside near the body. He couldn't even be positive that the bloody shirt was his own, saying, "I have fifty shirts." He also couldn't be sure that shoes found near the body belonged to him, noting, "I have forty pairs of shoes."

He curtly dismissed assistant Crown attorney Peter Westgate's suggestion that he met with a friend to get their stories straight before giving a statement to police. Arcuri said he met with the friend on November 28, 1996, simply "because there was lots of time and I went to see him just to kill some time."

Arcuri said he did his best to co-operate with police to get to the bottom of his friend's murder. Then he talked again of his poor health. "I don't see well today," said Arcuri, who had the lens of his glasses over his left eye covered with a patch. "I don't even remember what I ate last night."

The Crown admitted that it was basing its case on circumstantial evidence, such as the DNA on the blood-stained shirt, feathers, a package of gum, and the hand-stitched hem on some pants. That circumstantial evidence led police to suspect that a farm on Weston Road was likely the murder scene. "There is no eyewitness or smoking gun," assistant Crown attorney Lee-Anne McCallum told the jury. "There is no motive," she said. "This is a circumstantial case."

In the end, the jury believed the old grandfather Arcuri. The murder of his long-time friend remained unsolved.
See also: **Enio Mora, John "Johnny Pops" Papalia, Paul Volpe.**

Arviv, Harold Haim: Hot on the Dance Floor – He managed the trendy $1-million disco called Arviv's on Bloor Street in downtown Toronto. However, he liked insurance money even more than dancing, and so he levelled the place with thirty sticks of dynamite at 5 a.m. on January 9, 1980.

After he was found guilty of the explosion – and before he was sentenced to prison in September 1986 – the tanned, Israeli-born criminal spent much of his time dancing at a central Toronto disco (that he had not blown up) and sunning himself aboard his $170,000 powerboat *The Problem Child*, which was moored at Ontario Place on the Toronto waterfront. The vessel had a full-time boat boy, whose duties included passing out T-shirts with the stencilled message "100 per cent Bad Boys." Previous watercraft owned by Arviv were named *Misbehaviour* and *Monkey Business*.

Testimony by Satan's Choice biker Cecil Kirby, who did dirty jobs for mobster Cosimo Commisso and his brother Rocco Remo Commisso of Toronto, helped secure Arviv's conviction.

Judge Arthur Whealy was decidedly unimpressed by an innovative sentencing proposal involving Arviv's estranged wife, Kathryn. Through defence lawyer Edward Greenspan, she graciously offered to drop a lawsuit to collect $2 million in insurance money for the disco if the judge would agree to a maximum sentence of only thirty months.

The judge slammed the offer as "audacious, repugnant and abhorrent," and went on to fume, "It can only be described as an attempt to buy a shorter sentence.... This is a court of law, not a fish market.... Only the rich could make such an offer."

Arviv earnestly told the judge that "my life was never the same after I was charged in September 1982. I lost three businesses, my wife and children.... I hope that once I've done my time that society will let me go."

Upon hearing his sentence of four years, the expensively dressed prisoner was smiling again, and blew a two-handed kiss to the crowded spectator gallery in District Court in Toronto before he was led away in handcuffs.

After his release, he built a friendship with boxer Eddie Melo. The beaming buddies posed for pictures in March 1994, when Melo announced he would be returning to the ring at age thirty-four. Arviv was supposed to be his boxing manager for a pugilistic tour of Europe, but the ring comeback never materialized, and Melo and Ariv eventually had a bitter falling out over the stock business. Arviv missed Melo's 2001 funeral, as he was out of the country on holidays. *See also:* **Cosimo Commisso, Rocco Remo Commisso, Cecil Kirby, Eddie Melo.**

L'Association des témoins spéciaux du Québec: Angry Informers – There has always been an uneasy relationship between authorities and informers, and this was never more evident than when Hells Angels hit-man-turned-informer Stéphane "Godasse" Gagné was called to the witness stand in Montreal in April 2004 to testify in the trial of Wolodumyr

"Walter" "Nurget" Stadnick and Donald Stockford of the Angels elite Nomads chapter.

Instead of testifying against Stadnick and Stockford, Gagné used the occasion to tell the court that authorities had not respected his informant's contract, denying him courses and time outside his cell.

He spoke as a member of a newly formed informants' group, l'Association des témoins spéciaux du Québec, which claimed to speak for between ten and fifty informants, many of whom were recruited during the Hells Angels–Rock Machine biker war.

Their association published a newsletter, called *Journal L'Informateur*, which included news on lawsuits filed by themselves and their families against authorities, and also a pamphlet, with the question "Did they shortchange you?"

Others in the group included former Hells Angels hit man Serge Quesnel, who admitted to killing five people and plotting the murders of thirteen others, before signing an informant deal in 1995 that gave him $390,000 over the fifteen-year life of the contract.
See also: **Stéphane "Godasse" Gagné, Wolodumyr "Walter" "Nurget" Stadnick, Serge Quesnel.**

Atlantic City – *See* **Paul Volpe.**

Auger, Michel: Shooting the Messenger – The reporter, who had chronicled Montreal's underworld for three decades, was unloading his car on September 3, 2000, when a man dressed in black pumped six bullets at him and hustled away across the parking lot at *Le Journal de Montréal*. The gun was hidden in an umbrella, which slightly deflected the bullets, and probably saved Auger's life.

"I saw someone without a face and a ball of smoke near his belt," Auger said later. "While he was fleeing ... I immediately knew that my work was the cause of the pains in my back." He staggered but did not fall, and managed to pull out his cellphone and call for help.

Auger recovered, and kept on writing in *Le Journal de Montréal* about the deadly and escalating biker gang war in Quebec. By the time Auger was shot, in fact, some 160 people – including innocent bystanders – had already been murdered during eight years. Biker gangs forced farmers to grow marijuana, muscled in on small-town drug markets, beat up bar owners, killed two prison guards, and plotted the murders of judges, police officers, prosecutors, and journalists.

"I received threats in the past," Auger said. "I was taking precautions. I was not expecting to be shot. I was expecting maybe my car would be blown up. . . . I thought in Colombia, life is more dangerous, but not here in Canada."

The last article Auger wrote before his shooting was about how Hells Angels murdered people who told their secrets, and it included the passage "The dead don't talk."

Michel Vézina, a Hells Angels gunsmith, made the gun used to shoot journalist Michel Auger

See also: **Maurice "Mom" Boucher, Jean-Pierre Charbonneau, Hells Angels, Rock Machine, Nomads.**

B

Bader, Stanley: Fatal Sting – The Toronto loan shark and diamond dealer went to his grave in 1984, regretting the day he ever heard of "Johnny Pops" Papalia or his associates in the Cotroni crime family of Montreal.

Papalia had convinced Bader in 1973 that the Cotronis wanted to have him severely beaten, and that he had better pay him $300,000 to call off the contract. If not, Johnny Pops darkly warned, Bader would be left so injured he could never work again.

Cotroni crime boss Vic Cotroni and his right-hand man, Paolo Violi, were not the authors of Papalia's hoax. However, when they heard of it, they demanded a cut of the action, since their crime family's fearsome reputation was what motivated Bader to turn over the money.

When the Montrealers confronted Papalia, he protested that he made only $40,000 out of the scam, and that the rest went to a partner who worked with him.

On Bader's information, Cotroni, Violi, and Papalia were each eventually sentenced to six years in prison for extortion and conspiracy, although Cotroni and Violi had their sentences overturned on appeal after six months.

Understandably, Bader wanted to get far away from all of them. He fled to Florida, where he was an executive in a firm that dealt in precious gems. In early 1982, he received a string of threatening phone calls, including one that warned, "Look over your shoulder. You won't live out the week. . . ."

Bader might have been nervous, but, for some reason, when someone called at his luxury townhouse around two in the morning on March 16, 1982, he opened the door – and was shot dead.

The murder remains unsolved, but police considered Papalia a prime suspect – something that made Papalia livid.

In 1986, he told Peter Moon of the *Globe and Mail* that he had no love for Bader, but didn't kill him either. "Bader was a treacherous snake," Papalia said. "But whatever you write, don't say I ever killed anyone. I've never murdered anyone."

Then he drew a distinction that only a mobster could appreciate, telling Moon: "It wasn't an extortion. It was a swindle. That's not the same thing. A party owed some money and I helped out. That's all it was."

Papalia gave the reporter a copy of an affidavit Bader signed in Florida in 1980, which stated that he and the woman he was living with at the time of Papalia's extortion trial were pushed by the RCMP into testifying against Cotroni, Violi, and Papalia. The affidavit concluded with Bader saying that Papalia was not a part of the extortion conspiracy, a statement that contradicted Papalia's words to Cotroni on the wiretap.

"At no time was I threatened by, or forced to give funds to John Papalia," Bader said, "and, it is my opinion that he was the victim of an overzealous law enforcement agency whose actions were misguided."

Ironically, as he gave the affidavit to Moon, Papalia managed to sound like a victim himself. "I will not be set up again," he vowed.

See also: **Vincenzo "Vic the Egg" Cotroni, John "Johnny Pops" Papalia, Paolo Violi.**

Baker, Owen "Cannonball," a.k.a. George Nolan: Rum-Row Killer – A West Coast rumrunner in the early twentieth century, Baker was convicted of boarding a boat, the *Beryl G. Morris*, in Puget Sound, killing the two men on board, tying their bodies to an anchor, and then heaving them overboard.

This was in order to hijack 240 cases of whisky in the hold of the wooden freighter. The liquor had been bought for $6,000 and would sell for ten times more in the Prohibition-era United States of the 1920s.

Blood on the boat helped steer police to Baker, who was executed on January 14, 1926, in Oakalla Prison, along with his accomplice, Henry Sowash.

As the noose was placed around his neck by the executioner (who hid behind the pseudonym Arthur Ellis), Baker said, "Step on her, kid. Make it quick."

Bandidos: Enemies of the Hells Angels – Formed in the summer of 1965 in the Texas fishing community of San Leon in Galveston County, the Bandidos were the brainchild of dockworker and former Marine Donald Eugene Chambers. There was no Hells Angels presence to speak of then on the Texas Gulf, or local bikers would likely have joined that gang rather than copy the Angels by setting up a gang of their own. Despite – or perhaps because of – their similarities, the two clubs would become bitter rivals.

For their crest, the Texans looked to the Frito Bandito character used to sell corn chips, and adopted a cartoon drawing of a portly Mexican with a sombrero, sword, and pistol. For a motto,

they chose "Our colors don't run," and also enjoyed shocking people by saying, "We are the people our parents warned us about."

Many of the Bandidos original members were Vietnam War veterans, in much the same way that the original Angels were made up of footloose Second World War veterans. The Bandidos grew to become the third-largest motorcycle gang in the world, behind only the Hells Angels and the Outlaws, the oldest of the gangs, who were formed under the name The Outlaws Motorcycle Club near Chicago, at Matilda's Bar on Route 66, in 1935. The Bandidos used the Internet to tighten ties with Canadian biker clubs before moving into Canada in December 2000, absorbing the Rock Machine, who were locked in a war in Quebec with the Hells Angels, and thus entering a bloody struggle with the Angels themselves.

However, by the spring of 2004, most members of the gang in Quebec were behind bars or being sought on criminal charges that included conspiracy to commit murder. For the first time since the war between the Angels and the Bandidos (formerly the Rock Machine), one side was totally out of commission. Bikers were sought for murder, gangsterism, narcotics trafficking, and selling cocaine, heroin, ecstasy, marijuana and Viagra, the erectile-dysfunction drug.

See also: **Hells Angels, Red Zone, Rock Machine, Maurice "Mom" Boucher, Edward Warren Winterhalder.**

Nellie J. Banks: **Last of the Rum-Runners** – The schooner *Nellie J. Banks* was a familiar sight in the waters of Murray Harbour on the coast of Prince Edward Island in the 1930s.

When she dropped anchor, local seamen knew they would soon be unloading a cargo of smuggled rum and cigarettes.

The rum trade arrived at the perfect time for the small villages of the Atlantic coast. They had been suffering through a downturn in the fishery, and booze smuggling meant sailors

Nellie J. Banks *(Public Archives and Records Office of Prince Edward Island)*

could make more money running one load of rum to the U.S. eastern seaboard than in a year of toil on the fishing boats.

The *Nellie J. Banks* was one of many smuggling schooners sailing the perilous route south from the tiny French outpost of Sainte-Pierre and Miquelon off the Newfoundland coast. Many of the rum-running vessels were painted in drab tones to avoid detection, and sat low in the water to provide extra storage space.

Canadian and American authorities had cutters with superior speed and firepower, but like the East Coast pirates of centuries before, rum-running schooners like the *Nellie J. Banks* had the pick of the best crews. She would silently disappear into the coves and bays along the coastlines, and the Dicks brothers who captained her – Ed and John from Georgetown, Prince Edward Island – had allies on shore only too happy to help hide the contraband.

The peak years of schooners like the *Nellie J. Banks* off the shore of Prince Edward Island were from 1923 to 1938, but rum-running was a common practice long before Prohibition. In

1901, Prince Edward Island became the first province in Canada to institute strict measures against alcohol, and it became illegal for anyone to manufacture it, sell it, or have it in their possession. Soon rum-running was considered by many to be a very necessary part of life, despite harsh fines and the fact that ships and cargoes would be impounded.

The *Nellie J. Banks* was finally confiscated by authorities on August 9, 1938, when she became the last rum-runner seized off Atlantic Canada. *See also:* **Sainte-Pierre and Miquelon.**

Barillaro, Carmen: Ally of "Johnny Pops" Papalia – Barillaro trafficked drugs, put out a "hit" on an enemy, and made a point of not missing Sunday dinners with his widowed mother and his brother.

Barillaro was born July 24, 1944, in Italy and moved to Canada at age nine. He lived in Niagara Falls, Ontario, and spent his career in the orbit of Mob boss "Johnny Pops" Papalia of Hamilton. Like Papalia, he was considered a "made member" (actually part of the group, higher than an associate) of the Niagara Region Mob, answerable ultimately to the Magaddino organization of Buffalo.

An innovator of sorts, Barillaro once hired a woman to carry out a contract on a man who owed him a drug debt. The hit person, Faye Fontaine, didn't follow through and ultimately turned informer, and Barillaro was sentenced to three years in prison on January 24, 1989, for counsel to commit murder against Roy Caja of Niagara Falls, an ex-member of the Outlaws motorcycle gang. So ended an underworld version of affirmative action.

That wasn't Barillaro's first – or second – brush with the law. He received a two-year sentence in 1978 for conspiracy to traffic in heroin. Released on mandatory supervision in 1979, he was behind bars again in 1980 with a new three-year sentence, after selling approximately three ounces of heroin to an undercover operator.

Unrepentant and pumped up from lifting weights, Barillaro emerged from prison to extort Greek gambling clubs in the Pape-Danforth area of Toronto with Papalia, Enio Mora, and others. One of his associates in that

Carmen Barillaro

enterprise could bend coins with his mouth, a skill that terrified some gamblers into paying up. Barillaro also ran a restaurant and bar in downtown Niagara Falls, Ontario, and was even more exacting than kitchen guru Martha Stewart when it came to food preparation, once beating up an employee for defrosting food with cold water rather than a microwave, as he had been instructed. Later, he was the silent backer of a Niagara Falls roadhouse. He had to remain off the paperwork since his criminal record meant he couldn't have a liquor licence.

In the late 1980s, RCMP Cpl. Reg King ranked Barillaro about seventh or eighth out of 275 Mafia figures in Ontario, with his boss, Papalia, being at the top of the list. Barillaro's prime activities with Papalia were gaming and drug trafficking.

He was back before the courts yet again in St. Catharines in May 1992. Police in Canada and the United States said that he had imported several kilograms of cocaine and 900 kilograms of marijuana, with a wholesale value of about $3 million into Niagara Falls, Ontario, from various locations, including Buffalo and Florida.

In that case, police placed a listening device in a parking meter outside his restaurant-bar but had to go back and plant a new one after a drunk driver smashed his car into the meter.

Barillaro ultimately pleaded guilty, but his was a guarded *mea culpa*. He admitted once meeting a U.S. drug dealer acting only as an honest broker for a relative, and he pleaded guilty to conspiracy to import cocaine. For this, he was fined $10,000. That case was called a dry conspiracy because no drugs were seized.

Despite all his crimes, Barillaro made a point of meeting for Sunday dinners with his brother, a teacher in the separate school board of Welland and Niagara Region, at their widowed mother's house. At a bail hearing, his priest, Father Malachy Smith, had kind words for him, calling him a good father to his two daughters, with solid roots in the community, a solid marriage to a woman who was active in the church, and a sincere desire not to disappoint his wife.

On Wednesday, July 23, 1997, the eve of his fifty-third birthday, Barillaro was alone in his home when a stranger knocked on his door and asked about buying his Corvette, which was parked in the driveway. The man was Ken Murdock, a street tough in the employ of Pat and Angelo Musitano of Hamilton, who were close to Montreal Sicilian mobsters who were spreading their influence into the Toronto area.

Barillaro didn't usually welcome strangers to the door, and was particularly guarded when Murdock came to call, since his associate Papalia had been murdered by the Musitanos a month earlier. As Murdock pulled out a gun, Barillaro struggled with him, but his middle-aged muscles were no match for the hit man. When his wife and daughters returned home, they found Barillaro's body lying inside the front doorway, shot dead.

See also: **Stefano Magaddino, Eddie Melo, Enio Mora, Angelo and Pat Musitano, John "Johnny Pops" Papalia.**

Black Bart – *See* **Bartholomew Roberts.**

Beaudry, Paul: Deadly Contract – Beaudry was an RCMP constable-turned-criminal-lawyer whose life ended when someone shot him point-blank in his Old Montreal law office in September 1991.

He stumbled through a hallway in pursuit of the pair of gunmen, taking the elevator before collapsing in a pool of blood outside the building entrance. The father of two died several hours later at Montreal General Hospital.

Beaudry, an RCMP officer for ten years, had been working for a couple of months at the law firm of prominent Montreal criminal lawyer Claude F. Archambault, who specialized in drug cases.

See also: **Sydney Leithman, Frank Shoofey.**

Bellamy, Charles: Exploited Slaves – Daniel Defoe, the author of *Robinson Crusoe*, is also believed to have written a book on piracy, in

which he described how eighteenth-century pirate Charles Bellamy used slave labour to set up his headquarters in what was likely the St. Andrew's area of modern-day New Brunswick. The author wrote that Bellamy, who needed a sheltered area to repair his ships, drove the slaves with whips, "after the same manner as the negroes are used by the West Indian planters."

Bellamy first appeared in the summer of 1717 off the shores of New England and the Bay of Fundy on Canada's Atlantic coast. The captain brought with him three ships and grand visions of setting up a new nation, which – of course – he would run.

Upon his arrival, he began capturing and sinking fishing boats and trading ships near Fortune Bay, on the south shore of Newfoundland, near the French islands of Sainte-Pierre and Miquelon. One day, by mistake, he attacked a French ship in the Gulf of St. Lawrence that had thirty-six mounted guns. After a three-hour sea battle, he managed to escape under cover of the night to the west of Placentia Bay in Newfoundland, where he set up a new pirate fort.

He stayed there about a decade, and then it's speculated that he retired with his spoils. He's often confused with a pirate named Samuel Bellamy, who worked the Cape Cod, Massachusetts, area.

See also: **Eric Cobham, Cupids, Peter Easton, High Island, Edward Jordan, Captain Kidd, Mogul Mackenzie, Henry Mainwaring, Sheila Na Geira, Samuel Nelson, John Phillips, Gilbert Pike, Pirates, Bartholomew "Black Bart" Roberts.**

Benvenuto, Giuseppe Croce: New Mafia Strain – A native of Palma Di Montechiaro, Sicily, Benvenuto fled Italy in 1990. Authorities there wanted him on charges of killing Judge Rosario Livantino in Sicily on September 21, 1990, as well as for Mafia associations and for questioning about the murder of a police officer.

First he went to Germany, where he managed to evade arrest when two others also charged with Livantino's murder were picked up in the Mannheim-Dusseldorf area. His associates were sentenced to life in prison, while he flew to Toronto, where he passed himself off as a businessman.

Italian authorities considered him to be a member of the Stidda (which means "Star"), a new hybrid of the Sicilian Mafia that gained prominence in international drug trafficking in the late 1980s and early 1990s. When Benvenuto was finally scooped up at the Fiumicino airport in Rome on a trip back to Italy, author Antonio Nicaso said, "This is the first case of the Stidda in Canada." It was also the last reported case of the group operating in Canada.

The Stidda started in part because of the ferocity and autocratic ways of Sicilian Mafia boss Salvatore "Toto" Riina. Some members of the new group had five tiny marks between their thumbs and forefinger as identification.

Bienfait, Saskatchewan: Prairie Hideaway – New York City mobster Dutch Schultz (a.k.a. Arthur Flegenheimer, Beer Baron of the Bronx) spent a week in southern Saskatchewan at the Bienfait hotel near the American border during the rum-running days of Prohibition, according to a source quoted in James H. Gray's book *Booze*.

Schultz undoubtedly wished he was back in Bienfait instead of at the Palace Chop House in Newark, New Jersey, on the night of October 23, 1935. There he was caught in a shootout with rival gangsters from a group with the ominous name Murder, Inc. The shooters were Charles "Charlie the Bug" Workman, Emanuel "Mendy" Weiss, and a driver known only as "Piggy."

The gunplay left Schultz dying at the Newark City Hospital. His deathbed statements, recorded by a police stenographer, were a glossary of mobster jargon, and some scholars called them American folk literature while others might call them delirious ramblings. Among his fascinating but tough-to-decipher utterances was the comment "Mother is the best bet and don't let Satan draw you too fast." *See also:* **Samuel Bronfman, Moose Jaw Capone Tunnels, Annie Newman, Rocco and Bessie Perri.**

Big Beaver, Saskatchewan – *See* **Big Muddy Badlands, Dutch Henry, Sam Kelly, Sundance Kid.**

Big Circle Boys (Dai Huen Jai): Criminal Ring – Members of the Big Circle Boys typically were recruited into the notorious Red Guards in China as children. The group's name refers back to the height of the bloody purges of the Cultural Revolution of the mid-1960s to mid-1970s, when the Red Guard overran Guangzhou (Canton) by first encircling the entire city in tents.

In Hong Kong, the gang became notorious for evading capture by throwing grenades at police. Then, in anticipation of Hong Kong's switch from British to Chinese rule in 1997, gang members took advantage of Canada's loose entry laws in the late 1980s and early to mid-1990s.

Some gang specialists liken the structure of the Big Circle Boys (BCB) to that of a pickup basketball team, where players come together informally in playgrounds and often meet each other on the court for the first time. While it is an organized group, the BCB have a considerably looser and less-hierarchical structure than traditional Chinese criminal societies, or Triads, or than the Mafia. BCB often co-operate with individual criminals or even rival organized-crime groups.

Toronto police started to learn about them in late 1988 while investigating a sudden rash of pickpocketing on the subway and in downtown Chinatown. Thousands of dollars and hundreds of credit cards were lifted, doctored, and then used to buy luxury goods for resale, while others were used for calls to Hong Kong gangsters. Police estimated that Bell Canada was being defrauded of an estimated $10,000 a month by the gang.

The gang quickly moved into smuggling drugs and aliens into Canada, and set up strongholds in Toronto and Vancouver. In the Toronto area, Big Circle Boys ran brothels in downtown Chinatown and Scarborough that lured impoverished Malaysian women into the metropolitan area by advertising positions as maids.

More than five hundred Chinese-born BCB members, all from the city of Guangzhou (Canton), lived in Canada by the early 1990s, and many of them were known criminals who travelled frequently to New York, smuggling heroin and counterfeit credit cards.

In a 1990 sting operation, Canada's Asian Organized Crime Squad – in co-operation with American authorities and the Royal Hong Kong Police – revealed a network that had smuggled more than twelve hundred Chinese into Canada, including at least one hundred Big Circle Boys.

In the early 1990s, the gang had an aggressive presence in Toronto's Chinatowns, often swaggering into restaurants, dining on $300 meals, and then walking out without paying. They also collected money for "window-cleaning." In this protection racket, the "window-cleaning" service was really a threat that they would shatter windows if the restaurateurs didn't pay.

Gang members also entered Asian immigrants' homes, pistol-whipped them, then stole jewellery, money, passports, credit cards, and anything else of value. Gaming houses and wedding parties were also targets.

The gang tried to murder at least one Toronto police officer with a bomb, and ventured into kidnapping-for-ransom. Victims ranged from poor waiters to millionaire businesspeople. For the Canadian police, it was a challenge to convince victims that the police forces in their new homeland were different from those they had experienced back in Hong Kong and Taiwan, and that they didn't take bribes from gangs.

By 1996, the Criminal Intelligence Service Canada (CISC) – which gathers and analyzes crime from across the country in order to spot trends and assist police – issued a report on organized crime that described the gang as a major importer of heroin, adding, "There are clear indications Asian heroin traffickers such as the Big Circle Boys (BCB) are co-operating with Vietnamese gangs, Laotian, Fukienese and Taiwanese criminals, Italian organized crime, Hells Angels and with any criminal organization that will buy drugs."

By 1999, the Big Circle Boys were working in Toronto with Russian organized-crime groups to sell drugs and weapons and pass counterfeit money. They had spread across Canada and that year, police pointed to the Big Circle Boys as part of the reason why Edmonton then led the country in the number of drug-related gang shootings. They were also linked to crimes in British Columbia including exportation of stolen Native art.

A 1999 CISC report noted that organized crime in Alberta was linked to highly mobile criminals based in Vancouver and Toronto, including the Big Circle Boys, the Lotus Gang, and numerous other Vietnamese and Chinese gangs.

In December 2000, a White House report complained that Chinese gangs were using Canada as a gateway to enter the United States illegally. The International Crime Threat Assessment report by key American security agencies pointed at Canada as a key venue for Triads engaged in credit-card fraud, heroin trafficking, illegal migration, and software piracy.

The report highlighted what it considered Canada's lax rules for newcomers, particularly a plan aimed at attracting foreign investors, and pegged the Big Circle Boys as the most active Asian criminals in Canada.

In January 2001, police named Vancouver a leading centre for credit-card fraud after the Organized Crime Agency of British Columbia raided what they called a factory for creating counterfeit credit cards, which they suspected was run by the Big Circle Boys.

Such crimes were unheard of a decade before, but now fake cards made in Canada were approaching the quality level of the Asia-Pacific region. The card-makers were able to use data taken from genuine credit cards by corrupt merchants, gas-station attendants, and restaurant staff in the Vancouver area. Police said money from credit-card fraud helped pay for the gang's operations in prostitution, illegal gambling, the smuggling of handguns and aliens, and the drug trade.

By 2002, the Big Circle Boys operated across Canada, in possession and production of illegal drugs, in credit-card scams, and in extortion and immigrant smuggling. A group broken up in British Columbia that year had made some $200 million in fake credit cards and trafficked hundreds of kilograms of marijuana into Washington State from a Vancouver Island marina, while a gang in the Eastern Townships of Quebec smuggled 200 to 500 pounds of marijuana into the United States each week.

They were also then involved in the large-scale manufacture of counterfeit credit cards, computer software, CDs and DVDs, and had almost cornered the market on heroin impor-tation, human smuggling, and significant sales of ecstasy and domestic marijuana.

See also: **Born to Kill, 14K Association, Lau Wing Kui, Lotus Gang, Kung Lok, Kwok Ka, Lai Changxing, Sun Yee On, Trung Chi Truong.**

Big Muddy Badlands: Criminal Retreat – Antelope, white-tailed deer, coyotes, golden eagles, and prairie falcons love this sandy region that lies just north of the international border between southcentral Saskatchewan and north-eastern Montana.

Fugitives have also been drawn to the Big Muddy Valley, a 55-kilometre (35-mile) gap that's up to 3 kilometres (1.8 miles) wide and 160 metres (500 feet) deep where the Big Muddy River ran south into Montana and the Missouri River basin. Dotted with prickly pear cactus, it isn't great for farming, but for years has offered an excellent hideout from Canadian and American authorities.

Sioux chief Sitting Bull went to the Big Muddy Badlands to live after his victory over Custer and the Seventh Cavalry in the 1876 Battle of Little Bighorn. The valley was also an

Big Muddy Badlands

attractive retreat for outlaws like Butch Cassidy, Sam Kelly, and Dutch Henry.

Cassidy made Station #1 on the Outlaw Trail a ranch just south of Big Beaver in Saskatchewan's Big Muddy Badlands, and just north of the Canada-U.S. border, which stretched from Saskatchewan to Mexico. Cassidy borrowed a concept from the Pony Express, and had fresh horses at friendly ranches every ten or twelve miles along the route, so that lawmen chasing him were almost always left in his dust.

A landmark in Big Muddy is Castle Butte, a 70-metre-high (200-foot-high) sandstone-and-clay formation just outside the hamlet of Big Beaver, which was used for navigation by Indians, surveyors, North-West Mounted Police, outlaws, and settlers. The butte is dotted with caves, which are ready-made hideouts. Even when the North-West Mounted Police set up a detachment, it was no easy matter to patrol the area on horseback.

Outlaws would steal horses in Canada, move them through the Big Muddy Valley, and then sell them in Montana. Then they'd steal more horses in Montana and take them back through the valley to sell in Canada, where they knew there was a horse shortage of their own making. *See also:* **Big Beaver, Frank Carlyle, Butch Cassidy, Sam Kelly, Ed Shufelt, Sundance Kid.**

Black Hand: Early Mafia – A letter sent in 1904 to the Montreal office of Antonio "King" Cordasco, a banker, steamship agent, and labour recruiter, displayed a menacing drawing of a black hand, pointing to the letters M and A. It was accompanied by a crude sketch of a coffin, two skulls-and-crossbones, and what appeared to be a snake under the hot sun.

Cordasco knew it was an extortion threat by the Black Hand, the forerunner to the modern Mafia. The Black Handers were small, potentially violent groups that preyed upon their own immigrant community. How Cordasco dealt with the threat remains a mystery, but it's a safe bet that he didn't take it lightly.

In 1906, a Hamilton grocer named Salvatore Sanzone began receiving Black Hand extortion letters, and they continued for the next three years. Finally, in the fall of 1909, the Black Handers found themselves in court. Ralph Rufus and Joseph Courto turned King's evidence, with Rufus telling the court that he was ordered to write the threatening letters by John Taglerino, who ran an "Italian boarding house" and store on Sherman Avenue North in Hamilton.

Courto told the court that he also wrote threatening letters on orders from Taglerino. According to his account, Courto was forced into the gang because he owed money to Taglerino. When the extortion attempt against Sanzone failed, Courto said the gang decided to hold up the store instead. He felt badly and went to the grocer to warn him of the upcoming robbery. The men were all convicted of extortion.

In 1908, a baker named Louis Belluz was targeted by Black Handers when he received a letter in the wilderness town of Fort Frances in northwestern Ontario. This letter was written in red ink and demanded $100. If it wasn't paid, the letter warned, he would be killed and his buildings burned. There was an odd postscript to the letter, saying that the Black Handers would, however, settle for $50, if that was the best Belluz could manage.

A year later, during a housebreaking investigation, the Ontario Provincial Police learned of the inner workings of the Black Hand society that had targeted Belluz. They were told that two men, Frank Tino and Frank Muro, forced a number of Italian immigrants to pay $25 to join the society, although Nicholas Bessanti said he could only pay $10, and that was accepted.

Bessanti told the police, "In joining the Society we took a solemn oath that we would obey our leader's orders: would rob, burn, kill, as he directed, that we would protect one another from the hands of the law, to disobey these orders we would expect to be punished by death or otherwise decided upon by the Society.

The Society met every Saturday night in the west end of a freight shed and there they decided what to do to raise money."

Tino and Muro didn't do so well with the scheme in Fort Frances, so they moved on to Port Arthur, and then Duluth, Minnesota. Finally, they were deported back to Italy.

Toronto got a taste of Black Hand violence in 1911. A man named Frank Tarro was shot to death by Frank Griro in the city's downtown, near Front and Church Streets. Griro said he was being extorted by Tarro, and that he acted out of fear. Chief Justice Falconbridge clearly took his words seriously, and issued a stern warning to any organized criminals who might be operating in Canada:

> He [the defendant] will urge that he was being hounded down by members of the Black Hand, or Camorra, as they commonly are called. Now, I may say here that if there are any importations of these people to this country, this is not the clime nor the soil for them. These people need have no doubt of the result of their operations. They will be vigorously wiped out. There will be no comic opera accessories and they will be dealt with severely and sent to the gallows or behind prison walls as the case may be.

The accused Griro was acquitted by a jury.
See also: **Joe Musolino, Rocco and Bessie Perri.**

Blackwood, Robert (a.k.a. Errol Codling): Nasty Tune – He was a musician of sorts, recording the 1980 reggae dance-floor hit "Hey Fatty Bum Bum" under the name Ranking Dread.

However, he was best known to authorities in Canada, Britain, the United States, and his native Jamaica as a deadly fugitive wanted on murder charges, who used more than twenty aliases while on the run – including Ranking Dread. Performing songs with rude titles was the least of his crimes.

In 1990, Blackwood made history of a sort when he became the first Jamaican ever to claim refugee status in Canada, saying that either Jamaican police or political enemies would kill him if he returned to the island. At that point, Blackwood had been a fugitive for a dozen years, after being charged with fatally shooting a member of the Jamaica Constabulary Force. Exactly how he found time to record the dance song while on the lam remains a mystery.

For his part, Blackwood told Canadian reporters in 1990 that Jamaican police "trumped up" charges that he shot at them in 1973. He said the force wanted him dead, because he supported the opposition Jamaica Labor Party.

"They're going to murder me. I can't go back to Jamaica now with all the press [coverage]," Blackwood told reporters at a news conference at the front doors of the Inn on the Park.

Jamaicans are born into political parties according to the neighbourhood in which their parents live, and the wrong address can mean death, Blackwood said. "I've seen too many people die, kids, women, men, even dogs sometimes, because of politics. Once you're born in a community, you automatically become a politician, whether you're high-profile or low-profile."

Blackwood, who then had eleven children in the United States, Canada, and England, said he only wanted to make a new home in Canada with his favourite daughter, two-year-old Nicola. He lost his plea.

Canada was the third country to kick him out. He was deported from the United States on drug charges, and from Britain on counterfeiting charges and as the suspected leader of the violent Yardies drug posse, which controlled much of the crack-cocaine trade in London. The Yardies got their name because some Jamaicans refer to their homes – and, when abroad, their country – as their "yard."

His comments in Canada came two years after he had been deported back to Jamaica from Britain in November 1988. He was known in Britain as Errol Codling, and he had such a high profile as a criminal there that a half-dozen British newspapers carried the news of his deportation on their front pages.

At the time of his 1988 deportation, he was branded the most dangerous foreign national in Britain.

At his 1990 Toronto press conference, Blackwood sniffed at the mention of how he was arrested in Albany, New York, in June 1983 on marijuana charges. Blackwood said he was arrested for "just a spliff," a marijuana cigarette, and insists it was part of his Rastafarian religion, like wearing his hair in long dreadlocks. "That's why I don't have dreadlocks no more," added Blackwood, whose hair was then closely cropped. "Religion got me in trouble, so I don't practise that religion any more."

However, police would argue that drug dealing, not religion, was the basis of his problems.

By March 2003, he was still a fugitive and stood accused of killing more than thirty people. He was also blamed in part for Yardie violence as crack-cocaine sales grew in Scotland, where the press called him "the Godfather of British Yardies."

Authorities also linked him to a bizarre plot with the Irish Republican Army to assassinate Margaret Thatcher when she was prime minister. He allegedly met senior IRA members in Dublin several times in 1987 to arrange the smuggling of a well-known American gangster to Britain to carry out the killing of Thatcher before the general election.

His ties were forged with the IRA through a series of lucrative drug deals, published reports said. He and an American assassin, under the guidance of two senior IRA men, toured London, looking at Thatcher's official residence on Downing Street and the Houses of Parliament. After British agents were tipped off about the plot, a massive security cordon was thrown around Thatcher and the threat eventually fizzled.

See also: **Jamaican Posses.**

Blass, Michel: Deadly Antiques Dealer – He was a hired killer for the Hells Angels, who had executed a dozen people before becoming a police informant. In the final days of his life, however, he just wanted to be an antiques dealer.

Blass defected from the Hells Angels after the gang eliminated its drug-ridden Laval chapter by machine-gunning or beating to death six of its members and dumping their bodies into the St. Lawrence River. He figured he would be dead soon unless he did something drastic, and so he turned on his former gang and became a police informer.

Another of the defectors was Yves "Apache" Trudeau, who rigged a VCR with explosives and had Blass deliver it to a downtown Montreal apartment. Four mobsters died in the blast, just across the street from a police station.

In the 1986 case, Blass pleaded guilty to manslaughter in twelve killings, and, after seven years in jail, he was given a new name, Michel Simon, and resettled.

He lived quietly as an antiques dealer for eleven years, until, in March 1997, he failed to report to his probation officer.

Four months later, on July 5, 1997, after an intensive search in a wooded area northeast of Montreal, Quebec Provincial Police discovered his bones.

See also: **Hells Angels, Yves "Apache" Trudeau.**

Blass, Richard "The Cat": Mass Murderer – The brother of Michel Blass, Richard Blass grew up to be a terrifying criminal in his own right. In 1974, he escaped from prison for the second time in two years, after jumping his guards and hijacking a postal truck. Then, Blass entered the Gargantua Bar-Salon in Montreal and shot two men whom he accused of helping put him in jail, and set fire to the building, killing eleven others. In January 1975, he died in a shootout when police raided his hideout.

See also: **Michel Blass, Gargantua.**

Bluestein, Max: Nearly Executed – It was billed in the Toronto underworld as "The Near Execution of Maxie Bluestein." The setting was the Town Tavern in downtown Toronto, a block east of the current site of the Eaton Centre, on the night of March 21, 1961.

"Johnny Pops" Papalia of Hamilton badly wanted a cut of the gambling operations run by Bluestein, which authorities estimated grossed $13 million yearly. It was also a time when North American–based La Cosa Nostra mobsters like Papalia were muscling in on established local – and often Jewish – independent gentlemen gamblers like Bluestein.

Many of the hundred patrons in Town Tavern knew that everything that night rested on what Bluestein did when Papalia sent him over a drink. If it were accepted, there would be peace and Bluestein would be working for Johnny Pops. However, if the beverage were refused, then Bluestein would find himself on the receiving end of billy clubs, brass knuckles, and iron bars.

Patrons saw Bluestein curtly wave off the "hand of friendship" from Johnny Pops.

What followed was, in the words of *Toronto Star* columnist Pierre Berton,

> as terrible a beating as it is possible to give a man without killing him. . . . Iron bars with ropes attached to them for greater leverage rained down on Bluestein's head and across his forehead, eyes and cheekbones. His scalp was split seven or eight times. Knuckledusters smashed into his eyes and a broken bottle was ground into his mouth. When Bluestein dropped to the floor he was kicked in the face. His overcoat, torn and slashed, was literally drenched in his own blood. . . . When I saw Bluestein, some 10 days after the affair, he looked like a piece of meat.

Berton's writing triggered public outrage that such a thing could happen in the middle of the city, and police used the public outrage as an excuse to crack down on the Mob, arresting Papalia's associate Alberto Agueci before the Hamilton boss finally turned himself in.

By that time, Papalia was being probed in the French Connection heroin-smuggling case, and the Town Tavern beating didn't net him any extra prison time.

Bluestein's fate was far sadder. He became so paranoid that he suspected even his wife and two sons of murder plots, and he studied waitresses to make sure they didn't slip poison into his coffee. In a dark bout of paranoia, Bluestein shot his long-time friend David "Tex" Stillman to death, when Stillman dropped by on a Sunday afternoon for a visit.

Bluestein was found not guilty by reason of insanity, and died of carbon-monoxide poisoning in his garage on October 30, 1984.

Two years later, Papalia showed no remorse for the 1961 beating, telling *Globe and Mail* reporter Peter Moon, "Bluestein started it. He had a stiletto and he stabbed [Papalia associate Frank] Marchildon twice. We had to defend ourselves. Bluestein was greedy. He wanted it all for himself."

See also: **Alberto Agueci, John "Johnny Pops" Papalia.**

Bonanno, Joseph "Joe Bananas": Banana's Empire – Growing up in Castellammare del Golfo, Sicily, Joseph Bonanno was proud that his father had chosen a life in the Mafia over one in the priesthood. "He could have been more self-centred, placing personal tranquility over sacrifice," he bragged. "Instead, he chose to help his family."

In 1964, Bonanno tried to immigrate to Canada from the United States in 1964, telling authorities he was thinking of buying into a cheese-making enterprise. J.K. Abbott, director of inspection service for the Department of Citizenship and Immigration, wrote in his report, on May 27, 1964:

> His record ranges from a 1930 arrest in New York City for transporting machine

Joe Bonanno

and Vito Agueci who were arrested in New York City for narcotics violations. Vito Agueci is now serving a fifteen-year prison sentence for narcotics and his brother, Alberto, was brutally murdered in a gangland slaying near Rochester, New York, at the time of his trial.

During Bonnano's [sic] recent stay in Canada, and prior to his application for permanent landing, there have been indications that he has been associated with criminals in the Montreal area.

Abbott might have missed a few things, but he had the right idea. In Montreal, Joe Bonanno associated with the Cotroni crime family, since Vic Cotroni functioned as his northern branch-plant manager.

He detested his nickname of Joe Bananas, but his family took some pride that *The Godfather* characters Vito and Michael Corleone were supposedly patterned on him and his son, Bill.

He died peacefully in his Tucson, Arizona, hospital bed of heart failure in May 2002, at age ninety-seven.

See also: **Alberto Agueci, Cotroni Brothers, Carmine Galante, Stefano Magaddino, John "Johnny Pops" Papalia.**

guns for the Capone mob in Chicago to attendance at the Mafia organized crime conference which was held in Binghamton, New York, in 1956. During the U.S. Senate hearings on organized crime and illicit traffic in narcotics which were held in September and October of 1963 in Washington, Bonnano [sic] was named as the leader of a major segment of the crime organization exposed by Joseph Valachi.

The criminals who are reported to be members of Bonanno's crime group have been involved in crimes which include extortion, strong arm and murder, counterfeiting, gambling and narcotics.

He has been associated with Carmine Galente [sic] who is at present serving twelve years for narcotics violations and one-time owner of the Bonfire restaurant in Montreal and a major figure in illegal gambling.

He has also been connected with Toronto-based criminals John Papalia and Alberto

Bonanno, Salvatore "Bill": Loyal Son – For a while, it looked as if Bonanno wasn't going to follow in the Mafiosi footsteps of his grandfather in Sicily and his father, New York City Mob boss Joseph Bonanno. Bonanno attended private school and then the University of Arizona, where he was a leader of the ROTC cadet squad.

When it came time to marry, however, Bonanno moved back into Mob circles. He chose for his bride Rosalie Profaci, niece of Brooklyn Mob boss Joe Profaci, who had supported Bonanno's father in the mid-1960s, when there were reportedly threats on his life.

Bonanno was soon pulled deep into his father's orbit, which brought him to Montreal on November 28, 1966, to meet Paolo Violi and the Cotroni brothers. He was stopped by police at eleven that night at the corner of Jean-Talon and Hutchinson Streets, with bodyguards Carlo Simari and Peter Magaddino, a cousin of his father's bitter rival, Stefano Magaddino, and a couple of others. Police found three loaded revolvers in the car, and Bonanno was rushed back into New York by immigration officials.

In his book, *Bound by Honor: A Mafioso's Story*, Bonanno said his father was involved in Democratic Party politics from the 1930s on, and worked to help elect Franklin D. Roosevelt and John F. Kennedy.

See also: **Vincenzo "Vic the Egg" Cotroni, Stefano Magaddino, Paolo Violi.**

Born to Kill: Chinatown Warriors – At lunchtime on December 27, 1990, two men sauntered into the cramped Kim Bo restaurant on Toronto's Bathurst Street, across from the Toronto Western Hospital. One had a tattoo on his arm of a coffin and three lit candles – the logo of the BTK (Born to Kill) gang.

"Don't fuck with my *dat lo* [gang leader]," one of the men said to a table full of Vietnamese immigrants. Then he opened fire. When the shooting stopped, Dan Vi Tran, thirty-one, lay dead, and two other diners were wounded. The attack was first believed to be revenge for a shooting at a funeral in Linden, New Jersey, two months before, but the motive was never clearly established.

Tran's murder was the opening volley in the bloodiest chapter of gang violence in Toronto's downtown Chinatown, during which eight more people were killed in the summer of 1991.

The Born to Kill Gang in Toronto had tight links to the BTK gangsters who terrorized Asian communities in New York City in the early 1990s with a staggering array of robberies, extortion, and murder, which stopped only when New York leader David Thai was convicted.

Their territory was then taken over by rival gangs, including the Gum Sing (Golden Star) and Big Circle Boys.

In the Kim Bo slayings, a jury convicted Tat and Son "Sonny" Long of first-degree murder in May 1992, and they were given automatic life sentences. Both men strongly protested their innocence, even as they were being sentenced.

Eight years later, they were free men, when the convictions were quashed by an appeal court. In an eighty-four-page judgment, Mr. Justice David Doherty of the Ontario Court of Appeal wrote that "no reasonable jury, acting in accordance with the law, could have convicted either appellant."

Only one of the Crown witnesses identified the accused as the two men who fired the shots. The jury relied almost entirely on that witness – whose identity was protected by the court – to reach their verdict and Justice Doherty dismissed her testimony as "incredible."

He noted that her story changed at least three times. "The changes were dramatic and related to matters of central importance," he wrote. "No plausible explanation was offered for these dramatic changes."

"Indignation at the thought of cold-blooded killers getting away with murder is not . . . a substitute for hard evidence," Doherty wrote.

The murders remain unsolved.
See also: **Big Circle Boys, Ghost Shadows, Lai Changxing, Lau Wing Kui, Kung Lok, Sun Yee On, Asau Tran, Triads, Trung Chi Truong.**

Boucher, Maurice "Mom": Bloody Reign – It was while buying three bouquets of flowers in June 1997 that this Quebec Hells Angels leader learned that one of his men had murdered Diane Lavigne, a mother of two who worked as a prison guard.

Boucher was upset – not over news of the mother's murder, but because the east-end Montreal florist didn't serve him quickly enough.

"Fags are just like women. They are always late," Boucher told hit man Stéphane "Godasse" Gagné in the flower shop. Then he picked up his flowers and listened to Gagné provide details of Lavigne's murder.

Maurice "Mom" Boucher on his Harley-Davidson

When Boucher and Gagné met up with a group of bikers outside the shop, Gagné seemed a bit sheepish that he had gunned down a woman. Boucher told him not to worry – he simply had wanted a guard murdered. The sex of the victim didn't really matter.

"That's good, Godasse," Boucher whispered in his ear. "It doesn't matter that she had tits."

Boucher had wanted guards murdered to destabilize the justice system. As he strolled down the street with the flowers, he talked about how they had to be careful. "Don't talk of this to anyone," Boucher warned. "Because it is twenty-five years in prison. If the death penalty still existed . . ."

Then he made a gesture of a rope hanging someone.

Another Hells Angel congratulated Gagné, and a group of them went to the Chez Parée strip club in downtown Montreal for lunch.

It was just another scene in the life of Boucher, who was nicknamed Mom because he pestered people to pay attention to details, a bit like an overbearing mother. Others called him Les Lunettes, because of his steel-rimmed designer eyeglasses, which make him look a little like a graduate student.

Killing innocent women didn't lower Boucher's status in Montreal's outlaw biker world, Hells Angel-turned-informer Serge Boutin later testified. "Mr. Boucher was considered like a god," Boutin said. "When I'd see other Hells Angels around him, they were full of admiration for him."

Boucher was born on June 21, 1953, in the tiny Gaspé community of Causapscal, one of eight children of an ironworker who could be severe with his family. He grew up in the east end of Montreal, in Hochelaga-Maisonneuve, a working-class neighbourhood in the shadow of the Olympic Stadium, and wasn't much of a student, dropping out of school in Grade Nine at age seventeen.

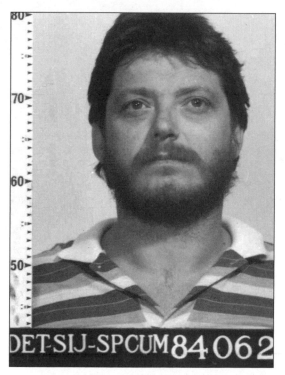

Mom Boucher in 1984

Much of his later teens were spent aimlessly, in a haze of hashish, LSD, cocaine, heroin, amphetamines, and Valium.

Boucher began his criminal career in 1973 with the theft of $200, and never looked back. He would appear before the courts forty-three times for crimes, including shoplifting, weapons possession, and armed robbery, before he was brought to justice for the Lavigne killing. At that point, the most time he had spent behind bars was forty months for an armed robbery in 1976.

He first got a taste of power and camaraderie through membership in the SS motorcycle gang, which disbanded in 1984. He then drifted toward the Sorel chapter of the Hells Angels, Canada's original Angels chapter. The members were known as the Popeyes before they received their Angels death-head patches on December 5, 1977.

The Quebec Angels had forbidden the use of cocaine by members, on penalty of death, and Boucher valued the club more than his drug use so he went cold turkey. On May 1, 1987, he became

a full member of the Angels and, by the early 1990s, his natural leadership ability had propelled him to the top of the Angels Montreal chapter. In the mid-1990s, he helped form the notorious and elite Nomads chapter. The Nomads' task was to spearhead the Angels expansion into Ontario and to lead the war over downtown Montreal drug turf against the Rock Machine.

He had come a long way from his teen years in Hochelaga-Maisonneuve. He moved onto an estate with horse stables on Montreal's south shore and listed his occupation alternately as a used-car salesman, real-estate manager, cook, and construction worker. No one who knew him took those job titles seriously, since everyone in his world knew Mom Boucher was a full-time Hells Angel.

He was also known in Acapulco, Mexico, where he bought property and nurtured contacts with notoriously corrupt police.

A fitness buff, he liked to work out at a gym that was favoured by police. Showing his face to them there, while flanked by several gang members, was just another way to taunt authorities. The Hells Angel leader, with his close-cropped silver hair and muscular frame, liked to make himself a familiar sight to officers in the Crimes Division in the Montreal Urban Community Police. The police offices were atop a shopping mall, with only a glass window separating homicide investigators from the shoppers below. Boucher liked to drop by with an entourage for lunch at the food court below, knowing his very presence made the officers' blood pump a little faster.

He loved to present himself as above authority. When the home of Nicole Quesnel, warden of the Sorel Detention Centre, was destroyed by arson in June 1995, Boucher and his men were the sole suspects. Apparently Boucher viewed this as revenge for treatment he had received at Sorel when he was serving six months for a firearms conviction.

His gang's bloody drug turf war with the Rock Machine killed some 165 people between

Mom Boucher salutes the camera

Mom Boucher's obituary card, which he prepared himself

1994 and 2000, including 30 people who had no involvement in crime. The Angels tried twice to plant large bombs in public places, despite widespread public revulsion after eleven-year-old Daniel Desrochers was killed by a biker-related car bomb in 1995. On August 23, 1996, the Hells Angels tried without success to blow up a van, disguised as a Hydro-Québec truck and loaded with 181 kilograms of explosives, next to the Rock Machine's Montreal clubhouse. On October 30, 1997, police discovered 130 dynamite sticks hidden in the conference room of defence lawyer Gilles B. Thibault, where several Rock Machine members were to gather.

In 1997, Boucher hatched the Machiavellian plan to ensure the loyalty of his men that led to Gagné's murder of Lavigne. Boucher wanted members to kill prison guards, prosecutors, judges, and police – all crimes for which there was a mandatory life term. That way, he reasoned, there was little chance of them turning informer.

He didn't try to corrupt the system from within like the Italian Mobs. Instead, he attacked it head-on. In April 1999 he planned to plant five bombs outside Montreal police stations. The explosives didn't go off, but it was still the largest bomb scare in Quebec since the days of the Front de Libération du Québec three decades before.

Despite his murderous attacks on innocent people, Boucher attained folk-hero status in certain parts of Quebec society. After his acquittal on charges for the double-murders of prison guards, he appeared in full biker colours with an Angels entourage at the Molson Centre in downtown Montreal for the Canadian middleweight title fight between Dave Hilton and Stéphane Ouellet. To the disgust of police, who also attended the fight, Boucher sat in the front row of the stadium and received a standing ovation from the crowd.

He also enjoyed opera and pop-music concerts, including those by Luciano Pavarotti and Phil Collins, and between biker meetings his appointment book noted travel to condos owned by the Angels in Mexico.

In the winter of 2002, Boucher was back in court for the murder of Lavigne and fellow guard Pierre Rondeau and the attempted murder of guard Robert Corriveau in 1997. The star witness against him was Angels killer Stéphane Gagné, the biker from the east-end flower shop.

The two men traced their association to their days as inmates at the Sorel Detention Centre in the early 1990s. Back then, Boucher had organized a hunger strike because he was sick of shepherd's pie, and when an inmate refused to join in, Gagné beat him severely. Now Gagné was the Crown's key weapon against Boucher.

A cell in the wing of a women's jail was renovated to house Boucher. His lawyer complained that he was slipping into a depression and eating junk food because of his solitary confinement and lack of exercise facilities. Others thought it wasn't depression but caution that pushed him to eat bag after bag of potato chips. The junk food was vacuum sealed, making it tougher to poison. Authorities also took special care of security; in the courtroom, jurors were protected from his view by an opaque screen.

This time, when the verdict came in, Boucher heard himself sentenced to life imprisonment with no chance to apply for early release after fifteen years (the so-called "faint hope" clause). His strategy of choosing a crime with no early parole had backfired.

Behind bars, Boucher was attacked once by a Native gang member, who some said was upset that he hadn't been allowed into the Hells Angels. The man went after Boucher with a knife in an eating area, and was beaten and stabbed several times by Boucher supporters.

There was a second attack in the fall of September 2002. This time it was by someone who helped guards deliver meals. The attacker pulled out a crude homemade bazooka and fired on Boucher through a small opening to his cell. The Indian Posse – a Native gang active in Alberta and Manitoba – was blamed. Boucher wasn't seriously injured in either attack, and didn't need medical attention.

See also: **Michel Auger, Bandidos, Serge Boutin, Salvatore Cazzetta, Stéphane "Godasse" Gagné, Hells Angels, Dany Kane, Diane Lavigne, Nomads, Aimé Simard, Wolverine.**

Boutin, Serge: Informer from Hells – Informer Serge Boutin described his time in the Hells Angels in the 1990s as a feudal lifestyle, where serfs and vassals gave absolute loyalty to their superiors and followed a well-defined code of conduct.

"What does a [biker] patch represent to you?" Boutin was asked in court.

"Power," he replied.

It also meant between $5,000 and $10,000 a week, tax-free, from drug dealing, said Boutin, who estimated he raked in about $12 million over a decade, and he had all the luxury items that money could buy, including a $16,000 wristwatch and a rare coin collection. In the late 1990s, he oversaw drug trafficking in two east-end Montreal neighbourhoods, Hochelaga-Maisonneuve and the Gay Village, and estimated he had about a hundred men working under him, though he had contact with only ten to fifteen of the more senior ones. "I knew they worked for me, but I didn't know them personally. Not because I was snubbing them, but for security reasons," he explained.

When he turned informer – he had pleaded guilty to assisting in the February 2000 slaying of Claude De Serres, who supplied information to the police while working for the Hells Angels – Boutin cut a deal to serve a life sentence for manslaughter in a provincial jail instead of a federal penitentiary. The transfer to a provincial prison made it easier for Boutin to gain escorted day passes and humanitarian leaves – at the discretion of the wardens.

See also: **Maurice "Mom" Boucher, Claude De Serres, Hells Angels, Dany Kane, Nomads, Webmasters.**

Boxing in Quebec – Professional boxing in Quebec has been riddled with mobsters for as long as anyone could remember. Fights were probably fixed. Managers and promoters were often hucksters who bilked athletes and the public. Those were some of the grim conclusions of a March 1986 Quebec government report, commissioned by former Quebec justice minister Pierre-Marc Johnson.

"If this happened in baseball or football or hockey, it would be a national scandal," said Judge Raymond Bernier, president of the Quebec Sport Safety Board and head of the committee that drafted the report.

It was no secret that many of the judge's scathing comments concerned the activities of Montreal mobster Frank "Santos" Cotroni, a ringside regular at amateur and pro fights throughout the 1980s. Cotroni's friends included the boxing Hilton family of world junior middleweight champion Matthew Hilton and slugger Eddie "The Hurricane" Melo, who called Cotroni "my biggest fan."

The judge's report drew from interviews held with 105 people between October 1984 and April 1985. Only part of the report was ever officially released, but large portions of the remainder were leaked to *Le Journal de Montréal* reporter Michel Auger. Even parts that weren't illegal were troubling to the judge.

"Some of these managers and promoters get as much as 50 per cent of a boxer's earnings," Bernier said, "and this even includes money earned at other jobs a boxer may have totally unrelated to boxing."

Bernier criticized the Montreal Athletic Commission for having allowed Don King, a flamboyant U.S. promoter with a past that included numbers running and manslaughter, to come to Montreal to promote the Hilton brothers. "I was very disappointed by that decision," Bernier said, "especially since I had expressly asked that he not be allowed [to come to Montreal]."

In confidential portions of the report, the commission concluded that King and Cotroni, who was then fighting extradition to the United States on heroin-smuggling charges, controlled several boxers, including the Hilton brothers. Confidential sections also said that several other boxers in Quebec and Ontario had links with organized crime.

The unreleased portions of the report identified Cotroni as "the guiding spirit" of pro boxing in Montreal, and said that the Hiltons lost "hundreds of thousands of dollars," because of their contract with King.

The report concluded that Cotroni looked after the financial needs of the Hilton family and supervised their boxing careers. There were numerous accounts of Cotroni's generosity to the family of Dave Hilton, Sr., a chronic alcoholic, whom Cotroni had known for thirty years. The report noted that Cotroni apparently paid for everything, from groceries to rent to insurance bills to clothing to furniture.

Sections 3 through 6 of the report described the boxing milieu as a prestigious recreational activity for mobsters like Cotroni, who used boxing matches as a cover for clandestine meetings with other organized-crime associates. Cotroni had underworld summit meetings at boxing matches, including in Cornwall, Ontario, and in Winnipeg. He travelled under an assumed name, but was greeted as a potentate the instant he stepped off the plane.

The final premise of the report contained the allegation that Cotroni and his associates "have a percentage of certain boxers' revenues." In a conversation with a close associate, Cotroni was reported to have said in November 1981 that Dave Hilton, Jr., would soon be sharing half his purse with Cotroni to the tune of $100,000.

The Quebec report said Cotroni "invested" $100,000 in the careers of the four Hilton boxing brothers and recouped his money in an exclusive contract between the Hiltons and King. It also stated that the Hiltons were victimized by their youthful ignorance and their thirst for glory in January 1985, when they signed the exclusive deal with King.

Cotroni was in jail when the King contract was signed, but the Quebec report said he was constantly involved in the contract talks, nonetheless. The report detailed a meeting in New York on January 29, 1985, involving Dave Hilton, Sr., a New York lawyer acting for Cotroni, and the American promoters. Two days later, the Cotroni lawyer came north to Montreal and visited Cotroni in jail. Later that day, the lawyer met with Hilton and an executive of Don King Productions, at the Sheraton Hotel in downtown Montreal.

The commission concluded that lawyer Frank Shoofey was virtually cut out of the contract talks with the Hiltons, whom he had represented for years. Shoofey was opposed to any exclusive deals involving his clients, advising them it was in their best interest to sign for one or two bouts at a time.

"The Hiltons have conceded all and received little in return," the report said. "For example, the minimum purse for an eventual championship fight is ridiculously low, $150,000." The estimated real value of a championship fight was more like $500,000.

Bernier suggested that, for three years preceding the January 31, 1985, contract-signing with King, Cotroni had contemplated selling the contracts of Dave Junior, Alex, Matthew, and Stewart Hilton to King for several hundred thousand dollars.

In reaching his conclusions, Bernier discounted testimony from Hilton family and friends that Frank Cotroni was the only man capable of controlling Dave Senior, who had a severe drinking problem. According to Montreal boxing promoter Henri Spitzer, he held frequent meetings with Cotroni in the period preceding these fights because, "the father was always drunk and I needed Cotroni's help to keep him in line."

In the period preceding the January contract-signing with King, police surveillance recorded the presence of close Cotroni associates Tony Volpato and Giuseppe "Joe" LoPresti. Volpato, described in the report as an "iron fist in a velvet glove," was found to be "a greater and greater presence around the Hiltons" while Cotroni was in jail. The report said Volpato helped consolidate Cotroni's "complete control over the Hilton family."

LoPresti, a lieutenant in Montreal's Sicilian Mob, was grilled by the inquiry on his connections with King. At the time, LoPresti was out on $200,000 bail for a New York heroin-trafficking charge related to the celebrated New York Pizza Connection heroin-smuggling case.

Cotroni's New York lawyer attended the contract signing after conferring with Cotroni at Montreal's Parthenais Detention Centre, where he was being held while his lawyers contested an extradition request. U.S. authorities wanted him on a 1983 heroin-trafficking charge in Connecticut.

After the negotiations, police intercepted a call from Cotroni to the Hiltons at the hotel, in which Cotroni told Hilton the contract was "a good one."

Shoofey left no doubt he was unhappy with the deal with King. A month after it was signed, he told the *Globe and Mail* that he would "have been much tougher with the promoter. I would have gotten a million-dollar guarantee for the boys, with big bonuses up front."

For his part, Hilton family patriarch Dave Senior made no apologies for his friendship with Frank Cotroni, which dated back more than two decades. "There were times I needed money for rent. It was always there, with no questions asked. He's helped a lot of amateur boxers and amateur teams."

Not everyone described Cotroni as so benevolent to members of the boxing fraternity. Cotroni hit-man-turned-informer Réal Simard said that Cotroni plotted to kill Montreal boxing promoter George Cherry, because of a misunderstanding over a debt that another Cotroni hit man, Richard Clement of Longueuil,

Quebec, owed Cherry. Told of Simard's comments, Cherry described Simard as an arrogant bully. He had nicer words for Cotroni, saying he sought to solve problems quietly through mediation. "With the name he's got, that's his job," Cherry said.

Among those who testified before Bernier was Frank Shoofey, who was under no illusions about boxing. "Polo is the sport of aristocrats and boxing is for bums," he once said.

Shoofey was shot dead outside his Montreal law office the night of October 15, 1985.

In an interview with the *Globe and Mail*, Cotroni, who was then out on bail awaiting judgment from the Quebec Court of Appeal on his extradition, described the Bernier report as a blatant attempt to get him.

"I'm not a gambler and I have never put a penny on the Hiltons," he said. "I just want the boys to have money because you should see how they suffered when they were young. People know what I do for the poor people, not just the Hiltons."

Cotroni called Bernier's thesis that King paid him to secure the Hiltons' contracts "crazy. No one's going to get paid before they fight. The only money from King was a cheque to the father and mother as a gift." Financial records show that King gave a $50,000 bonus to Dave Hilton, Sr.

Meanwhile, the Shoofey murder remains unsolved.

See also: **Frank "Santos" Cotroni, Giuseppe "Joe" LoPresti, Eddie Melo, Frank Shoofey.**

Boyd, Edwin Alonzo: Smiling Bank Robber – Canada's most famous bank robber had a simple explanation for his choice of vocation. "What it came down to, was that they had the money and I wanted it," said Boyd, who admitted to robbing at least eleven banks from 1949 to 1952.

Boyd was born in Toronto on April 2, 1914, and began school a year later than most children, after his mother forgot to enrol him. He made it to Grade Eight, and was deeply affected

when his mother died during a scarlet-fever epidemic shortly before his sixteenth birthday. His father, a First World War veteran and respected Toronto police officer, sent him to work on a farm north of the city, and that was the last time he lived in what was left of the family home.

Like many young men of his generation, Boyd rode the rails west in 1932, seeking work in the Great Depression. He was arrested for panhandling and for a "dine and dash" – when he ordered a meal and then bolted without paying. Shortly after that, he got two and a half years in the bleak Saskatchewan Penitentiary in Prince Albert for robbing a gas station.

Released in 1939, he enlisted in the Royal Canadian Regiment and served in the Second World War as a dispatch rider. Later, he took commando training and showed so much ability in unarmed combat that he was called upon to teach others. He was promoted to the rank of sergeant in the military police, but his sorry attitude soon saw him busted back down to private.

When the war ended, Boyd returned to Canada with a war bride and eventually found a job as a streetcar driver for the Toronto Transit Commission. His wife, Doreen, had high expectations of him, and he grew despondent at being unable to fulfil them or better provide for his three children. He dreamed of being an actor like Jimmy Cagney, and then one day read about a mentally handicapped teenager who robbed a Toronto bank simply by demanding money. "He just told the teller it was a holdup and they gave him the money," Boyd later said. "If it's so easy to rob a bank, what the hell am I working for?"

Boyd took out a Luger pistol he had lifted from a dead German soldier in France and robbed his first bank on September 9, 1949, netting $2,256. He worked alone at first, often affecting disguises by stuffing his cheeks with cotton and painting his face with makeup. Once, he tested the effectiveness of a disguise by walking back into a bank he had just robbed without the makeup on and approaching the same teller, to see if she could recognize him. She didn't and soon he was back in a fresh disguise, robbing the bank again.

Boyd's first arrest for bank robbery came shortly after he changed the pattern of his crimes and took on a partner. While in the Toronto (Don) Jail, he met Willie "the Clown" Jackson, a mugger, and Lennie Jackson (not related), another bank robber, who had opened fire with a machine-gun on Ontario Provincial Police pursuers. It was in the Don Jail that Boyd hatched the idea of forming a gang, rather than working alone or with a single partner.

Lennie Jackson walked with the aide of an artificial limb, and while behind bars, someone sent him a new foot. It wasn't just to help him walk, as it concealed several hacksaw blades, which the newly formed gang members used to saw through the bars and slide to freedom on a rope made of bedsheets November 5, 1951.

Soon afterwards, they added Steve Suchan, a doorman at Toronto's posh King Edward Hotel, to their ranks. They were able to scout out which banks would have payroll moneys coming in, which suggested they had some inside information. They liked to work banks in the suburbs, reasoning that police there had longer distances to respond. Managers in suburban banks often carried guns, but it was a risk Boyd and his associates considered manageable. During a heist, Lennie Jackson would stand at the door with a machine-gun, while others in the gang filled pillowcases with cash, once netting more than $46,000 – the largest cash haul in Toronto history to that date.

Boyd was nimble enough to leap over a bank counter in a single bound, and did calisthenics to stay that way. His wife wasn't the only one who thought he looked like screen star Errol Flynn, and his good looks and dashing exploits caught the attention of the *Toronto Daily Star* and *Telegram* newspapers, which were locked in a circulation war. The public had scant sympathy for the banks, and Boyd's heists were seen by many as daring, victimless crimes.

Despite their success, Boyd didn't like Suchan, whom he considered too cocky, and Boyd rarely socialized with other gang members, other than to plan new heists. Boyd's reservations about Suchan were borne out on May 23, 1952, when Suchan gunned down Toronto Det. Edmund Tong, before Tong could draw his gun. Tong lingered near death for seventeen days before dying.

Suddenly, members of the gang were no longer seen as romantic figures, but as hardened killers. Suchan and Lennie Jackson were captured in separate shootouts in Montreal and were returned to Toronto, to stand trial for Tong's murder.

Boyd was still at large when he wrote a letter March 14, 1952, that stated he believed Toronto police "will use an order of 'shoot to kill,'" but that "death means nothing to me when I am fighting for my family." The letter warned police to look for him "in your every shadow. Start guarding your families, they are your weakness, for I am no longer a respecter of persons." Boyd added that he had pressed his inked fingers to the page. "My fingerprints are on this paper. This will prove I'm not kidding."

The letter was unmailed the next day, when Toronto Sergeant of Detectives Adolphus Payne crawled into Boyd's apartment near a church at 6 a.m. on March 15, 1952, and woke up the bank robber by thundering, "You sonofabitch, if you grab your gun, I'll blow your head off."

In the bedroom near Boyd was an open briefcase holding $23,329 in bank loot, two .38-calibre and one .455-calibre Smith & Wesson revolvers, a 7.35 Beretta automatic, and a 9 mm Luger. All the pistols were loaded and all their handles were pointing up, making them easy to grab.

Giddy with the news of the capture, Toronto Mayor Allan Lamport ordered the police to keep Boyd in the apartment until he could arrive with an entourage of reporters and photographers. When they were finally ready to take him away, Boyd looked at Payne and said, "You fellows did a fine job."

September 8, 1952, was the eve of the trial date for Suchan and Lennie Jackson to face charges of murdering Tong. It was also the first night of CBC-TV *Newsmagazine*, hosted by Lorne Greene. Years before, Boyd had thought of attending the Lorne Greene acting academy in hopes of imitating Jimmy Cagney. Now, stentorian-voiced Greene interrupted his evening newscast with a scoop from reporter Harry Rasky – the Boyd Gang had just broken out of the Don Jail again.

It was the *Daily Star*'s ace crime reporter Jocko Thomas who coined the name "Boyd Gang," and now the *Daily Star* hailed Boyd as Canada's original television star with a September 9 story headlined, "BOYD FIRST STAR AS TV STARTS SMOOTHLY."

The gang were recaptured, tried, and convicted, even though their counsel were two of the finest lawyers in the nation, with Arthur Maloney representing Jackson and J.J. Robinette defending Suchan. While Jackson didn't pull the trigger, he was found guilty of murder for being Suchan's accomplice. The date of their executions was set for December 16, 1952, in the Don Jail, from which they had twice escaped. Jackson requested that his final meal be the same as what Christ dined upon at the Last Supper: lamb, unleavened bread, and wine. The jail superintendent turned him down, as alcoholic beverages were forbidden, and so Jackson agreed on the same meal that Suchan had ordered: fried chicken, peas, mashed potatoes, and apple pie.

This time there would be no escape or reprieve. Suchan and Lennie Jackson were hanged back to back at 1 a.m. Boyd, who wasn't present when Tong was shot, was sentenced to eight life sentences, which translated into fourteen years behind bars, before he was paroled. Boyd resettled into British Columbia under an assumed name, and he was well into his eighties when he told author Brian Vallée that he killed two people in 1947 and put their bodies in the trunk of a car that he dumped in Toronto's High Park.

The victims were Iris Scott, a twenty-one-year-old former Miss Toronto beauty pageant contestant who worked as a clerk at an automobile dealership, and George Vigus, Sr., thirty-nine, a father of two who worked as foreman at a Toronto box factory. "After I left the TTC, I did a few things that could have got me hung, but I just kind of didn't mention them or I didn't think about them, so . . . ," Boyd told Vallée.

In another conversation with Vallée, Boyd expanded a little more, saying that sometimes he would go on walks alone, wearing gloves, a German Luger pistol, and lengths of sash rope. "I was out practising," he said. Vigus was struck on the forehead and garrotted with the slash rope, while Scott was strangled with the killer's bare hands. "Back in those days, it didn't bother me," Boyd said. "I'd just got out of the army a short time."

By the time Boyd made the grisly confession, one might argue that he was a different man. He had divorced his first wife shortly after his release from prison, and in 1970, he married a wheelchair-bound woman whom he met while driving a bus for the disabled. Six years later, they built a house in Sidney, British Columbia, which they shared with another disabled woman. Boyd cared for them both, until his own health began to fail.

He died of pneumonia in a hospital near Victoria in 2002, at age eighty-eight. He later credited his second wife with enriching his life enormously in his final years. "Meeting my [second] wife is the best thing that ever happened to me," he told *Toronto Star* reporter Dale Brazao in 2000. "It kept me out of trouble. It gave me something worthwhile to do."

Brigante, Natale: Violi Victim – The carpenter was shot to death in 1955 by Paolo Violi, in a final outbreak of bad blood that dated back more than five years to their native Calabria in southern Italy. He was shot twice in a dispute over a woman and left to die in Toronto in the gutter at Howard Park Avenue and Dundas Street in Toronto.

Natale Brigante

Arrested when he went to a Welland hospital for treatment of a chest wound, Violi pleaded self-defence, and was acquitted when police witnesses proved uncooperative at the trial.

Brigante's murder brought Violi to the attention of police, and he would remain in their sights for another quarter-century until he too was murdered.

See also: **Paolo Violi.**

Broeker, Cal: Undercover Agent – In the early 1990s, when he came in contact with Montrealer mobster Réal Dupont, Broeker was a grocer, restaurateur, antiques-shop owner, and upstanding citizen in Chateaugay, New York. His life changed forever, one day in the summer of 1994, when Dupont handed him U.S.$10,000 in counterfeit cash. Dupont's move put him in an uncomfortable position. He could either pass on the money, and commit a crime, or go to the police, and turn Dupont against him.

Broeker immediately contacted the New York State Police organized-crime task force, and they

told him to give back the money. Broeker tried, but this sign that he was not "onside" brought a death threat against his family.

Broeker's bank manager called in the U.S. Secret Service, which set up a meeting between Broeker and the Mounties. Soon the antiques dealer was working as an undercover agent for the RCMP.

His private life also underwent a major change. He began living with a Native woman in Kahnawake, where reserve criminals were forging ties with the Hells Angels, the Mafia, and the Russian Mob. In October 1994, Broeker's undercover work took him to Bulgaria, where a military official told him he'd like him to move arms from Canada into the United States through his connections on the reserve.

While at Kahnawake, Broeker worked undercover on Operation Orienter, which targeted Larry Miller, an enormously wealthy cigarette smuggler in New York State. When that operation ran its course, Broeker moved to Toronto, where he worked with bikers connected to the Hells Angels, whom he knew by names like Shark and John the Bat. They offered work on dope deals and money laundering.

Broeker blamed red tape and roadblocks from above for the fact that the RCMP did not move quickly enough against a man who wanted him to launder $100 million for the Mob. Disillusioned, he decided to retire in September 2000, and wrote *Smokescreen* with writers Paul William Roberts and Norman Snider about his seven years of undercover work.

See also: **Larry Miller.**

Bronfman, Samuel: Thirst Quencher – During American Prohibition the future head of the Seagram's Corporation and renowned philanthropist worked – in the words of American Mob architect Lucky Luciano – "bootleggin' enough whisky across the Canadian border to double the size of Lake Erie."

No matter how much booze Bronfman supplied through the prairies to Luciano's associate

Abner "Longie" Zwillman, it never seemed to be enough to quench the thirst to the south. Bronfman wasn't the only one cashing in. One of his competitors, Lewis Rosentiel, would one day turn his bootleg enterprise into the Schenley Corporation.

Bootlegging was profitable but sometimes dangerous work. Bronfman's brother-in-law Paul Matoff was shot during a battle between rival bootleggers in southern Saskatchewan in 1922.

Bronfman booze went south in a variety of ways; by ship to the East and West Coasts, by speedboat across the St. Lawrence–Great Lakes waterways, and by car across to New York, Michigan, Montana, and North Dakota.

None of this was breaking the law, since it was legal to manufacture liquor within Canada, and also legal to sell to anyone of age who would pay for it. Bronfman later told *Fortune* magazine, "We loaded a carload of goods, got our cash, and shipped it. We shipped a lot of goods. I never went on the other side of the border to count the empty Seagram's bottles."
See also: Bienfait, Saskatchewan; Moose Jaw Capone Tunnels, Annie Newman, Rocco and Bessie Perri.

Brook's Bush Gang – *See* James Brown.

Brown, James: "Sad Connection" – On the afternoon of Saturday, March 30, 1861, duck hunters found a body floating in a bay between the mouths of the Little and Big Don Rivers of Toronto. After examination by a coroner, it was determined to be the remains of John Sheridan Hogan, a Member of the Provincial Parliament and newspaper publisher who had been missing since December 1859.

Police suspected he had been murdered, and that the crime had been committed by the Brook's Bush Gang, a motley group of male and female drifters who often inhabited the city's drunk tanks when not living in the Don Valley.

One of the gang, a woman named McGillich,

heard that there was a reward for information on the crime, and promptly gave police the story they wanted.

On April 2, 1861, Brook's Bush regulars James Brown and his common-law wife, Mary Crooks, were arrested for the murder in Kingsbury's Tavern on King Street East in downtown Toronto.

It was the first – and last – serious brush with the law for Brown, who was born near Soham in Cambridgeshire, England, on February 28, 1830. He immigrated to the United States in 1852, first working on a farm near Rochester, New York, then quickly blowing his earnings in Buffalo. He found more work in shipyards in the Niagara Region, Toronto, and Port Dover.

It was in Port Dover, Ontario, while on the job, that he suffered a serious injury that made it difficult for him to walk. Rather than recuperate in a hospital, he regained his strength in the Collin's Tavern in Port Credit.

Mobile again, he drifted into an area of Toronto in the Don Valley known as Brook's Bush. Later he recounted in court how he hooked up with what police grandly called the Brook's Bush Gang: "Heard a noise in an old stable; went to see what it was; was invited to get into the stable by some girls; find a number of men and women; they made me feel welcome; asked me to send for some drink; I did so, and remained there for a month. This marks my sad connection with Brook's Bush Gang – a connection I most deeply deplore."

His hard-drinking new friends stole what clothes he wasn't wearing and sold them while he was in the Toronto drunk tank. Not long afterwards, he was fingered for what police considered the murder of Sheridan.

He freely admitted to being a member of the Brook's Bush Gang, but repeatedly swore that he never killed anyone. When he was convicted of the murder of Sheridan, Brown told jail authorities, "When I was asked to state what are the causes that have brought me to my present unhappy condition, I would answer in one brief sentence, 'Intoxicating drink and bad company.' "

This bad company sold him out for the reward, or what Brown called "filthy lucre" – even though he was not guilty, he swore.

His execution by hanging was set for 10 a.m. on March 10, 1862. On the evening of March 9, 1862, a reverend named Fish and missionaries came to visit him in his cell in Toronto's Don Jail. When they asked how he was, Brown shook their hands and replied, "As well as can be expected."

"I have every confidence in the Lord, and I know He will be with me and sustain me when I come to die," Brown continued.

For the past few days, he had been able to hear construction of a scaffold on the west wall of the jail. Now, the gallows were complete and it rained violently on what was to be the last night of his life, which he spent praying and singing hymns.

As execution time neared, his visitors looked distraught, but the *Globe* described Brown as "calm and collected." Now he was counselling the religious men who were in the jail to give him comfort. "He told them to prepare themselves, to be steadfast in the faith, and to meet him in Heaven," the *Globe* reported. "He repeatedly told them that he was prepared to die."

After a breakfast of coffee and cake, Brown was anxious again. He pleaded with the religious men to find his common-law wife, Mary Crooks, and to, in the words of the *Globe*, "entreat her to turn from her sinful life, to endeavor to get a situation as servant in some respectable family, and by living a righteous and holy life be prepared to meet him in Heaven. He urged Mr. Fish more particularly to write his aged father in England, to tell him that he died happy, with the sincere hope in his blessed Redeemer."

Outside, Brown could hear the murmur of a crowd gathering to watch the spectacle. He dropped on his knees to pray yet again. "When I go through that drop, into the Shadow of death, be Thou with me."

The executioner arrived in the cell to put a white cap on Brown's head and to tie his elbows behind him. The *Globe* reported the hangman was "a little man with a frightful mask upon his face, and with his whole person so carefully concealed that it was impossible to say who he was, or whether his skin was white or black . . . the 'white folks' are pretty sure he was negro, and the negroes are equally certain that he belongs to the pale-faced race."

Brown knelt and prayed yet again. Outside, there was a tolling of the bell from St. Lawrence Hall to announce it was 10 a.m.

"That's ten," people on the grass outside the jail said, knowing that it was Brown's final hour.

A female prisoner shrieked when Brown was led past her cell, and the *Globe* reported that he stopped for a second, "and a shade of surprise seemed to cross his countenance – perhaps that any human should care at all for him."

The crowd of five thousand outside the jail included nurses with babies, school kids, respectable women, and farmers on carts. They were still as he prayed, and then he spoke in a soft voice to a sea of their upturned faces.

Few of the crowd could hear him, as he said, "I have been a very bad man, and now I am going to die. I hope it will do you good. I hope this will be a lesson to you, and to all people, young and old, rich and poor, not to do those things that has brought me to my last end. Though I am innocent of the murder, I am going to suffer for it. Before two minutes are gone I shall be gone before my God, and I say with my last breath, I am innocent of the murder."

The twang of the rope brought a shudder from the spectators and most of them had hurried away by the time Brown's body was cut down at 10:30 a.m.

It was Toronto's last public hanging.

Brûlé, Étienne: Fur-Trading Outlaw – The man who began the pre-Confederation outlaw tradition of the coureurs de bois was brought to New France in 1608 by Samuel de Champlain, when

Étienne Brule (C.W. Jefferys, National Archives of Canada)

de Champlain founded the colony of Quebec. In de Champlain's early journals, he affectionately called him "my boy" and "my servant."

Before too long, the two men would be bitter enemies.

At the time of their arrival, there were already Basque traders on the lower St. Lawrence River, who had no or little respect for the French charter or rules against trading with the Natives without official permission.

Brûlé, who was from peasant stock, quickly picked up the Cree and Huron languages, and his comfort in the Native communities opened up fur-trading opportunities for him as well.

England and France were at war in 1627, and King Charles I gave a charter to a soldier of fortune, David Kirke, to capture New France. Kirke began his attack on the colony in 1627 and, by the spring of 1628, New France was desperately short of supplies. Brûlé sided with the probable winners and guided Kirke's ships to Quebec, where de Champlain had to surrender without firing a shot.

Before he returned to France, de Champlain denounced Brûlé as a traitor and an outlaw, while Brûlé tried to argue that the English forced him to help them. Champlain rejected the explanation and darkly predicted Brûlé would die "abhorred by both God and man."

Kirke's younger brother Lewis became governor of Quebec, and Brûlé made him rich with huge supplies of furs. Brûlé was the first from the New France colony to see two of the Great Lakes, and roamed the area between Chesapeake Bay and Lake Superior, living in Indian territory and trading furs.

In 1632, war between England and France ended, and New France was returned to France. Brûlé was now on his own to ponder his future.

De Champlain returned to New France in 1633, the year Brûlé was taken captive by Hurons in the village of Toanche on Penetanguishene Bay and executed. Folklore says that his body was eaten by the Hurons, who wished to share his strength.

His outlaw tradition of the coureurs de bois lived on for the next hundred years in New France, operating outside the rules of the Catholic Church and rulers of New France, and risking penalty of death if ever captured.

See also: **Coureurs de Bois, Sieur des Groseilliers, Pierre Radisson.**

Buscetta, Tommaso: Super Informer – In the 1980s and early 1990s, Buscetta's testimony would send hundreds of Mafiosi and a former Italian prime minister to prison, and he would

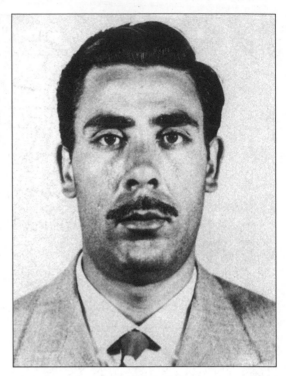

Tommaso Buscetta

be described in the Italian press as "*Principe dei Pentiti*" – "prince" of the repentant Mafia figures.

However, Buscetta attracted little attention when he lived on residential Northcliffe Boulevard in an Italian neighbourhood in Toronto in 1964. He was there after fleeing Sicily, along with many Sicilian Mafiosi, in the wake of the 1963 bomb blast in Palermo's rural Ciaculli district that killed seven police officers and three bystanders and caused police to stage a massive crackdown on the Mafia.

His Canadian associates included Giuseppe "Pino" Catania, who was tightly tied to Montreal's Cotroni family, as well as some of the old French Connection characters, including ex-Gestapo agent Auguste Joseph Ricord.

When he lived in Toronto, Buscetta was separated from his wife and living with a vivacious Italian television personality. He left Canada briefly to go to Mexico City for plastic surgery, but the results were barely noticeable. Buscetta slipped from Canada into the United States, where he lived for a time in New York City before going to Brazil.

A native of Palermo, Buscetta turned Italian state witness in 1984 after he was arrested in Brazil on murder charges and extradited to Italy. Once he decided to talk, he went on for forty-five consecutive days, revealing some of the Mafia's darkest secrets, including its alleged relationship with Italy's political elite. By the time he was done talking, he was widely regarded as the most significant informer in the history of the Sicilian Mafia.

In the 1980s Pizza Connection trial in New York, Buscetta gave damning testimony against twenty-two people charged with smuggling $1.65 billion in heroin to the United States. The drugs were sold through a network of pizza parlours in the American Northeast and Midwest.

Buscetta told the court of many conversations he had had in Brazil in 1982 with one of the defendants, Gaetano Badalamenti, who was convicted of running the international drug ring and sentenced to thirty years in prison.

Buscetta continued to be a star witness in a series of trials in Italy in the late 1980s that convicted more than 350 Mafia figures. He lived under a new name in an undisclosed place in the U.S. Witness Protection Program, and appeared again in Italy in the 1990s to testify in two cases against former prime minister Giulio Andreotti, claiming the politician had met top Mafia bosses.

Buscetta died of cancer at age seventy-one in April 2000. He was living in the United States by that point, but his life was so secretive that his lawyer would not say where he died.

See also: **Alfonso Caruana, Giovanni Falcone, French Connection, Giuseppe "Joe" LoPresti, Gerlando Sciascia.**

Buteau, Yves "Le Boss": Popeyes President – On August 14, 1976, when he was twenty-five years old, Buteau was among the mob arrested at a hotel in Saint-André-Avellion, Quebec, when almost fifty members of the Popeyes bike gang trashed the establishment.

Despite the cartoonish name, the Popeyes were no joke, and were regarded as Montreal's strongest biker club at the time. It wasn't surprising that they were picked to become Canada's first Hells Angels chapter on December 5, 1977.

Buteau got his colours from Hells Angels legendary founder Sonny Barger himself, and was the only Canadian authorized to use the title of "Hells Angels International." Angels hit man Yves "Apache" Trudeau, who would later turn informant, said that he, Buteau, and two other bikers killed Daniel McLean of the Outlaws gang and his girlfriend, Carmen Piché, by planting a bomb on their bike in Verdun on May 9, 1979, then detonating it after the couple climbed on board.

As an Angels president, Buteau established contacts with many biker gangs who would eventually become Hells Angels chapters. He worked to move the Angels from beer-swilling brawlers to an organized criminal enterprise, and urged members to shave, keep lower profiles, and avoid hassles. In the spring of 1982, he prohibited the use of cocaine by members. The penalty for breaking this rule was death, and the rationale behind it was simple: drug addicts weren't reliable.

On the evening of September 9, 1983, Buteau was drinking with a fellow Hells Angel and a Satan's Choice member. When they finally left the bar, a small-time drug dealer opened fire, and two bullets tore into Buteau's chest, killing him. Angels from the United States and England accompanied Quebec bikers as they rode from Sorel to Drummondville in a show of homage to Buteau. The drug dealer who killed him was promoted to membership in the rival Outlaws gang.

See also: **Hells Angels, Outlaws, Popeyes, Satan's Choice, Yves "Apache" Trudeau.**

C

Caccamo Papers: Criminals' Code – When police searched the home of Francesco Caccamo and reached into the cookie jar, they found themselves a major treat. Inside was a loaded .25-calibre handgun, six counterfeit ten-dollar bills, and – most importantly – what later became known as the "Caccamo Papers," a twenty-seven-page document that experts from Italy identified as the secret rules and regulations of the Calabrian Mafia.

Written in archaic Italian, it outlined the initiation rites of the 'Ndrangheta, or Calabrian Mafia, warning that any member who revealed the secrets of the society would be killed. Italian and Canadian police said that only four copies of the code were known and that all were in the hands of the Mafia, according to their sources.

Caccamo, whom Canadian authorities tried unsuccessfully to deport, was an important 'Ndrangheta member, the *mastro di giornato*, who made sure members complied with the rules and that spoils of crime were fairly divided, police said.

Among the rules was one that forbade members from telling anyone they belong to the 'Ndrangheta. Meetings begin with the disarming of members and a reminder to keep what is said secret. If members fail to give up their weapons at the beginning of a meeting, they may be disciplined by a beating on the back with a pointed stick.

See also: **Giacomo Luppino, 'Ndrangheta, Michele "Mike" Racco.**

Calgary Hells Angels: Fighting City Hall – A senior Hells Angel and at least one underling plotted in 1999 to blow up the homes of Alderman Dale Hodges, a Calgary city-hall staffer and a member of a community organization, and counselled a thug to assault Hodges and another person.

The bikers were angry with the alderman for his opposition to their former clubhouse in the Bowness area of Calgary. The clubhouse had been ordered destroyed because it failed to comply with local building codes. The plot was uncovered before the beatings could take place, and the bikers were sent to prison.

Capone, Al – *See* **Samuel Bronfman, Moose Jaw Capone Tunnels, Rocco Perri, Antonio Papalia, Quadeville, Sainte-Pierre and Miquelon.**

Cappuccitti Brothers: Rich Blood – Daniel Vincent and Vincent David Cappuccitti were born into an extremely wealthy family that was involved in the potato-shipping and the hotel businesses in the Toronto area.

The brothers were sent to prison in 1991 for the 1989 plot to kill boxer Eddie Melo and Frank Natale Roda of King City. Crown attorney Hugh Campbell said Danny Cappuccitti, then twenty-six, was "a dangerous psychopathic personality who led the conspiracy."

See also: **Eddie Melo.**

Carlyle, Frank: Coulee Namesake – He had been an officer with the North-West Mounted Police around the turn of the twentieth century, but was thrown off the force for being too friendly with horse thieves. He also got along well with train robbers, and in 1905, he was part of a scheme to rob a train near Plentywood, Montana. Carlyle's job was to blow up a railway bridge, and other members of his gang were to rob the train when it stopped.

The plan was spoiled when Carlyle got drunk and staggered off in an alcoholic haze, infuriating gang leaders Sam Kelly and Frank Jones.

On Christmas Day three riders showed up at a ranch in the Big Muddy Badlands of southern Saskatchewan, which Carlyle was visiting. They seized Carlyle, rode off into the hills with him to an area now known as Carlyle Coulee, and shot him dead.

See also: **Big Muddy Badlands, Dutch Henry, Sam Kelly, Sundance Kid, Outlaw Trail.**

Caruana, Alfonso: "Mafia's Rothschild" – Former pig farmer and international money launderer Alfonso Caruana wasn't in an expansive mood when grilled by Revenue Canada lawyer Chantal Comtois during an income-tax hearing in Montreal in March 1997. Comtois asked if Caruana was the Mafia's godfather.

"If only it were true," Caruana replied.

Comtois pressed on: "Is it true that you owned 160 square kilometres of land in Venezuela near the Colombian border?"

"Everything is false," replied the fifty-one-year-old Caruana, who now lived in the community of Woodbridge, north of Toronto. Revenue Canada was demanding $29.8 million in unpaid taxes and penalties, but Caruana countered that he made just $400 a week – net – washing and waxing vehicles at a car wash he owned.

Caruana was pressed to explain why people kept bringing him huge sums of money, and why some of that money found its way to Switzerland.

"You went back and forth – Venezuela, Montreal, Switzerland?" the judge asked.

"No, I had it brought to me," Caruana replied.

"By whom?" the judge asked.

"By travellers," Caruana replied, declining to elaborate.

Superior Court Justice Derek Guthrie noted that some $21 million had passed through Caruana's bank account in 1981 – one of several years when he didn't file an income-tax return. Caruana seemed puzzled. Despite the large sums of money going through his accounts, Caruana had declared bankruptcy.

For much of his life, Caruana had been able to escape such unwanted attention. His father had learned the ways of Mafia stealth in Agrigento, Sicily, from don Giuseppe Settecase, the same man who was sent to Montreal to try to mediate the Paolo Violi–Nick Rizzuto feud back in the 1970s. Caruana's family originally came to

Giuseppe Settecase

Canada around 1967, when he was a teenager. He had arrived in the Montreal courtroom via a winding route, from the dusty Sicilian village of Siculiana in southern Sicily to Montreal, South America, and a posh Sicilian enclave in Woking, outside London, England, in a district nicknamed the Stockbroker Belt. He had left Europe shortly before a wave of money-laundering and drug-trafficking arrests hit his business associates. Along their travels, the Caruana and Cuntrera families of Siculiana kept intermarrying, creating, in the words of academic researcher Tom Blickman, "a curious mix of Sicilian old-fashioned patriarchal clannishness (which protects them from infiltration) and modern global enterprise in illegal commodities."

By 1997, tax problems weren't the worst of Caruana's woes. The rival Corleonesi Mafia clan of Sicily wanted to kill him, because they thought he had become too rich and too arrogant, while Italian authorities sought to lock him up for almost twenty-two years for his conviction *in absentia* for drug trafficking and Mafia association.

Alfonso Caruana

When the 1997 Montreal tax hearing was over, the news wasn't so bad for Caruana. Guthrie ordered him to pay only $90,000 of the tax bill over the next three years. "I don't believe a word he said . . .," Guthrie concluded. "I don't believe the bankrupt [Caruana] and his wife, whose testimonies were full of holes, hesitations and incomplete explanations, but I must render my judgment based on proof, not suspicions."

Within a year, on July 15, 1998, Caruana was arrested with thirteen others on charges of conspiracy to import cocaine, conspiracy to traffic in cocaine, and importing cocaine in a series of pre-dawn raids carried out simultaneously by some two hundred officers in Toronto, Montreal, the United States, and Mexico.

Police said that, when Caruana wasn't washing cars or raising pigs, he moonlighted as the head of a multi-billion-dollar Mafia group, one of the most powerful in the world, that specialized in drug trafficking and money laundering. His group had bases throughout the world, including Toronto, Montreal, New York, Miami, Houston, Mexico City, Venezuela, Aruba, Spain, France, England, the Netherlands, Germany, Italy, India, and Thailand. The sophisticated organization moved drug profits from accounts in Toronto and Montreal to Miami, Houston, and Mexico City, through numbered accounts in Lugano, Switzerland, and from there to Colombia. Arrested along with Caruana, then fifty-two, for conspiracy to import cocaine were his brothers Gerlando, fifty-four, of St. Leonard, Quebec, and Pasquale, fifty, of Maple, Ontario.

The Cuntrera-Caruana clan was called "the Mafia's Rothschilds" by journalist Giuseppe D'Avanzo in the Italian newspaper *la Repubblica*. Canadian police called their effort to bag them Project Omerta. *Omerta* means "conspiracy of silence" in Italian, so the project name was wholly appropriate for one targeting such a tight-lipped man.

Until that point, despite his notoriety in police circles, Caruana enjoyed relative privacy in his $400,000 home on Goldpark Court in Woodbridge. He and his family had no record of violence and were Mafia financiers and facilitators, not gunmen. In a milieu where leaders had nicknames like The Executioner and The Beast, Caruana was known as The Ghost.

His brother-in-law Pasquale Cuntrera had also been arrested that spring in Spain. He was in his seventies and confined to a wheelchair, but that didn't stop him from somehow escaping custody in Italy in May while awaiting sentencing in a drug-trafficking case, causing a national scandal.

When Caruana was sentenced to eighteen years in prison, police could say that they had lopped the head off a state-of-the-art, multi-billion-dollar, transnational crime enterprise. They couldn't, however, say that they had killed his organization or others like it. Authorities estimated that some $17 billion was laundered in Canada each year, making Canada, in the words of RCMP Chief Supt. Ben Soave, head of the Toronto Integrated Intelligence Unit, "a haven for organized crime."

Part of the reason it was considered a haven was light prison sentences for mobsters. When he pleaded guilty in February 2000, Caruana was somehow eligible for parole because of time already served. The board, however, exercised some discretion and did not let him walk out of the courtroom a free man the day of his conviction.

In July 2003, Mr. Justice Ian Nordheimer denied Caruana bail, saying he was too rich and powerful to be allowed out of custody, since he still had access to enormous drug profits. Instead, he had to stay in custody to see if he would be deported to his native Italy, where he faced nearly twenty-two years in prison on drug trafficking and Mafia conspiracy charges.

Alfonso's brother Gerlando Caruana became eligible for accelerated parole in February 2003, but was arrested on a warrant from Italy in April while inside Fenbrook Institution, a medium-security prison north of Toronto.

The Office of the State Attorney General in Palermo, Sicily, called Caruana "a front-line participant in managing a colossal heroin traffic, the drug being produced in clandestine Sicilian laboratories and transported to the United States." The Palermo attorney general said "a river of money" was used to buy morphine to turn into heroin. "Thereby, [they] kept up a non-stop circuit of drugs to the U.S.A. and of money to Switzerland and thence to Sicily."
See also: **Tommaso Buscetta, Enio Mora.**

Cattle Rustling: New West Crime – Brand inspectors said organized-crime syndicates were behind $1.6-million worth of suspected cattle-rustling cases in Alberta in 2000, and that many more cases likely went unreported.

Sometimes, thieves just drove up to a field and loaded cattle onto trucks. At other times, they waited until the cattle were herded into lots at auction markets. Some owners made things easy by not branding their animals. Others left them out to graze from spring until fall.

Cazzetta Brothers: Biker Innovators – Salvatore Cazzetta was a member of the tiny SS biker gang in Quebec in the 1980s, of which fellow members included Maurice "Mom" Boucher.

When the SS dissolved in 1984 and became part of the international Hells Angels organization, Cazzetta wanted to try something new. He was thirty then, old enough to be experienced but young enough to be flexible. He convinced his brother Giovanni, twenty-seven, to quit the Outlaws biker gang, and together they would start up a new kind of biker club. Gang vests and crests only seemed to invite trouble, so they were out. He still liked tattoos, jewellery, and clubhouses, so they stayed.

Salvatore Cazzetta spoke fluent English, French, and Italian, and had wide-ranging, influential underworld contacts, including members of the Montreal Italian Mafia, the French-Canadian Dubois brothers, and the mostly Irish West End Gang.

Rock Machine founder Giovanni Cazzetta (left) by Johnny Plescio, Salvatore Cazzetta, and Renaud Jomphe

By 1990, his new group had a name – the Rock Machine – and a crest, a bald eagle. Members wore rings with the eagle crest on them instead of colours, and displayed eagle logos at their businesses. The Rock Machine didn't have weekly meetings like the Angels, and didn't have membership lists, which Cazzetta felt only helped identify members when they fell into police hands. He and Giovanni built up more than one hundred associates in their network between Montreal and Quebec City in the early to mid-1990s, and Cazzetta did well enough moving drugs that he could buy a house worth more than $2 million in L'Epiphanie, while the Rock Machine had a $1.3-million fortified clubhouse in southwest Montreal on Hudon Street.

His brother Giovanni pleaded guilty to possession of three kilograms of cocaine worth $2.25 million in the spring of 1993, and Salvatore was arrested in Fort Erie, Ontario, on May 1994 and charged with importing eleven tons of cocaine. With its two leaders in jail, the Rock Machine was under attack from Maurice "Mom" Boucher, Giovanni's former ss brother, for their drug distribution turf in downtown Montreal, along Saint-Laurent Boulevard, Sainte-Catherine Street, and Saint-Denis Street.

The Rock Machine took a pounding in the war that followed, and finally, in December 2000, they were absorbed into the American-based Bandidos gang. By that time, the two Cazzetta brothers were in jail for drug trafficking.
See also: **The Alliance, Bandidos, Maurice "Mom" Boucher, Dark Circle, Fred Faucher, Dany Kane, Nomads, Paul Porter, Rock Machine, Wolverine.**

Charbonneau, Jean-Pierre: Brave Survivor – The Montreal reporter for *Le Devoir* newspaper survived a shooting attempt on him in his newsroom from a mobster connected to the Cotroni family and rebounded to write a thick tome on organized crime in 1976. *The Canadian Connection* exhaustively chronicled drug trafficking in Canada from the 1930s onwards.

Charbonneau's book was crammed with names of criminals, providing a virtual who's who for police, prosecutors, and fellow reporters. During the Pizza Connection heroin-trafficking trial of the mid-1980s, in which prosecutors included future New York City mayor Rudolph Guiliani, New York Police Department investigator Charles Rooney leafed through the index of the book and found the name Salvatore Catalano. The entry helped them understand the international scope of the criminal who lived in their jurisdiction, describing him as "an important international trafficker." It continued, "Catalano, a Brooklyn resident, had been exposed in 1963 by Italian authorities as a dangerous member of the Mafia." It noted that Catalano had been listed by the American Bureau of Narcotics and Dangerous Drugs as an associate of Tommaso Buscetta, a Sicilian Mafiosi, "and several other U.S. and Italian crime chiefs."

The account by Charbonneau explained that Catalano had been caught on a Canadian police wiretap trying to set up a Mexican company to import sardines, tomatoes, pasta, or anything else. "That doesn't matter," Catalano said on the phone. He said the man in Mexico would understand, as this was simply a front for drug trafficking. With this report, American investigators were able to better understand their targets in the massive Pizza Connection case.

Charbonneau went on to become minister of intergovernmental affairs for the Province of Quebec. His long-time friend, and former rival in journalism, Michel Auger was shot by a gunman connected to the Hells Angels in 2001, and also survived to write again.
See also: **Michel Auger, Tommaso Buscetta.**

Cheema, Ranjit: Almost Stung – A mysterious Pakistani man who called himself only "Khan" went to the U.S. Drug Enforcement Agency (DEA) in the late 1990s with a plan for what police call a reverse sting. In such an operation, police or their agents offer to sell contraband to a target whom they consider an organized criminal.

The mysterious Khan made his living by setting up illegal drug shipments, arranging deals with police, and then collecting rewards from them. Khan's plan was to smuggle $12 million in heroin from Pakistan to Los Angeles and then into Canada.

Reverse stings are legal in the United States, but the Canadian law allowing them was overturned around January 1997, right in the middle of the joint DEA-RCMP operation involving Khan that had targeted Ranjit Cheema of Vancouver and others. By that time, plans were already in motion for a shipment of two hundred kilograms of heroin from Pakistan to Canada, using Khan as the middleman. The Mounties hoped that Parliament might pass legislation to allow reverse stings so that they could stay in the operation, but this didn't happen.

Meanwhile, Khan received $35,000 plus expenses from the Canadian police for helping the project, which was officially terminated on February 25, 1997. Six years later, American authorities were still fighting to extradite Cheema and two co-accused to face charges of conspiracy to distribute heroin and conspiracy to possess it with intent to distribute.

Cheng "Big Sister" Chui-ping: Human Cargo – On the Chinatown streets of Toronto and Manhattan, Cheng Chui-ping looked like any other matronly, slightly chubby housewife from a rural Fujianese village.

Her reputation, however, was quite extraordinary. Depending on whom you asked, she was alternately a saint, an international organized criminal, a liberator, a kidnapper, a folk hero, an exploiter, or a heaven-sent reuniter of families.

Born in the poor farming village of Shengmei in Fujian province, she had little education and few prospects when she first came to Canada as an illegal migrant in the early 1980s.

These were fortuitous times for her as she moved to Manhattan. Ties between China and the United States were warming, opening up trade, travel, and tourist links. Before this, the only way out of China was to work as a seaman and then jump ship, but now Cheng recognized the business potential in offering to guide Chinese outside the country, and then allow them to disappear.

In 1989, things went horribly wrong, after she arranged for several groups to enter Canada and be held in a safe house in southern Ontario, before heading into the United States. One group of women and children were driven to the banks of the Niagara River in midwinter and put on a flimsy $69 rubberized raft. En route to the U.S. side, the raft capsized, and four passengers died.

She was convicted of conspiracy to smuggle aliens into the United States, and sentenced to six months in prison. While serving time, she became an FBI informant, providing information on other migrant smugglers – called "snakeheads" – as well as on a violent and powerful Chinese gang, the Fuk Ching.

Once freed, she returned to Manhattan's Chinatown, where she puttered around her Yung Sun restaurant and Tak Shun variety store, set amongst a confusion of restaurants, jewellery, clothing, electronic, and produce shops in the heart of the East Broadway Chinese district. She sold cheap clothes and food in the neighbourhood, which was the largest base for illegal immigrants leaving China, and home to thousands of newly arrived Fujianese.

During lunch hours, Cheng chopped vegetables, washed dishes, waited on tables. At other times, she could been seen weaving among fellow Fujianese and Cantonese pedestrians along East Broadway, with bales of clothes to sell at her general-merchandise store. While she was rich enough to own the $3-million building that housed her restaurant, she continued to work

and live there, and chose the subway over chauffeured limousines.

Along East Broadway, she was known as "Dajie Ping" or "Big Sister Ping" – a term of endearment among those thankful for her role in helping them to the United States. She had a reputation for finding jobs for people and for helping them figure out their new surroundings. She was also capable of providing loans faster than the Bank of China.

However, officials said she made U.S.$40 million on the backs of illegal Chinese immigrants, who were poor, vulnerable, and unsophisticated. Police said she ran her immigration business by buying off corrupt immigration, tourist, and other officials and using fake or purchased papers. She charged a small down payment, and hopefuls promised to borrow the rest of the money upon arrival from family members already in the United States. Those who couldn't pay were found jobs at restaurants and garment factories and allowed to pay off the debt, with interest, in instalments. In the 1980s, according to police, the fee for the trip to America was $18,000, the price of a one-way ticket would hit $60,000 by 2003.

The 1989 Tiananmen Square crackdown created a boom in Cheng's business. The amnesty granted by President George Bush to Chinese living in the United States established a huge legal population that could afford to pay to bring family and relatives over. As demand accelerated, larger criminal gangs learned that smuggling people was more profitable and legally less risky than smuggling drugs.

Quickly the nature of the game changed. Gangs with bases in Hong Kong and China entered the field. Immigrants were recruited en masse, even if they couldn't afford a down payment. And when they couldn't keep up the payments or find jobs in a recession-racked America, they were kidnapped, tortured, and sometimes killed. To accommodate the demand, snakeheads pooled resources and bought old, unseaworthy ships and stuffed the holds with people who would spend months at sea in horrific conditions.

During one month in 1993, at least twenty-five ships, carrying thousands of immigrants, set off from Fujian crammed with human cargo. One of them was the *Golden Venture*, a dilapidated freighter that had been won in a poker game by Gu Liang-chi, who went by the street name Ah Kay, the leader of a Fujianese street gang that controlled East Broadway.

Cheng's fortunes changed forever, when on June 6, 1993, the *Golden Venture* hit a sandbar off the shore of the Rockaway Peninsula in Queens, New York City. After three months at sea, it had travelled 25,750 kilometres and now was just 200 metres from the shores of America, and within sight of the Statue of Liberty, when it started to take on water.

Ten passengers either drowned or died of hypothermia. Images of hundreds of immigrants jumping ship and huddling in blankets on the beach helped spark an American crack-down on people smuggling, and inspired tougher immigration laws.

Cheng watched the tragedy of the vessel hitting a sandbar on TV news reports in her New York home, said an alleged associate involved in the operation. "When I arrived Sister Ping told me she had a bad feeling about the boat," Weng Yu-hui said in a court statement. "I told her she shouldn't worry too much, because she only had two customers on board. She said she worried nonetheless, because she had had a run of bad luck recently."

The U.S. Court of Appeals described the con-ditions on the ship as unsanitary and danger-ous. "Nearly 300 passengers were crammed into the 40-foot-by-20-foot hold. . . . A single sta-tionary ladder provided access to the deck. No life boats or life preservers were available. Water and food were severely rationed. . . . The male passengers were required to use the deck of the boat as a latrine," the court said.

The tragedy launched a six-year manhunt for Cheng, who returned to the People's Republic of China a couple of months later for an anniversary celebration of the Communist Party. Much to her surprise, she was arrested upon her arrival, but bribed her way out of custody.

In December 1993, she was named in a six-count federal indictment for smuggling aliens and for illegal money transfers. Cheng retreated to a three-storey house, No. 398 in Shengmei village, constructed with money sent back to China over the years. Her home, complete with pagoda, dwarfed the other houses, made mostly of mud in the farming village.

Interpol agents had begun checking passen-ger lists on flights between Hong Kong and New York after she eluded arrest. But in the end it was not her name but that of her son that would prove to be her downfall.

With forty agents staked out in the Hong Kong airport on the morning of her son's flight hoping that Cheng too would arrive, she was spotted and arrested. At the time of her arrest she was found to be carrying three false pass-ports for Hong Kong, the United States, and the state of Belize.

Prosecutors say Cheng hired members of the notorious Fuk Ching gang in Chinatown to hold immigrants hostage in safe houses until they paid up to $30,000 apiece. Authorities said gang members sometimes threatened to dis-member their captives.

Finally returned to a New York City court-room in September 2003, Cheng struck a humble pose before the court in a black suit, with her head down and hair drawn into a low ponytail, pleading not guilty to people smug-gling. She looked quite ordinary, and not like someone accused of masterminding smuggling attempts involving as many as three thousand immigrants.

By the time of her court appearance, Ah Kay, the leader of the East Broadway Fuk Ching gang, was already serving a twenty-year term for his role in the *Golden Venture* tragedy, after plead-ing guilty to smuggling people and racketeering.

Chourt, Médard – *See* **Sieur des Groseilliers.**

Chu, Wai Hing "Kitty": Kitty Cathouses – On the night of September 10, 1997, police swept more than a dozen brothels throughout the Toronto area and, before the night was over, some twenty-two women – including alleged ringleader Wai Hing "Kitty" Chu, thirty-three, faced a total of 750 prostitution and immigration-related charges. All of the women were Asian and few spoke more than a couple words of English.

Simultaneous raids were conducted in Vancouver, British Columbia, and San Jose, California.

Chu was no stranger to authorities. She claimed refugee status in Canada after arriving from Hong Kong in 1987 but was able to extend her stay in Canada by appealing her refusal to the Federal Court and then to the immigration minister on humanitarian and compassionate grounds. Those appeals were also rejected.

In the meantime, she was convicted of several prostitution-related offences in Canada and she was ordered deported in the summer of 1995. The Immigration Department was working on arrangements to have her removed from Canada at the time of the brothel raids.

There were reports that the women had been pressed into service as prostitutes to pay for their passage to North America, but later reports said that many knew exactly what kind of work they had been recruited to do. Soon after the story broke, most of the women were released on their own recognizance and vanished from public view.

Chu was identified by Canadian police as the head of the Toronto chapter of a prostitution ring working in California in the late 1990s.

According to police, they were tipped off to the Toronto operation by an informant who knew several people in the Canadian operation, and who helped police learn that members of the ring in Thailand and Malaysia recruited the women for a $40,000 fee and brought them into Canada, where they were eventually delivered to brothels to work off their indebtedness to the ring.

Canadian authorities say Chu was connected to the Big Circle Boys, and that her prostitution ring brought the women into Canada via Vancouver on visitors' visas. When they arrived in Vancouver, they were met at the airport and put on another plane to Toronto, where they were escorted to one of a series of houses or apartments in North York, Scarborough, and Markham.

Bawdy-house operators paid between $7,500 and $15,000 in U.S. currency for each woman delivered to Canada, and the women, some as young as sixteen, were exchanged among the bawdy houses and in some cases were sold to brothels in the United States.

"You can buy any girl in the place for $15,000 [U.S.]," RCMP Staff Sgt. Larry Tronstad said.

Once the debt was repaid, police said, the women were theoretically free to go, though many continued to work in the brothels and massage parlours.

See also: **Big Circle Boys.**

Cobham, Eric: Pirate/Magistrate – When it was clear his death was coming soon, he summoned a priest to make a confession. Then he urged the priest to have his confession transcribed and put into book form.

Almost all copies of his exploits as a pirate in the Gulf of St. Lawrence between 1740 and 1760 were quickly bought up – by his own family. They considered themselves respectable, and did not want it broadly known that their wealth came from two decades of savagery on the high seas.

One copy survived purchase – and burning – by the Cobham family, and it was safeguarded in the French Archives. Its contents were backed up by contemporary accounts.

Born in Poole, one of the channel ports of England, Cobham went to sea as a boy. He may have worked in the Newfoundland fisheries at the age of fourteen or fifteen before joining a smuggling gang running brandy from France to England.

When he was about nineteen or twenty, he was caught, flogged, and sent to Newgate Prison for about two years. Upon his release, he worked at an inn in Oxford, where he robbed a wealthy traveller of a bag of gold coins.

The innocent innkeeper was accused of the theft, and Cobham didn't step up to clear his name. While the innkeeper was hanged for the theft, Cobham used the loot to buy a small, armed boat in Plymouth. There he recruited a nasty crew from the docks, and set sail for the Irish Sea, where they were lucky enough to find a ship carrying a golden cargo.

Showing the brutality that became the signature of his pirate career, Cobham sank the ship and drowned the crew, then set sail for the French Mediterranean to forge contacts with pirate brokers.

When he returned to Plymouth, he met Maria Lindsey, and the association made him even more ruthless. Together, they found a fresh pirate crew and set sail for the New World.

They first landed in New England in the whaling community of Nantucket, and soon afterwards sailed north past the tip of Cape Breton Island. There, they discovered the supply route to New France, where there were cargoes of furs and fish, and virtually no competition from other pirates.

They chose to make their home on the west coast of Newfoundland in Bay St. George at Sandy Point, which was guarded by a mass of shoals. This put them two days' sail from their favourite theatre of mayhem, between Cape Breton and Prince Edward Island.

Since they didn't want to risk frequent ocean crossings, they regularly unloaded some booty at Percé on the eastern point of the Gaspé Peninsula, where there was an active black market.

Cobham later boasted that he operated for twenty years without ever being caught. That's because he followed the pirate motto "Dead cats don't meow," and slaughtered all potential witnesses, then sank their ships.

His partner, Maria, was likely insane. Cobham's memoirs say she poisoned one ship's crew. Other captured sailors were sewn into sacks and thrown overboard alive, or were tied up and used for pistol practice.

Piracy was a young man's crime, and when it came time to retire, Cobham and Maria sailed for France, where they bought a grand estate near Le Havre from the Duc de Charters. There, they purchased status amongst the landed gentry, with a private harbour, servants, and a yacht.

However, the old ways died hard, and on one cruise, Cobham snuck onboard a brig sailing the English Channel from the West Indies. He and his servants overpowered the surprised crew, slaughtered them, and threw them overboard. It was more for old time's sake than money, as Cobham had plenty of that already.

After that last spasm of violence, Cobham settled into life as a pillar of respectability. He was appointed a magistrate in the French county courts, a position he held for a dozen years.

He and Maria grew apart as they grew more respectable. He wenched with enthusiasm and no discretion, while she often numbed herself with alcohol laced with laudanum, a then popular mixture of alcohol, sugar, and morphine. She became increasingly withdrawn, and her body was found one day in the sea under a cliff, her system full of laudanum. Apparently, she wanted to make doubly sure of her suicide.

Cobham's final working years were spent as a magistrate in France, where he died a natural death.

See also: **Charles Bellamy, Cupids, Peter Easton, High Island, Edward Jordan, Captain Kidd, Mogul Mackenzie, Henry Mainwaring, Sheila Na Geira, Samuel Nelson, John Phillips, Gilbert Pike, Pirates, Bartholomew "Black Bart" Roberts.**

Coderre, Judge Louis: Gloomy Judgment –
Many Montrealers in the early 1920s were disgusted with rampant drug peddling and prostitution on their streets. They were also certain that things couldn't be so blatant without corruption among the police and municipal authorities, and presented Superior Court with a petition bearing 158 signatures, calling for an investigation.

Judge Louis Coderre agreed to the investigation, which involved 162 days of testimony from criminals, police, and the public, beginning on October 6, 1924. When it was over, the horrified judge wrote that "vice spread itself across the city with an ugliness and insolence that seemed assured of impunity."

Comeau, Gary: Loyal Brother – The bar in Port Hope, Ontario, was full of bikers in 1978 when someone pumped three bullets into Bill Matiyek, sergeant-at-arms for the Golden Hawk Riders motorcycle club. When police tried to interview witnesses, several of whom were members of the Satan's Choice biker club, no one co-operated.

Six members of the Satan's Choice were charged with the shooting, and none of them took the stand in his own defence, since loyalty to the club forbade it.

After the longest murder trial in Canada to that date, Gary Comeau and Rick Sauve of the Satan's Choice were each convicted of first-degree murder, and Merv Baker, Jeff McLeod, Larry Hurren, and David Hoffman, all of the Choice, were found guilty of murder in the second-degree.

Lorne Campbell, another Satan's Choice member, swore that he shot Matiyek, but he had once been found guilty of perjury, and his confession wasn't believed.

Hoffman was eventually freed when a police wiretap showed he wasn't even in Port Hope on the night of the killing.

Comeau's claims of innocence were defended in a book by author Mick Lowe, *Conspiracy of Brothers*, which inspired songwriter Steve Earle to write the song "Justice in Ontario," and the case was also taken up by the Association in Defence of the Wrongly Convicted.

Finally, in September 2000, Comeau was the last of the six men jailed in the murder to get parole. If he knew who did the killing, he wasn't saying, choosing nearly a quarter-century in prison to ratting on a biker brother.
***See also:* Satan's Choice.**

Commisso, Cosimo Elia: Business and Personal Plots – Born in Calabria, Italy, in 1945, Commisso has a Canadian criminal record that includes three convictions for conspiracy to commit murder and counselling to commit murder in 1981.

The convictions came for plotting the murders of Toronto Mob boss Paul Volpe and his driver, Pietro Scarcella. Those two murders were planned for business reasons, while a third murder plot against American hairdresser Helen Nafpliotis was strictly personal. She had a romantic involvement that did not meet with Commisso's approval.

Cosimo Elia Commisso

Other convictions for Commisso include extortion, explosion with intent, arson, counsel to extortion, aggravated assault, and wilfully setting fires. He was considered a member of the Siderno crime group in Toronto, and by 1976 was ranked as *capo bastone* (boss). His undoing came when family enforcer Cecil Kirby of the Satan's Choice biker gang turned against him and co-operated with police.

See also: **Girolomo Commisso, Rocco Remo Commisso, Cecil Kirby, 'Ndrangheta.**

Commisso, Girolomo: Fallen Father – He had been considered *sgarrista* or *camorrista* or a higher-than-average soldier in the Calabrian Mafia of southern Italy when he was murdered in his mid-twenties in 1948, leaving behind a widow and three sons.

His sons – Rocco Remo, Cosimo Elia, and Michele – eventually moved to Toronto, where they had relatives and family friends. While his murder was never officially solved, it was widely believed to have been carried out by Salvatore Scarfo, a member of the Antonio Macri *cosca* (Mafia group) and his associate Michele Alberti, fifty-eight, who fled southern Italy for Argentina.

Alberti finally returned to Calabria in 1982, at which point there was a lunch meeting on the patio terrace of Gourna Restaurant in his birthplace of Siderno. With the dinner, finally peace seemed possible, after more than three decades of tensions.

Those feelings of goodwill lasted about as long as it took to get through the entrée. Then someone shot Alberti to death and, even though the restaurant was busy and there were more than twenty people at his table, police could find no witnesses.

Diners at his table that day included about a dozen Toronto residents, many of whom were close to the children of Girolomo Commisso. They included a manager of a Toronto-area linen-rental firm, who said he couldn't remember who arranged the lunch and that he didn't really know the victim. There were also two Toronto brothers in their thirties, one of whom said he felt lucky that he left the table shortly before the murder. "What does it take [for a stray] bullet to catch another guy?" he asked, adding he also did not know who invited the victim to his final meal.

Other diners included Vincenzo Figliomeni of Brampton, who would be murdered in November 1988, and Vincenzo "Jimmy" DeLeo, who ran a Toronto bakery shop. DeLeo said he visited Rocco Remo and Cosimo Elia Commisso in Kingston Penitentiary immediately after returning from Italy, but they didn't discuss the killing. DeLeo said he and another Toronto man were en route to the restaurant's washroom when the victim was shot. The old baker added he did not know the victim well. "I didn't know there were going to be all of those people there," DeLeo said. He shrugged his shoulders innocently when asked if he knew Alberti was a prime suspect in the murder of Gerolamo Commisso. "Oh my gosh, no . . . I came to Canada in the 1930s."

See also: **Cosimo Commisso, Rocco Remo Commisso, 'Ndrangheta.**

Commisso, Rocco Remo: New World, Old Problems – He immigrated to Canada in 1961 at age sixteen with his mother and two brothers, Cosimo Elia, then twenty-three, and Michele, then thirteen. The community he was leaving, Gioisa Ionica in the Italian province of Calabria, was dominated by the 'Ndrangheta (Calabrian Mafia), and Commisso's father, Girolomo, had been a senior member until his murder in 1948.

His uncles in Toronto ran a bakery and, during the 1960s, young Commisso was very close with them. It wasn't until 1970 that police noted him, and suspected he was using strong-arm tactics to pirate bakery contracts from other bakeries.

He was particularly close to old Mafia don Michele "Mike" Racco. In 1971, a power struggle was developing between the *cosca* of Marina di Gioiosa and Commisso's birthplace of Gioiosa

Rocco Remo Commisso

Ionica. That October, Commisso was visiting in Calabria with Salvatore Aquino, head of Gioisa Ionica *cosca*, when someone opened fire on them.

The next year, he returned to Calabria, and again was fired upon.

During this period, Toronto appeared to have two cornerstones – one under Michele Racco and that of Rocco Zito, to which Commisso appeared closer. The Zito group also had a close working relationship with Sicilian mobsters with tight ties to Montreal.

Rocco Remo Commisso was a pallbearer at Mike Racco's 1980 funeral. The next year, things started to go badly for him. In May 1981, he and his brother Cosimo Elia were arrested for counselling Satan's Choice biker Cecil Kirby to murder Toronto La Cosa Nostra leader Paul Volpe and his driver, Pietro Scarcella.

During the prison stint that followed, he showed himself to be well read by criminal standards, and worked in Kingston Penitentiary library.
See also: **Girolomo Commisso, Cecil Kirby, 'Ndrangheta, Michele "Mike" Racco, Rocco Zito.**

Cooper, Darin: Official Disgrace – This organized criminal was a member of the Toronto police department and, between December 1999 and March 2000, he and five associates pretended to be police officers on drug raids in order to commit crimes. Cooper, a ten-year police veteran, would flash his badge and then enter a residence, a police-issue Glock pistol hanging from his belt and a phony search warrant in his hand. Then he and his gang would rob and threaten drug dealers.

Their plan was to use money from the robberies to import 200,000 ecstasy pills from Europe, and then sell the tablets to dealers for a profit of about $1.2 million.

The gang was formed in a gym where Cooper became hooked on steroids and other drugs, according to his lawyer, Edward Greenspan. When the crimes were committed, Cooper claimed he was taking as many as nineteen different pills and tablets and five injections daily to satisfy his drug habit, at a cost of almost $800 weekly.

Cooper stole police equipment for the other men and used department databases to obtain information about their intended robbery targets. This strange and ugly chapter in the history of the Toronto force ended in February 2001, when Cooper, thirty-one, hugged his mother in the courthouse and was led away to serve a nine-and-a-half-year prison term.

Chief Julian Fantino noted that his Toronto police force moved quickly and strongly against Cooper. "[This case] casts a shadow over Cooper, the individual involved. We're not about to assume guilt for his wrongdoing."

Most of Cooper's prison time was to be served in "super segregation," because, as a former police officer, he was a prime target for other inmates.

Cooper had graduated in the top 5 per cent of police officers in his class and had no criminal record until his crime spree.

Costa, Giovanni: Born Unlucky – Costa wasn't a criminal, but he died a criminal's death nonetheless.

Costa had the profound misfortune of being related to mobsters involved in a four-year-long gang war in Toronto and Calabria, Italy, over drug turf. In June 1991, members of the five major Mafia groups operating in Toronto were believed to have been consulted before the father of three was shotgunned to death on June 27, 1991, making him the forty-ninth victim in the feud between Siderno's rival Macri-Commisso-Caccamo-Romeo and Costa-Lombardo-Figliomeni crime groups. By the time Costa was killed, criminals were targeting innocent family members, such as a deaf-mute in the Costa family.

While Giovanni Costa wasn't a criminal, two of his brothers were tied to the Calabrian Mafia ('Ndrangheta) in Toronto and Siderno, and he was the fourth Costa brother murdered in bloodshed that began on January 21, 1987, with the murder of his brother Luciano, thirty-two.

Another Costa brother, Giuseppe, was also an organized-crime figure who operated in Toronto in the early 1970s. Giuseppe, known in Toronto as Peppe and Joe, was close to established families in the Toronto area, including the crime group once directed by the late Giacomo Luppino of Hamilton.

Hostilities had begun to heat up after Luciano and Giuseppe returned to Calabria from Toronto and began challenging traditional crime groups operating in drug trafficking in Siderno. Giuseppe aligned himself with crime groups in a neighbouring Calabrian province with control over an airport and an ocean port, which gave them influence in heroin trafficking.

Giovanni wanted to escape the violence and give his family a peaceful life when he appeared in Toronto on August 16, 1986. He was granted landed-immigrant status five years later, and worked as an ornamental iron worker.

Italian sources said the underworld ambitions of his brothers, Giuseppe and Luciano, did not grate on Toronto organized criminals as much as on Calabrian criminals, after their return to Italy. "In Toronto, there's a place for everybody," said author Antonio Nicaso, who has studied links between organized-crime groups in Calabria and Canada. "In Siderno, with only 20,000 people, the interests of each individual are more restricted."

See also: **Rocco Remo Commisso, Giacomo Luppino, 'Ndrangheta.**

Cotroni, Frank "Santos": Recipe for Crime – He was nicknamed "Le Gros," French for the Big Guy, and "Il Cice," Italian for the tender, life-giving core at the centre of a hard nut.

The youngest of six Cotroni children, he was certainly a hard nut himself and big in businesses involving vending machines, ceramics, strippers, restaurants, labour racketeering, and – primarily – drug trafficking. Because of his high profile and constant criminality, he spent half of his life behind bars.

While in custody in Quebec, he made the best of the situation, driving a golf cart and preparing meals in his own cooking area. When not thus employed, he maintained links to cocaine suppliers in New York; Miami; Cali, Colombia; and Lima, Peru.

In the early 1980s, Cotroni looked at expanding into Toronto, and it was rumoured for a time that mobster Paul Volpe was murdered to clear the way. In the end, the theories blaming the Cotronis for Volpe's murder were discounted, since Volpe would have been a potential ally for them in Ontario. Toronto had replaced Montreal as Canada's largest city, with its growth accelerated by businesses fleeing the uncertain business climate of Quebec.

Cotroni grumbled more than once that one of the few bad points about Toronto the Good was a dearth of police officers on the take.

His Toronto contacts included Rocco Zito, a grandfather who had been a member of the Calabrian underworld before he immigrated to Canada three decades earlier. Roy McMurtry,

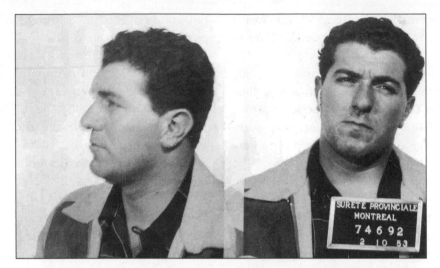

Frank "Santos" Cotroni in 1953

From left: Guido Orsini, Frank Cotroni, Carlo Arena

Frank Cotroni posing with Nancy Sinatra

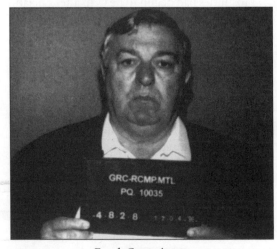

Frank Cotroni, 2002

then Ontario Attorney General, was told in a meeting with southern Ontario police chiefs just before Christmas 1983 that Frank Cotroni was a man to watch. "By far our greatest concern must be the Cotroni family of Montreal. . . . Needless to say, we consider [Frank] Cotroni our most serious threat," reported an internal police document.

In 2001, the National Parole Board refused him parole, saying he had made no effort to reform. "Despite your age, family and health problems, your criminal tendencies are at the same point as when the offence was committed," the board ruled.

By 2003, Cotroni was free from prison, having served at least half a seven-year sentence for drug trafficking. That sentence came on the heels of time served for ordering five contract killings.

It was in September 2003, less than a week from his seventy-third birthday, that publisher Les éditions du Trécarré announced that "Le Gros" Cotroni was writing a cookbook. While he was best known as the author of at least five underworld killings and an international drug trafficker, he was also handy in the kitchen. Recipes did not include "Broken Leg of Lamb" or "Informer's Tongue."

"Of course, he's a gangster, but he likes to cook," Anne Béland, a spokesperson for Éditions du Trécarré Inc., said. "Even in prison he cooked. He wants to be remembered for other things than crime."
See also: Boxing, Giuseppe "Pep" Cotroni, Vincenzo "Vic the Egg" Cotroni, Eddie Melo, Réal Simard.

Cotroni, Giuseppe "Pep": Big Crimes, Big Prison Times – The younger brother of Montreal Mafia leader Vic Cotroni, and the elder brother of Frank, Pep's health never recovered from more than a dozen years in Stony Mountain Penitentiary in Manitoba for a late-1950s $9-million securities heist and possession of heroin valued at $8 million. At the time, these were considered the biggest drug-trafficking

Giuseppe "Pep" Cotroni

and securities-fraud cases in the history of Canada.
See also: Frank "Santos" Cotroni and Vincenzo "Vic the Egg" Cotroni, Luigi "Louis" Greco, Lucien Rivard.

Giuseppe Cotroni

Cotroni, Vincenzo "Vic the Egg": Branch-Plant Manager – Vic Cotroni was fourteen in 1924 when he arrived in Canada with his parents, two sisters, and younger brother Giuseppe "Pep" from Mammola, Calabria. He spoke neither English nor French, and never went to school.

Montreal was often the first stopping point for Italian immigrants, and the Cotroni's new neighbourhood was one everyone aspired to leave quickly. They settled at the corner of Ontario and St. Timothée Streets in a three-storey brick row house, in Montreal's original Italian section. It was an area of urban decay, a seamy spot for frequent violent crime, a flourishing bootlegging trade, gaming houses, and brothels. More affluent Italian immigrants understandably preferred to settle in the new Italian section in St. Leonard around Madonna della Difesa church.

In 1929, Cotroni became a naturalized Canadian at the same time as his parents. His father, Nicodemo, worked as a carpenter and listed his income at $35 a week. All of the

*Paolo Violi (left) and
Vincenzo "Vic the Egg" Cotroni at dinner*

family's possessions were valued at just $1,500.

Young Vic and his father had plenty of minor brushes with the law for selling bootleg booze in Montreal and in 1928, when Vic was eighteen, he was arrested on a charge of violating a teenaged girl for refusing to marry him. She

A young Vic Cotroni

became his bride while he was free on bail awaiting charges, after he paid a $1,000 bond to keep the peace for twelve months, and they would remain married for the rest of his life.

A couple of months later, he spent thirty days in jail for illegally selling liquor, and in 1931 he was convicted of passing a bad cheque. In 1934, there was another six months in jail for possession of counterfeit money, which he later said consisted of just two fake fifty-cent pieces.

He worked for a time with his father as a carpenter, then became a professional wrestler under the name Vic Vincent. He was trained by wrestler Armand Courville, who remained a friend and associate for the rest of his life. When not perfecting half nelsons and body slams, Cotroni was learning how to get a hold on gambling houses, blind pigs (booze cans), and brothels, as well as crooked politicians.

In 1936, he was found guilty of assaulting an election officer, his last conviction for almost four decades. He and Courville had been hired by the Liberal party and the Union Nationale in "baseball-bat elections" to clear balloting rooms of their rivals and to stuff ballot boxes.

Throughout this period, Cotroni's name appears in Montreal court records alternately spelled as Cotroni, Catroni, Catoni, and Coutroni, with Cotroni the most common version. (The spelling "Cotrone" appears on Vic's headstone.)

He was heavily involved in nightclubs and gambling in the 1940s, and he was considered a benefactor of Québecois music at a time when much of the entertainment was American and English-language.

Ironically, crime inquiries and investigations in Quebec and the United States in the 1950s only helped Cotroni's underworld career. Potential rival Frank Petrula disappeared after a 1954 police raid uncovered a list of politicians and journalists who had been paid $100,000 to defeat then mayoralty candidate Jean Drapeau. Drapeau, at that time a young lawyer, was a target because of his zeal in running the Mob into the ground for a vice inquiry set up in 1953 to clean up Montreal's reputation.

Crime probes in the United States during the same time period pushed Carmine Galante of the New York City Bonanno family north to Montreal. Police estimated Galante was soon collecting gambling profits in Montreal worth about $50 million a year.

Galante and Cotroni became friends and, by 1960, Cotroni was a well-established local underworld chieftain, left in virtual control of the Bonanno family's northern "subsidiary." His powers were like that of a chairman of the board of local criminals.

The 1970s were a devastating, sometimes humiliating decade for Cotroni. He sued *Maclean's* magazine for an article that fingered him as a Mafia boss, and won the case in 1972. However, the victory brought only more embarrassment, for the judge awarded him just $2 in damages – $1 for the English version of the offending article and another $1 for the French – on the grounds that Vic Cotroni did not have much of a reputation to sully.

The following year saw the launching of the Quebec inquiry into organized crime. The hearings dragged on for years, and witnesses accused him of being involved in prostitution,

Pietro Sciara, Cotroni adviser

loan-sharking, gambling, extortion, and a host of other crimes. Cotroni responded by playing dumb and telling the inquiry that he was just a humble sausage-maker. "If I'm such a bad criminal, why am I walking around free?" he asked. It didn't help him that a wiretap captured his voice offering one of his tips for success: "I act stupid." This time it didn't work, and he got a year for contempt of court, a sentence that he beat on appeal.

At five-foot-five and 135 pounds, he certainly didn't look dangerous. Even when he spoke, he remained true to the code of silence. "What is the Mafia?" the little grandfather once asked a reporter. "I made my money in clubs and in gambling. All the rest is nothing but talk."

But he didn't seem so benign during a wiretapped conversation with "Johnny Pops" Papalia of Hamilton, as Cotroni pressed Papalia for money from an extortion bid.

"I don't care what he says," Papalia said. "He didn't give it to me, Vic."

"Let's hope because, eh, we'll kill you," Cotroni replied.

"I know you'll kill me, Vic," Papalia said. "I believe you'll kill me."

Tired and sick, he slowly withdrew from his role as businessman and "chairman of the board." The Quebec government in 1975 revoked his licence to operate his meat business. In 1977, Pietro Sciara, a Sicilian adviser who worked for Cotroni, was murdered outside a theatre where he had just seen the Italian-language version of *The Godfather*. In 1978, Paolo Violi, another Cotroni associate, and Cotroni's handpicked successor, was shot dead in his ice-cream and espresso-coffee bar.

By 1980, the old Cotroni organization was in severe decline, as various upstart groups, ranging from motorcycle gangs to brutally ambitious local hoods, warred for control of turf he once dominated.

As cancer racked his body, however, Cotroni remained the equivalent of a chairman of the board of the Montreal Italian mob. He retained respect, loyalty, and potential power, if he chose to wield it. His death was a victory of sorts, since he went to his grave peacefully, unlike many of his associates.

See also: **Bill and Joe Bonanno, Frank "Santos" and Giuseppe "Pep" Cotroni, Armand Courville, Faison D'Or, Carmine Galante, Luigi Greco, Willie Obront, Paolo Violi.**

Coureurs de Bois: Runners from the Law – Canadian schoolchildren read of them as romantic figures of the Canadian wilderness, whose name translates as "runners of the woods."

In their own time, however, they were far less affectionately regarded by the state and church powers of New France. It was illegal in New France in the seventeenth century to trade with the Indians, and this carried the threat of fines, imprisonment, or hanging.

A coureur de bois
(C. W. Jefferys, National Archives of Canada)

Armand Courville

The first of their number was Étienne Brûlé, who died in 1633.

While coureurs de bois were technically criminals in New France, the law regarding trading with Indians was rarely enforced, since they were vital to the economy of the colony. Historians Harold Horwood and Ed Butts credit them with keeping New France solvent in the seventeenth century, since, without them, there would have been no fur trade. The money they were paid never left the continent and their trading generated taxes that went back to the cash-strapped government.

Part of the problem they had with the Quebec state was sexual. Jesuit priests were disgusted by their custom of taking Native wives, and living with them outside the church. There were also business jealousies. At least one coureur de bois was hanged after he sold furs to a governor's trade rival. They were finally given legal status in 1700, and after that, those who followed this trade became known as voyageurs.

See also: **Étienne Brûlé, Sieur des Groseilliers, Pierre-Esprit Radisson.**

Courville, Armand: Grappling with the Law – Courville was also a successful amateur and then professional wrestler, who taught at the Club St. Paul de Ville, where he had about forty students, including young Vincenzo "Vic the Egg" Cotroni. Together, they also learned the fine points of organized crime that would help them gain a hold on Montreal's underworld.

One of the first big lessons they learned was that it paid enormously to have provincial, municipal, and police contacts. At one point, Courville bragged to *La Patrie* newspaper, "J'étais le chef de la 'police' du parti Liberal," "I am the chief of police for the Liberal party."

He went into the restaurant business with Vic Cotroni in 1941, opening up the Faison Doré and Café Royal. He was considered the right arm of Cotroni, and was well known in Montreal's East End, with his fine cars and rolls of bills, which he would peel off with flare.

He also had an interest in gaming clubs with Cotroni, and was generous to parish priests and community groups. If he suffered from low self-esteem or remorse, he certainly didn't show it.

When a crime commission pressed him about his livelihood in the 1970s, he replied, "If the Mafia exists in Montreal, it's probably like the Knights of Columbus."

His association with Cotroni lasted for a half-century, and they owned meat-packing firms together with Paolo Violi. Courville was one of the culprits in the scam that brought tainted meat to the concession stands of Expo 67.

His nephew, Réal Simard, became a hit man for Frank Cotroni, and then turned informer. By the time Courville died in 1991, Simard was in a witness-protection program.

See also: **Vincenzo "Vic the Egg" Cotroni, Réal Simard.**

Cuntrera-Caruana Family – *See* **Alfonso Caruana.**

Cupids, Newfoundland: Loved by Pirates – Originally founded by the English in 1610, it was known as Cuper's Cove. That name gradually morphed into "Cupids."

Not long after its founding, the settlement was discovered and raided by rich pirate Peter Easton, and the pirates kept coming back. In 1810, a Mrs. LeGrow reported unearthing a box of English and Spanish gold coins, which had been buried in her garden.

See also: **Charles Bellamy, Eric Cobham, Peter Easton, High Island, Edward Jordan, Captain Kidd, Mogul Mackenzie, Henry Mainwaring, Sheila Na Geira, Samuel Nelson, John Phillips, Gilbert Pike, Pirates, Bartholomew "Black Bart" Roberts.**

Customs Scandal: Criminal Clearinghouse – In November 1924, the barge *Tremblay* docked at the Port of Montreal with 16,000 gallons of alcohol hidden in its hold. That's more than enough liquor to fill a backyard swimming pool, and no duty had been paid on any of it. Soon, Walter Duncan, an investigator for the Department of Finance, revealed that several customs officers were raking in bribes of $100 a week.

In Ottawa, William Lyon Mackenzie King appointed his customs minister, Jacques Bureau, to the Senate, called an election, and narrowly clung to power. Duncan kept digging into corruption and passed on more damaging evidence to veteran Conservative MP Harry H. Stevens, whose revelations of widespread corruption in the Customs Department sparked the formation of a parliamentary committee to study the charges.

The committee found that much of the liquor shipped from Canadian ports was smuggled back into Canada. That cost taxpayers untold millions of dollars, since excise tax was not paid on exported liquor.

Prime Minister King faced loud calls to explain the apparent indifference of customs ministers. The Commons passed a motion censuring the government, moved by Harry Stevens. At this point, King decided that he could no longer hold together his minority government, and appealed to the Governor General, Lord Byng, to dissolve Parliament, but Byng refused. King subsequently resigned on June 28, 1926, and the Governor General invited Arthur Meighen of the Conservative Party to form a government.

Meanwhile, investigators found even more corruption within the ranks of customs officials, such as officials accepting bribes as Montreal mobsters smuggled liquor into New York State, and then picked up goods to smuggle into Canada. This was a time of a transportation boom, and mobsters used fast cars and trucks to tighten ties between the underworlds, while corrupting customs officers in between.

D

Dai Huen Jai – *See* **Big Circle Boys.**

Dark Circle: Hit Squad – This group of Montreal bar owners wanted to take back drug-trafficking turf in their establishments from the Hells Angels in the mid-1990s. They also set up a biker club, the Palmers, to fight the Angels' puppet club, the Rockers. The Dark Circle became the hit squad for the Alliance, an association of independent drug gangs, bar owners, and the Rock Machine.
See also: **The Alliance, Cazzetta Brothers, Hells Angels, Nomads.**

Davis, Harry: Corrupter of Public Officials – His headquarters at the White House Inn in the southwest Montreal suburb of Lachine was Montreal's biggest illegal gambling joint in the early 1930s, and his nightclub, Frolics, did

Harry Davis

nothing to tone down Montreal's gaudy image for vice.

The fun came to a crashing halt in April 1932 when Davis was arrested for trafficking 852 kilograms of opium, morphine, and heroin. Some of his operations involved diverting drugs from legal manufacturers. In addition to the drug charges, he was also accused of corrupting public officials. It took a jury less than an hour to find him guilty, and then a judge hit him with a prison sentence of fourteen years, plus ten strokes of the lash. This shocked the Montreal underworld, as no one in their ranks had ever received so tough a sentence unless he had pointed a gun at someone.

Among Davis's associates was Louis "Lepke" Buchalter of New York, who killed seven witnesses before turning himself in to police in 1939 after underworld associates Albert Anastasia and Meyer Lansky tricked him into believing they had made a deal for leniency with the government. In fact, they had simply grown weary of the heat that the police hunt for Buchalter had created for the underworld. Buchalter's sentence was far tougher than Davis's: he was found guilty of murdering a talkative witness and executed in the electric chair.

Davis walked free from prison in 1945, and within the year, someone tried to kill him with a bomb. On July 25, 1946, eleven days after the bomb attack, a gangster murdered Davis for refusing him permission to set up a gaming house. Montrealers weren't too shocked about vice, but the violence revolted them, and, in the midst of public outrage about the police corruption that had allowed Davis to flourish, lawyer Pacifique "Pax" Plante was appointed head of the Montreal police department's morality squad. He did an effective job and was fired eighteen months later.

See also: **Vincenzo "Vic the Egg" Cotroni, Harry Davis, Luigi Greco, Frank Petrula.**

Desrochers, Daniel: Innocent Victim – The eleven-year-old boy was killed by a bomb on August 9, 1995, during the Hells Angels–Rock Machine war, which ignited public opinion and sparked the institution of a tough new police biker squad, codenamed Wolverine. Daniel's mother, Josée-Anne, campaigned for a new anti-gang law, and refused a Hells Angels honour guard for her son. She also turned down their offer to pay for his funeral or her silence, and gave the same answer when the Rock Machine tried to buy her off.

"A life has no price," she said. "No one can buy Daniel from me."

See also: **Michel Auger, Maurice "Mom" Boucher, Serge Hervieux, Dany Kane, Diane Lavigne, Nomads, Rock Machine, Wolverine.**

De Serres, Claude: Computer Glitch – When the Ontario Provincial Police officer returned to his hotel room, the only thing missing was his laptop computer. Unfortunately, it was the most valuable thing there.

The police officer had just gone for dinner, taking a short break from surveillance of Hells Angels members in Sherbrooke, Quebec. When he saw what had been stolen, he quickly realized that, while he was spying on the bikers, they were also watching him. This is just one example of how the Angels and other outlaw biker gangs have grasped the advantages of the information age – and how they put that information to use.

In February 2000, within months of the computer theft, police agent Claude De Serres,

who was undercover among the bikers, was dead.

According to information revealed during the murder trial of Angels president Maurice "Mom" Boucher in 2003, the stolen OPP laptop landed in the hands of Normand Robitaille, one of the closest confidantes of the Angels leader.

When Robitaille read through the confidential files stored on the computer – including some personal information about him – it didn't take long to figure out that fellow biker Claude De Serres was talking to police.

Robitaille arranged a meeting with De Serres in February 2000 through one of his closest friends, a man who had vacationed with him in the Dominican Republic just days earlier. Police tried to follow their informant as he drove to the meeting in the Joliette area, about eighty kilometres outside of Montreal. Tragically, they lost him, and ended up hearing Des Serres's final words on his hidden body-pack recorder.

An unidentified voice said, "Listen, why do you work for the police and how long have you worked for police?"

"I have a problem," De Serres replied.

"You're not going to say anything," the unidentified voice said.

De Serres had an instant to think about his fate. Then there was a gunshot and he was dead.

See also: **Maurice "Mom" Boucher, Serge Boutin, Webmasters.**

Diefenbunker: There Goes the Neighbourhood – Former prime minister John Diefenbaker had the Russians and not the Hells Angels on his mind when he had underground bunkers constructed between 1959 and 1961 at the height of the Cold War – including one in Penhold, Alberta, just south of Red Deer.

Built as a refuge for political leaders in the event of an A-bomb attack, the Penhold bunker caught the eye of the Hells Angels long after the Russian threat had passed.

It seemed like easy money for Ottawa when the federal government sold the Penhold Diefenbunker in 1994 to two Red Deer–area

RÉCOMPENSE   REWARD
15 000,00$
DANIEL DESROCHERS
VICTIME INNOCENTE / INNOCENT VICTIM

RÉCOMPENSE 15 000,00$ REWARD

Si vous avez des informations visant à faire arrêter et condamner le ou les responsables de la mort de Daniel Desrochers survenu le 9 août 1995, S.V.P. contactez:

If you have any information leading to the arrest and conviction of the person(s) responsible for the death of Daniel Desrochers on August 9, 1995, please contact :

 Police (514)280-2777
(514)280-2052
SPCUM

 (514)842-6822

La récompense expire le 28 février 1996.   Reward expires February 28th, 1996.

Daniel Desrochers

businessmen for $312,000. However, thirty months later, the federal government scrambled to buy the structure back for $750,000 after the Hells Angels and a paramilitary group expressed interest in buying it. In 1999, Ottawa decided it would be best simply to destroy the structure.

Dorion Commission – *See* **Lucien Rivard.**

Dosanjh, Gerpal "Paul": Second Time Unlucky – His family was well known to Vancouver homicide investigators by the time a gunman shot the twenty-seven-year-old to death around 5 a.m. on Saturday, March 6, 2004, in a restaurant on East Hastings.

His older cousins were gang-leaders Ranjit "Ron" and Jimsher "Jimmy" Dosanjh, who were shot to death in separate attacks in 1994. Paul Dosanjh survived being shot in the head on August 16, 2003, in a clash at Vancouver's Loft Six nightclub between Hells Angels bikers and Indo-Canadian gangsters. Three people were killed and six were wounded, including several innocent bystanders, in the crossfire that night.

His murder remains unsolved.
See also: **Ranjit "Ron" and Jimsher "Jimmy" Dosanjh, Peter Gill, Bhupinder "Bindy" Johal, Lotus Gang.**

Dosanjh, Jimsher "Jimmy": Foiled Revenge Plans – Police surveillance first spotted him in the late 1980s, when they monitored the multi-ethnic Los Diablos street gang in Vancouver. He was arrested and charged with the March 14, 1991, murder of Teodoro Salcedo, who represented a Colombian cocaine cartel in Vancouver.

Witnesses refused to co-operate with police, and Dosanjh was soon back on the streets. During his absence, however, his associate Bhupinder "Bindy" Johal had taken over his drug turf. Soon, the word on the street was that Dosanjh had put out a contract on Johal.

Dosanjh thought he was going to buy stolen goods when he stepped out of his truck into an alley on February 25, 1994. Someone shot him

dead. Six weeks later, his brother Ranjit "Ron" was murdered, after threatening to kill Johal. Johal and five others were picked up and charged with killing the Dosanjh brothers, but acquitted.

On December 20, 1998, Johal was shot down in front of three hundred people at the Palladium Club in downtown Vancouver. That murder was never solved.
See also: **Ranjit "Ron" and Gerpal "Paul" Dosanjh, Peter Gill, Bhupinder "Bindy" Johal, Lotus Gang.**

Dosanjh, Ranjit "Ron": Politics and Drugs – He was a suspect when, on March 14, 1991, Sikh moderate leader Bikar Singh Dhillon, sixty-seven, was shot and wounded outside his Vancouver home. Drug dealer Ranjit "Ron" Dosanjh, also former head of the Vancouver branch of the International Sikh Youth Federation, was a political opponent of the wounded man.

Dosanjh threatened revenge after his brother, Jimsher, was murdered on February 25, 1994. He told a television reporter he would shoot Johal "right between the eyes" if he ever showed up at the Dosanjh home. Just six weeks later, however, Dosanjh was fatally shot in the face, when gunmen pulled up beside him and opened fire in a busy east Vancouver intersection in rush-hour traffic.
See also: **Gerpal "Paul" and Jimsher "Jimmy" Dosanjh, Peter Gill, Bhupinder "Bindy" Johal, Lotus Gang.**

Dubois Brothers: Brutal Clan – The Quebec Crime Commissions of the 1970s weren't sure whether the Dubois brothers were more powerful than the Mafia. The fact that this was even up for debate was quite a statement on the power of the Dubois family. This crime family from Montreal's working-class neighbourhood of St. Henri ranged in age from thirty to late forties at the time, and consisted of brothers Raymond, Jean-Guy, Normand, Claude, René, Roland, Jean-Paul, and twins Maurice and

Normand Dubois

Adrien. There was also a white sheep of the family, who worked for years as a civil servant, never straying into crime.

Their father was a poor bartender from south-end Montreal, but his criminal sons gained infamy after Montreal's 1975 Valentine's Day massacre, in which they fatally shot four rivals from the McSween gang at the Lapiniere Hotel.

Roland Dubois

A Quebec Crime Commission probe of organized crime dedicated almost a hundred pages of its final report to the Dubois clan. The report called the gang the most important criminal organization in Quebec, so vicious that it was feared by both motorcycle gangs and the Mafia.

The French-Canadian toughs had emerged from St-Henri in the early 1950s and, two decades later, controlled most of the city's rack-eteering, drug-trade, and prostitution business.

Claude and Adrien were particularly active, running their own gangs of several dozen members. Family rackets ranged from burglary, extortion, and armed robbery to drug importa-tion and loansharking. One early victim, a Greek restaurateur, refused to make extortion payments and his body was found with a cross carved into his chest. By the mid-1980s, the Dubois brothers had lost their power.

See also: **Vincenzo "Vic the Egg" Cotroni, Claude Dubois, Jean-Guy Dubois, Raymond Dubois, Claude Jodoin, Donald Lavoie, Paolo Violi.**

Dubois, Claude: Singing Killer – The former nightclub singer was the acknowledged leader of the Dubois clan of Montreal and was con-victed of the 1973 slaying of two relatives of Mafia boss Frank "Santos" Cotroni.

During his younger years, he worked as a doorman in a Mafia-controlled nightclub, and his rise in the underworld was later aided by the weakening of the Violi-Cotroni Mafia group, which allowed him to expand into the strip-club business and bars.

He ran his empire like a feudal despot, meeting his up to two hundred workers at his headquarters on St. Catharine Street East in downtown Montreal on Thursday, Friday, and Saturday from 7 to 9 pm.

At the same time that he was conducting a reign of terror in the Montreal underworld in the 1970s, he also enjoyed singing in cabarets. (Quebec had another singing Claude Dubois at

Claude Dubois

the time, but that rock star's only hits were in the music world.)

Brought up for sentencing in March 1989, the same week that his brother Raymond took his life, the Quebec Court of Appeal reduced the minimum sentence he would have to serve from twenty-five years to ten years.

See also: **Dubois Brothers, Jean-Guy Dubois, Raymond Dubois, Claude Jodoin, Donald Lavoie.**

Dubois, Jean-Guy: Another Family Killer – One of the notorious Dubois clan, he was convicted of the 1975 murder of a bartender, whose body was dumped in the Lachine Canal.

See also: **Dubois Brothers, Claude Dubois, Raymond Dubois, Claude Jodoin, Donald Lavoie.**

Dubois, Raymond: Deadly Big Brother – The eldest member of the infamous Dubois brothers died of an apparent suicide in March 1989 at age fifty-seven. His wrists were cut and his body surrounded by empty pill bottles in a suburban Montreal hotel room.

Dubois had had a criminal record stretching back to 1947, and Pierre Tremblay, a McGill University professor who specializes in the study of organized crime, called the death "most unusual and fascinating." "Those types of

people don't usually die of anything as peaceful as suicide," he said.

According to testimony before the Quebec Crime Commission, Dubois's specialty was extortion. He was a suspect in hundreds of crimes but, despite his brash tactics, was rarely convicted.

In November 1976, he drove his limousine through twelve consecutive red lights and, after his arrest, managed to grab a police officer's finger, which he twisted slowly until it broke.

Dubois faced murder charges in 1974 but was acquitted.

See also: **Dubois Brothers, Claude Dubois, Jean-Guy Dubois, Raymond Dubois, Claude Jodoin, Donald Lavoie.**

Raymond Dubois

E

Easton, Peter "The Pirate Admiral": Pirate/ Marquis – Perhaps the richest buccaneer in the Golden Age of Piracy and for several years in the early seventeenth century, his headquarters was a tiny village in Newfoundland.

Easton was from a prominent English family that had produced a bishop, and he was sponsored early in his career by John Killigrew, the first governor of Pendennis Castle on the Cornish coast of England, outside Falmouth. The Killigrews were called by some the "robber barons of Land's End," and helped Easton assemble a private armada of forty ships.

The British Crown granted him a letter of marque, which meant he could aid in the British war effort against Spain by plundering Spanish galleons. Other state-sponsored privateers included Sir Francis Drake and Sir Walter Raleigh. With Easton, they helped defeat the Spanish Armada in 1604 and make Great Britain the most powerful nation on the sea.

The end of the Spanish War brought drastic cuts in funding for the British navy. Easton found himself in Newfoundland with many former English officers who now had no income. An oath of blood brotherhood was sworn by the sailors, including Easton, who set their sights on potential plunder on the Spanish Main of the Caribbean, in the Gulf of St. Lawrence, and in the English Channel.

The Gulf of St. Lawrence offered the attractions of valuable cargoes of fish and the salt needed to preserve them. Far more importantly for Easton, however, was the skilled manpower which the Canadian coast offered for his fleet. For the outport men, the hope of riches at sea through sailing with a successful skipper like Easton was clearly better than the grind of working in the fisheries, which meant eighteen-hour days that barely paid enough for them to survive. When he wasn't satisfied with the level of volunteering for his crews, Easton simply "shanghaied" sailors into his ranks.

Easton's first appearance off the Newfoundland coast was in 1602 and, by 1610, he was the most powerful pirate in the western hemisphere, with a fleet of forty ships and thousands of crewmen. He shifted his attentions back toward England, setting up a stronghold near Bristol at the mouth of the Avon River. From there, he could hold up all the traffic in the English Channel, extracting tribute for safe passage. Bristol merchants pushed the Lord Admiral, the Earl of Nottingham, to get rid of him. When offered a pardon to go straight, Easton sniffed that he would not "bow to the orders of one king, when he himself was, in a way, a king as well."

Not wanting a battle with the British navy, Easton returned to Newfoundland, where Canada's first English colony was founded in 1610 at Cuper's Cove on the northern shores of the Avalon Peninsula. It wasn't long before they were visited by Easton, who demanded "protection money" in the form of livestock. John Guy, founder of the first English colony in Newfoundland, recorded in his diary that Easton returned to the island in 1610 and 1612 with his fleet.

His ship, the *Happy Adventure*, flew the flag of St. George rather than the Jolly Roger, and he rarely had to attack ships. They simply respected his force and let him board without a struggle, in exchange for their lives.

Easton carried himself as a ruler, not as a bandit. He used a captured cannon to fortify Harbour Grace Bay, and built a fort just east of Caplin Cove. His headquarters were across the bay from Harbour Grace on Kelly's Island.

In 1611, Easton was returning to Harbour Grace aboard the great Spanish galleon *St. Sabastian* with plunder from the Spanish Main when he was attacked by five Biscayan and French pirate ships. Easton sank the *St. Malo*, the largest of his attackers' ships, by forcing it onto Eastern Rock, which from that time on became known as Easton's Rock.

Between 1612 and 1614, the Pirate Admiral effectively ruled northeastern Newfoundland and, in one raid, he captured thirty English, Portuguese, and Jersey Island ships in St. John's harbour. More importantly, he scooped up Sir Richard Whitbourne, the sheriff who had been dispatched from England to arrest him and bring justice to Newfoundland. Whitbourne was from a lower social class in England, and likely felt obligated to listen to Easton, even if he happened to be a pirate.

Sir Richard later wrote that he was held on a ship by Easton for eleven weeks. Some people captured by pirates were tortured unmercifully, but Sir Richard was feted in an effort to convince him to become Easton's first lieutenant. Sir Richard refused, but did agree to go to England to support a petition for pardon, so that Easton could spend his days living in splendour on his loot.

In 1612, Easton shifted his base of operations to the more secure area of nearby Ferryland on the southeast coast of the Avalon Peninsula, after deciding that Harbour Grace was too vulnerable to sea attack, should the Crown decide to send a fleet against him. He settled in what was locally called the "Great House" on Fox Hill. From there he commanded his armada of forty ships from a fortress that was virtually unassailable, sheltered by Isle au Bois.

Once secure, he gave England an ultimatum: He could either continue to rule the high seas or he could get a pardon and settle quietly in England. The government of England buckled and wrote out the pardon, but for reasons unknown, it never arrived.

Gaston spent two more years in Ferryland, waiting in his palatial home on Fox Hill, and keeping some of his fleet in nearby Aquaforte. His sources in the English court were excellent, and he heard that the Crown had dispatched Henry Mainwaring to capture him.

Now, Easton set sail for the Azores to attack Spanish treasure ships, then sailed off for the Barbary Coast, where in 1614 he captured fourteen ships full of riches. He joined forces with the King of Algiers, fighting against Spain.

Finally ready to retire, he set sail for the pirate kingdom of Savoy – at Ville Franche, near Monaco. There he lived in luxury until his natural death at an advanced age. Captain John Smith, who colonized Virginia, noted in 1629 that Easton lived his final years with the title Marquis of Savoy.

The federal government has erected a monument for Easton at Harbour Grace, with a bronze plaque that reads,

Peter Easton 'The Pirate Admiral' fortified this site in 1610 and made Newfoundland his base until 1614. He defeated a French squadron at Harbour Grace in 1611, recruited five thousand fishermen from this colony into his crews, and raided foreign shipping as far as the Caribbean. In 1614 he intercepted the Spanish fleet at the Azores, captured three treasure ships, and divided an immense fortune among his crews. He was twice pardoned and invited home by James I, but retired instead to southern France where he became Marquis of Savoy and lived in great splendor.

His surname remains a proud one on the island, adopted by many who sailed under him.

See also: **Charles Bellamy, Eric Cobham, Cupids, High Island, Edward Jordan, Captain Kidd, Mogul Mackenzie, Henry Mainwaring, Sheila Na Geira, Samuel Nelson, John Phillips, Gilbert Pike, Pirates, Bartholomew "Black Bart" Roberts.**

Ellis Family: Early Toronto Brothel-Keepers – In 1802, Stephen Ellis and his wife, identified only as Mrs. Ellis, became the first recorded case of what might be considered organized crime in the town of York, which later became Toronto.

The couple was charged with running a brothel. Stephen was acquitted, but his wife was sentenced to the stocks and six months in jail. Despite her sad example, and Toronto's strict Protestant roots, vice marched on, especially prostitution and grog houses.

In 1831, Catholic journalist and Progressive Reformer Francis Collins railed in his *Canadian Freeman* about brothels.

More shameless debauchery was never exhibited in Sodom and Gomorrah, than is carried on in this town at present. Houses of infamy are scattered thro' every corner of the town – and one of them had the hardihood to commence operations next door to our office, in a house under the control of a Police magistrate! So besotted are some would-be gentlemen, that they crowded to it at noon-day and in open day on the Sabbath.

Emond, Richard "Crow": Biker War Casualty – Other bikers in Montreal were keeping a low profile in September 1995, for the streets were hot with drive-by shootings and bombings.

That wasn't the way Emond, president of the Hells Angels' Trois-Rivières chapter, did things. As he walked alone across a Montreal parking lot with neither a handgun nor bulletproof vest, someone pumped six bullets into his back.

His funeral in Trois-Rivières was fit for a statesman. He was buried in his biker garb, which included his "Filthy Few" patch, noting he had killed for the gang. His coffin, draped with the gang flag, was borne into the church, as "The Sound of Silence" was played by fellow biker Claude Berger, a trumpeter with the Quebec Symphony Orchestra.

Before Emond's murder, a total of twenty-two people had been killed in the biker war, but most of them were associates or hangers-on of the Hells Angels or their archrivals, the Rock Machine. Emond was the first full-fledged member of the Hells Angels to die in the battle for control of drug turf and, with his death, violence escalated enormously.

See also: **Hells Angels, Nomads, Rock Machine.**

F

Faber, Claude: Cotroni Insider – Considered the right-hand man of Montreal mobster Frank Cotroni, Faber was married to Cotroni's niece.

When he stayed in Toronto in the early 1980s, his tab was paid by Local 75 of the Hotel and Restaurant Employees Union, even though he didn't have a union title.

By the late 1980s, Faber was in jail after pleading guilty to cocaine trafficking and to the 1982 Montreal gangland slaying of Claude Ménard.
See also: **Frank "Santos" Cotroni, Hotel and Restaurant Employees Union, Eddie Melo, Réal Simard.**

Faison D'Or: Mob Hot Spot – A Montreal hot spot at the corner of St. Catherine and St.

Claude Faber (back) behind Frank Cotroni

Laurent, it was purchased in 1944 by Vic Cotroni and his long-time friend and associate Armand Courville.

Another Cotroni spot was Vic's Café, which became Vic's Pal, which became Pal's Café, also on St. Catherine near St. Laurent.

French-Canadian singers and comedians were highlighted at the Faison D'Or, earning Cotroni the title "Papa des artistes."
See also: **Vincenzo "Vic the Egg" Cotroni, Armand Courville.**

Falcone, Giovanni: Illustrious Corpse – Crusading Italian judge Giovanni Falcone knew that the better he got at his job, the sooner he would be murdered.

He was working against the Sicilian Mafia, and his efforts were more dangerous to him than to his quarries. Only the time and method of his murder seemed in doubt.

He had between seventeen and sixty bodyguards for himself and his wife, Francesca, and they were an elite group, with cool nerves, quick reflexes, and, generally, no spouses or children to slow them down. Sometimes they watched over Falcone's home by helicopter as well as by land. Commonplace activities, like jogging or walking to a corner store alone for a newspaper, were out of the question. When he did go out for coffee, Falcone would order ten cups and drink just one, reasoning this would cut the chances of being poisoned.

His Palermo neighbours feared they would get caught in a crossfire and some pressured him to move off their street. Through it all, Falcone maintained a quiet sense of humour, although his hair was prematurely grey, he smoked constantly, and he admitted to sometimes being lonely.

Falcone often travelled to Canada, both for business and for relaxation. Aside from Montreal, he spent time in Ottawa, where the RCMP are headquartered, and in the Toronto area, where the Sicilian Mafia had made heavy investments in real estate, food stores, factories, and restaurants. At times, he would speak to the RCMP about men like the Cotronis, Nick Rizzuto, and the Cuntrera-Caruana clan, but his real focus was to show that corruption and the Mafia were inextricably linked.

He told Canadian police officers that the Sicilian Mafia could move to different countries, but its mentality and structures remained rigid and Sicilian. He also spoke of how major crime groups were already working together and police must also learn to co-operate. He noted that Mafia members were acting as financiers and money launderers for emerging Colombian cocaine cartels and established Asian heroin-trafficking groups. In the end, whoever controlled the money held the most power and was the hardest to catch.

Falcone found a peace in Canada he could never enjoy in his native Sicily. He loved to drive through the prairies to Banff National Park, sharing space only with his wife and one RCMP bodyguard.

In the spring of 1992, Falcone was being touted as the next man to take charge of a new anti-Mafia agency. He was already Italy's first national anti-Mafia prosecutor. It was common knowledge then that he and his wife often returned to Palermo on weekends, and there was only one highway from Punta Raisi airport to Palermo's downtown.

He was on that road with his wife on Saturday, May 23, 1992. No one had paid much attention when a work crew tore open a stretch of the highway earlier that week, then repaved it. Also unnoticed was a man perched somewhere on the rocky white cliffs overlooking the highway that afternoon. With a press of a button, a ton of dynamite hidden under the highway ripped open an entire five-hundred-yard section of pavement, leaving a gaping forty-foot-deep crater just as Falcone drove over it. Falcone somehow managed to survive until shortly after he reached hospital, while Francesca clung to life for five hours.

Promotions in Falcone's work were both honours and death sentences, and on July 20, 1992, Falcone's heir apparent, Judge Paolo Borsellino, was murdered while visiting his mother in Palermo. On July 29, 1992, Giovanni Lizzio, head of Catania's anti-extortion team, was slain. It was a truism in the underworld that someone's ripe for murder when they are both isolated and dangerous, and that's how Italian law-enforcement officials must have felt that horrible summer.

Judge Liliana Ferraro, Italy's director of penal affairs for the minister of justice, appealed in March 1993 to the *Toronto Star* for Canada to tighten up its extradition laws. "It is impossible to win this war without co-operation from other countries," she said.

See also: **Michel Pozza.**

Faucher, Fred: Bandidos Booster – This explosives expert was an original member of the Rock Machine. He dreamed of being a big-time biker, and was impressed by what he heard of a war in Scandinavia between the Hells Angels and the Bandidos. Soon, he wanted his Rock Machine to be part of the Bandidos.

He was brushed off when he went to the Bandidos headquarters in Houston, Texas, with his merger idea, but eventually the plan took hold. The Rock Machine joined the Bandidos in 2000, and gained full status on December 1, 2001. Meanwhile Faucher was sentenced in December 2000 to eleven years in prison, after pleading guilty to twenty-eight charges. Half of the charges related to cocaine dealing and he also admitted to taking part in seven bombings in 1996 and 1997 during the biker wars.

See also: **Salvatore and Giovanni Cazzetta, Hells Angels, Nomads, Rock Machine.**

Fino, Ron: Mob Union – Toronto construction union leader Giancarlo "John" Stefanini was lucky to be alive after American Mafia chiefs hotly debated whether they should put a contract on his life in 1987, said Ronald M. Fino, who was described by the Federal Bureau of Investigation (FBI) in Buffalo as a long-time organized-crime figure and son of a Mob chieftain.

According to Fino, at one point, $100,000 was offered for the murder of Stefanini, and the hunt for a contract killer was conducted in Buffalo, Chicago, New England, and New Mexico.

Fino, who ran Local 210 of the Laborers in Buffalo for fifteen years, detailed the alleged bid to kill Stefanini, long-time business manager of Labourers Local 183 in Metro Toronto, in two one-hour phone interviews with the *Toronto Star* in 1990.

Fino said he thought the man seeking the killer "came very close to having Stefanini dumped a couple of years ago. 'Dumped' means killed."

After a year, American mobsters connected to the union decided Stefanini should be allowed to live, said Fino, who added that he considered the 1983 murder of Toronto mobster Paul Volpe linked to the Buffalo Mob.

Told of the murder plot, Stefanini replied, "I certainly hope it's a joke. Holy cow! There's no question we had extremely big rivalries in the 1980s [over] union philosophies."

Stefanini said his 14,000-member local – the largest construction local in Canada – had vigorously resisted Mob pressures. "We as a union fought these people and we cleaned the union out," Stefanini said. "We're extremely proud of our high standard."

Fino, under constant FBI guard at an undisclosed location, has proved a reliable witness in a number of cases involving relations between organized crime and labour in Buffalo, Cleveland, New Jersey, and New England, said G. Robert Langford, Buffalo's FBI chief.

Fino was the son of the late Joseph "Ebe" Fino, a former Local 210 official who was described by U.S. authorities as boss of the Buffalo crime family from 1968 to 1972. Fino stressed that he was positive Stefanini was not in the underworld. "He was not an organized-crime member," Fino said. "I would have known that out of respect [that would have been shown him]."

Fino said his father used to drop the family off at the Canadian National Exhibition while conducting Mob business in Toronto. Often that meant visits with mobster Paul Volpe, sometimes on a boat on Lake Ontario. Volpe helped the Buffalo mobsters, both financially and by giving them information.

Fino's father was shunted aside by New York–based mobsters in the 1970s and narrowly missed being murdered himself, Fino said. The elder Fino died of natural causes in 1984.

He thought his father's fall from underworld grace made it possible for Metro Mob rivals to murder Volpe.

Fino, who also ran a hazardous-waste disposal company, said union funds from Canadian workers were used in a variety of Mob-controlled scams in Canada.

Among them were:

- pumping union benefits funds into insurance companies, then using influence with insurance companies to win bonding and liability insurance for Mob companies;
- putting benefits funds into Mob-backed businesses;
- mixing hazardous wastes with fuels and reselling them in Canada, or selling asbestos-contaminated metals for scrap in Hamilton;
- taking kickbacks from brokers on stock deals involving union money; and
- using union money to manipulate stock prices. "The union takes it on the chin," Fino said of any investment losses that ensue.

Fino said he could not come to Toronto or Hamilton after becoming an informer for fear of being murdered. "I know too many people. I'd be recognized. It wouldn't be too long before I was in serious trouble."

See also: **Giacomo Luppino, Stefano Magaddino, John "Johnny Pops" Papalia, Paul Volpe, Waisberg Commission.**

Five Dragons: Corrupt Police – There was a time in the 1970s when it seemed the only thing that distinguished Hong Kong police from criminal Triad members were the taxpayer-funded uniforms.

However, in the mid-1970s, the British government formed a graft-busting organization called the Independent Commission Against Corruption (ICAC), which focused its attack on five station staff-sergeants called the Five Dragons.

The Five Dragons, led by former staff-sgt. Lui Lok, fled Hong Kong in the late 1960s and early 1970s. They felt it was only a matter of time before they would face charges from the newly formed ICAC, a civilian agency targeting the colony's endemic corruption. They reinvested tens of millions of dollars in real estate, construction, and the hospitality industry in Toronto and Vancouver, and police suspected they worked with criminal Triads to traffic drugs and launder money. In Toronto, at least $50 million was invested in a high-rise tower on Bay Street, near Chinatown.

Given the reputation of the police in Hong Kong, not surprisingly, many Hong Kong immigrants living in Canada found it hard to trust the authorities.

One of the Five Dragons was Hon Kwing-Shum (a.k.a. Hon Shum or Hong Sum), and he entered Canada in the 1970s under the entrepreneurial-sponsorship program. At that time, police said, he had made a fortune taking protection payments from opium dens, gambling halls, merchants, and prostitutes, which he reinvested in Canadian real estate.

In 1977, Hong Kong began extradition proceedings to have Hon returned to his homeland to face corruption charges. Arrested in Vancouver, he jumped bail to abscond to Taiwan, where fellow Dragons had fled.

After Hon's death in Taipei in August 1999 of natural causes, Hong Kong's High Court denied his family his riches, saying his assets were purchased with dirty money and would become the property of the government.

See also: **Triads.**

Fontaine, Faye – *See* **Carmen Barillaro.**

Fort Whoop-Up: Prairie Slaughter – The southern Alberta fort was founded in 1869 and named by Montana rotgut-whisky trader John J. Healy, who was described by Pierre Berton in *Klondike* as a former "hunter, trapper, soldier, prospector, whisky-trader, editor, guide, Indian scout, and sheriff." Healy was also an innovative fighter. When American wolf-hunters, known as the Spitzee Cavalry, attacked Fort Whoop-Up, Healy held them off by holding a lit cigar over a keg of gunpowder, creating the impression he wouldn't mind them all entering eternity together.

Healy was clearly an organized criminal. He trafficked in illegal whisky and weapons, breaking the laws of Canada and the United States. His base of operations was located at the junction of the Oldman and St. Mary Rivers, near present-day Lethbridge, Alberta, and was the first and worst of the so-called "whisky forts" that existed to make quick money through the illegal liquor trade with Native people. Whisky traders sold a vile and often lethal form of alcohol to Natives, which often blended raw alcohol, tobacco juice, red ink, painkillers, pepper, ginger, and laudanum, a mixture of opium and alcohol.

The first fort at the site of what became Fort Whoop-Up was called Fort Hamilton, and it was burned to the prairie by the Blackfoot people of the area. In 1870, it was rebuilt and given the less grand name of Fort Whoop-Up. In 1869 and 1870, the whisky trade from the fort greatly demoralized the local Native people, who traded buffalo hides for rotgut liquor.

The whisky trade was also a politically destabilizing force. The Hudson's Bay Company had maintained relative peace in the area, but with Confederation, its influence was gone, and now there were fears that the Americans would claim the territory as their own.

On June 1, 1873, life around Fort Whoop-Up plummeted to a new low, when whisky traders and wolf hunters slaughtered men, women, and children of the Nakoda First Nation in what became known as the Cypress Hills Massacre. This was the final straw. It was decided that policing was essential for the area.

The newly formed North-West Mounted Police reached Fort Whoop-Up in the fall of 1874, lead by guide Jerry Potts. The Mounties yelled into the fort that they were prepared to reduce it to rubble, but nothing happened. Then Potts rode up to the door and knocked. Finally a thin man with a scraggly beard appeared, and invited them inside for supper. The rotgut whisky traders, fearing a fight, had fled the area a few weeks before.

See also: **Whisky Runners, Wolfers.**

14K Association: Mobile Triad – They were big in the United States, but small fry in Toronto compared to the rival Big Circle Boys and Vietnamese gangs. In the early 1990s, they bolstered their strength by actively recruiting criminals of Vietnamese descent and also formed links with traditional Mafia groups.

In December 2000, a White House report drawn up by a number of American agencies – including the Central Intelligence Agency, the Federal Bureau of Investigation, the Secret Service, and the Customs Service – pointed harshly at what it considered Canada's lax rules for newcomers, particularly a plan aimed at attracting foreign investors, and said that the two largest Hong Kong Triads, 14K Association

and Sun Yee On, made substantial property investments in Canada during the 1990s.

The Toronto-based 14K, according to the report, was the fastest-growing Triad in Canada, with links to Asian criminal activities in New York and other American cities, while "Sun Yee On members are involved in trafficking heroin and methamphetamine, as well as alien smuggling, to the United States, where the triad has ties to New York's Tung On Gang," the report said.

Prominent 14K members from Hong Kong and Macau have emigrated to Canada, and Sun Yee On members have settled in Toronto, Edmonton, and Vancouver.

See also: **Big Circle Boys, Ghost Shadows, Lau Wing Kui, Kung Lok, Sun Yee On, Triads.**

French Connection: Heroin Highway – American mobsters Carmine Galante, Joe Bonanno, and Lucky Luciano met with Sicilian crime boss Salvatore "The Pope" Greco and rising Sicilian Mafioso Gaetano Badalamenti in 1957 at the best hotel in Sicily, the marble-lined Grand Hôtel des Palmes in Palermo. Also meeting on the hotel's lush red carpets was

Lucky Luciano

Grand Hôtel des Palmes, Palermo

Tommaso Buscetta, who would one day become one of the greatest informers in Mafia history. They dined at the equally luxurious Spano restaurant nearby, as they plotted what would become known as the French Connection. This drug pipeline would become famous through the book and movie of the same name.

Despite its immortalizing in literature and film, the French Connection was anything but glamorous. The mobsters were planning how to send Turkish opium to the French port city of Marseilles, where it was converted into heroin in makeshift labs on the sandy cliffs overlooking the ocean. Once converted, it was sent into Montreal and into the United States.

French-Corsican gangsters were brought on board with the promise of the seemingly unlim-ited American market. The profits were enor-mous: a kilogram of opium, bought for $35 in Turkey, sold on the streets of Harlem for up to $225,000. For the underworld, it meant mobsters were now looking beyond their neighbourhoods and becoming international entrepreneurs. Mob bosses had a tougher time controlling ambitious young gangsters, who saw the possibility of arranging deals on their own, and almost imme-diately becoming rich and powerful. Drugs also meant bigger prison terms than were handed out for old Mob activities like gambling. With the threat of big prison time came more vio-lence. The Mob would never be the same.

See also: **Alberto Agueci, Joe Bonanno, Tommaso Buscetta, Carmine Galante, John "Johnny Pops" Papalia, Benedetto Zizzo.**

G

Gagné, Charles: "Low-Risk" Hit Man – This Quebec man was regarded by federal officials as a low-risk parolee when he murdered Toronto boxer Eddie Melo and Melo's friend Joao "Johnny" Pavao.

The National Parole Board granted Gagné a day pass on December 12, 2000, even though he was serving a ten-year sentence for robbing a grocery store in 1995 with an AK-47 assault rifle while unlawfully at large. "The board is persuaded that your risk is not undue upon such a release," the board ruled, although the decision added, "Your criminal history includes a number of weapons offences, which involved guns on all occasions and negative associates."

Calling his previous behaviour "impulsive" and "thrill-seeking," the parole board decision continued, "As well, you have demonstrated a comfort with a criminal lifestyle that includes guns and negative peers who make 'big promises' of easy money." Nonetheless, the board concluded that Gagné, then twenty-seven, had mellowed since he stuck up the supermarket with the AK-47. "Your institutional performance over-all has been good, which the board takes as evidence that you are less impulsive and better able to choose your associates, . . . all of which suggest that risk is manageable."

Four months later, on April 6, 2001, Gagné was in a Mississauga parking lot, firing close-range shots into Melo and Pavao. He hadn't met either man before but was willing to end Melo's life for $75,000, and the promise of future criminal work. He threw in the Pavao murder for free because Pavao was a witness.

In September 2003, Gagné turned on the man whom he said had hired him, a long-time neighbour and sometime friend of Melo. For this, Gagné was allowed to plead guilty to two counts of second-degree murder, which offered the hope of further parole in twelve years. A first-degree murder conviction would have meant no parole for twenty-five years.

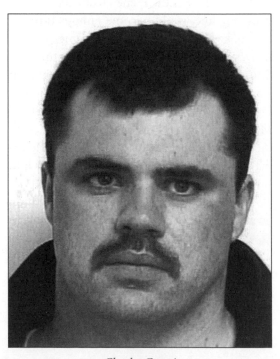

Charles Gagné

"The Crown is accepting Gagné's plea to second-degree murder, in what is clearly a first-degree murder case, because of the need to call Gagné as a Crown witness in order to seek justice in that related case," Crown prosecutor Stephen Sherriff told the court. Gagné's lawyer, John McCulligh, said his client, who was now HIV positive, "renounced the life he lived."

On December 16, 2003, a man from Melo's old west Toronto neighbourhood, fifty-year-old Delio Manuel Pereira, pleaded guilty to conspiracy to commit murder in connection with Melo's contract murder.

Pereira admitted that the plot involved three other men, including Gagné. His sentencing will not take place until after June 2004.

At the time of Gagné's arrest on July 14, 2003, for the Melo and Pavao murders, he was on a day pass from a prison in Gatineau, Quebec, where he was serving a new ten-year sentence for aggravated assault for shooting up a Quebec chalet while collecting a drug debt.
See also: **Eddie Melo.**

Gagné, Stéphane "Godasse": Football Team – The first time Gagné met Hells Angels boss Maurice "Mom" Boucher was in the mid-1990s in a downtown Montreal store. He instantly recognized Boucher and passed him his pager number, asking Boucher to call him.

Gagné, whose nickname means "dirty shoe" in French, had a twelve-year criminal history of theft and drug convictions. After the chance meeting with Boucher, he was approached by a member of the Rock Machine while in the Bordeaux Jail in Montreal. The Rock Machine member asked him to stomp on a picture of Boucher, and Gagné refused.

"I was an independent [drug dealer] at this point in the biker war," Gagné later told court. "They asked me to choose between the Rock Machine and the Hells Angels and I chose the Hells Angels." Gagné was quickly hurt in a fight, but took his revenge later by attacking a Rock Machine inmate with a pipe. Transferred to

Sorel Detention Centre, he met Boucher again, and they soon were taking Alcoholics Anonymous and drug-rehab sessions so that they could talk.

When they were both free again, Gagné stole a Jeep Cherokee for Boucher. Soon, Gagné was moving in Boucher's circles. On weekends, he would help bring the *ti' gars*, or "little guys," who were the lowest-ranking dealers in their crews, to Boucher's home. The *ti'gars* would clear his yard of unwanted foliage and bushes, making the place tidier and, far more importantly, making it more difficult for intruders to hide.

During get-togethers for *les hells*, junior bikers acted as gofers and waiters. It was a feudal arrangement, and lower-tier bikers like Gagné had to make sure their higher-ups were properly fed and refreshed. "As long as there are members who are up, you stay up to serve them," Gagné said.

Gagné soaked up the nuances of biker culture, such as how, when bikers of equal rank met, they would shake hands and hug, patting

Stéphane Gagné

each other's backs. However, a lower-ranking biker must not do that to a superior. Someone of his rank had to keep his hands off the gang patch on the back of a senior biker's vest.

Gagné felt he was part of something big now. One meeting in 1997 was at Bistro à Champlain, which had a 35,000-bottle wine cellar. Seventeen bikers dined on foie gras, Bordeaux, and Burgundy, then paid the bill of more than $8,000 in cash.

To explain how they could own houses and cars without real jobs, the bikers invested in a range of businesses, ranging from dry cleaners to taverns. There were also fake jobs, and Gagné arranged for a company to issue him bogus pay slips and T-4 forms. Boucher sometimes claimed in court cases that he was a used-car salesman working on commission. "Me, I've never seen Mom sell a car," Gagné later told the court.

Gagné felt as if he belonged in Boucher's world, and even named his son Harley-David after the Harley-Davidson motorcycles the bikers rode. "I wanted to make money and become a Hells Angel," he said. "I'd go out each night, buy rounds, give money to my relatives, drive the latest car of the year."

Gagné said that Pierre Provencher of the junior club, the Rockers, recruited him to the Angels' "football team," a euphemism for the Angels' death squad. Provencher was among a group of Rockers fighting to gain control of drug turf in Verdun during the late 1990s. The Rock Machine was already well-entrenched in the area, and the battle for Verdun became a focal point in the biker-gang war.

In early 1997, Gagné and another biker tried to kill a Rock Machine drug dealer in the woods. They shot him and tried to suffocate him when he kept talking. To Gagné's shock, the man was somehow still alive the next day.

In June 1997, Gagné met with Boucher again, and was told to stay out of jail for a while. "He told me it was important that I stay clean for other things than stealing cars," said Gagné.

"For more important things, the big jobs."

The "big jobs" included murdering an unarmed mother simply because of her job as a prison guard. On June 26, 1997, Gagné and André "Toots" Tousignant shot guard Diane Lavigne dead as she left her work. She hadn't done anything personally to offend the gang. They didn't even know her. The mother of two was murdered simply because she was a jail guard, and the murder was part of a plan of Boucher's to destabilize the justice system.

Two days later, a twenty-nine-year-old civilian employee who conducted Alcoholics Anonymous meetings at St. Vincent de Paul Penitentiary in Laval, north of Montreal, was wounded in similar circumstances. Two men on a motorcycle fired four times at him, but he escaped with severe injuries.

When another guard was murdered, Gagné asked two more-senior bikers about the attack. They didn't say exactly, but Gagné left the conversation with the impression that they had a hand in it. They were later promoted to the Nomads, the highest Hells Angels rank, before going to jail on other murder charges.

Gagné later told police that he was preparing to kill defence lawyer Pierre Panaccio when he was arrested December 5, 1997. According to Gagné, Panaccio fell out of favour after influential members of the Rockers accused the lawyer of defending them poorly, and wanted to recover some or all of the advance they gave him. Gagné said the issue was brought to the attention of Boucher. As Boucher and Gagné added up drug proceeds, Boucher wrote on a message board, "Must do Pinocchio."

When Gagné was arrested for the Lavigne murder, he pleaded guilty and was given a twenty-five-year sentence. He cut a deal with the Crown for $140 a month to be paid to his prison canteen privileges and $400 a month for his son. For that, he agreed to be the Crown's main witness in Boucher's first-degree murder trial in the spring of 2002, for the murder of the two prison guards.

Gagné learned of the Hells Angels leader's conviction as he watched TV behind bars. "I shouted 'Yes' and went into the prison yard to work out and get some sunshine," Gagné recalled. "Justice has been done."

See also: **L'Asssociation des témoins spéciaux du Québec, Maurice "Mom" Boucher, Diane Lavigne, Nomads, Rock Machine, André "Toots" "Peanuts" Tousignant.**

Galante, Carmine: Deadly Ambassador – Born in 1910 in the slums of East Harlem, New York, Galante was the son of an immigrant fisherman from the town of Castellammare del Golfo in Sicily. That scenic community was also the birthplace of American Mob bosses Joe Bonanno of New York City, Stefano Magaddino of Buffalo, Joe Profaci of Brooklyn, and Joe Aiello of Chicago. Soon Galante (whose name is often also spelled Galente) would follow in their footsteps.

Carmine Galante

By the age of ten, he was an incorrigible delinquent and by seventeen, he was in Sing Sing Penitentiary in Ossining, New York, for assault. At twenty, he was accused of the murder of a police officer, but the case was dismissed for insufficient evidence. In 1939, still under thirty, he was paroled on his third prison stint – this one for assault and robbery.

By then, organized crime in New York City was governed by the Mafia Commission, which oversaw the activities of the five major families, and Galante lusted for a strong role in the new order. He freelanced his criminal services for underworld bosses Bonanno, Profaci, Vito Genovese, and Lucky Luciano, until Genovese gave him his big break. Genovese wanted Carlo Tresca, the New York editor of *The Hammer* newspaper, murdered. The feisty anti-fascist newspaperman had infuriated Italian fascist leader Benito Mussolini, and Genovese wanted to curry favour with "Il Duce."

Shortly after the murder, Galante was Joe Bonanno's driver, a position of some status. It wasn't long after that, in 1952, when Galante moved north from New York City to Montreal. He brought with him a fearsome reputation, top-level Mob contacts, and a desire to escape the relentless publicity caused by the Kefauver hearings on organized crime in the United States. His job was to expand the operation of the Bonanno family north.

Galante wanted to make Montreal the focal point in the drug trade. Montreal had great promise for the American underworld, if someone could bring some measure of order to it. There was the lure of the long, inviting shoreline along the St. Lawrence, harbours for ocean-going ships, and fast highways on the 385-mile drive to the rich drug markets of New York City.

At that time, branch plants were coming to Canada in the auto, radio, and appliance industries, and Galante wanted to do the same thing with organized crime. He worked out of an electronics firm, guarded by Frankie Carbo, considered the dean of boxing. Soon Galante was pulling in protection money from underworld gambling dens and blind pigs (after-hours drinking spots).

His boss, Bonanno, was particularly interested in gambling profits. Police estimated that Galante helped collect some $50 million yearly in gambling profits in Montreal, earning him the titles of Bonanno's underboss and foreign minister.

There was clearly a shakeup underway in Montreal. Gambler Frank Petrula brought a huge amount of heat on his associates when police raided his home in 1954 and found a notebook that contained a list of municipal politicians and journalists who were bribed a total of $100,000 to defeat then mayoralty candidate Jean Drapeau, who was a reformer against the Mob. Petrula was never forgiven for this sloppiness, and it was feared he might start cooperating with authorities. Soon, he was missing and presumed dead as the era of gen-

Frank Petrula

tlemen gamblers like Petrula was gone, replaced by more hardened business people like Galante.

Galante didn't last too much longer in Canada, but by the time he was deported to New York City in 1955, he had firmly planted the Bonanno family flag in Montreal. Vic Cotroni was installed as its branch-plant manager, and this relationship was cemented when Galante became godparent to one of Vic Cotroni's children, and vice versa. Galante was five-foot-five, an inch taller than Cotroni; together, the two were the little Napoleons of the Montreal underworld.

Also at the top of the Cotroni family was pizzeria owner Luigi Greco, a Sicilian. With the Calabrian Cotroni and the Sicilian Greco working together atop the Montreal Bonanno family, there was a lid to any ethnic fighting between Sicilian and Calabrian mobsters.

Galante was arrested along with Bonanno at the 1957 Appalachian Mob meeting in upper New York State, when state troopers and federal agents sent the sixty or so crime delegates fleeing through the bushes. Publicity from this forced FBI Director J. Edgar Hoover to admit the existence of the Mafia, which he had denied for almost three decades.

Galante was also in Palermo in 1957 when plans were set up for the French Connection heroin route, to bring Turkish opium to Marseilles, where it was refined, and then shipped to New York City and Montreal. Others in attendance included Bonanno, Lucky Luciano, Sicilian crime boss Salvatore Greco, rising Sicilian Mafioso Gaetano Badalamenti, and Tommaso Buscetta, who later became one of the Mob's most dangerous turncoats.

Galante also used this trip to spread the word that ambitious young Italian Mafiosi could come to New York and form their own crews under his wing. By the mid-1960s, many of these newcomers were setting up businesses or working in bakeries and pizzerias around Knickerbocker Avenue in Brooklyn. They became known as "Zips" for the quick way they talked, and ultimately they would determine Galante's own fate.

Galante also worked on a Cuban drug route through Havana and Florida, getting permission from the Batista government to use Cuba as storing spot for mainland-bound heroin. Although he was unschooled, he could speak Spanish, French, and Italian dialects fluently, which helped him set up drug deals. His habit of never writing things down made him hard to convict.

He was often seen with his pants held up by a rope, although he also had hand-tailored suits and loved smoking Don Diego cigars, which earned him the nickname Mr. Lillo, which translated to "Mr. Cigar."

He had a mistress of more than twenty years, but considered himself a Roman Catholic, and refused to divorce his wife. Instead, he made an underling marry his common-law wife to legitimize their children. Of his so-called religious beliefs, an associate was once quoted as saying, "Lillo would shoot you at noon during high mass."

He was able to walk around New York City with no bodyguards, as there were so many police tailing him he didn't need them. He gave his police shadows a workout, changing cars as often as other men changed shirts. At one point, police followed him to Disneyland, where they found him riding go-carts with another mobster.

Though unschooled, he was said to enjoy the writings of Descartes and St. Augustine, although he was never bogged down by conventional morality. A prison psychiatrist diagnosed him as a psychopath, a mass murderer who managed to see himself as a good Catholic and a good patriot. Detectives would estimate he had been involved – directly or indirectly – in some hundred underworld executions, and that he carried out eighty of them himself.

He was rumoured to have dreams in the late 1970s of uniting New York City's five families under him, as boss of bosses. There had been a vacuum left by the death of Carlo Gambino, and Galante hoped to fill it himself. Not surprisingly, there were plenty of whispers that other mobsters – including those in his own crime family – were out to kill him and his ambitions.

In 1979, Galante told a journalist, "No one will ever kill me – they wouldn't dare. If they want to call me boss of bosses, that's all right. Between you and me, all I do is grow tomatoes."

Four days later, he was murdered at age sixty-nine. The killers were from his crew of Sicilian-born "Zips," whom Galante considered his own private army.

As a final indignity, the church refused him funeral mass.
See also: **Joe Bonanno, Vincenzo "Vic the Egg" Cotroni, French Connection, Luigi Greco, John "Johnny Pops" Papalia.**

Galliardo, Don Totto: Postwar Don – He ran an established Sicilian crime family in southern Ontario after the Second World War, and a police report from the time called him "one of many italians [sic] who never work, living on the proceeds of bootlegging and criminal activities." Totto Galliardo's brother Joe was the family enforcer. Based in Toronto's downtown Ward district (around York Street in today's financial district), his allies included a powerful Niagara Falls Sicilian crime figure, named in police reports throughout 1920s as Don Simone, and his rivals were the Calabrian Mob.
See also: **Interned in the Second World War, Giuseppe "Joe" Musolino, Bessie and Rocco Perri.**

Gang of Eight: Legal Debacle – In the early 2000s the federal Justice Department decided to make their suit against this gang a test case for Canada's newly minted anti-gang law, which made it illegal for anyone to be part of a criminal organization.

For ten months, Edmonton city police and RCMP tapped the phones of the members of an alleged crime family. In all, the police taped 281,000 conversations, very few of which were in English, but rather Cantonese, Mandarin, Vietnamese, and Chiu Chow, a dialect spoken in China's Guangdong province. To make things more complicated, many of the conversations involved street code and slang. More than 65,000 person-hours were spent between 1999 and 2002 to translate, transcribe, sort, and photocopy those conversations.

In September 2003, the case collapsed under its own weight, as Justice Doreen Sulyma stayed charges against eleven more defendants of the alleged crime family, ruling that things had dragged on so long their right to be tried within a reasonable time had been violated. At that point, they had been awaiting trial for four years, and the starting date for any trial was well off in the future.

Three more defendants in the case pleaded guilty to lesser charges. That left eight – the so-called "Gang of Eight" – still awaiting trial.

The *Edmonton Journal* concluded that "the police and the Crown ended up with too many defendants, too much evidence, too many witnesses, and not enough resources to cope with any of it."

The *Journal* also noted that, in September 1999, the same month the police arrested the defendants, management consultants Price-waterhouseCoopers completed a confidential report for the federal cabinet that said that the RCMP's ability to fight organized crime was in peril because of five years of budget cuts. What the force needed was 189 more officers and $125 million to effectively fight organized crime, the report concluded.
See also: **Manitoba Warriors, Nomads.**

Gargantua: Underworld Slaughter – In 1975, thirteen people were herded into a storage room in Montreal's Gargantua nightclub. Some were shot, but most died of suffocation when the building was set on fire by underworld figure Richard "The Cat" Blass.

Blass, a prison escapee, was really at the bar to kill two men he blamed for putting him in jail. The other eleven victims were eliminated as potential witnesses.

It was Canada's worst mass murder until December 6, 1989, when Marc Lepine, twenty-five, walked into L'École Polytechnique, the engineering school of the Université de Montréal, and methodically murdered fourteen women.
See also: **Michel Blass, Richard "The Cat" Blass.**

Ghost Shadows: Student Extortionists – By the early 1990s, this gang had amalgamated with the 14K Association in Toronto and were rearing their heads at the expense of the rival Kung Lok. Many Canadian Ghost Shadow members belonged to wealthy families and were in Canada on student visas. Others were waiters and busboys who hoped that a connection with the Triads would win them respect.

Gang members often assaulted fellow students, then asked for "*lo mo*" – slang for extortion payoffs.
See also: **Big Circle Boys, 14K Association, Kung Lok, Sun Yee On, Triads.**

Giglio, Salvatore "Little Sal": International Troubleshooter – He moved north to Montreal from New York City in 1956 to watch over Bonanno family interests after the deportation of Carmine "Mr. Lillo" Galante.

Giglio grew so close to Montreal criminal Lucien Rivard that Rivard was his best man when Giglio married a waitress at El Morocco, a nightspot run by a Cotroni family lieutenant. Giglio's duties included making sure the heroin traffic of the Cotroni family and Rivard ran smoothly. He also assisted Cotroni and helped to connect him to other significant underworld figures. Giglio paid visits to Rivard in Cuba in the 1950s, before Rivard was deported back to Canada.
See also: **Joe and Bill Bonanno, Giuseppe "Pep" Cotroni, Carmine Galante, Lucien Rivard.**

Gill, Peter: Freedom Lover – More than fifty Vancouver criminals had been slain in a gang war in the 1990s when Gill appeared in court to face murder charges, which included brothers Ranjit "Ron" and Jimsher "Jimmy" Dosanjh, heads of a lower B.C. mainland criminal organization, who were gunned down within six weeks of each other in early 1994. One of the victims of the gang fighting was shot dead at his own wedding, and another inside a barber shop. Yet another hit was in front of three hundred people in a crowded nightclub, but no witnesses came forward.

Gill walked free from the murder charges, and later it was learned that he had had an affair with one of the jurors, Gillian Guess.

In May 2002, Gill was found guilty of obstruction of justice for intimidating a witness in an assault case in Calgary, his new hometown. *See also:* **Gillian Guess, Bhupinder "Bindy" Johal.**

Ginnetti, John Ramon "Ray": Rough Company – Ray Ginnetti wouldn't have minded that a dozen Hells Angels wore their colours to his May 1990 funeral, including sergeant-at-arms Lloyd Robinson.

Ginnetti, who began his career as a car salesman in East Vancouver, loved the high life in Vancouver nightclubs and eateries, and made headlines once by getting into a restaurant shoving match with actor Sean Penn. He often hinted at his connections with organized crime (although was never a member of either the Mob or the Hells Angels), and boasted he earned his living by collecting on loans and by betting. Later, he worked as a stockbroker for several Vancouver brokerage houses, doing nothing to bolster the already-shaky image of the city's financial traders.

Ginnetti was involved in promoting a questionable Vancouver Stock Exchange offering of a telemarketing company. When investigators raided it in 1986, they found a boiler-room operation, complete with phone banks, "sucker lists" of potential clients, and sales records. They also found a bag containing $50,000, but before they could confiscate it, a man grabbed it and threw it out the window to Ginnetti, who caught the loot and ran. Not surprisingly, the B.C. Securities Commission slapped a cease-trading order on the firm.

Ginnetti ceased trading altogether at the age of forty-eight, when someone shot him execution-style with a single bullet to the head from a .380-calibre semi-automatic handgun. His body was found by his wife of ten years, Barbara, on the afternoon of May 9, 1990. stuffed in a closet at their $750,000 West Vancouver home.

Shortly after Ginnetti was escorted to his grave by a dozen Hells Angels, police were investigating yet another gangland murder. On May 15, 1990, small-time Russian mobster Sergey Filonov, an accused cocaine trafficker who allegedly bragged about being involved in the Ginnetti killing, was himself slain.

The Filonov murder didn't close the books on the Ginnetti hit. In June 1995, authorities charged thirty-five-year-old Jose Raul Perez-Valdez, who listed his home as Hollywood, California, with first-degree murder in connection with the killing.

At the time he was charged, Perez-Valdez, a Cuban American, was sharing living quarters with 1,800 other inmates in the federal penitentiary in Lompoc, California. As prisoner number 24900-086, he was serving a ten-year sentence imposed for a Seattle-area kidnapping and for possession of cocaine with the intent to distribute.

It would take a flowchart to follow who was killing who and why. Police concluded Perez-Valdez was a professional hit man, who, along with another Cuban, was hired to kill Ginnetti by a notorious Vancouver-area underworld enforcer, Roger Daggitt, who subcontracted the job after being hired himself to kill him.

Daggitt, thirty-nine, who was once described in court as a top enforcer for the Hells Angels, could offer no clarification on the murder, since he was killed himself in a Mob-style hit in the beer parlour of the Turf Hotel in Surrey, British Columbia, in October 1992. He was shot three times in the back of his head as his son watched.

No further details of the murder emerged when Perez-Valdez was charged in 1995, but tantalizing new information surfaced the following year, when hit man Serge Robin pleaded guilty to killing enforcer Daggitt. Knowledgable *Vancouver Sun* crime reporter Neal Hall wrote, "One theory is that Daggitt was killed [by Robin] to even the score" for the Ginnetti murder. Daggitt "had once worked as a body-guard for Ginnetti," Hall reported. "An inform-ant told police Daggitt was the driver for the man who killed Ginnetti."

Exactly why Ginnetti was slain remains unclear. Police wondered if perhaps there was a link between the murder and that of former stockbroker David Ward, who was found shot in the head in an idling truck in Vancouver in 1997.

See also: **Vancouver Stock Exchange, David Ward.**

Gold Key Club: Hamilton Hot Spot – If you had made it inside the east-end Hamilton hot spot at Main Street East and Wentworth, you would have rubbed shoulders with lawyers and busi-ness people and plenty of mobsters connected to "Johnny Pops" Papalia.

If you had looked across the street to a doughnut shop, you might have seen police craning their necks in an attempt to watch the goings-on.

The Gold Key Club was operated from the mid-1970s to the early 1980s by Papalia, who married, and then divorced, a waitress there. One of the club's other hostesses, tall, blonde, comely Shirley Ryce, penned her memoirs, *Mob Mistress: How a Canadian Housewife Became a Mafia Playgirl*, with veteran organized-crime writer James Dubro.

Ryce, a bookie's daughter, said she tried to show less-experienced mob women "how to act

like a lady." "There's a lot more to me than just horizontal," she explained to *Toronto Star* inter-viewer Susan Kastner.

See also: **John "Johnny Pops" Papalia.**

Greco, Luigi "Louis": Historic Meetings – Greco and gambler Frank Petrula had been bodyguards for Harry Davis when Davis was a major narcotics trafficker in Montreal in the 1940s. After Davis was murdered in 1946, they hooked up with Vic and Giuseppe Cotroni and took over some of Davis's rackets.

In 1950, Greco and Petrula were believed by police to have met with internationally power-ful mobster Lucky Luciano that year in Naples.

Greco and Vic Cotroni backed Carmine Galante of New York when Galante enforced his rule of Montreal's nightclubs, booze cans, gam-bling dens, bookies, hookers, and thieves. Greco and Cotroni's younger brother, Giuseppe, led the Canadian contingent to the 1957 Appalachian Conference, a major Mafia get-together in upstate New York, which was crashed by police.

Luigi "Louis" Greco

Greco was accidentally killed on December 7, 1972, in a freak solvent fire when he and some workers were replacing the floor of his north Montreal pizzeria. At his funeral, attended by the top figures of the Montreal underworld, his crony, Conrad Bouchard, sang Franz Schubert's "Ave Maria."

See also: **Vincenzo "Vic the Egg" Cotroni, Harry Davis, Carmine Galante, Frank Petrula, Michel Pozza.**

Grim Reapers: Prairie Bikers – The Grim Reapers motorcycle club was founded in 1967 as Calgary's first outlaw motorcycle club. Two other clubs, the Rebels and the King's Crew, followed in 1969.

One of the club's most notable members was Gerry Weldon, who joined in 1973 and would later become president of the Edmonton chapter of the Hells Angels.

While with the Reapers, Weldon also publicly challenged police to charge his members or leave them alone. Police took him up on his challenge in June 1998, when Weldon, forty-seven, was riding his Harley-Davidson and stopped at a giant roadblock ten kilometres south of Edmonton. Auto-theft experts in the police traced the serial number of his Harley engine to one stolen three years ago in Surrey, British Columbia, and impounded the bike.

He had more luck in 1990, at the end of a twenty-nine-month fight to recover weapons that were seized by police. Police seized the guns when working to prevent what they said was an imminent war between the Grim Reapers and the King's Crew.

In Calgary, police seized seventy rifles, including two AR-15 assault rifles, and four handguns, while Red Deer raids netted twenty-three rifles, twelve shotguns, four handguns, three crossbows, and an explosive device. In Edmonton, police scooped up twenty-two rifles and shotguns, three semi-automatic weapons, a flintlock musket, and ammunition. All of the weapons seized in Edmonton had valid registrations.

Police then said they believed there were tensions in Alberta because the Hells Angels were trying to open up an Alberta branch, and were deciding whether to hitch their fortunes to the Grim Reapers or the Rebels.

Ironically, when Weldon got his club's guns back in 1990, he praised the legal system, saying, "In the end, it's the judges that decided. It's in the courts where we got justice."

In July 1997, the Calgary and Edmonton Hells Angels were finally established when they absorbed twenty-three Grim Reapers, becoming Canada's thirteenth and fourteenth chapters. Weldon became a member of the elite Nomads within the Hells Angels.

See also: **Hells Angels, Nomads.**

Sieur des Groseilliers: English Hero, French Outlaw – He was born in France in July 1618 and christened Médard Chouart. He became Sieur des Groseilliers after he inherited a patch of family land where there were many gooseberry bushes, or *groseilliers.*

Like early coureurs de bois (runners of the woods) Étienne Brûlé and Pierre-Esprit Radisson, Groseilliers has had an honoured place in English-Canadian history as a great adventurer and explorer.

He arrived in Canada in 1641, and in 1647 married Hélène Martin, daughter of Abraham Martin, for whom the Plains of Abraham was named. Through his marriage, he became acquainted with fur traders of Acadia, the de la Tours. His wife died soon after the marriage, and he was remarried in 1653 to the half-sister of Pierre-Esprit Radisson, who then was a captive of the Iroquois.

At this time, New France was money-starved, and the wilderness areas of the west offered great promise. Fur-trading saved New France from bankruptcy, even though the state and Jesuits disapproved of its residents moving to live with the Indians.

Groseilliers was jailed with Radisson (who had been freed by the Iroquois in 1653) and most of his furs were confiscated in the summer of 1660, when he returned from the longest and most successful canoe journey of any white person of that time, a journey that had taken him to present-day Wisconsin and Minnesota. He sought redress from Paris, but was denied, and turned in frustration to the English as sponsors.

In yet another reversal of loyalties, he and Radisson went back to the French in 1675. They received pardons, and then helped organize a French rival to the English Hudson's Bay Company, known as the Compagnie du Nord.

He and Radisson were schemers of the highest order and, in 1681, Radisson returned to London to work as a spy for the powerful French smuggler Charles de la Chenaye.

Toward the end of his life, Groseilliers faded into obscurity, and alternate theories have him dying in the community Hudson Bay or, more likely, in New France as late as 1697.

See also: **Coureurs de Bois, Pierre-Esprit Radisson.**

Guess, Gillian: Fresher Evidence – When the attractive blonde had an affair in 1995, the fireworks weren't restricted to the bedroom. Her lover, Peter Gill, was ten years her junior, and on trial for a gangland murder.

Making things even hotter was the fact that Guess worked with the North Vancouver RCMP counselling crime victims, and she was on the jury that was hearing Gill's case at the same time she was secretly sleeping with him.

Her clandestine trysts with Gill became tabloid fodder, and the first-time offender drew an eighteen-month sentence – of which she served three months – despite having no

Gillian Guess (Alex Waterhouse-Hayward, for Saturday Night, *January 27, 2000)*

previous brushes with the law. Meanwhile, Gill walked on the murder charges. With that, Guess became the first juror in North America and the Commonwealth convicted of wilfully attempting to obstruct justice. Her couplings with the gangster were even the subject of a Harvard Law School Web site.

Guess did nothing to escape the spotlight, even setting up a Web site of her own that reproduced articles about her, coupled with her own musings. The affair started, she said, because of mutual curiosity. Then, as things advanced, Guess explained, she feared Gill and felt trapped. He encouraged her to convict two of his co-accused, including his brother-in-law, Bindy Johal, who was gunned down in a nightclub three years later.

The sordid affair reached the B.C. Court of Appeal, where five justices studied a photograph by Vancouver photographer Alex Waterhouse-Hayward, which showed Guess luxuriating in a bathtub, showing off a naked leg displaying an electronic-monitoring ankle bracelet. The photo was introduced by defence lawyer Ian Donaldson to show Guess sought media attention, despite her earlier protests to the contrary. "This is even fresher evidence," Justice George Cumming joked when he saw it.

See also: **Peter Gill, Bhupinder "Bindy" Johal.**

Gyakuzuki – *See* **Project Gyakuzuki.**

H

Hall's Harbour – *See* **High Island.**

Hamel, Normand "Biff": Family Horror –
Hamel was with his girlfriend and child when
he was approached by two gunmen men in front
of a health clinic in Laval on the outskirts of
Montreal around three in the afternoon of
April 27, 2000.

As his girlfriend and child watched in horror,
the gunmen chased him around the parking lot
before they cornered him and sprayed him with
bullets.

Hamel, who had twice been acquitted of
conspiracy to commit murder, was a founding
member of the elite Nomads chapter and a top
lieutenant and long-time friend of the Angels'
Quebec leader, Maurice "Mom" Boucher.

His murder made him the highest-ranking
Hells Angel killed in the turf war with the
Bandidos over the lucrative drug trade.

A member of the Angels for fifteen years, he
had also stood guard while five members of the
Angels' Laval chapter were gunned down at
the Lennoxville clubhouse in the spring of 1985
because of the enormous drug debts they'd
amassed.
See also: **Bandidos, Maurice "Mom" Boucher,
Hells Angels, Nomads.**

Hart, Pearl: "Girl Bandit" – She attended a fine
finishing school in Lindsay, Ontario, in the late
nineteenth century, then shocked the town by
running off as a teenager with a man who was
not her husband.

Things only got more scandalous from there.

After dumping her lover, she hung around
for a time in Colorado with "Calamity Jane"
Cannary, a hard-drinking, straight-shooting
woman who often dressed as a man.

On the morning of May 30, 1899, two masked
bandits – Pearl and boyfriend/pimp Joe Boot –
held up the Globe, Arizona, stagecoach. Even
though it was a gold-mining area, they managed
to pick a stage holding no gold, and they got
only $431 in cash from the passengers. With that
feeble haul, she became the West's only female
stagecoach robber, as well as its last female
stagecoach robber.

There wasn't much wealth, glory, or freedom in the titles, just the prospect of free
housing in a prison. Hart and Boot, who had no
horses, were easily captured in the hills the next
morning.

At her trial, she wove a sad story of how she
had committed the crime to pay her mother's
medical bills, then shouted out a statement that
endeared her to feminists for generations to
follow: "I shall not consent to be tried under a
law which my sex had no voice in the making!"

Boot received a thirty-five-year sentence for
the crime. Perhaps because Hart, though
twenty-seven, looked only nineteen, the jury
sentenced her to a mere five years in Yuma
Territorial Prison.

Pearl Hart (Arizona Historical Society)

Pearl Hart (background right) and fellow Yuma Penitentiary inmates

Hart was apparently not intimidated, or repentant, inside the eight-foot-thick adobe-and-stone walls of Yuma, where a guard stood watch at the main tower with a repeating rifle capable of firing six hundred rounds a minute. There, Hart welcomed reporters and photographers, sometimes posing with a brace of pistols and a Winchester lever-action repeater. The warden's wife of the almost all-male prison wasn't amused, and decreed, "We'd better keep that woman far away from the other inmates. She'll shock them with her language and corrupt their morals."

The warden's wife was apparently on to something. When Pearl was finally released, it wasn't for good behaviour in the traditional sense, but for what some others in the prison might consider really good behaviour: she had become pregnant.

Freed after serving less than two years, Hart embarked on a national lecture tour, speaking on "What My Life of Crime Has Taught Me," and starring in a play called *Pearl Hart, Girl Bandit*. The press loved her, calling her a "spitfire" and "Pearl Hart, the Arizona Bad Girl." She hadn't made much money for her crime, but she was able to make a living re-enacting it. More than once she boasted, "I'm the only woman who's ever robbed a stagecoach."

When her play finally ran its course, she disappeared, although in the 1920s she was reported to be running a bawdy house in Mexico. After that, there were equally unconfirmed reports that she turned respectable, living under another name, and had married a wealthy farming husband.

Hells Angels: Constant Wars – A group of B-17 bomber pilots stationed in England at the end

Hells Angels, 1983

Murdered Members of Hells Angels Laval Chapter

Jean-Guy "Brutus" Geoffrion

Michel "Willie" Mayrand

Laurent "L'Anglais" Viau, president of the Laval chapter

Jean-Pierre "The Weasel" Mathieu

Guy-Louis "Chop" Adam

of the Second World War called their aircraft "Hell's Angels." The name proved a popular one, and was picked up by other Allied fighter groups, including one that served with U.S. Marines stationed in Asia. When the Marines returned home to California, they hit the road on motorcycles together, keeping the name.

The first chapter of the Hells Angels motorcycle club appeared in 1948 in San Bernardino County, California. In 1957, Ralph "Sonny" Barger formed the Oakland chapter. The Angels made Oakland their headquarters and Barger became leader.

The Angels first displayed their colours in Canada on December 5, 1977, when the Popeyes gang, who had been warring for two years with the Satan's Choice and the Devil's Disciples over drug turf, became the Angels' Montreal chapter. They immediately began to fight with the Outlaws as well, who were bitter enemies of the Angels.

This gave the Quebec Angels about three dozen members and, on July 23, 1983, the Angels expanded into British Columbia. In 1984, they absorbed the Thirteenth Tribe gang in Halifax.

A year later, in 1985, they shocked the public and other gangs by executing six members of the Laval Angels chapter for rampant drug use. The bodies of five of them were found in the St. Lawrence River, in weighted-down sleeping bags.

By the time the Montreal chapter celebrated its twenty-fifth anniversary on December 5, 2002, the Canadian Hells Angels were connected to stockbrokers, bankers, and lawyers. They were particularly wealthy in British Columbia, where gang members owned such businesses as cellphone stores, stripper agencies, and porn sites on the Internet, and displayed a key interest in stock-market fraud.

Their drug-smuggling operations in Halifax, Montreal, and Vancouver were aided enormously by the federal government, which dismantled its ports police in the 1990s, despite strong warnings from major police forces, the

provinces, and some of their own advisers. Authors Julian Sher and William Marsden of *The Road to Hell: How the Biker Gangs Are Conquering Canada* estimated in 2003 that forty-three Hells Angels and associates worked in the Port of Vancouver, at least eight of them as foremen and one as the training officer for longshoremen. Other gang members worked on docks in trucking, maintenance, laundry, and garbage service. While the Angels beefed up their presence in the ports, Ottawa simply walked away.

While Ottawa was dismantling the ports police, the Hells Angels of Quebec were proving themselves to be the most violent Angels on the planet. They were locked in the 1990s in a war with the rival Rock Machine that left some 165 people dead and another 300 injured, including innocent bystanders. The war was over control of downtown Montreal drug-trafficking net-

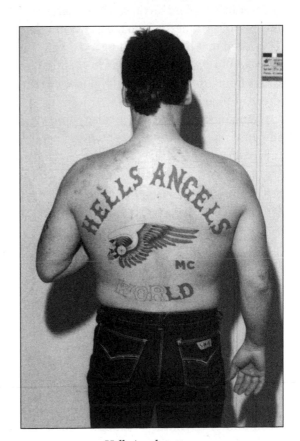

Hells Angels tattoos

Hells Angels in Mexico

works. Angels hit man Serge Quesnel told his biographer, Pierre Martineau, that there was a businesslike ruthlessness to the gang's murders. "I noticed that before executing a criminal, the guys would often 'borrow' large quantities of drugs from him. As a result, they pocketed hundreds of thousands of dollars."

Gang members were particularly interested in gathering intelligence on potential enemies, and police in Montreal found gang members had rented a room overlooking the employee parking lot of the RCMP, using high-powered lenses to note and record licence numbers of cars coming and going.

By the end of the millennium, they spanned the country from coast to coast. Their almost six hundred Canadian members made up about a quarter of the membership of the Hells Angels around the world, and the Toronto area had the highest concentration of Angels in the world.
See also: **Michel Auger, Maurice "Mom" Boucher, Yves "Le Boss" Buteau, Daniel DesRochers, Stéphane "Godasse" Gagné, Nomads, Popeyes, Rock Machine, Red Zone, Wolodumyr "Walter" "Nurget" Stadnick, Wolverine.**

Dutch Henry: Badlands Bad Guy – The real name for the Swiss-born, stocky cowboy with the hooked nose and German accent was Henry Yuetch, or Ieuch, but he was known in the Big Muddy Badlands of southern Saskatchewan as Dutch Henry. His brother Pete apparently also found the family name cumbersome and went by the moniker Coyote Pete.

Dutch Henry fought in one of the defining battles of the American West on November 25, 1864, at Adobe Walls on the Texas Panhandle plains, alongside Christopher "Kit" Carson, Wyatt Earp, Quebec-born Bat Masterson, a man known simply as Frenchy, and twenty-three others against Comanche and Kiowa. While the whites were vastly outnumbered, they had far superior firepower, including howitzer repeating rifles. When the day-long battle was over, scores of Indians had been slaughtered and more than 170 Kiowa lodges were destroyed, along with their winter provisions and buffalo robes. Also gone were the Natives' hopes of a unified stand to protect their lands.

The 1880s were a time of drought on the American prairies. Beef prices dropped and once-rich ranchers were suddenly broke.

Cowhands – even skilled ones like Henry – were released from their jobs, and some formed gangs to rustle cattle, rob trains, and terrorize ranchers.

Henry drifted north in 1888, to the Badlands area of Montana and Saskatchewan, which was a rustlers' paradise. Criminals could steal as many as two hundred horses on one drive in Montana, alter their brands, and resell them in Canada. Then they could resteal them and sell them again in Montana and the Dakotas, where they knew there was a shortage – of their own creation.

Henry had a keen sense of humour and many friends along the border. Law-enforcement agencies weren't impressed that he gave money and beef to poor families, noting that the gifts had often been stolen from someone else.

A bounty of $12,000, enormous money for the time, was promised for capture of his band of horse thieves. When in Canada, Henry's gang often hid out in a wolf den near Peaked Butte in the Big Muddy Badlands, close to the American border. They dug out the den until it was big enough for the outlaws and their horses.

Henry was credited with naming Plentywood, Montana, when he was camped by a creek, and impatient that a cook couldn't get a fire started. "Go upstream a couple of miles, and you'll find plenty of wood," Dutch supposedly said, and the place where the wood was found became known as Plentywood.

One of his partners in crime was Ed Shufelt, a cowboy who exhausted his life savings successfully bribing a jury after pumping four bullets into the back of a dying man in a saloon he ran in Saco, Montana. Shufelt began working in Canada in the Big Muddy town of Willow Bunch at the ranch of respected citizen Pascal Bonneau.

A grassfire in 1902 forced Bonneau to winter his horses in Montana. He left the herd with Henry and another cowboy, but when he tried to retrieve them in the spring, Henry stuck a gun in his back and told him to go home. Henry then sold the horses to his friend Shufelt, giving him a bill of sale.

Bonneau wasn't easily intimidated, and the next time Shufelt showed his face in the Willow Bunch area, the Mounties were ready to arrest him.

"When Shufelt went to trial in Regina for his role in the horse theft, cowpuncher friends filled the courtroom and intimidated witnesses," as Barbara Hegne writes in *Border Outlaws of Montana, North Dakota and Canada*. The judge had to dismiss the first jury because of threats, but finally a trial was held and Shufelt was sentenced to five years in prison. He died before completing his sentence.

Henry escaped unscathed, and joined forces in 1903 with Sam Kelly and a motley crew of others, including characters named Bloody Knife and Pigeon Toe Kid. In 1905, Henry gave an ornately engraved, ivory-handled Bisley Colt .45 to a boy named Alfred Watkins near Loring, Montana.

"If I never come back, kid, it's yours," Henry told him.

He also left his buggy and $100 with Watkins, supposedly so he would have an emergency weapon and transportation safely stashed at the Watkins ranch. A few months later Henry wired Watkins from North Dakota, saying he needed the money quickly. The next day, however, Henry was reportedly shot to death by an associate. What was believed to be Henry's body was discovered in 1907 in a shallow grave with a gunny sack over his bullet-riddled head.

There were other reports that the real Dutch Henry was killed in 1910 by a Mountie on the Big Muddy River near Moose Jaw, and also that he fled to South America. Whatever the case, he never came back for the pistol.

Ironically, the gun that Henry used to rob ranchers became an economic plus for Malta, Montana, attracting tourists to see it in a glass case in the Phillips County Museum. "It's not just any revolver," explained Gary Wilson, a Montana author of books on outlaws. "This is tied to economic development for this town."

Henry's character was dramatized in director Anthony Mann's classic 1950 movie, *Winchester '73*, in which he was played by Stephen McNally. *Winchester '73* revived the career of James Stewart and also featured a young Rock Hudson, playing an Indian chief, and a dance-hall girl played by Shelley Winters.
See also: **Bat Masterson, Big Muddy Badlands, Frank Carlyle, Sam Kelly, Outlaw Trail, Sundance Kid.**

Hervieux, Serge: Deadly Mistake – He looked up when a visitor to the northeast Montreal car-rental outlet where he worked called out the name "Serge." Seconds later, the father of two lay dying from gunshot wounds, because bikers connected to the Hells Angels mistook him for a rival Rock Machine member they were seeking.

Serge Hervieux, thirty-eight, had no criminal record or known affiliation with biker gangs, and police called his murder a case of mistaken identity.

Other innocent victims of the biker wars included eleven-year-old Daniel Desrochers, who was killed when a bomb went off outside a Hells Angels hangout in 1995. Two years later, two prison guards were shot in an intimidation campaign. In January 1997, Montreal security guard Guy Lemay was fatally shot in his apartment building, after being mistaken for a neighbour who was a Rock Machine sympathizer.
See also: **Michel Auger, Daniel Desrochers, Diane Lavigne, Nomads, Red Zone, Rock Machine.**

High Island, Haut Isle: Deadly Mysteries – There are a couple of notable points about this tiny island about twenty kilometres off the Nova Scotia shore. One is that its appearance constantly changes because of a phenomenon called refraction. The other is that it was a former stopping point for American pirates, including Captain Kidd and Ned Lowe.

It was called Ile aux Morts by the Acadian-French settlers, meaning the "Island of the Dead," since it was a trap for ships trying to enter north or south channels of the bay and offered scant hope of escape for trapped sailors. Tides here often hit fifty feet, and run like the current of a great river. The island has only one landing place, and the rest of its shores are ringed by cliffs from eighty to two hundred feet high.

Local folklore said that American pirate Capt. Samuel Hall left treasure nearby. Hall, who raided Nova Scotia settlements during the American War of Independence, was a privateer with American letters of marque, meaning he could legally attack and loot enemy ships from his sloop, the *Mary Jane*. When the *Mary Jane* was captured by the British, its strongbox was missing and presumed to be buried somewhere around Hall's Harbour.
See also: **Charles Bellamy, Eric Cobham, Cupids, Peter Easton, Edward Jordan, Captain Kidd, Mogul Mackenzie, Henry Mainwaring, Sheila Na Geira, Samuel Nelson, John Phillips, Gilbert Pike, Pirates, Bartholomew "Black Bart" Roberts.**

Hotel and Restaurant Employees Union: Grim Distinction – This was the only union ever thrown out of the Quebec Federation of Labour (QFL) for ethical misconduct, which was quite a distinction, considering the QFL also included the Seafarers' International Union of Hal C. Banks, which was rough enough to merit a federal commission of inquiry into its behaviour.

The Cincinnati-based hotel union also had problems with authorities in the United States, and a 1984 report by a permanent Senate subcommittee on investigations concluded, "that the almost 400,000 members of the union have suffered as a result of some officers who have been corrupted."

Reformers were eventually swept to power in Montreal, Vancouver, and Toronto, after the old guard was accused of vote-rigging, negotiating poor contracts, stealing money from members, and maintaining tight links to organized crime.

During the union's bad old days, top Quebec mobster Claude Faber had his hotel, drinks, meals, and movies billed to the Toronto-based union local. An invoice from the Delta Chelsea Inn in Toronto shows that Local 75 of the Hotel and Restaurant Employees Union was billed for the $75.79 tab for Claude Faber of Ste. Adèle, Quebec, during a February 19 and 20, 1981, visit. The bill covered the room, beverages, phone calls, four movies, and meals.

Faber had been identified as the right-hand man to Montreal Mafia boss Frank Cotroni during the Quebec Police Commission inquiry into organized crime in the 1970s. A year after his stay at the Delta Chelsea, Faber had his accommodations subsidized by the taxpayers, as he was in jail after pleading guilty to the 1982 Montreal gangland slaying of Claude Ménard and to cocaine trafficking.

It didn't help the union's image that its organizers in Toronto in the early 1980s included Eddie Melo, a former boxer who was a close friend and associate of Cotroni. Melo once threatened a bartender to force him to sign a union card. He didn't deny making the threat, but did argue that he didn't pull the .38 revolver that was found in his home. Then he gestured with his fists toward investigating officers and added, "I have my own weapons – these two."

See also: **Frank "Santos" Cotroni, Claude Faber, Eddie Melo.**

I

Iakoubovski, Dmitri Olegovich: Russian James Bond – In August 1993, someone fired three shots at the palatial mansion belonging to Dmitri Iakoubovski in the Bridle Path area of Toronto. A note in Russian was found inside the gates of the $5.3-million home, warning Iakoubovski, twenty-nine, a former senior Russian government official, to stop complaining publicly about corruption in Russia.

With the bullets and note began a dizzying series of international investigations that included a multi-million-dollar baby-food scam, theft of priceless books, alleged forgeries of taped conversations, secret Swiss bank accounts, and the top levels of Russian politics.

Within a month of the shooting, Russian President Boris Yeltsin cited Iakoubovski's allegations of corruption when he fired Vice-President Alexander Rutskoi and first deputy prime minister Vladimir Shumeiko.

Yeltsin was referring in part to the baby-food scam, in which Russian-produced cotton, valued at $20 million on Western markets, was allegedly traded to an Austrian company. In return, the Austrian company was to provide baby food for Russia, but the baby food had a value in Russia of only $10,000. Profits from the deal were allegedly transferred through a bank owned by a Toronto-based firm to a secret trust account in a Swiss bank.

Throughout the dizzying allegations and counter-allegations, it became quickly apparent that Iakoubovski – dubbed the "Russian James Bond" by one Moscow newspaper – wasn't an ordinary crime victim. He certainly wasn't ordinary and he wasn't even much of a victim, either.

Born just outside Moscow on September 5, 1963, he was the son of a mid-ranking army officer who died when Iakoubovski was in his teens from lingering damage due to exposure to toxic fumes from rocket fuel.

The year of his father's death, Iakoubovski entered a Soviet military academy, but was refused readmission for a second year. Apparently, the KGB security service gave him a bad report card, because his mother was Jewish.

He then turned to law and, by his late twenties, he was legal adviser to the prosecutor-general, a post roughly equivalent to that of deputy minister. After June 1992, his career was skyrocketing upwards, and he was made the liaison between the Russian government and its security forces, the former KGB and police. Then, his career stopped as suddenly as it had taken off. By September 1992, he had left both his job and his country.

He resurfaced in one of Toronto's swankiest neighbourhoods, enjoying cream cheese and bagels poolside at his Bridle Path mansion, which was close to that of media mogul Conrad Black and watched over by security cameras and off-duty police officers.

Not yet thirty, he was involved in a Swiss-Canadian company at the centre of a storm of corruption allegations that were racking the Russian government, and still hailed as a hero by a Russian presidential commission charged with exposing and stamping out corruption. "I did not stop when I was asked to stop, and continued to go further," Iakoubovski told reporters through an interpreter shortly after the shooting. He then went on to deny he has received any government money that was illegally spirited out of Russia, and said his lavish lifestyle was supported by "consulting work" and a wealthy family.

Within a year, he was back in Moscow, booking an entire floor of the capital's most luxurious hotel for his law office. Then, in December 1994, his fortunes took yet another sudden reversal. Russian police charged him with participating in the theft of $130 million worth of rare and ancient European, Hebrew, Chinese, and Tibetan manuscripts from a St. Petersburg library.

As if the plot wasn't thick enough, before his case went to court, the body of his defence lawyer, Yevgeny Melnitsky, was found by neighbours in his small apartment in Moscow. The lawyer's throat was cut and his head bludgeoned and, according to the Interfax news agency, Iakoubovski now feared "the next corpse in his case will be himself."

He survived the trial to be convicted in 1996, and was sent to a luxury jail in Siberia, whose inmates had included fallen members of the political elite. Upon his release in 1998, Iakoubovski boasted that his political enemies had failed to defeat him. "They were all punished by God. Some lost their posts, some lost their families."

Within a few weeks of his release, he was pouring champagne at the debut of his new career as a television celebrity. He was host of a weekly show called *Arrest and Release*, inspired by his four years in Russian jails.

He said he planned to give legal advice and support to the country's legion of convicted criminals, estimating that 15 per cent of all Russians have spent time in jail and 50 per cent have a close relative who served prison time. "It's the biggest electorate in Russia these days," he said.

He was also author of a new legal textbook, *What Is Arrest and How to Fight It*, and was featured on the cover of a popular Russian tabloid with his blonde wife, Irina, who sported only a black bikini brief, matching stiletto shoes, and a coil of barbed wire. The new Mrs. Iakoubovski – his fifth – had met him when she was his defence lawyer, and married him in a prison chapel a year before his release.

See also: **Vyacheslav Kirillovich Ivankov, Joseph Sigalov, Vyacheslav Marakulovich Sliva.**

Iannuzzelli, Louis: Depressed Loan Shark – When Iannuzzelli disappeared in October 1985, Niagara Regional Police suggested to reporters that he might have committed suicide. Iannuzzelli, who had interests in a wax museum in Niagara Falls, Ontario, and in a cruise boat, was also involved in loansharking, and police said he owned a large amount of money to "Johnny Pops" Papalia of Hamilton, who was horning in on his business.

"I'm sure he was depressed," a police intelligence officer said to Peter Moon of the *Globe and Mail*. "You'd be depressed too, if you thought Johnny Pops was mad at you for some reason. He didn't commit suicide. He was killed. And with him gone, there's no competition for John in Niagara Falls."

For his part, Papalia told Moon he had known Iannuzzelli for forty years and was aware that some police suspected him in the disappearance. "I had nothing to do with it," Papalia told Moon, "and that's presuming he is dead."

See also: **Carmen Barillaro, John "Johnny Pops" Papalia.**

Ieuch, Dutch Henry – *See* **Dutch Henry.**

Interned in the Second World War: Mafia Roundup – In the Second World War, Ottawa feared an unholy alliance between mobsters of Italian heritage and Fascists. The RCMP submitted secret lists to the federal government on hundreds of Canadians with suspect loyalties, and mass roundups and internments followed quickly.

It was a time of rampant anti-Italian prejudice. In one case, a Toronto man was confined for two years for no greater offence than playing the Italian lawn-bowling game of bocce with Fascist sympathizers. But the intelligence files also included an inventory of the Ontario Italian underworld, and confirm that, despite later denials by politicians, Ottawa clearly considered Mafia association a serious security threat. Giovanni Durso of 200 Hess Street North in Hamilton was described in a secret RCMP report as a "criminal-minded Italian and a member of the Mafia." Charles Calogero Bordonaro of Hamilton was listed as "the leader of the Maffia [sic] at Hamilton," and Domenic Belcastro, Thomas Rasso, and Domenic Longo of Guelph were listed as "members of an international gang."

Among those interned at Camp Petawawa were Rocco Perri, Hamilton's King of the Bootleggers, who was not released until October 17, 1943, on a special order signed by then Justice Minister Louis St. Laurent. Also scooped up in the seventeen police cars that swept into Hamilton's Italian community were Perri's lieutenant Frank Sylvestro (alias "Frank Ross"), a bootlegger; Antonio "Tony" Papalia, a bootlegger, Perri associate, and father of "Johnny Pops" Papalia; and Calogero "Charlie" Bordonaro, believed to be a Black Hand bomber and Perri supporter.

From Niagara Falls, internees included Vincenzo "James" Sacco, a bootlegger and Perri associate; "Black Peter" Sacco, a gambler and bootlegger; and John (a.k.a. "Archie" and "Czar") Saccone, an alien smuggler. From Guelph, there was suspected arsonist and counterfeiter Domenic Belcastro and Domenic Longo, a bootlegger and Perri ally.

But while about a dozen Ontario residents are bluntly listed as Mafia members by Mountie intelligence, none of the hundreds of Montrealers interned during the war were listed as having Mafia ties. The closest the intelligence material comes to mentioning Montreal underworld figures was in June 1942 letters to the government, suggesting that Luigi, Michele, Vincenzo, and Giuseppe Soccio be granted freedom only if they do "not belong to, or have any relationship with any secret society, band or gang, or any illegal organization."

Almost everyone on the RCMP list from Montreal was a pro-Fascist immigrant of Sicilian heritage connected with the Sons of Italy. This was relatively easy information to get. The omission of criminals of Calabrian heritage, such as Vic Cotroni, was more an indication of police ignorance than underworld passivity.

See also: **Black Hand, Antonio "Tony" Papalia, Rocco Perri.**

Ivankov, Vyacheslav Kirillovich: "Little Japanese" – He exercised control in Toronto in the 1980s even when he was locked up in a Russian gulag for murders and hundreds of extortions.

A senior member of *vor v zakonye* (Russian Mafia), he even stole his nickname Yaponchick, "Little Japanese," as it had been used earlier by the legendary Russian bandit Mishka Vinnitsky, who ran the Jewish underworld in the Black Sea port of Odessa in pre-revolutionary times.

While in maximum-security prison in Siberia, Ivankov continued to expand his crime empire and, with the help of two associates in Toronto, he was able to persuade Russian banks and investors to put $5 million into phony shares for a Siberian gold-mining company. Furious bankers sent a hit man to Toronto to kill one of his co-conspirators, but the hit man was arrested by the RCMP.

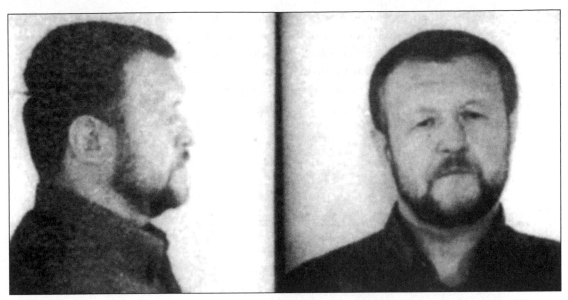

Vyacheslav Ivankov

Ivankov and his associate Vyacheslav Marakulovich Sliva headed to North America after the breakup of the former Soviet Union. Ivankov moved from Moscow in 1992 to the Brighton Beach area of Brooklyn and became the most powerful Russian Mob leader in the United States, while Sliva settled in an exclusive condominium near Finch and Bayview Avenues in Toronto in 1995.

The FBI were having enormous difficulty gathering enough evidence to support a request to wiretap Ivankov's telephone, since Mob leaders in Brighton Beach used a go-between to carry messages rather than communicating by phone.

However, the FBI was helped out by the Mounties in Toronto, who caught Ivankov in a conversation with his old associate Sliva.

Ivankov, fifty-seven, was arrested in June 1995, after an investigation that involved in part these wiretaps of his conversations supplied by the RCMP. Because of the Canadian help, a jury found Ivankov guilty of trying to shake down two businessmen who owed a $4.8-million debt to a Moscow bank.

Ivankov was sent to prison for nine and a half years after being convicted in an extortion con-

spiracy, but Sliva and Sigalov were not charged. The stocky, bearded Ivankov blurted out obscenities at FBI agents and government lawyers as he was led out of the courtroom.

Even before Ivankov's arrival on North American soil, there were dark mutterings from law-enforcement officials about the spread of *vor v zakonye*. Insp. David Veness, head of Scotland Yard's organized-crime unit, warned in 1993 that the world was facing an organized-crime threat on a scale it never had seen before from Russian mobsters from the former Soviet Union.

By 1995, the Criminal Intelligence Service Canada (CISC) noted that Russian-organized criminal syndicates had planted roots in Toronto and other Canadian cities, and that they were well on their way to changing the agenda of law enforcement everywhere in North America. "The international scope of the organized crime groups demands a co-operative strategy between law enforcement agencies around the world," RCMP Cmsr. J.P.R. Murray, chairman of the CISC, said in his introduction to a special report on Russian organized crime.

Journalist Stephen Handelman, the *Toronto Star*'s former Moscow bureau chief and author of *Comrade Criminal*, an incisive look at the Russian *mafiya*, wrote that the 1999 "victory" by the West in the Cold War lulled North Americans into believing that the new Russia would soon become a carbon copy of capitalist democracies.

Handelman noted that the early reports out of Moscow about a "crime wave" set off few alarm signals. Most observers concluded the explosion of muggings, murders, and racketeering was the price Russia was paying for its transformation into a new society. Almost no one paid attention to the special characteristics of what Russians were even then calling the *mafiya*.

Meanwhile, the new powers were smuggling abroad billions of dollars gained from profiteering in Soviet property and strategic resources. Handelman wrote that some of that money was coming to Canada as early as 1991 and 1992. It aroused few suspicions, as it was often associated with the establishment of legitimate companies or real-estate investment.

Canada's comparatively relaxed banking and investment laws made the country one of the world's money-laundering havens – alongside such notorious money-laundering spots as the Cayman Islands.

By the time of his 1995 arrest, Ivankov already had set wheels in motion for his Russian Mob, presiding over a meeting of Russian gangland chiefs in Miami that law-enforcement authorities here privately compared to the Appalachia meeting of U.S. organized crime bosses in the 1957.

See also: **National Hockey League, Joseph Sigalov, Vyacheslav Marakulovich Sliva.**

J

Jamaican Posses: High-Rise Horrors – Noted by police in Toronto in the early 1990s, posses have names like Striker, Spangler and Shower, and have ties to New York, Miami, Houston, Dallas, Washington, and other American cities where they exercise absolute, murderous control of the crack-cocaine trade.

Other gangs of young people aren't so organized, but use the term *posse* as a scare term, particularly in large Toronto apartment complexes.

Apartment complexes are appealing to posses because they house large numbers of youths, who are a ready-made market for the $20 to $60 "rocks" of crack the posses sell.

The posses smuggle in guns – especially 9 mm automatic pistols and the small submachine guns seen in many Hollywood movies – from the United States via the same route as the cocaine cooked up for crack.

The Toronto police have countered by recruiting Jamaican-born police officers who can understand the Jamaican *patois* picked up on wiretaps.

The posses are noted to be hard-core criminal gangs, born in the depressed areas of Jamaica and nurtured on free-enterprise drug markets. Membership is confined to Jamaicans, and each posse confines its members to Jamaicans – "Yardies" – from a particular geographic area, all of whom know each other.

Often, gangs use impoverished women as expendable couriers – "mules," in drug parlance.

Typically, the posse supplies a rental car, train, or bus ticket to New York to the woman. There cocaine is picked up and smuggled back over the border. Air tickets to Jamaica or Florida are provided for women who are lured by the promise of a holiday.

See also: **Robert Blackwood.**

Jaworski, Doug: Big Sting – The tiny private airstrip in rural Burtts Corner, New Brunswick, looked just right to the Colombian drug barons.

The Medellín cocaine cartel planned to use rural New Brunswick as a North American distribution base in the late 1980s, and the plot was approved by cartel kingpin Pablo Escobar, reportedly the world's richest criminal.

Instead, it became the site of the largest cocaine seizure in Canadian history. Unknown to Escobar and his workers, Doug Jaworski, the man who they thought was buying the tiny airstrip for them, was actually an undercover agent for the RCMP, directed by Insp. Wayne Blackburn.

Jaworski was one of only a handful of non-Colombians trusted by the drug lords. He sold many of them airplanes from a dealership he ran in Florida. He delivered planes to Colombia, and gradually got to know key cartel figures. They were impressed with his quick mind regarding technology, and he helped them with cellphone scramblers and wireless fax machines and was able to show them how a plane might find seams in radar systems to avoid detection. Eventually, however, Jaworski flipped and agreed to turn on the cartel in exchange for $200,000 and an agreement by U.S. authorities not to prosecute him on tax charges.

He told authorities he had previously earned between $300,000 and $400,000 from the Medellín drug cartel for "illegal activities" between 1984 and 1988. He said the cash was payment for ferrying drugs, selling and maintaining aircraft, and laundering "millions" in drug profits through Swiss banks.

Jaworski helped the cartel adapt to modern technology, like how to use portable FAX machines, multibranch banking, cellular phones, and transmitters that detect police bugs.

Now, the drug lords wanted him to study any weaknesses in Canada's ability to track airplanes off its East Coast.

While working undercover for the Mounties, Jaworski helped organize a shipment of five hundred kilograms of cocaine from Colombia to New Brunswick. Backroads of rural New Brunswick had been used by bootleggers during Prohibition, and now the Colombians planned to use them for cocaine.

In April 1989, Blackburn and a crew of Mounties were hiding in the snow as the first drug plane to attempt to land in the Maritimes brushed a tree, then touched down at the secluded airstrip.

Not long after the pilots were jailed, the cartel sent up a hit team to free the jailed pilots. One of them later told police the cartel "intended to kill the informer, his wife, and cat and dog," even though Jaworski was in witness protection.

The hit team was captured because of an alert gas-station attendant – also a moonlighting newspaper reporter – who called police about a van full of suspicious men.

Jaworski's knowledge of internal cartel operations was so extensive that he was questioned by U.S. authorities who were preparing a drug-trafficking case against former Panamanian strongman Manuel Noriega, and West German police tapped him for help in putting together a money-laundering trial involving cocaine that was hidden in shipments of pricey artichoke hearts.

He also helped American authorities prep for a trial involving the cartel's reputed "finance minister," Eduardo Martinez Romero, who was extradited from Colombia on charges of laundering or conspiring to launder $1.2 billion of cartel drug money.

Seized airplane in New Brunswick

Seized cocaine

The RCMP rated the potential risk against people on a scale from zero to seven. Jaworski, had a 6.5 security rating, just 0.5 below that of American President George Bush and the Pope and 1.5 above Prime Minister Brian Mulroney.

Fears that the Mounties were abandoning Jaworski's parents drove the family to take their case for protection to the Supreme Court. Jaworski had threatened to sabotage the case from the witness stand unless he felt his parents were adequately protected and compensated for their losses in the case. The 1990 case was so sensitive that it caused the only secret hearing in the history of the Supreme Court of Canada.

Probably Jaworski's strongest Canadian critic was Sydney Leithman, the Montreal lawyer for convicted Colombian cartel members and other underworld notables, including Mafia leader Frank Cotroni and Claude Dubois of the infamous Dubois brothers. Leithman slammed Jaworski in court as a liar, criminal, and a "tarnished and paid informant." He also accused Jaworski then of having "a giant-sized ego," and said he was "flippant, arrogant and insulting."

For his part, Jaworski was unapologetic, saying he did Canada a service with his role in the sting. Police never had any evidence against him, so he could have just walked away, he said.

As Jaworski was beginning life under a new identity, the Mounties scrambled in June 1991 to assess the damage of one of his RCMP bodyguards, who they worry acted as a double-agent

for the cocaine cartel. The officer under investigation faxed in his resignation and fled Canada for Portugal shortly after the May 13, 1991, contract-style slaying of Leithman, who had apparently taken on a huge retainer and then didn't deliver in court. The murder remained unsolved.

Meanwhile, Jaworski's old cartel friend Caycedo was also reportedly murdered in Colombia.

See also: **Sydney Leithman.**

Jodoin, Claude: Too Close to the Story – He grew up in east-end Montreal, studied law at McGill University, then chose a career in journalism. In 1967, two years after he began his reporting career, Jodoin met Claude Dubois, who was well on his way to becoming one of the province's most feared criminals. The two men became friends, a bond that would influence both of their lives.

Jodoin was making $120 a week as a reporter, and crime was a hot beat. This was a time of "New Journalism," when reporters were often encouraged to live the beat they were covering. Jodoin found himself growing closer to Dubois, who was moving up in the Montreal underworld.

The Dubois family became a household name in 1975 when the Quebec Crime Commission inquiry into organized crime described Claude and his eight brothers as the driving force behind a bloody war for control of underworld activity in Montreal.

Around this time, Jodoin was sacked by *Le Journal de Montréal* for becoming too close to the mobsters. He got a job running two bars for his underworld friends.

Police couldn't find anyone to testify against the Dubois brothers in court until November 1980, when Donald Lavoie, a self-admitted underworld hit man, came to them. Lavoie, forty-two, had just narrowly escaped an attempt on his life, and was seeking police protection. He told police – and later admitted on the witness stand – that he was a hired gun for the Dubois brothers for ten years, plotting several killings and personally gunning down so many people that he had lost count.

Local underworld figures were panic-stricken when Lavoie started talking. Some went into hiding and others plotted revenge.

"I didn't like what I was hearing," Jodoin told the *Globe and Mail* in 1982. "Some were talking about murders to shut Lavoie up, including the killing of women and children. I was getting in deeper and deeper and they were asking me to do things I didn't want anything to do with. I had to get out."

Finally, he contacted police, who needed someone to corroborate Lavoie's testimony about the murders of Richard Desormiers and Jacques-André Bourassa. Both men were connected to mobster Frank "Santos" Cotroni and both were slain at a Montreal nightclub in 1973.

With Jodoin's help, prosecutors were able to lay murder charges against Dubois and two of his associates nearly nine years after the killings.

For this, police gave Jodoin $4,000 when he began working with them, then weekly payments of $400, to a maximum amount of $25,000.

Before the murder trial, Jodoin worked for eight nerve-racking months as a double-agent, feeding information to police after meeting with underworld figures. "Dubois thought I was helping him build his defence, when in fact I was doing just the opposite," Jodoin recalled.

When the trial was over, and Dubois was convicted, his former friend Jodoin retreated far from Montreal, where he lived under the constant protection of bodyguards. "I'm not nervous about the prospect of being killed [by the underworld]," Jodoin told the *Globe and Mail*. "If it's going to happen, then it's going to happen."

But life in protective custody has other drawbacks. Jodoin moved "somewhere in the country in a prison without bars. . . . All I see out in the country is trees. I'm getting to hate them. I'm a city boy. I'd rather look at buildings."

See also: **Dubois Brothers, Claude Dubois, Donald Lavoie.**

Johal, Bhupinder "Bindy": Gang-War Victim – This B.C. gang leader was involved with co-defendant Peter Gill in the longest criminal trial in Canadian history. The trial was better known for the publicity around Gill's liaison with juror Gillian Guess than for the outcome, when Johal, Gill, and others walked free after being charged with hits on alleged gangsters Ron and Jimmy Dosanjh.

Johal was gunned down in a crowded Vancouver nightclub in December 1998. At the time of his murder, he was facing charges for the kidnapping of the younger brother of a rival gang leader. Johal's next-door neighbour had earlier been shot dead while walking his dog, and police believe he was mistaken for the drug dealer.

See also: **Ranjit "Ron" and Jimsher "Jimmy" Dosanjh, Peter Gill, Gillian Guess.**

Johnston, Bill: Accidental Patriot – A pirate by profession and a patriot by accident, Johnston was born in Trois-Rivières, Quebec, on February 1, 1782, and his family settled in 1784 in Bath outside Kingston. He worked as a farmer and merchant before finding his niche as a smuggler on the St. Lawrence River, where the Thousand Islands offered (and offer) countless hiding spots from authorities.

In the War of 1812, when he was suspected of smuggling goods to the American enemy, Johnston's property was confiscated and he was jailed in Kingston. He escaped from custody and, livid over the loss of his property, offered his services to the Americans as a spy and raider, using his six-oared boats to attack boats on the St. Lawrence. He also robbed mail coaches on land.

When the war ended, he settled in New York in the community of French Creek, which later became known as Clayton, New York State. Ostensibly, he was a merchant, but French Creek was a notorious smugglers' roost, and Johnson looked every inch the river smuggler, with six pistols and a Bowie knife tucked into his belt. He did his illegal work from a twenty-eight-foot, twelve-oared boat that could hold twenty men, and was light enough to be hauled overland.

When rebellion broke out in Upper Canada in 1837, rebels hoped for help from Americans, and Johnston the pirate found himself with the grand title of "commodore of the Navy in the East" for the rebel side. With a cloak of respectability from American authorities, Johnston terrorized the waterways, and in July 1838, Lady Durham, wife of the Governor General of British North America, travelled up the St. Lawrence and wrote to Countess Grey, "Our voyage by the Thousand Islands has been most prosperous, no appearance of Pirates or ill-disposed persons, but we heard afterwards that Bill Johnston, the most dreaded of these robbers, had been very near us."

It was around this time that Johnston became involved with the Hunters, a patriot lodge whose members used secret signs to identify themselves and swore oaths "to promote republican institutions throughout the world."

Johnston took part in an ill-conceived effort by the Hunters to invade Canada through Prescott, Ontario, in November 1838. Their plot – and boats – literally ran aground, and Johnston surrendered to Canadian authorities near Ogdensburg, New York, on the condition that he could give his six pistols, twelve-shot rifle, and Bowie knife to a son.

Again he bolted from custody, but he was recaptured and tried in Albany for murder and piracy. Found guilty, he received a one-year sentence and a fine of $250. Six months into his term, he escaped yet again, and rather than being punished for his crime, he was granted a pardon by American President William Henry Harrison, who fought in the War of 1812.

Johnston's final years were spent in French Creek. He owned islands in the area, which he called Ball, Shot, and Powder. He died in French Creek at age eighty-eight, on February 17, 1870.

Jones, Frank – *See* **Sam Kelly.**

K

Kane, Dany: Double Life, Double Death –
When Hells Angels hit man Dany Kane was
found dead in August 2000, a reporter asked Sgt.
Guy Ouellette, a Quebec biker expert with the
Sûreté du Québec, for his reaction.

"Curious," Ouellette said, and he certainly
wasn't exaggerating.

The death of Kane, thirty-one, born in St.
Luc, Quebec, a village about thirty kilometres
south of Montreal, was nothing if not curious.

Kane reportedly died of carbon-monoxide
poisoning in his Mercedes in his garage, but his
family noted that his face had apparently been
severely beaten.

His private life was equally curious. He was a
family man, but also had a gay lover. Professionally, he killed at least two people for the gang
and supplied explosives that were used in at least
another nine killings between 1994 and 1997, but
he was also a long-time RCMP informant, with
source number 3683. He left a note for his RCMP
handlers which read, "Who am I? Am I a biker?
Am I a policeman? Am I good or evil? Am I het-
erosexual or gay? Am I loved or feared? Am I
exploited or the exploiter?"

Kane's death wasn't particularly big news at
the time, but eight months later, it leaked out
that he was a major informer behind Operation
Springtime, a massive crackdown by police on
122 Hells Angels across Canada.

In the trials against seventeen Angels that
followed in May 2002 in Montreal, the court
heard that police had offered Kane $1.75 million
to infiltrate the Quebec Hells Angels. He was a
"source agent" who wore a wire, recorded biker
meetings, photocopied documents, and gave
videotaped testimony for the police. As part of
his cover, the RCMP sponsored his gay sex magazine, although some members of the Mounties
feared that he might be a Hells Angels plant,
spying on police for his biker mentor, David
"Wolf" Carroll of Halifax.

Kane began co-operating with the RCMP in
1994, around the time of an unsuccessful effort
by the Angels to move into Ontario. The bikers
wanted to expand into Toronto, Canada's

Dany Kane

richest drug market, but they had no chapters in Ontario. Angels national president Wolodumyr "Walter" "Nurget" Stadnick set up a puppet (support) club called the Demon Keepers, whose sole mandate was to prepare the ground for the Angels' expansion into Ontario.

Kane was made president of one of its chapters, although he was only in his early twenties and spoke very little English. It was during this expansion attempt that Kane was stopped in Belleville on April 1, 1994. He served almost six months in custody for having two loaded revolvers in his car.

Sometime either while in custody or shortly afterwards, he agreed to work undercover with the RCMP, apparently having soured on the biker lifestyle. Meanwhile, the Demon Keepers were disbanded, and Kane joined the Rockers, also a puppet club for the Hells Angels.

By the time of the mega-trial of 2002, his evidence had led police to the Hells Angels' main Montreal counting-house, which was processing as much as $1 billion yearly. As a result, forty-odd associates of *les hells* pleaded guilty in drugs cases.

Partly because of Kane's work, police were able to compile a list of 135 people the bikers were trying to assassinate. In April 2002, in a Montreal courthouse, it took ten minutes for the court clerk to read the list aloud.

Much of this evidence was gathered when Kane wore a body pack – a hidden microphone taped to his torso that helped investigators penetrate the most secret of biker meetings – what they called "mass" – where all the killings and drug business were discussed.

Kane captured five of those masses on videotape, including one of a top member of the Nomads chapter named Normand Robitaille, whom Kane was supposed to be guarding.

On the tapes, Robitaille was recorded telling others that the price of a kilogram of cocaine was increasing to $50,000, with no room for debate. The price of a quarter-gram of coke on the street jumped from $20 to $25.

"The price of a kilo is now $50,000. I made a deal with the Italians. That's the price now," Robitaille said. This represented a $10,000 increase in the price.

Kane apparently killed himself before he could collect the full amount owed to him by police, but defence lawyers for the Angels suggested he didn't really die at all, and that he had really been given a new identity before his closed-casket ceremony.

See also: **Maurice "Mom" Boucher, Demon Keepers, Nomads, Aimé Simard, Wolodumyr "Walter" "Nurget" Stadnick.**

Kelly (also spelled Kelley), Sam (a.k.a. Charles "Red" Nelson): Butch Cassidy Cohort – You can still stand inside the caves in the Big Muddy Badlands of southern Saskatchewan where Kelly and fellow lawbreakers, including Frank Jones and the Sundance Kid, hid out at the turn of the twentieth century. And if you bring a horse, it can still fit into the separate, neighbouring cave that the gang had for their mounts.

Because of the crimes of Kelly and his cohorts, the North-West Mounted Police was pushed to set up a detachment in the Big Muddy Valley, near the hamlet of Big Beaver.

Kelly's band kept busy stealing horses and cattle on one side of the border and then selling them on the other. Occasionally, they broke the routine by robbing trains loaded with gold, and they sometimes also worked with outlaw groups like Butch Cassidy's Wild Bunch.

Their hideout in the Big Muddy Valley became known as the "Sam Kelly Caves." The caves, which had once been wolf lairs, were big enough to hide horses as well as humans, and the caves' location, across from Peake's Butte, on an elevated patch of land, gave them an expansive view of the area, including the trails used by Mountie patrols.

When members of the gang saw the Mounties coming, they had plenty of time to flee back across the border into the United States and out of Canadian jurisdiction.

Sam Kelly Caves, Big Muddy Valley

Kelly was born in Nova Scotia and it was not clear how he ended up on the prairies. What was clear is that he kept himself – and pursuing lawmen – busy. On May 25, 1895, he and another man watched the jail in Glasgow, Montana, where two associates were being held. After Deputy Sheriff "Hoke" Smith left town with a heavily armed posse in search of Kelly, Kelly and his friend rode calmly up to the jailhouse with two extra horses and freed their friends with a key, which had been shaped from tallow and made from tin.

One of the gang tipped his hat at the sheriff's wife before they made their escape.

Around 1909, Kelly moved out of the caves and onto a ranch he bought in the Big Muddy Valley. Four years later, he moved north to a homestead near Debden, about seventy-five kilometres (forty-five miles) northwest of Prince Albert, bringing with him some horses and three friends from Montana. The area where they settled became known as Kelly's Lake.

Kelly was accurate with a gun, although he didn't enjoy the act of killing like his partner, Frank Jones. It was said in Debden that Kelly could dehorn a steer at a hundred yards with a rifle.

He was apparently well behaved in the Debden area, although the final few years of his life were sad. He was found, hungry and confused, at the bus stop in Smeaton, Saskatchewan, and committed to the Saskatchewan Hospital in Battleford, where he died and was buried in October 1937, at age seventy-eight.

See also: **Big Muddy Badlands, Frank Carlyle, Dutch Henry, Outlaw Trail, Sundance Kid.**

Kerrivan, Peter – *See* **Masterless Men.**

Captain Kidd: Respectable Pirate – There was a time when William Kidd was the very model of respectability.

A founding member of the Trinity Church in lower Manhattan, at Wall Street and Broadway, he donated equipment to help hoist stones for its construction, and also bought a pew there, as befitted his status as one of the wealthiest and most influential members of New York society in the 1690s.

At the time, Trinity Church was the tallest building in lower Manhattan, and was used as a landmark by ships, which was appropriate, since Kidd made his fortune on the high seas.

Home for Kidd was a well-appointed, three-storey mansion nearby on Wall Street, the city's best street, where he lived with his wife, the beautiful Sarah Bradley Cox, who had been New York's wealthiest widow, and their daughter, Sarah.

Legend has it that William Kidd was born the son of a Calvinist minister in Greenock, Scotland, in 1645, but in fact he was born on January 22, 1654, in Dundee, Scotland. His father was a sea captain who died when William was five, and his once-wealthy family was reduced to poverty.

Young William headed off to sea, mostly working ports and ships in the Caribbean. One of his captains may have been Captain Henry Morgan (of rum fame), who was granted a knighthood for his relentless attacks on Spanish ships.

Morgan, and later Kidd, were privateers, not pirates, which was a subtle-but-important distinction, because privateers were knighted, while pirates were hanged. Privateers were commissioned by governments to attack ships of enemy nations, while pirates were truly outlaws.

Put in the best possible light, the profession of privateer was respectable and patriotic, although their ships were often crewed by former pirates. Indeed, the states of New York and Massachusetts often dispatched Kidd to clear their coasts of enemy vessels.

Five years later, in London, Kidd was granted a royal commission to hunt pirates who preyed upon the ships of the East India Company in the Red Sea and in the Indian Ocean. France was at war with England, and plundering her ships in the name of England was nothing short of patriotic.

His sailing brought him into Canadian waters. On one voyage from England to New York, Captain Kidd and his warship, the *Adventure Galley*, fired a shot across the bows of a French fishing vessel off the coast of Newfoundland. Its crew was captured and, in that brief encounter, Kidd had managed to pay for his entire voyage.

Kidd tried to serve in the Royal Navy in 1695, but instead was commissioned by the Crown and by four members of Britain's upper crust – the Earl of Shrewsbury, the Earl of Romney, Lord John Somers, and Admiral Edward Russell – to hunt pirates. At that point, piracy was proving a real threat to England's growing trade empire.

His employers included King William III, a consortium of English lords, and some of America's most influential individuals, and his job was to track down pirates and recover their spoils. In short, he had a licence to steal – but only from thieves.

Out on the high seas, life was anything but easy for Kidd. The pirates he was hunting would often rather die than surrender. He had to travel in a lone ship, manned by former pirates, many of whom had friends and relatives serving on the pirate ships Kidd was chasing. His ship's articles didn't allow him to punish his crew, except with a vote of the entire crew. The Royal Navy didn't trust him, because he was a civilian, while the powerful East India Company considered him an interloper.

On top of that, he was a Scot trying to keep discipline over English and Dutch sailors. Once he rounded the Cape of Good Hope on his way to the India Ocean, the only ports were pirate ports. Despite all the challenges, he was somehow expected to find pirate ships in the twenty-eight-million-square-mile Indian Ocean, and he had just a year to do so, and pay back his impatient financial backers. Then things got worse, with storms, run-ins with ships from the East India Company, sickness, and, ultimately, a mutiny.

Back in England, his financial backers betrayed him with a cutthroat ferocity that would have made a pirate proud. The booty he collected wasn't distributed through official channels. Instead, his backers took it all for themselves, and this act of greed proved to be his downfall. This undercut him to the point that the East India Company managed to get him officially declared a pirate and a wanted man. Usually, past sins were forgiven in the form of a pardon for the right money, and Kidd certainly had far fewer sins in his past than many other wolves of the sea who managed to purchase pardons and even titles.

Kidd got the news that he had been declared a pirate while he was in a tavern in Anguilla, and wrote, "The news of . . . being proclaimed pirates put the crew into such consternation that they [afterward] sought all opportunities to run the ship upon some reef or shoal, lest I should carry her into some English port."

To make things worse, the former Trinity Church pew-holder had fatally struck a crewman during a shipboard quarrel, leaving him vulnerable to a murder charge. He was still confident he could clear up the misunderstanding, if only he could state his case, so he set sail for America. There he was arrested and shipped to London for trial.

Kidd's backers were nervous now, and didn't want it exposed that they had cheated the government out of money. Documents that should have cleared him mysteriously vanished, and Kidd didn't have enough treasure to pull the aristocracy behind him.

When he was sentenced to death in May 1701, Kidd told the court: "For my part, I am the innocentest Person of them all, only I have been sworn against by Perjured Persons."

As he was led on May 23 from Newgate Prison to Execution Dock at Wapping, East London, a jeering mob pelted him and fellow condemned men with food and dead cats covered in excrement. Standing in the gallows, with a rope around his neck, he had to listen to a noose break during an execution attempt of a fellow prisoner. He said he loved his wife and daughter, and then it was his turn. This time, the rope held. His body was left to rot in a cage by the Thames as a warning to would-be pirates.

Salty yarns tell of secret coves where Kidd buried treasure, like Gardiner's Island off Long Island, or the depths of Money Pond on Montauk Point, or along the banks of the lower Hudson, or off the coast of Nova Scotia on High Island, or Haut Isle. The truth may be considerably less romantic. Author Richard Zack concluded that whatever treasure he left gathered dust in an Admiralty warehouse before it was auctioned off.

See also: **Charles Bellamy, Eric Cobham, Cupids, Peter Easton, High Island, Edward Jordan, Mogul Mackenzie, Henry Mainwaring, Sheila Na Geira, Samuel Nelson, John Phillips, Gilbert Pike, Pirates, Bartholomew "Black Bart" Roberts.**

Kiev Embassy – *See* **Kyiv Embassy.**

Kirby, Cecil: Mafia Nightmare – The last words that Rocco Remo Commisso spoke to Kirby were reassuring ones, as he later recalled.

"Don't worry. We'll take care of you," Kirby said he was told. "You know we respect you as a brother. Don't worry."

At the time, Kirby was a killer, bomber, thug, enforcer, former Satan's Choice biker chapter vice-president and road captain, and perhaps the sole non-Italian in the Toronto Mafia's inner circle.

He was also, unbeknownst to Commisso, a police informer.

At the time Commisso spoke those words, on May 16, 1981, Kirby later recalled in court, Commisso thought Kirby had murdered Toronto mobster Paul Volpe for him. However, he had merely faked the killings.

Volpe had agreed to co-operate with police and handed them his wallet when told that he was a murder target. Then Kirby went to the home of Rocco Remo Commisso. Before they began to talk in earnest, a bathroom faucet was turned on to thwart any police listening device. Despite the precaution, this conversation was captured on a hidden recorder worn by Kirby:

"Volpe, he's dead," Kirby said.

"How come?" Rocco Remo Commisso replied.

"I just killed him an hour ago. . . . Cosimo told me you and he wanted it," Kirby responded.

"You should never come here," Commisso said.

"I need some money, okay, and I'm broke, okay . . . I need some money and I want to get . . . out of the country," Kirby said.

"Tell me when I'm going to get it to you?" Commisso asked.

"Well a thousand or something just to get me out of here. . . . I took this right out of his back pocket, okay," Kirby said, referring to the wallet.

"You should have thrown [it] away. . . . All right, don't worry. We'll take care of you," Commisso said.

Volpe remained on the street as the brothers went to prison.

As a result of Kirby's undercover work for police, there were guilty pleas by brothers Rocco Remo, Cosimo, and Michele Commisso to plotting to murder two people in Canada. Rocco Remo and Cosimo were sentenced to eight years in jail, while Michele and a fourth man, Antonio Rocco Romeo, thirty-two, all of North York, who were involved with Cosimo to kill Helen Nafpliotis, a former hairdresser in Stamford, Connecticut, received sentences of two and a half years.

The three Commisso brothers also admitted in a negotiated plea that they conspired to murder mobster Paul Volpe and Pietro Scarcella, a Toronto cheese distributor and Volpe's driver.

Cosimo Commisso pleaded guilty to hiring Kirby to beat up a man called Lillo, a North York furniture-store owner.

The Chief Justice of the Supreme Court of Ontario did not mince words as he sentenced the four men. "This is a gangster case," Chief Justice Gregory Evans said. "It is a contract killing case and we can feel little clemency or mercy with those involved in this case. . . . (I would) remind those who are similarly inclined that contract killing in this province is a very reprehensible offence."

During one meeting with Cosimo Commisso, Kirby testified that he was told he would be put on the payroll. His salary would be $500 a week, with bonuses for crimes committed for the crime family.

Cosimo told Kirby that Volpe was to be killed, and later promised $20,000. He added that Kirby would have to decide on his own whether to kill Volpe's wife if she were present.

Kirby knew it would also endanger his own life, since his old bosses would want to conceal their crime and avoid paying some $20,000 for Volpe's death.

Among other things, Kirby told police:

- it took only a bottle of whisky to get a friendly postal worker to steal credit cards and driver's licences;
- in just two hours, bikers could find unlisted phone numbers, thanks to a sympathetic Bell Canada employee;
- a dispatcher with the Ontario Provincial Police was feeding the gang information;
- information could be culled on extortion targets through a banker who supplied credit information and the contents of bank accounts;
- bikers could check licence numbers of cars they suspected were unmarked police vehicles, thanks to an employee at the Ministry of Transportation and Communications; and
- bikers carried the phone number of a woman with access to CPIC, the central Canadian police computer.

A decade after the murder plots, Kirby sat in a Toronto restaurant with his back to the window, like a man without a worry in the world.

"I'm happy, a changed man," Kirby said in an interview with the *Toronto Star*. "I haven't committed a crime for about ten or eleven years. I don't intend to, either."

At that time, Kirby was in hiding.

Kirby admitted his past included supplying guns to criminals, maybe even the gun used to kill Const. Michael Sweet at the Bourbon Street Tavern on Toronto's Queen Street West on March 14, 1980.

He had also beaten, threatened, and bombed people who wouldn't knuckle under to criminals. A bomb he planted at the Wah Kew Chop Suey House on Elizabeth Street killed cook Chong Yim Quan and injured three others in May 1977.

Kirby admitted that he didn't turn on the Mob for moral reasons, but because he knew too much and his own life was in danger. He also didn't bother to fake great remorse. "If it's past it's past," he said of the hurt he had caused. "I could tell all these people I'm sorry for the hurt I caused them. But what will that do? They would probably want to spit on me."

Aside from the Commisso brothers, Kirby also helped jail Toronto disco bomber Harold Arviv and more than a dozen others, including Charles Yanover, who was convicted of trying to overthrow the government of Dominica.

Kirby was right about the danger to his own life. By 1982, police heard of four separate contracts of $100,000 for his death and a figure of $250,000 was later mentioned. In 1985 some bikers almost cashed in when they discovered where Kirby lived, but he was able to flee before they could kill him.

Kirby joked that the price for his death has probably gone up: "What's a contract worth? With GST, the end of the recession, and inflation? It must be some good bucks now." But he noted with pride that he wasn't living in fear. Once, he even slipped into a Toronto Mob restaurant, sipped a cup of cappuccino, and strolled out unnoticed, feeling pepped up by adrenaline as well as the coffee.

"I don't worry about dying," Kirby says. "I never did. I think I'm less concerned now than I used to be. Now, I've got [moral] conviction. I've got remorse. But I still don't care if I die."

Asked what he would say to his former Mob associates, if he could have one last conversa-tion, he smiled and his eyes twinkled. "Go to confession."

See also: **Harold Arviv, Rocco Remo and Cosimo Commisso, 'Nndrangheta, Pietro Scarcella, Satan's Choice.**

Krowetz, Russell: Slain Manitoba Biker – Robert Blaine Tews cut a chilling figure, even in the world of outlaw bikers and street drug dealers. At fourteen, he was bigger and stronger than most men – tough enough to beat up some of the nastiest men in Winnipeg's downtown.

By his late teens, he had slit the throat of a Winnipeg taxi driver from ear to ear. A decade later, after spending much of his prison time pumping weights, he weighed more than three hundred pounds and was doing guard duty for the Manitoba Warriors, a Native group that in the mid-1990s appeared to be the biggest oppo-sition to the Hells Angels.

That set Tews against Russell Krowetz, a member of the Redliners, a puppet gang set up by Hells Angel Wolodumyr "Walter" "Nurget" Stadnick, who had moved to Winnipeg from Hamilton, Ontario, to oversee Angels' interests. Krowetz and fellow Redliner Stefan Zurstegge had been running hookers in a downtown area known as the "low track."

After ugly words in an after-hours drinking spot, Tews, Roger Sanderson, vice-president of the Warriors, and Robbie Sanderson, a junior member of the Warriors, made a late-night visit to Krowetz's home on August 6, 1996.

When the three men left the house, Krowetz had been stabbed thirty-six times – so often that investigators wondered if the killers were trying to lop off his head. Two of Krowetz's visitors – who weren't Redliners – were also tortured and murdered. One was hacked thirty-four times, the other ten times.

When police arrested Tews, an officer had to hook two sets of handcuffs together so that they could reach behind his massive, bulked-up body. Tews and the two Sandersons were sen-tenced to life terms, and an officer involved in the arrest grimly joked that he would ask to go into a witness-protection program if Tews was ever released.

An elderly couple moved into the Semple Avenue house where the murders took place. The couple, who have no connection to bikers, have painted the trim of the house pink and planted a tree as a memorial to the slain men. Once a year, they hang a memorial wreath on the front door.
See also: **Warriors, Redliners, Wolodumyr "Walter" "Nurget" Stadnick, Zig Zag Crew.**

Kung Lok Triad: Unlikely Name – *Kung Lok* means "mutual happiness," but the society has a three-hundred-year history of murder, narcotics, extortion, abduction, forcible confinement, fraud, robbery, and gambling.

The Triad arrived in Canada from Hong Kong in 1974, in the form of Lau Wing Kui. He moved to Toronto, with thirteen "boys" or cell leaders under him, and quickly expanded Kung Lok operations from Vancouver to Saint John, New Brunswick. By 1979, the Canadian Kung Lok had 150 hard-core members, who collected "protection" money from illegal gambling houses, and extorted money from Chinatown businessmen and recent immigrants and students from Hong Kong.

In 1980, Kui was declared *persona non grata* and deported, but his organization remained intact. Although the Kung Lok went through a period of infighting after the loss of its founder, its new leaders kept expanding in the early 1980s, and forged pacts with triads in Boston and Los Angeles.

In 1981, Toronto was represented when Triad chieftains met in Hong Kong, at what has been likened to the Mafia's 1957 Appalachian meeting, when Mob figures from across North American gathered in Upstate New York to map out their territories and operations. "The meeting resulted in a recognition of territories and an agreement to assist one another when necessary," a 1986 U.S. presidential report on organized crime said.

"The participants 'burned the yellow paper,' a ritual that symbolizes brotherhood and the start of a new venture."

Toronto police investigating an extortion and beating in 1983 discovered a hundred-year-old book on initiation rites to the secret Kung Lok Triad. It gave them a glimpse into an initiation ceremony that called for aspiring members to swear three dozen oaths and drink a mixture of their own blood, wine, chicken blood, cinnabar, sugar, and ashes.

In the mid-1980s, the rival Ghost Shadows group had joined forces with the 14K Association and they were asserting themselves in Chinatown, at the expense of the rival Kung Lok.

During the early 1980s, Vietnamese gang members were recruited by old-style Triad members to stand guard at gaming houses across Toronto, some of which grossed $50,000 in nightly earnings. But the guards turned on their bosses and gaming house patrons and owners were often beaten and robbed.

By the early 1990s, Triad members entered Canada in the entourages of pop singers from Hong Kong, using their visits to smuggle drugs, launder drug money, and import prostitutes. "We simply do not know who among actors, singers, crew, technicians, dancers, musicians, choreographers, electricians, camera person, director, etc., that are part of groups who go to Canada regularly are triad members," a Canadian police report said. "Their roles and actual purpose in going to Canada can be so easily disguised."
See also: **Big Circle Boys, 14K Association, Ghost Shadows, Lau Wing Kui, Sun Yee On.**

Kyiv Embassy: *Mafiya* **Gateway** – In the late 1990s, fraud and mismanagement at the Canadian Embassy in Kyiv (formerly Kiev) meant suspected organized-crime figures and other illegal immigrants were able to slip into Canada.

The problems first came to light in August 1998, when the Canadian Security Intelligence Service and Citizenship and Immigration

Canada officials complained that the Kyiv embassy in Ukraine didn't check to see if visa applicants had organized-crime connections. A year later, immigration officials complained further that the embassy had issued visas to two more people without properly screening them for ties to the East European *mafiya*. "One of these individuals was suspected of involvement in money-laundering on a massive scale," Derek Fraser, Canadian ambassador to Kyiv, said in a February 2001 report.

Kyiv and Moscow were considered major bases for East European organized-crime groups active in financial fraud, prostitution, auto theft, drug smuggling, and money laundering. The RCMP found evidence that an employee in the trade section in Kyiv had taken bribes in exchange for providing business visas to bogus businessmen, bypassing regular security screening procedures.

The Kyiv case wasn't the only case of bribery and corruption problems at Canada's overseas missions. Almost two hundred cases were investigated from 1996 to 1999, and forty-five staff members were found to have engaged in misconduct in Syria, Pakistan, Kuwait, Los Angeles, Hong Kong, Ivory Coast, the Philippines, and elsewhere. Despite the huge damage they could cause, corrupt embassy employees were seldom subject to criminal charges.

L

Lai Changxing: Gambling on Canada –
Fourteen prisoners in shapeless green prison shirts and shorts and slippers dropped their heads as a Chinese tribunal in Beijing sentenced them to death on November 8, 2000. The prisoners, all former state officials, were accused of taking part in a multi-billion-dollar smuggling scheme that was considered the worst corruption scandal to hit China since the People's Republic was proclaimed in 1949.

Officials accused the group's ringleader, Lai Changxing, of bringing more than U.S.$6 billion of cars, oil, cigarettes, textiles, and electronic goods into China without paying import duties. The scandal was said to hit the highest echelons of the party, involving as many as six hundred government, police, customs, and Communist Party officials. Not surprisingly, cynics in Beijing recalled a glum saying, which went: "If the government is serious about locking up corrupted officials, they can simply convert all the government buildings into jails."

Some of the accused in court wept upon hearing their death sentences, but the man Chinese authorities wanted to punish the most wasn't among them. Lai was in Niagara Falls, Ontario, playing games of chance at Casino Niagara. He lost nearly $18,000 at the tables the day the death sentences were passed, a marked improvement from the $85,000 he dropped three days before. However, the fact that the alleged mastermind of the smuggling mega-scandal was alive and outside of China was a major jackpot for him.

The high-roller at Casino Niagara was nothing less than China's top fugitive. In an effort to get him transferred back to China, Premier Zhu Ronji guaranteed Canada that Lai wouldn't be executed if he was extradited. Canada and China had no extradition treaty, so the premier had to appear gentle if he ever hoped to land Lai.

Arrested by the Mounties at Casino Niagara, Lai contended he had done nothing illegal, but the chubby former well-digger and blacksmith had certainly done well financially for someone with a Grade Six education. His critics said his success was aided by a practice of heaping wine, women, and yuan on local Communist Party officials.

At the time of his arrest, Lai had been living in Canada for more than fifteen months, entering the country on August 14, 1999, with a legal visitor's visa issued on his Hong Kong passport. While in Canada, he had no visible job, and was often seen in B.C. casinos, sporting baseball caps and dropping big bets. He was eventually barred from casinos in British Columbia after the B.C. Lottery Commission suspected him of loansharking. He had received word from a senior Chinese police official that investigators were coming to arrest him, and a couple of hours later, he was on a speedboat, fleeing to Hong Kong, and then to Vancouver.

He had settled in comfortably in his new country, paying cash for a $1.3-million mansion in Vancouver's ritzy South Granville area, while his three teenaged children were enrolled in private school, at a cost of $6,000 each. His wife, Tsang Mingna, also accused of corruption in China, deposited U.S.$1.5 million to get a local bank account started.

While his new Canadian digs were certainly comfortable, they were a far cry from the U.S.$8-million, seven-storey headquarters known as the Red Mansion, which he built in his home city of Xiamen, 1,100 miles south of Beijing. After his flight, Chinese officials converted the marble-floored, red brick pleasure palace into an exhibit to warn cadres of the dangers of corruption, although some might argue it only encouraged further wrongdoing. Touring visitors could tour its banquet halls, saunas, karaoke rooms, massage parlours, "two-people dance floors," private cinema, and big-screen televisions for "pornographic film viewing" – along with built-in secret escape routes.

Back in his heyday in the 1990s, Lai was Xiamen's most important private businessman, chauffeured about with bodyguards in a fleet of bulletproof Mercedes-Benz limousines, and rich enough to buy a pro soccer team and move it to his hometown. The Chinese government said he also bought local officials and involved them in games of a different sort, supplying them with women in the Red Mansion, then videotaping their activities.

He contended that he and his businesses were singled out by ambitious Party officials seeking to make him an example, and that he was nothing more than a victim of murky backroom politicking. In their request for refugee status, Lai, his wife, and their three children contended that they had a "well-founded fear of the Chinese government because Lai had refused to cooperate in a government scheme to falsely incriminate an official in the central government."

Meanwhile in China, Zhu Rongji relaxed his stance on Lai slightly. At first, the premier said

Lai should be put to death ten times over, but later softened the figure to execution just three times over.

In 2002, the Canadian refugee board ordered Lai and his family deported. "Mr. Lai and Ms. Tsang are common criminals who headed one of the largest smuggling operations in China," the board said in a written decision. The board said it believed that Lai and Tsang "committed a serious non-political crime outside Canada, including smuggling, fraud, tax evasion, and bribery."

By July 2003, Lai was in limited house arrest in a Vancouver condominium, denying all charges against him. He and his wife were not allowed to be out of the apartment at the same time, and they were continually monitored by video cameras. Immigration lawyers have claimed the couple were associates of members of the Big Circle Boys and the Kung Lok Triad, two Asian-based crime syndicates active in Western Canada, and argued they must be watched closely because these gangs might be able to assist the pair in fleeing Canada. They were also not allowed to attend casinos or associate with members of the Big Circle Boys and Kung Lok Triad.

While critics said he was taking advantage of lax Canadian immigration laws, he said he was simply seeking fairness. "A friend recommended I come to Canada, saying the laws here are more democratic and just," Lai told the *Washington Post*.

At the time Lai was praising Canada's immigration laws, a Canadian court considered his appeal. At least eight of the prisoners who were condemned in his case in China had already been executed, as Lai fought for refugee status in Canada.

See also: **Big Circle Boys, Lau Wing Kui, Kung Lok, Sun Yee On, Triads.**

Lassandro, Florence: Fatal Gamble – In 1923, Lassandro had the sad distinction of being the first and last woman hanged in Alberta.

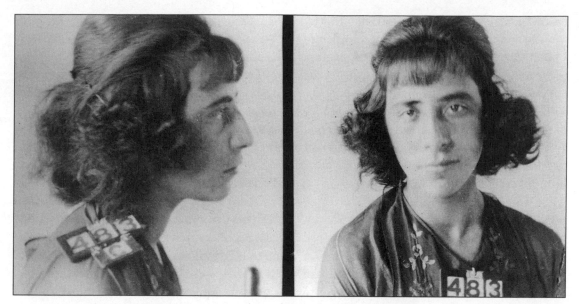

Florence Lassandro, 1922 (Glenbow Archives, NA-3282-2)

The Temperance Act was in force then in Bible Belt Alberta, meaning that big money could be made smuggling booze over the Rockies from British Columbia. Demand for bootleg liquor was particularly high in the coal-mining towns of the Crowsnest Pass region, where Italian immigrant Emilio "Emperor Pic" Picariello ran an extensive rum-running operation out of his hotel in Blairmore.

By some reports, Lassandro was his mistress but, whatever her relationship with Emperor Pic, she often tagged along with him and his teenaged son, Steve, as they ran carloads of booze over the Continental Divide through Phillips Pass.

One night, in September 1922, Steve Picariello headed over the pass, unaware that the Alberta Provincial Police lay in wait. A chase ended in the town of Coleman, where Steve received minor injuries in a shootout. Someone mistakenly told Emperor Pic that his son had been killed. Emperor Pic was beside himself with anger and grief, and raced into Coleman with Lassandro at his side to confront Const. Steve Lawson, whom he thought was his son's killer.

It was never certain who fired the fatal shot that killed the officer on the street, but Emilio was a good guess. In an effort to save him from the gallows, the defence suggested that it had been Florence who actually pulled the trigger. No woman had ever been hanged in Alberta, and Emperor Pic's lawyer wagered that the judge would not break tradition now. The ploy failed, and both were sentenced to be hanged in May 1923 at Fort Saskatchewan Jail.

"Why are you doing this to me?" Lassandro asked plaintively, shortly before she and her lover dropped to their deaths.

Her tragic death became the subject of an opera staged in the 2002–2003 season by Calgary Opera, entitled *Filumena*, by John Estacio and John Murrell. It was billed as being about "love, deception, crime, and danger in a poor Alberta coal mining town in the early years of the 20th century . . . More than a thrilling crime tale, it is the story of how Filumena came to love the mountains and big sky as emblems of spiritual freedom, which even her tragic public fate could not tarnish."

Regret over her execution – and a fear of more violence in the bootlegging trade – sped up the end of Prohibition in Alberta.

***See also:* Samuel Bronfman, Moose Jaw Capone Tunnels, Emilio Picariello.**

Lastman, Mel: Handshake from Hell – Exactly why the Toronto mayor felt the urge to rush into a hotel lobby and shake the hand of a member of the notorious Hells Angels in full gang regalia in January 2002 remains a mystery.

Lastman, a flamboyant mayor with a history of gaffes, first said they appeared to be "good guys," and that he was unaware that the bikers were associated with anything shady, like prostitution, drug dealing, or murder.

In another version, the mayor portrayed himself as a concerned leader with a full bladder. In that explanation, the mayor said he bumped into the bikers after a trip to the downtown Toronto Holiday Inn men's room. Lastman said he paid a visit to the hotel's manager to ensure there were no problems before he was approached by a gang member in Angels regalia. Exactly what problems he was searching for was not explained.

"I said to him, 'Why don't you prove me wrong and the people of Toronto wrong . . . and show us that you guys are great and you're not here to make trouble?'" Lastman said. "He said, 'We're definitely not here to make trouble,' and he put out his hand, and I shook his hand."

The mayor also said he was overcome by nerves when he shook the gang member's hand. "They scare me. I'm just a little guy," the five-foot-five mayor said of the Hells Angels. "What am I going to do? Not give them my hand? My parents may have had ugly children, but they didn't have stupid ones."

There was also the curiosity answer: "I'm curious. I'm concerned. I'm the mayor of this city, and I wanted to make sure the city was operating well and there were no problems." Reporters were also offered the common-courtesy explanation: "Please understand, I never turned my back on anybody who gave me their hand. Do I welcome you when I shake your hand, if you come over to me and say hello? Have I ever refused anybody to shake their hand? I don't do that. I've never done that in my life."

A photo of Lastman shaking hands with the Hells Angels member made the front pages of

Mel Lastman with Hells Angel (Dave Lucas, Toronto Sun)

newspapers and outraged police forces across the country – particularly in Quebec, where gang leader Maurice "Mom" Boucher was about to go on trial for murder. "Memo to the mayor: The Hells Angels aren't the Shriners. They're not people you should be welcoming to town, not while your police force is trying to chase them out," wrote the *Toronto Star*. Authorities and editorial writers across the country expressed disgust at the mayor's actions. In Montreal, the front page of *Le Journal de Montréal* shouted out: "THE MAYOR OF TORONTO IS THE FRIEND OF HELLS!"

By the time the bikers' convention weekend in Toronto was over, police, politicians, the entire province of Quebec, and even the Hells Angels themselves were demanding apologies from Lastman.

The bikers were incensed because he publicly threw a souvenir T-shirt they gave him in the garbage after the public outrage about his handshake. In a letter sent to the mayor, the bikers said Lastman's decision to throw out the T-shirt was the "pinnacle of poor taste."

Lau Wing Kui: Triad Pioneer – By the time he was deported to his native Hong Kong in 1980, Lau had established the first major Triad in Metropolitan Toronto, its members bound together by secret rituals and blood oaths under the Triad symbol of the three primary forces of the universe: heaven, earth and man.

This was the Kung Lok (mutual happiness) Triad, which police intelligence reports said grew to some four hundred members who were involved in extortion against businessmen and recent immigrants and students from Hong Kong, as well as in "protection" and the entertainment industry in Chinatown.

By the time of Lau's deportation, the Kung Lok was being led by former associates of Lau who were close to Triad and gang leaders in New York, Boston, San Francisco, and Hong Kong. The Toronto Triad gained control of some of the protection rackets for entertainers who come through Toronto from Hong Kong and China. In a subtle form of extortion, it also provided guards for some of the many illegal Chinese gambling houses in the Toronto area.
See also: **Big Circle Boys, Kung Lok, Triads.**

Lavigne, Diane: Murdered Prison Guard – She was murdered by the Hells Angels in 1997, simply because she worked as a prison guard. The Hells Angel who pulled the trigger on orders from gang boss Maurice "Mom" Boucher could see only her uniform as he fired into her car, and that was all that mattered to him.

Her father, Leon Lavigne, a retired prison guard himself, was in the front row of a packed courthouse as he watched Boucher get a life sentence for his role in the crime. "It's one of the most beautiful days of my life," Lavigne told reporters outside court. "I'm very happy it's over. I'll turn the page from now on. . . . It took five years."

Boucher was also found guilty of the first-degree murder of fellow guard Pierre Rondeau and attempted murder of guard Robert Corriveau. Many people in the courtroom had worn small pins in memory of Rondeau and Lavigne throughout the trial. After hearing the sentence, a family member said the past five years had been especially difficult on Diane Lavigne's two children, then twenty-four and twenty-six.

The Crown case was based on the theory Boucher did not pull the trigger himself but ordered the shooting deaths of the two guards in an attempt to destabilize the justice system and was thus equally guilty.

This was Boucher's second trial on the charges. He was acquitted the first time, and the prosecution appealed. When the guilty verdict was registered, Leon Lavigne spoke warmly of the twelve ordinary people on the jury who found Boucher guilty, after eleven days of deliberations. "I thank the jury for having the guts to give the guilty [verdict]," said Leon Lavigne. "I hoped all the time, but I didn't know."

"Finally, peace," his wife, Helen, said. "Justice and peace."

See also: **Maurice "Mom" Boucher, Serge Boutin, Daniel Desrochers, Stéphane "Godasse" Gagné, Pierre Rondeau, André "Toots" "Peanuts" Tousignant.**

Lavoie, Donald: Forgetful Killer – When Lavoie testified in court as a defence witness in October 1981, *Globe and Mail* columnist William Johnson wrote: "He is an unusual witness. Donald Lavoie is 39 and looks like a college professor."

Lavoie had worked for a dozen years as a killer for hire, and couldn't tell the court exactly how many people he had murdered. Perhaps the number was about twenty-seven, he ventured, noting there were also assaults, armed robberies, and drug use and sales.

The testimony came during the extortion and confinement trials of Jean Tremblay and Micheline Pelletier-Travers, who were accused of holding the wife and mother-in-law of a Canadian Imperial Bank of Commerce accountant for ransom in December 1980 in a motel until the bank paid about $135,000 for their release. Lavoie said he was part of the Dubois gang at the time, working with the extortionists.

Then he said he got wind that the gang had taken out a contract on him. He said the decision was made by Claude Dubois and others. "Mr. Dubois wouldn't dirty his own hands. He would have it done by others."

Lavoie had plenty of theories why the Dubois family might want him dead. Claude Dubois had given him $4,300 for a sale of hashish, but he was supposed to get more than $8,000 for the deal, and he had pointed this out to Dubois.

Things only got worse with Dubois after that, he said. It was nothing less than a "war," in Lavoie's mind. "I was afraid for my family, I was afraid for myself, and I'm still frightened."

"The criminal world no longer accepts me, so I went over to the other side," he said under cross-examination by noted criminal lawyer Léo-René Maranda.

Maranda drove home the point that Lavoie was a liar and a killer, although that was never much in dispute. The lawyer recalled how Lavoie had told one of the abducted women that he had respect for women.

"Did you have a great respect for Linda Majore?" Maranda asked.

"I didn't know her," Lavoie replied.

"Did you kill her?"

"Yes."

"With how many knife stabs?"

"I don't know."

Maranda also noted that Lavoie's respect for women didn't stop him from trying to kill his first common-law wife with an axe.

See also: **Dubois Brothers, Claude Dubois, Claude Jodoin.**

Leithman, Sydney: Murdered Lawyer – Leithman was on his way to his office to present his final arguments in a trial involving Colombian drug traffickers on May 13, 1991. Driving alone in his black Saab convertible at 6:48 a.m., Leithman was just a minute from his home in Mount Royal when suddenly a car cut him off at a stoplight at the corner of Rockland Road and Monmouth Avenue.

Then a young man walked toward him from near a telephone booth, pulling out a

Sidney Leithman

.45 automatic pistol. The gunman kept firing methodically at Leithman until he was leaning right into the Saab. When the shooting finally stopped, a bag of smoked meat was thrown onto the body. Perhaps it was an anti-Semitic flourish, or perhaps the gunman had tried to squeeze in a snack before the murder and misjudged the time. Whatever the case, the murder remains unsolved.

Naturally, Leithman's clients figured high on the list of potential suspects, as he was unable to save many of them from jail time. He had often appeared at the side of Montreal's most notorious underworld figures. He and fellow lawyer Rolland Blais had presided over a press conference in November 1975, when some of the infamous Dubois brothers of St.-Henri stripped in front of reporters and photographers, arguing they had been beaten by police.

Leithman also poured drinks for guests at a press conference in the early 1970s, when mobster Frank Cotroni tried to clear up what he called misconceptions about a trip he had made to Mexico.

Leithman's clients also included Colombian drug traffickers, with connections to the world's most wanted criminal of the early 1990s, Pablo Escobar of the Medellín cartel.

His name was also mentioned darkly in connection with a top police officer. In December 1992, RCMP Insp. Claude Savoie committed suicide after learning that he was going to be questioned by officers from the force's internal-affairs division about allegations he funnelled information through Leithman to Montreal drug king Allan "The Weasel" Ross of the West End Gang.
See also: **Claude Dubois, Frank "Santos" Cotroni, Doug Jaworski, Allan "The Weasel" Ross, Claude Savoie, Frank Shoofey.**

Lemay, Guy: Tragic Mistake – When he opened the back door of his Montreal apartment to let his dog out on January 7, 1997, someone shot Lemay dead. He had been mistaken for a Rock Machine drug dealer who lived upstairs.

See also: **Daniel Desrochers, Diane Lavigne, Serge Hervieux.**

Lepage, Guy: Changing Sides – The cop-turned-biker was extradited to the United States from Montreal at the end of July 2002 to face drug charges in Miami that could land him in prison for life.

Lepage was a Montreal police officer from 1966 to 1974, then moved on to become a chauffeur for Hells Angels kingpin Maurice "Mom" Boucher. He was also founder of the Rockers, a Hells Angels puppet club, and served as its president. Police said he was also linked to the Nomads, a select chapter of the Hells Angels, commanded by Boucher.
See also: **Maurice "Mom" Boucher, Dany Kane, Nomads.**

L'Epiphanie, Quebec: Mob Summit – When they raided the house of Gerlando Caruana on Imperia Street shortly before midnight on December 14, 1971, police interrupted a Mafia summit in this community in northeastern Montreal.

The twenty-seven people inside included the city's top Mafia bosses, and five of the people present would be murdered over the next five years. Among the top topics for discussion that night was the role of Nicolo "Nick" Rizzuto, who had strong supporters internationally, including ties to the Caruana and Cuntrera Mafia families.

Among those present was Leonardo Caruana, who would be deported from Canada and who would be murdered in Palermo on the wedding day of one of his sons. Also attending the meeting was Pietro Sciara, a Sicilian mobster who was shot to death with an Italian shotgun, or *lupara*, in 1976 while leaving a movie theatre in little Italy belonging to a Cotroni sister. Ironically, he'd just seen the Italian-language version of *The Godfather*.
See also: **Vincenzo "Vic the Egg" Cotroni, Alfonso Caruana, Nick Rizzuto, Vito Rizzuto, Paolo Violi.**

Lindsey, Maria – *See* **Eric Cobham.**

Lui Lok – *See* **Five Dragons.**

Longabaugh, Harry – *See* **Sundance Kid.**

LoPresti, Giuseppe "Joe": Poor Joe – A wealthy contractor with solid Liberal party connections took LoPresti into the *Montreal Daily News* offices in 1989 and asked a senior executive for some help. In a slightly patronizing tone, the contractor called LoPresti "Poor Joe" and continued, "We all feel sorry for him and would like to get him into something."

That something was a plan to ship bundled newspapers to the Third World for recycling. The papers would be sent there in large containers, which seemed an extravagance. The idea was for the containers to then be shipped back, and no one was so rude as to point out that this would be a convenient way to import heroin.

The plan fell through, as the newspaper's parent company already had a newsprint plan, and LoPresti didn't seem particularly concerned when told the bad news. Perhaps that's because Poor Joe, who outwardly seemed a totally unremarkable man, had plenty of other businesses to keep him occupied, and he never seemed to be hurting financially.

Had the newspaper executive seen LoPresti's neo-Tudor-style, custom-built home, he might not have worried about Poor Joe's cash flow. There were only four houses on his extremely exclusive street in the posh Cartierville section of Montreal, and even in a depressed real-estate market, they were worth around $1 million each.

More interesting than his house were his neighbours. One of the houses was quietly occupied by sixty-five-year-old Libertina Rizzuto, who waited patiently for her fugitive Mafia don husband Nicolo "Nick" to return from Caracus, where he was being held on drug charges on a Venezuelan government minister's order. Nick's son, Vito, occupied another of the mansions,

and the other was for Paolo Renda, Vito's brother-in-law.

Police were certainly interested in that posh enclave. Clearly LoPresti had done well financially since he arrived in Halifax in 1969, one of many Mafiosi fleeing his birthplace of Cattolica Eraclea in Agrigento, Sicily, after an anti-Mafia crackdown.

LoPresti was always hanging around in the background in interesting locations. He was certainly close to Nick Rizzuto after the January 22, 1978, murder of Rizzuto's underworld rival Paolo Violi. More than one person with insights into the underworld considered Poor Joe at least partially responsible for the Violi hit.

LoPresti was also involved in promoting kick-boxing and boxing, according to an investigation, but police thought this was more of a diversion than the source of his considerable wealth. There were also his investments in video poker, but even that wasn't the real source of his

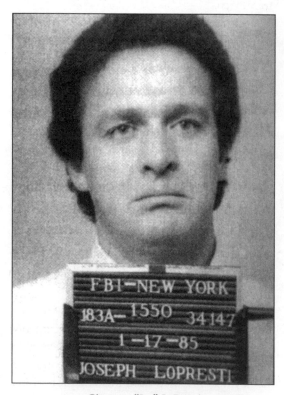

Giuseppe "Joe" LoPresti

power. What made Poor Joe a someone was that he was well connected to the Bonnano and Gambino families, as well as with a new wave of Sicilian immigrants, known as "Zips" in Brooklyn for their quick way of talking.

His "Zip" friends included Cesare "Tall Guy" Bonventre, the bodyguard for Mafia boss Carmine "Mr. Lillo" or "The Cigar" Galante, who extinguished The Cigar in July 12, 1979. Bonventre himself would end up in two pieces in an oil drum, possibly a crude symbolism for his double-cross, or perhaps just a way of fitting him into the drum.

LoPresti's New York City contacts also included Angelo "Quack Quack" Ruggiero, who was as loud as an angry duck and who was often told by Gambino family powerhouse John "Johnny Boy" Gotti, "You've got to keep your fucking mouth shut."

Connected with LoPresti and Ruggiero was Gerlando Sciascia, who held an undeveloped patch of land next door to Poor Joe on Antoine-Berthelet Avenue, on which he hoped to build a house, if he could settle legally in Canada.

In the early 1980s, LoPresti and Sciascia were breaking the rules of the Gambino family as well as those of the rest of society with their whole-sale drug dealing with Ruggiero. Gambino boss Paul Castellano had ordered his men to stay away from drug importing, since that meant the threat of big prison time, and the threat of big prison time brought with it the heightened chance of members turning informer.

To change the rules inside the Gambinos, up-and-coming family member John Gotti had Castellano murdered.

Unfortunately for them, LoPresti, Sciascia, Ruggiero, and more than a dozen others were soon facing heroin-importing charges.

LoPresti chilled in Montreal on bail as other defendants bought more time with jury tampering. Sooner or later, if authorities caught him, he would have to explain why he was picked up on a police bug reassuring Quack Quack that he had assured a heroin supplier in the Cuntrera-Caruana family that a shipment of heroin was coming. In that statement, made May 16, 1982, Poor Joe indiscreetly said, "He said he was 100 per cent certain that our load is coming. It's in Canada for a week and a half before it's here."

When Poor Joe finally faced trial in Brooklyn, security concerns meant jurors were identified only by numbers to cut the fear of intimidation or bribery. FBI agent John Flanagan told the court that the prisoners had "used the services of an investigator to trace the licence plates of juror's cars, many of which had been parked in a lot near the courthouse."

It didn't help that one juror had personalized plates, making him particularly easy to follow, and court officials only got more queasy when a juror said he was approached by a stranger and offered a new car for insights about how the case was going. Another juror said his mother was "panicked." More nasty than intelligent, co-accused Eddie Lino tacked a menacing note on what he thought was the door of a juror. He had the wrong address and the homeowner went to the FBI. Yet another juror told of being offered a $10,000 bribe.

The tactic of going after the jury still had some success. Andrew Maloney, U.S. attorney for the Eastern District of New York, said that one juror was compromised. Asked what he meant, Maloney replied bluntly, "Bought and paid for, in the bag."

The effort to scuttle the trial paid off in an acquittal on February 7, 1990, after the defence trotted out a technical expert who said it was possible that the incriminating tapes could have been tampered with in an undetectable way.

Two years later, on April 27, 1992, Poor Joe drove his cherry-red Porsche out of the driveway of his neo-Tudor-style home. He had likely heard of a meeting of top-level Calabrian mobsters in Montreal the day before, and perhaps that was on his mind. The Calabrians were all connected to Paolo Violi, and all would have heard the reports of LoPresti's alleged involvement in setting up the hit.

It was common for Poor Joe to drive off to racquetball courts, discos, construction sites, bakeries, and restaurants, and that day he was en route to a restaurant on Décarie Boulevard.

Whoever he met must have been trusted and a somebody, because LoPresti wasn't in the habit of spending time with just anyone, and he trusted the person he met enough to leave his car in the restaurant lot.

At 10:30 that night, a CN railworker saw a large plastic package lying on the tracks at Fifty-Fourth Avenue and Henri Bourassa Boulevard East in northeast Montreal. Wrapped inside the plastic was the body of Poor Joe, with a small-calibre gunshot wound to the head. Whoever did the killing was thorough enough to take his ID, which would be useful for the hit man to prove he carried out the job to whomever was paying him. However, $4,000 was left on the body, underlining the fact that this wasn't the work of a street punk.

Possible theories for the murder included an unexplained grudge from the Gotti family over the court cases. Or perhaps it was long-festering anger over the Violi murder, which would explain the meeting of Calabrians the day before. Toronto Sicilians who were close to LoPresti huddled to talk things over, then did . . . nothing. Perhaps they were just as confused about the motive for Poor Joe's murder as the police.

See also: **Boxing, Carmine Galante, Nicolo "Nick" Rizzuto, Vito Rizzuto, Gerlando Sciascia, Paolo Violi.**

Los Brovos: Manitoba Bikers – Formed in 1967 with twelve original members from the St. Boniface/St. Vital areas of Winnipeg, their original colours depicted a skeleton draped in a cape on a motorcycle.

Like the rival Spartans, the Los Brovos conducted some drug trafficking, but most of their money came from debt collections and the handling of stolen goods, especially Harley-Davidson motorcycles. The Los Brovos were also noted for their intelligence-gathering abilities,

which included keeping accurate account of police members' names, addresses, and vehicles.

In 1980, the Los Brovos began a massive recruitment, shortening the required prospect time from a year to just a month in some cases. The club's membership peaked at sixty-eight full members, with an average age of just twenty-five.

It was clear in the summer of 1980 that the Los Brovos were ready to end their peaceful co-existence with the Spartans and make their push to become the dominant gang in Manitoba. Both clubs began to make overtures to the Hells Angels, who had established their first Canadian chapter in Sorel, Quebec, three years before.

In July 1983, new Hells Angels chapters were granted in British Columbia, to White Rock, Vancouver, and Nanaimo, and the Los Brovos hoped they'd soon also join the larger gang. In late July, the Hells Angels attended Winnipeg en masse for the first time and, as part of the event, the Los Brovos sponsored drag races in Gimli, Manitoba. When the racing was over, some of the Angels called the Los Brovos "goofs," and the Los Brovos hopes of changing colours appeared to be in the ditch.

Within a month, the Los Brovos were in disarray. The club's mechanic was kicked out of the club in August. Three months later, a member abducted and raped a local woman with strong family ties to various active criminals. Now the gang's popularity plummeted in the local criminal community.

By February 1984, the Los Brovos were down to just thirty-eight members. There once had been a pact among the Los Brovos, the Grim Reapers of Alberta, and the Satan's Choice of Thunder Bay to fend off Hells Angels expansion, but by the early 1990s, this would weaken considerably.

Between 1991 and 1993, there were thirty-one acts of violence between the Los Brovos and Spartans. Among those injured was Hells Angels associate Donald Magnussen, the bodyguard for the Angels national president, Walter Stadnick.

Stadnick was so upset that he reportedly ordered the fighting to stop and negotiated a truce between the Los Brovos and Spartans. To secure the peace, he offered the Spartans the carrot of membership, while threatening the Los Brovos with the stick of retaliation.

By early 1994, most Los Brovos members were either facing charges or behind bars, as club fortunes sunk to a new low. The club's new leader, Jeff Peck, was arrested in 1995 for operating what was found to be the largest "chop shop" of stolen motorcycles ever located in Canada.

On May 10, 1996, Los Brovos members Shane Preston Jones and David Boyko attended a Hells Angels anniversary party in Halifax, Nova Scotia, as relations between the two gangs grew more cordial. That didn't last long. On May 12, 1995, Boyko was shot dead execution-style in a commercial area of Dartmouth.

The actual shooter may have been Donald Magnussen, now the bodyguard for Scott Steinert of the Hells Angels, or may have been a member of the Grim Reapers of Alberta. Whatever the case, the murder caused a major split in the Los Brovos. The gang's old allegiance to the Grim Reapers–Satan's Choice pact was now ended. Several old-time members of the Grim Reapers quit their club, while others began prospecting for the Hells Angels.

Stadnick and numerous senior members of the Hells Angels attended Winnipeg for Boyko's funeral. When they went with members of the Grim Reapers to the Los Brovos West Winnipeg clubhouse, they were told that the Grim Reapers could enter, but the Hells Angels must stay outside. As a result, both gangs left.

It was the Winnipeg health department and not rival gangs that ultimately shut the North clubhouse in May 1996. After repairs, it was rented out to members of the Manitoba Warriors bike gang for cocaine sales.

During this time, the Los Brovos supplied Native street gangs with both drugs and weapons, while the Native gangs allowed the Los Brovos to store their items on reserves to avoid detection.

The Los Brovos officially folded on July 24, 1999, becoming a prospect club for the Hells Angels. After six months, they became a full chapter. Their rivals, the Spartans, had disbanded after the mysterious disappearance of their leader, Darwin Sylvester, in June 1998.
See also: **Donald Magnussen, Redliners, Wolodumyr "Walter" "Nurget" Stadnick, Darwin Sylvester, Kevin Sylvester, Robert Blaine Tews.**

Lotus Gang: Drug Wholesalers – In a study released in early 1999, Simon Fraser University criminologist Rob Gordon found that the Lotus Gang had been active since the 1960s in street-level crime in Vancouver, like extorting Asian businesses, gambling, drug distribution, and prostitution.

By the 1980s, Lotus, which has a predominantly Chinese-Canadian membership, amalgamated with a 1970s street gang called Jung Ching, composed of ethnic Chinese from Vietnam. In the late 1980s, Lotus joined forces with the Los Diablos gang, which was originally composed of Hispanic members, to fight a street war over drug turf with the Gum Wah (Golden Chinese) gang and the now-defunct Red Eagles (Hung Ying), who were a mixture of ethnic Chinese from Hong Kong, the Philippines, and Vietnam.

By the early 1990s, Vancouver was home to thirty gangs with one thousand members, also including the Big Circle Boys, former members of the Chinese Red Army; Viet Ching, mostly ethnic Chinese from Vietnam; and two emerging groups, a gang known simply as Ethnic Vietnamese and the Maralatinos, Hispanics who had recently arrived in Canada. Those heavily armed gangs often banded together to smuggle drugs, run prostitution rings, and rob wealthy Asians.

The Los Diablos grew to include Indo-Canadian members and became known as the East Indian Mafia in the 1990s. By the mid-1990s,

Lotus had expanded to trafficking cocaine at the "wholesale" level to Bhupinder "Bindy" Johal and his East Indian Mafia, who sold cocaine on the street through a dial-a-dope operation.

Despite their attempts to work together, violence often flared up between the two groups. Johal kidnapped Randy Chan of the Lotus Gang during a 1996 drug deal that went awry, which pitted Chinese-Canadian and Indo-Canadians gangsters against each other. An associate of Johal felt that he was being cheated when he went to buy two kilograms of cocaine from Randy Chan and an associate. Johal felt that the cocaine had been "watered down" with a bogus white powder.

Johal took Randy Chan hostage, and at one point held him in the trunk of a car as he drove around Vancouver, repeatedly calling the pager of Chan's older brother, Raymond Man Yuen Chan, and demanding five kilograms of cocaine if he wanted to see his brother alive. The late Vancouver criminal lawyer Richard Israels was able to negotiate Randy Chan's safe release after being held for fifty-six hours.

Johal was gunned down in December 1998 in front of three hundred witnesses on a crowded dance floor of the Palladium nightclub in Vancouver. In May 2003, Raymond Chan was murdered at age thirty-one in a business-industrial section of Richmond, British Columbia, in what police called a "targeted gangland-style hit." Neither the Johal nor the Chan murders have been solved.
See also: **Bhupinder "Bindy" Johal.**

Lowe, Ned – See **High Island.**

Luppino, Giacomo: Wise Old Man – As a young man in the village of Oppido, Calabria, in his native Italy, Luppino was said to have cut off a man's ear in a fight. He carried the grisly trophy, which looked like a gnarled piece of leather, in his wallet, Canadian police were later told.

Although police were able to install a listening device amongst the tomato plants in his backyard on Ottawa Street North in east Hamilton, they didn't get enough evidence to charge him with any crime. What they did hear included the old don complaining about the performance of the Toronto Maple Leafs and saying that an underworld figure should be killed for cheating on his wife.

RCMP Insp. Dino Chiarot said that the old man once told his wife he wished he could speak English so he could set up a business, "as in his opinion, people here are much easier to cheat than in Italy." Inspector Chiarot continued that the organization looked with disfavour on members who attract the attention of police and quoted Luppino as saying that the Buffalo don, Stefano Magaddino, told him "He never wanted to be visited by the Canadian group, because certain things have been in the papers."

He said Luppino warned his associates "not to let anyone go to the States any more and be careful not to break the code." Then he noted that his own Montreal-based son-in-law Paolo Violi might be in danger for breaking underworld rules. "The way the code stands now, you may lose Paolo Violi. So be careful."

Luppino, who was considered as tough as the ear rumoured to be in his wallet, had been the Magaddino family's southern Ontario syndicate boss since the death of Santo Scibetta in the mid-1970s, according to investigators. The two had jointly ruled as godfathers through the 1950s and 1960s, with control passing to Luppino.

Luppino's daughter Grazia married Paulo Violi, who had risen to become arguably the most powerful crime boss in Montreal by the time he was killed Mob-style in 1978.

Luppino reportedly sponsored Paul Volpe in entering the Magaddino family. Volpe was killed and stuffed into the trunk of his wife's BMW parked at Pearson International Airport in 1983. Former biker and Mob enforcer Cecil Kirby, who later worked undercover for police, said that the Luppino organization also took Volpe out of the Mob, authorizing his execution. No one has ever been charged in that case.

The most attention Luppino ever got from the public was in March 1987, when his funeral attracted the glare of publicity he had shunned all his life. The man known as southern Ontario's Mob "godfather" was eighty-eight when he was carried to his grave in a shiny bronze coffin. It was arranged as a relatively low-key event, which he would have appreciated.

But it was not to remain low-key. Cadillacs, Lincolns, Mercedes-Benzes, and other high-end cars from Connecticut, New York State, and Quebec were among the funeral cortege of 130 vehicles. Some mourners arrived by taxi after flying into Hamilton Civic Airport aboard private aircraft.

Neighbours offered no complaints about the old man to reporters, noting that he would often sit on his veranda and pass out candy to neighbourhood children. "He had lots of visitors, but would never let them block our driveways," one neighbour recalled.

See also: 'Ndrangheta, Stefano Magaddino, John "Johnny Pops" Papalia, Michele "Mike" Racco, Paul Volpe, Paolo Violi.

M

Mackenzie, Mogul: Civil War Pirate – During the American Civil War, Mackenzie commanded the ship *Kanawha* off Canada's east coast, preying on Union ships. His reputation was that of a sadist who needed little reason to torture captives.

In 1865, when the Civil War was over, merchant seamen on the Atlantic coast reported that they were being harassed by a lean grey pirate ship that sounded suspiciously like the *Kanawha*. Their complaints sounded like something from the "Golden Age" of piracy from more than a century and a half earlier, before the British navy crushed piracy everywhere but in the Indian Ocean and the China Sea.

In May 1865, an American gunboat off the coast of Nova Scotia spotted a ship resembling the *Kanawha* and tried to overtake it, but the mysterious boat slipped through treacherous waters toward Sable Island.

Soon afterwards, another ship resembling the *Kanawha* tried to overtake a Nova Scotia schooner off Campobello, New Brunswick, but the schooner's pilot, a skilful sailor, fled to safety.

A few days after that, a whaler reported finding the trading vessel *St. Clare* abandoned in the Bay of Fundy, its sails still raised. There was no sign of her crew, but a small boat was tied to her planking with the name *Kanawha* on its side. The crew was feared captured or thrown overboard.

As the fate of the crew of the *St. Clare* was contemplated, a trading vessel from Boston arrived in Yarmouth, reporting a sighting of the *Kanawha* in the direction of Saint John, New Brunswick. The British warship H.H.S. *Buzzard* set off in pursuit, but lost sight of it near High Island. No trace of the *Kanawha* was ever found, although a naked sailor was found near death on the shore about fifty kilometres north of Yarmouth, his tongue cut out. The suspicion was that he had met up with Mackenzie, and had been tossed overboard.

See also: **Charles Bellamy, Eric Cobham, Cupids, Peter Easton, High Island, Edward Jordan, Captain Kidd, Henry Mainwaring, Sheila Na Geira, John Phillips, Gilbert Pike, Pirates, Bartholomew "Black Bart" Roberts.**

Magaddino, Stefano: Criminal Undertaking – Religious candles flickered in front of tabletop statues of saints when a judge visited Magaddino in the bedroom of his home in December 1968 to arraign him on tax charges.

Two pillows propped up Magaddino's head, as the seventy-seven-year-old, looking feeble and benign in his lime-green pajamas, drew oxygen from a tank at the foot of his bed. Two doctors stood watch at his bedside, ready to rush to his aid if his condition took a sudden turn for the worse.

The judge had to travel to Magaddino's bedroom because his lawyers said he was too ill to go to court himself. That day, FBI agents found a large safe in the basement of his home

Stefano Magaddino

The Old Man was certainly familiar to law-enforcement officials. His contact with police had dated back to at least August 16, 1921, when he was arrested regarding a homicide in Avon, New Jersey.

The visit by the FBI and the judge came a decade after a 1957 meeting of North America's top crime lords in the Appalachians, near Binghamton, New York. Magaddino was one of a handful of men who founded the Mafia's high commission, a group of twelve mobsters who met periodically to settle disputes, determine what crimes were allowed, and what families would control them.

Magaddino was a commissioner with this top rung of Mafia lords because of the strength of his "Arm," which reached into Niagara Falls, Buffalo, Ontario, and parts of Ohio and Pennsylvania. He managed to elude state police in their raid at the Appalachian conference, although his clothes were found at the meeting site.

As legitimate sidelines, when not running drugs, gambling, or construction rackets, The Old Man ran the Magaddino Memorial Chapel Funeral Home, the Power City Distributing Co. of Niagara Falls, and Camellia Linen Supply Co. of Buffalo, New York. He was said to have pioneered the double-decker casket, with a paying customer on the top, and the corpse of a murder victim secreted underneath.

The Magaddino Memorial Chapel Funeral Home on Niagara Street in Niagara Falls, New York, was the business front for Magaddino's criminal empire. When federal authorities illegally bugged the chapel in the early 1960s, they overheard that The Old Man's cut from gambling in an old Buffalo firehall on Seneca Street was $25,000 a week.

The bugs prompted police to recover $38,000 in alleged bookmaking profits at the chapel, but once it came out that the wiretaps were conducted illegally, all charges against Magaddino and his associates were dropped.

He was intensely suspicious – perhaps rightly so – of his New York City cousin Joe

on exclusive Dana Drive in Lewiston, New York, but when they opened it up, it was empty.

By the time the FBI agents made their bedroom visit, Magaddino had run his organization in the Niagara Falls–Buffalo area for a half-century. The organization was known on the streets of Buffalo as the Arm, and he was alternately referred to as The Old Boss, The Old Man, and Don Stefano.

His "Arm" had a firm grip that reached into Canada, although The Old Man never lived north of the forty-ninth parallel. Born October 10, 1891, in Castellammare, Sicily, he lived on the eastern seaboard of the United States briefly before moving to upper New York State, building his home adjacent to the equally luxurious home of his daughter and son-in-law.

According to the U.S. McClellan Committee on organized crime, his empire in Canada was said to include the organizations of John Papalia and of the Agueci and Volpe brothers.

Bonanno. After Bonanno applied for Canadian citizenship in 1963, Magaddino complained that he was doing this to cut in on his northern turf. "He's planting flags all over the world," Magaddino protested.

The Old Man was capable of enormous cruelty, as in the torture/murder of Alberto Agueci of Scarborough, Ontario, after Agueci threatened to become an informer. However, many considered him a soft-spoken gentleman, well-schooled in the ways of the Old World. He certainly was a smiling presence at his annual fall meetings at the now-demolished Andy's Café on Lower Terrace Street in Buffalo. As many as fifty men, members of the inner sanctum, shed their Borsalino hats and camel-hair coats to sit at four long tables, arranged in a square in Andy's backroom. "He wasn't loud or boisterous like a lot of others," one restaurant employee told the *Buffalo News*. "He was like Santa Claus. He smiled with his eyes."

While The Old Man avoided jail after the 1968 bedside visit, his power was clearly slipping. More than $500,000 in musty bills – in denominations from $1 to $1,000 – had been discovered in an attic trunk belonging to his son, Peter, and the discovery marked the beginning of a downward slide for the Buffalo Mafia.

At the time the bills were discovered, The Old Man had been complaining to his underlings that he was too poor to give them their share of the proceeds from their criminal enterprises. Understandably, news of his secret money cache stirred dissention in the ranks.

By the time of his death in 1974, The Old Man was out of power, but by Mob terms his life was a success, as he died in bed, without ever going to trial. None of his successors in the Buffalo Mob merited a seat on the Mafia's national high commission, as none of them were considered strong enough.

See also: **Alberto Agueci, Joe Bonanno, Ron Fino, Giacomo Luppino, John "Johnny Pops" Papalia, Paolo Violi, Paul Volpe.**

Magnussen, Donald: Angels' Muscle – He didn't live to see the Hells Angels officially set up quarters in Manitoba in July 21, 2000, but he played a significant role bringing *les hells* into the Keystone Province.

Magnussen, who was originally from Thunder Bay, was a bodyguard for the Angels national president, Walter Stadnick, in the early and mid-1990s, back when Stadnick was helping the gang expand across the prairies.

It was clearly a violent job. Magnussen was shot in the legs outside the Windsor Park Inn in Winnipeg about 2:30 a.m. on December 15, 1993, while waiting for a cab. Someone in a pickup truck belonging to a member of the Los Brovos motorcycle club squeezed off between ten and fifteen shots from a weapon believed to be a 9 mm semi-automatic handgun.

Only one of the bullets hit Magnussen, passing through both his legs as he ran to safety in the hotel. He refused to speak to police and discharged himself from St. Boniface General Hospital.

At the time, Magnussen was well known in Winnipeg as Stadnick's muscle. Magnussen, Stadnick, and another man had been charged in August 1993 with the beating of two off-duty Winnipeg police officers, after the officers taunted the bikers and one climbed on one of their motorcycles. Charges for beating up the police were dropped by the Crown, after it was determined that police picked the fight.

Magnussen moved on to Quebec, where he became bodyguard for Scott Steinert, a flamboyant, high-ranking Montreal Hells Angel and would-be porn star. Police warned Magnussen two times in 1996 that they had heard of a murder plot by the Hells Angels to kill him, in hopes of turning him informer, but he refused police protection. On November 4, 1997, Steinert called on Magnussen to go with him to a meeting. The two men vanished and, at first, police believed that Steinert was hiding to escape deportation to his native United States.

Then, on May 23, 1998, Magnussen's bound, decomposed body was pulled out of the St. Lawrence Seaway. Steinert's body surfaced in the river about a year later. Both men had been beaten to death with a ballpeen hammer, wrapped in plastic, and dumped in the Angels' unofficial burial ground, the seaway.

No one was explaining for outsiders exactly why the two were killed, although it's believed to have been part of an internal gang purge. Magnussen had apparently killed someone close to the Angels, a Winnipeg biker at an Angels party in Halifax, in 1996, over a personal grudge, and Steinert was also punished for not stopping him. It didn't help Magnussen's value with the Angels that he had also beat the son of a Montreal Mafia boss, creating unnecessary tensions.

See also: **Los Brovos, Redliners, Spartans, Wolodumyr "Walter" "Nurget" Stadnick, Scott Steinert.**

Mainwaring, Henry: Golden Thesis – When Mainwaring sat down to write a thesis on piracy, the Oxford-educated scholar certainly had a wealth of research to draw upon.

He was one of the pirates who prowled the rocky shores of Newfoundland in the seventeenth and eighteenth centuries, when the island's outports were a stopover point to and from the rich hunting grounds of the Spanish Main, now the Caribbean.

During his high-seas days, Mainwaring was commissioned by the British Crown to capture infamous pirate Peter Easton. However, when Mainwaring arrived in Newfoundland in the second decade of the seventeenth century, Easton had been tipped off by sources in the English court and had already sailed away.

Mainwaring's high-born family had been involved in the War of the Roses, over rights to the English throne back in the fifteenth century, and had even better contacts in the English court than Easton. Despite his noble pedigree, it wasn't long before Mainwaring turned pirate himself, moving into Easton's abandoned fort at

Harbour Grace and launching raids against Spanish, French, and Portuguese fleets.

Mainwaring made a king's ransom in piracy, and then was offered a huge amount of gold by the king of Spain to quit piracy to sail for the Spanish. Mainwaring's cocky reply? "I don't need the help of the Spanish king to lay my hands on Spanish gold."

Like Easton before him, he had his pick of the best of Newfoundland's sailors, and had six aspirants for every spot on his pirate ships. While he was feared on the seas, his expeditions were a welcome escape from the slavelike conditions Newfoundland workers experienced in fishing "plantations." Sailors were generally only too eager to flee that life to sail on his outlaw ships, despite the risk of being caught and hanged from a yardarm. For them, one successful raid meant more riches than a lifetime toiling in the fisheries. Stealing fish paid far better than processing them, as salt cod fetched a healthy return on the European black market.

Mainwaring eventually retired from his base in Newfoundland, with enough wealth to buy a pardon from King James I and return to England. He was knighted, made admiral of the British navy, and given the job of clearing the seas of piracy. He wasn't yet thirty years old.

When he wrote his thesis on piracy, his most valuable suggestion was a typically audacious one: the king should stop selling pirates pardons like the one Mainwaring had just purchased. After that suggestion was followed, the "Golden Age" of piracy withered, as pirates were treated as a menace and not as soldiers of fortune worthy of negotiating with monarchs.

Mainwaring's own personal fortune was also lost, since he exhausted his resources fighting for Charles I in the English Civil War, and he died in poverty in 1653.

See also: **Charles Bellamy, Eric Cobham, Cupids, Peter Easton, High Island, Edward Jordan, Captain Kidd, Sheila Na Geira, John Phillips, Gilbert Pike, Pirates, Bartholomew "Black Bart" Roberts.**

Manitoba Warriors: Test Case – Known on the street and in prison as the M-Dubs, some thirty-five Warriors and fifteen associates were tried in 2000 on a total of 142 charges, including drug trafficking, weapons possession, fraud, conspiracy, and prostitution in the first test of Canada's new anti-gang legislation passed in 1997.

The case ended in a partial victory for the system, as the gang-related charges were eventually stayed against most of the accused in exchange for guilty pleas to drug charges in a complicated and often-unwieldy court case.

In May 2001, the Manitoba Court of Appeal rejected the defence argument that this was "systemic discrimination" because of the gang's Aboriginal backgrounds, with Madam Justice Freda Steel writing on behalf of the majority, "While I agree this was a minor league gang whose major market was in inner-city hotels and dependent upon the distribution of welfare cheques, it was a methodically planned and ongoing business which distributed a large quantity of cocaine over time."

The Warriors, who were older and more established than their rivals in the IP, or Indian Posse, rebuilt themselves under the arm of the Hells Angels. The Warriors were also clearly a force behind bars. On April 25, 1996, the members of the Warriors and the Posse were involved in an eighteen-hour riot that caused about $8-million damage to Manitoba's Headingley Correctional Centre. Eight guards were injured, including four who had fingers chopped off, when inmates high on drugs broke into cell blocks housing sex offenders and informants.

See also: **Darwin Sylvester, Kevin Sylvester, Robert Blaine Tews.**

Masterless Men: Flight to Freedom – In the eighteenth century in Newfoundland, it was a crime punishable by flogging or even death for a worker simply to walk away from his fishing master or the British navy.

Some workers did so anyway, and soon became known as the Masterless Men. Master-less Men hid out in the Butter Pot Barrens, near where Butter Pot Provincial Park is today, which overlooks the town of Holyrood and waters of Conception Bay.

Their leader was Irish immigrant Peter Kerrivan, and they existed partly through plunder and partly through following herds of caribou. They traded surreptitiously with settlers in remote ports, swapping meat, hides, and furs for flour, molasses, and rum. When they couldn't swing a good trade, they stole nets, cord, guns, and ammunition.

Their flight made them the first Europeans to live in Newfoundland's interior. In order to shake off pursuit parties from the British navy, Kerrivan and his men built roads that led into bogs or heavy underbrush to confound search expeditions. There were at least three attempts by the navy to capture them, but Kerrivan was never taken. However, two of his men were scooped up and hanged in Ferryland around 1810.

The War of 1812 offered employment and opportunity to some of the Masterless Men, while others became settlers who were considered respectable. By 1820 they had disappeared, not through police action but through social change. Now, it was possible for a poor man without property to live independently without being bound to a fishing master or a ship's captain for legitimacy.

Masterson, Bat: Limping Legend – The legendary Wild West lawman was born November 26, 1853, in St. Georges of Henryville parish, Iberville County, Quebec, and christened Bertolomiew. He was the second of seven children.

A popular story had it that he became known as "Bat" while an army scout in Sweetwater, Texas, after he was shot in the leg in a dancehall brawl. The shooter was killed, but Masterson was left with a limp, so he started using a cane. Years later, when he was a peace officer, the cane was useful as a club to use on recalcitrant cowboy heads.

In fact, Masterson was called "Bat" back in his Quebec days, long before he was limping, for Bat and Bart are accepted diminutive forms of Bertolomiew.

Not long after his birth, his family moved to New York, Illinois, and eventually Sedgwick County, Kansas, around 1871.

Masterson began his legal career as Wyatt Earp's deputy in Dodge City, when cowboys off the trail, professional gamblers, and footloose killers offered a career challenge.

Masterson missed out on the famous gunfight at the O.K. Corral in the silver mining town of Tombstone, Arizona, on Wednesday, October 26, 1881, when three of Earp's enemies were shot dead.

At that time, Masterson was in Dodge City, drawn by a frantic wired message from his brother Jim, who co-owned a saloon there. Jim Masterson told him that his partner in the saloon wanted to kill him. Masterson shot Jim's business partner and one of his associates, but didn't kill them. For this he was fined $8 for firing a pistol on a city street.

His final years were spent as a sportswriter on the New York *Morning Telegraph*, and he was a familiar figure at top boxing matches. He died at his desk on October 25, 1921, in New York at the age of sixty-seven.
See also: **Dutch Henry, Sam Kelly, Outlaw Trail, Sundance Kid.**

Matticks, Donald: Cooked Beef – The son of Gerald Matticks, a powerful figure in the West Montreal underworld, Donald Matticks was one of fifteen men arrested on December 4, 2002, for allegedly importing an estimated $2.1 billion in drugs through the Port of Montreal. In the December 2002 busts, police alleged that 44 tonnes of hashish and 265 kilograms of cocaine arrived at the port in containers, and was loaded onto trucks and diverted through insiders to a warehouse off port grounds.

Matticks worked on port grounds, an employee of a trade association known as the Maritime Employers Association, and his job was a strategic one, directing containers at the port.

The police operation was dubbed Projet Boeuf – a tip of the hat to Matticks's nickname Boeuf, "Beef." At the time of the arrests, Matticks was already behind bars after being arrested in a huge nationwide sweep against the Hells Angels in the spring of 2001, when police alleged drugs imported from 1999 to 2001 were worth some $2.1 billion. Police said that his West End Gang brought those drugs into the country for distribution to the Hells Angels. Matticks, out on bail, awaits his drug-trafficking trial slated for September 2004.
See also: **Gerald "Big Gerry" Matticks, Richard Matticks.**

Matticks, Gerald "Big Gerry": Short Childhood – Born in 1940, he grew up in the predominantly Irish tenements of Goose Village in Montreal's Point St. Charles district, the youngest of fourteen children. His father drove a horse and buggy for the city while his mother was kept busy with the family. A school dropout by age twelve, he was married at seventeen and a father of four by twenty-one.

The Matticks brothers – Gerry, John, Fred, Robert, and Richard – were identified by a 1970s organized-crime inquiry as leaders of a truck-hijacking-and-robbery ring run out of western Montreal. They gravitated to the notorious West End Gang run by Frank "Dunie" Ryan, made up of English-speaking thugs.

Gerry and John Matticks faced attempted-murder charges in 1971, when a man said they shot him because they thought he was telling port police about their dockyard crimes. Matticks was acquitted when three witnesses said he was in a bar at the time of the shooting. One of those people offering alibis was a former RCMP officer who became a member of the West End Gang.

As his trucking firm, cattle farm, and beef-wholesaling company grew, he moved out of the

Point and onto a sprawling farm in La Prairie, Quebec, with surveillance cameras mounted on its nine buildings.

Although Big Gerry left the old neighbourhood, he never forgot his roots when he made it big financially, and gained a reputation as a Robin Hood of sorts. Every Christmas, he drove a decorated flatbed truck along South Shore streets, with a Santa who handed out gifts for poorer children. He also at times dressed up a truck as a sleigh and threw out dollar bills. His mint-condition vintage cars were often used in St. Patrick's Day parades and, during the 1998 ice storm, he gave out some two thousand free meals.

When Father Marc Mignault was overheard complaining one day about his presbytery's leaking roof, Big Gerry took care of it, then refused to charge anything. "I asked Gerry for the bill three times," Mignault told the court in 2002, when Matticks was facing drug-trafficking

charges. "He said it was lost in the mail. He took care of it."

"There is a little bit of devil and saint in all of us," Mignault said of Matticks.

Often, when Matticks gave food to the poor, he said it was damaged by his trucking company, and would have been thrown out if someone didn't take it. It wasn't uncommon for him to drop by the church with enough frozen turkeys to fill an eighteen-foot freezer.

"Did he come to church every Sunday? No," Mignault said. "Did he help out people? Yes. Did he practise his faith? Yes."

However, law officials saw a different side of him. When Matticks and brother Richard were arrested in 1994 for allegedly trafficking 26.5 tonnes of hashish, a lawyer offered Crown attorney Madeleine Giauque the bribe of an all-expenses-paid southern vacation – and perhaps a new Cadillac too – if she allowed Matticks out on bail.

When Giauque refused, the lawyer began talking about cement blocks and sleeping bags – standard means for hiding murder victims in the St. Lawrence River. "You'll never get out of this alive," Giauque was told, but she still wouldn't buckle.

Charges were dropped anyway, after police were found guilty of planting evidence.

Matticks was eventually sent to prison when his right-hand man, Elias Lekkas, turned police witness in 2001, prompting several South Shore bars to post photos of Lekkas with the words "Rat" or "Stool."

"Gerry is very powerful," testified Lekkas, a vitamin salesman who once sold stolen poultry for the gang. "He has contacts all over the place to eliminate anybody that he wants."

After he was charged, about six hundred people signed a petition in Point St. Charles and the South Shore saying he wasn't a threat to the community.

See also: **Richard Matticks, Allan "The Weasel" Ross, Frank Peter "Dunie" Ryan, West End Gang.**

Gerald "Big Gerry" Matticks

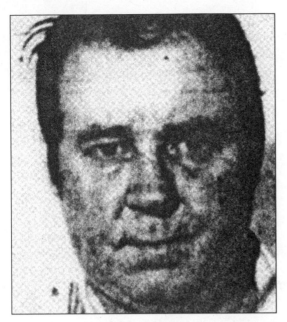

Richard Matticks

Matticks, Richard: West End Gang – Gerald's brother Richard was also a member of Montreal's West End Gang. The gang added an Irish flavour to the city's active underworld and had a near-mythic status in some of the city's rougher areas. At the top level of the West End Gang was the Matticks family, known for its influence in the ports.

Along with his brother, Richard had a reputation for hijacking, drug-trafficking, and enormous influence at the Port of Montreal. Richard was sentenced to three years for trafficking cocaine on June 17, 1997, his third trip to prison since 1957. Richard's soldiers, Frank Bonneville and Donald Waite, got four years and two years respectively while Giovanni Cazzetta, acting boss of the Rock Machine biker gang, was also pinched.

See also: **Giovanni Cazzetta, Donald Matticks, Gerald Matticks, Allan "The Weasel" Ross, Frank Peter "Dunie" Ryan, West End Gang.**

Melanson, Donald "Snorko": Debt Up to His Nose – He was paranoid during the last few years of his life in the late 1980s. This may have partly been a chemical reaction to the large amounts of cocaine he put up his prominent nose. Also, however, it must have been a realization that he couldn't afford to pay $900,000 for that inhaled cocaine – which the Hells Angels had fronted to him to sell, not snort.

Melanson, forty, was the president of the Vagabonds motorcycle gang on Gerrard Street East near Woodbine in east Toronto in the late 1980s, and he earned his nickname for his habit of snorkelling up ungodly long lines of cocaine.

"He used to make lines about two feet long," his old friend and fellow Toronto cocaine trafficker Saul S. said. "What a big nose he had. He was like a vacuum cleaner."

(Saul S. asked that his last name not be used. He now lives out of Toronto, under an assumed name after going into a witness-protection program to work with police against several high-level drug traffickers.)

On September 3, 1987, Snorko's body was found in a room he had rented in the Novotel Hotel in Toronto on Yonge Street, north of Sheppard, with two bullets in his head.

The killing remained officially unsolved, but Saul had no doubt which of his former underworld contacts pulled the trigger. It had to be Hells Angels, who lured him to the room with the promise of another deal, Saul reasoned. "Who else would do it? He owed them a big chunk of money."

Precisely because they feared this type of thing, the Vagabonds forbade their members from dealing with Hells Angels. The Vagabonds were the biggest, richest Ontario club that did not join Hells Angels during the mass conversion that began shortly after Christmas 2000.

Snorko knew the rule against dealing with the Angels well, but he also craved some of the planeloads of the narcotic they were getting from the Medellín cartel in Colombia.

So Snorko had got his old friend Saul to cut a deal with the Angels, and Saul then immediately passed on the cocaine to him. When Snorko scored the cocaine, his biker buddies didn't ask a lot of questions about its source.

"He used to give to everyone, but he didn't remember who he gave it to. He used to give a kilo, half a kilo."

There were a few meetings between the Angels, Snorko, and Saul in Toronto strip clubs and a posh restaurant. "They sent the top men from Montreal and the top men from Ontario," Saul said.

The out-of-towners, especially the tall, skinny one who did most of the talking, didn't look so rough. They looked more like businessmen, dressed Friday casual. Despite the difference in appearance, however, it was clear to Saul that rough-looking Snorko was the nervous one.

Snorko had remortgaged his house for $50,000 and Saul scraped together another $20,000, but it wasn't nearly enough, and Saul sensed it was a good time for a holiday in Tampa. "I didn't want to be in the middle of that mess."

While in Florida, Saul read in a Toronto newspaper that Snorko's body had been found by a cleaning woman at the hotel. Saul attended the funeral, which was the biggest in memory for bikers in Toronto, with some two hundred Harleys slowly cruising Steeles Avenue West from the St. Paschal Baylon Church. They came from as far away as Dallas, Edmonton, and Chicago and mourners wore the colours of the Lobos, American Breed, Penetrators, Scorpions, and Outlaws. No Hells Angels were to be seen.

Shortly afterwards, Saul became a police agent, working sting operations that netted dozens of traffickers in what was known as Project Amigo, Toronto's biggest drug haul.

Saul remembered Snorko as a simple man, who loved his Harley-Davidson motorcycle and whose big dream was to some day own a plumbing firm. Saul wasn't too impressed with Snorko's old biker friends, who left Snorko high and dry when the time came to pay his debt.

"They all ripped him off. He was too generous."

See also: **Hells Angels.**

Melo, Eddie "The Hurricane": "Always Fighting" – Melo was getting just a little chubby as he passed his fortieth birthday, but he didn't seem to mind. His personality seemed to be softening as well as his body. He bought new pews for St. Helen's Church in Toronto's Portuguese district, the same church where his preschool son, Eduardo, Jr., had been baptized. When Eduardo, Jr., was born, Melo told Eduardo's mother, his second wife, Rhonda, "I can't wait till he can love me back." Now that four-year-old Eduardo, Jr., could show affection, Melo relished every second of family life, like taking the family to the Golden Griddle every Saturday morning so Eduardo, Jr., could get his beloved waffle fries.

Melo had spent all of his life trying to be tough, but now that he wasn't so imposing, he seemed happier. However, with his past, it was difficult to age gracefully. "I wish I could be treated as a normal person," he once complained. "I always seem to be in a mess, with someone challenging or provoking something. I'm afraid to go out. I hate to fight. It goes on everywhere I go."

There was a time when Melo seemed to want nothing more than a tough image. He was a neighbourhood legend on the streets and in the gyms of Toronto's west-end Ossington Avenue area. "I was always fighting," Melo later said. "If I had a black eye, I didn't put on dark glasses to hide it. If I got a little scratch and came home bleeding, my mother would go crazy. But the way I figured it, you can't give pain to somebody else and not expect to get a little bruised yourself."

A construction worker's son and the eldest of five children, Melo quit school after Grade Nine and moved to Verdun, Quebec, where he turned pro in the boxing ring with a forged birth certificate. His ferocious, take-no-prisoner's boxing style brought him the nickname "The Hurricane" and the Canadian professional middleweight title, but, by his early twenties, he was a spent force, with early signs

Harold Arviv (left) with Eddie Melo (right)

of brain damage. There were criticisms that his managers pushed him too hard, too fast. Despite his impressive record of twenty-four knockouts in thirty-eight fights, many boxing insiders felt he might have had a world title shot, if he'd had better management. Melo was only twenty in 1982 when he quit pro boxing for the first time, a few months after being knocked out in a bid for the Canadian light heavyweight title. As it was, by the time he left the ring, he was married to a former Miss Montreal Alouette, drove a new Lincoln Continental, had $20,000 in jewellery, a new house in the Toronto suburbs, a newborn baby, and a job as an organizer with the Hotel and Restaurant Employees Union. He also had a furious temper and a tight friendship with Montreal Mafia boss Santos "Frank" Cotroni, whom he called "my number-one fan."

In the Toronto area, Melo ran Cotroni-related businesses that supplied strippers for bars and rented out video machines. He quickly grated on the nerves of Hamilton mobster "Johnny Pops" Papalia, who, according to a police source, told Frank Cotroni, "Put a leash on Melo or I'll kill him." Johnny Pops wasn't the only one who felt that way about Melo. In 1989, a group of young mobsters decided it was time for the ex-boxer to die, after Melo slapped one of them around in a College Street pool hall in

Toronto's Little Italy. A hit man was given a .357 magnum to kill Melo, and a smaller .22 for Melo's less-threatening associate, Frank Natale Roda. The murder plot was foiled by police, but it took a toll on Melo nonetheless.

Perhaps the stress of almost being slain was what finally ended Melo's first marriage. He and his first wife, Sine, separated, reconciled, and then split for good in April 1989. Shortly afterwards, she moved to the West Coast with their two young daughters, whom Melo dearly loved.

It was a truism among Toronto-area police that if they wanted to find trouble, they could always follow Melo. Surveillance officers noted him meeting at a trendy Yorkville eatery with a B.C. Hells Angel who was active in loansharking, and a 1993 police report from the Southern Italian province of Calabria listed him as a member of the Toronto Siderno Mafia group, even though Melo was born in Portugal and maintained tight ties with Cotroni.

In August 1994, a police wiretap caught Melo on the phone with Cotroni's associate Tony Volpato. It was easy to draw ominous references, as Melo told Volpato, "I went there when they had the meeting. I had a couple of guys. We took care of things. You know what I mean? . . . Went down and took care of things, so there is no problem. . . . So what I'm doing, I think, is the right thing here for us . . . and fuck the other guy."

As he approached middle age, Melo decided to return to a place where he had always felt in control and alive, the boxing ring. He planned to re-establish his name with bouts across Europe and South America, then earn the shot at a world title he had dreamed about more than half his life. His new manager was Harold Arviv, a Bay Street businessman whose past included prison time for blowing up his own Bloor Street disco for the insurance money.

However, around this time, Canadian police discovered that Melo, who had been brought to Canada at age six, had never taken out Canadian citizenship. He remained a Portuguese citizen, and now the government sought to deport him

to Portugal for criminality. He was a new father, and protested: "My parents brought me here for a better life. I did everything in Canada. Had two daughters and now a baby. And I have to add I got in a lot of trouble here, too."

He admitted to immigration officials that his friends included ex-boxer Joe Dinardo, known in police jargon as "a leg and arm man" with some thirty criminal convictions, stretching back to 1958, for arson, robbery, uttering counterfeit money to illegal possession of guns. When questioned by authorities, Melo had only kind words for Cotroni and his underworld associates, saying they never turned their backs on him, and were still his friends. He admitted that Volpato was in fact the godfather to one of his daughters. Melo added that he was the godfather of the daughter of Arviv, "the disco bomber" and would-be boxing manager.

Melo was asked in an immigration hearing if he would avoid the likes of Cotroni, Volpato, and Arviv, should he be allowed to stay in Canada. Clearly on the ropes, he replied, "All I know is that they've been okay with me. They've never asked me to do any criminal activity or get into trouble. They've only been supportive in whatever it was that I had to do."

Melo told Canadian immigration authorities in 1999, "I haven't seen anyone associated with the Mafia in three or four years. They're all in jail." By that point, Melo's old mentor, Cotroni, and his associate, Volpato, both of Montreal, were indeed both behind bars.

As he fought to stay in Toronto, Melo remained a celebrity of sorts, and posed for photos at the 1998 Toronto Film Festival with second wife, Rhonda, whom the press gushed was a lookalike to actress Pamela Anderson Lee. He told immigration officials that he was receiving regular psychiatric counselling and two types of medication – a chemical straitjacket – to control the anger that had worked so well for him in the ring.

He complained to the Immigration and Refugee Board that police harassment almost drove him out of the vending-machine business. Police noted that close associates were still active in that business, and couldn't help but be suspicious. He declared his income as exactly $24,000, yet somehow, he was able to maintain monthly condo expenses of $2,000 for his home on Lakeshore Boulevard West, another $1,500 monthly to his first wife, an undisclosed amount for a second condo on upscale Queen's Quay, and payments on his sport utility vehicle and sleek Jaguar.

The first week of April 2001, Melo stayed home from his job as a boiler-room stock promoter at a Bay Street brokerage firm to be with Rhonda. Thursday, April 5, was his fortieth birthday, and he and Rhonda were going to celebrate the next night with tickets for tenor Andrea Boccelli at the Air Canada Centre. That afternoon, he and Rhonda went to see a lawyer friend for lunch at the Mövenpick restaurant on downtown York Street.

They returned to their condo overlooking Lake Ontario at about 5 p.m. Within fifteen minutes, Melo took Rhonda's Cherokee to a nearby coffee bar at a tiny plaza near the Queen Elizabeth Highway to meet with his long-time friend Joao "Johnny" Pavao, a salvage-truck driver from the Toronto suburb of Mississauga. The restaurant was called the Amici Sport Café – amici is Italian for "friends" – where, in Rhonda's words, he "used to go to drink cappuccino and hang out." He wasn't going to be long, as the concert was starting at 7.30 p.m.

Melo left Amici at 6:25 p.m. and was in the Cherokee chatting with Pavao, who stood in the parking lot, when Charles Gagné, an armed robber on parole, climbed into the backseat of the Jeep and shot Melo in the head, then turned the gun on Pavao. The job done, Gagné hijacked a red 1990 Honda Civic and fled.

It was the first time Gagné had ever met Melo or Pavao. He had been promised $75,000 for the killing, plus more criminal work.

Normally, in a homicide investigation, police start with the victim's family and friends and

work outwards, and Melo's inner circle certainly gave them plenty to work with. "There's a lot of history between a lot of people," was Det. Steve Gormley of Peel Regional Police's understated comment.

It would be two years before Gagné was charged with the murders, and two months later, a long-time acquaintance of Melo's from the old College-Lansdowne area was charged with hiring him. When the arrests took place, Gagné was already under arrest in Hull for trying to collect a drug debt with a gun. There had been more than one thousand interviews done by police at this point.

Melo's daughter Jessica made a point of flying out from British Columbia to be in Toronto for Gagné's court appearance. For Jessica, a criminology student at Simon Fraser University, it was important to remind people of the Eddie Melo that she knew and loved. "He was the most amazing father, friend, confidante, supporter, everything," she said. "I couldn't ask for a better person to be my father. . . . I was with him for nineteen years. I went everywhere with him."

Jessica and Rhonda wept repeatedly when Gagné pleaded guilty in court on September 30, 2003, after cutting a deal to testify against the man who hired him in return for the chance of parole after twelve years.

Melo's younger brother, Joey, thirty-nine, said his brother was killed over jealousy, not underworld ties. Two men from the family's old neighbourhood were charged with hiring Gagné. "It had nothing to do with bikers and it had nothing to do with mobsters," he said. "It was the jealousy of a little man."

"Eddie walked into a lot of places and people respected him," Joey Melo said. "These guys could never face him one on one, even if my brother only had one arm and one leg."

"At least we have some closure, but there is still only going to be two people at the dinner table tonight," Rhonda said. "This is not a day for celebration. My son still has no father."

Ironically, Melo might have still been alive if he hadn't recently won his fight with Canadian authorities to keep from being deported to Portugal. He wasn't famous or feared over there, but then nobody there wanted him dead either. *See also:* **Harold Arviv, Boxing, Charles Gagné, Frank "Santos" Cotroni.**

Menard, Bob – *See* **Paolo Violi.**

Mennonite Triangle: Unholy Trade – There was a time when authorities on the Mexican-American border would simply wave at Mennonites in their pickup trucks as they crossed from Mexico into El Paso, Texas, loaded down with traditional furniture and "Queso de Chihuahua" (cheese).

The pious, plain-living, German-speaking Mennonites had a well-earned reputation for valuing simplicity and peace, and it was those values that first brought them from Canada to Mexico in the early 1920s. They moved from southern Manitoba to Cuauhtemoc in the high sierra of Chihuahua state, in Mexico, two hundred miles south of El Paso, Texas, to avoid conscription and compulsory education in English, which they feared would transmit "worldly" ideas.

The Mexican Mennonite community of more than fifty thousand was reeling from drought and crop failure in the late 1980s and early 1990s, and the North American Free Trade Agreement only made things worse, as in January 1994, they lost government subsidies for products like cheese and furniture. When the peso collapsed later that year, many of the once-proud farmers were impoverished and nervous. Their religion forbids contraception, meaning the hundred thousand acres they originally bought from the Mexican state wasn't big enough to support their ever-growing numbers.

So perhaps it shouldn't have come as a total shock when a few members of the community turned to drug trafficking instead of beginning factory work for $10 a day like others in their

order. The first sign was in 1989 when a drug-sniffing dog at a border checkpoint in El Paso found more than two hundred pounds of marijuana in a truckload of Canada-bound traditional furniture. Further seizures came as the illegal weed was found in bricks of cheese and trailor-loads of fertilizer.

By the end of the 1990s, customs officers estimated that 20 per cent of the Mexican marijuana that reached Canada was carried by Mennonites, who ran a drug pipeline between southwestern Ontario, Manitoba, and Mexico dubbed "the Mennonite Triangle." In the early 2000s, police feared what they called "the Mennonite Mob" was working with biker gangs to transport highly addictive methamphetamine. Competition from highly potent "B.C. Bud," produced in B.C. indoor grow houses, has caused many involved in the Mennonite drug pipeline to shift their energies to cocaine, which produces higher profits and is more concentrated and easier to conceal.

Michipicoten Gang: Railroaded Town – Workers on the Canadian Pacific Railway in Northern Ontario in the late nineteenth century sweated for low wages in thick forests and swamps, tormented by clouds of blackflies that all but blocked out the sun. Their diet was so wretched that some suffered from scurvy.

Not surprisingly, many of them welcomed the chance to escape into a drunken haze, even though the CPR did not approve and the Public Works Act didn't allow the sale or possession of liquor within ten miles of the rail route.

The work crews were a magnet for bootleggers, hookers, gamblers, con men, and thieves. Whisky that sold for fifty cents a gallon in Toronto fetched five dollars a pint by the rail lines.

Sudbury was a base for liquor smugglers, who bribed or bound railway detectives, and moved contraband whisky, gin, brandy, and beer in barrels labelled "vegetables." Between September 1883 and October 1884, one Sudbury magistrate levied more than ninety bootlegging-related convictions.

Worksites on the north Superior received supplies from steamships out of Sault Ste. Marie and little ports like Peninsular Harbour and Michipicoten, an old Hudson's Bay Company post on the northeast shore of the lake. The ports soon became smuggling hubs, as booze arrived in barrels marked "coal oil."

There was a jail in Michipicoten, but it was only a root cellar for storing vegetables as well as lawbreakers. In the summer of 1884, railway contractor James "Bulldog" Commee locked a bootlegger named Bond in there for six months, and emptied his $600 worth of liquid wares into Lake Superior.

Bond won his release when he argued that Commee had no authority to do this, but Commee simply arrested him again, and then searched the law books to see if he had the authority to have Bond flogged. He found he didn't have this power, so he settled for sentencing Commee to life imprisonment in the root cellar.

It was about this time that Commee learned that his head constable, Charles Wallace, thirty-six, a former cook known as Montana Charlie, moonlighted as a top bootlegger, and had been using his official position to further his illegal business. Wallace was fired, but when Commee had to leave town temporarily on railway matters, Bond was sprung loose again.

In Commee's absence, Wallace pulled together a tough gang that included Harry Leland, a fugitive from Michigan State Penitentiary, "Little Dick" Goldsberry of Ireland, and Canadians Gordon Doherty and Arthur Asselin (a.k.a. McGillvery), an escapee from Stony Mountain Penitentiary in Manitoba.

By October 1884, Wallace's gang had virtual control of Michipicoten, using a spirited combination of bribes and beatings. Liquor sales were conducted in the open, and Wallace collected taxes from other liquor sellers for his "corporation." Hoodlums flocked into town

from Peninsular Harbour to be part of a thriving community, run by criminals for criminals and fuelled by illegal booze.

Lawmen were ordered out of town, and fired upon to speed their exit. Wallace's gang actually posted notices that made it clear the lives of law enforcers were in danger, should they choose to stay. The posters sounded official, as they were marked "By Order of the Vigilance Committee," which was Wallace's gang.

However, Canadian Pacific agent Alexander Macdonald and Ontario magistrate Captain Burden refused to abandon town. On the night of October 10, 1884, thirty-five masked men opened fire on the building the two used as their office and living quarters. Some three hundred bullets were pumped into the building, but the lawmen survived.

The mob rioted and the unarmed, untrained civilian constables couldn't handle that. They turned to Toronto for help and, on October 17, 1884, Captain Burden met with Mayor Boswell in Toronto and Major Draper, Toronto chief of police, who sent up eleven officers, armed with carbines, bayonets, and revolvers. The bootleggers were unfazed, telling a reporter they could easily pick off the police as soon as they arrived in the harbour.

Hostile words, not snipers, greeted the police, however, as most of the town apparently preferred booze to justice. News of the impending cleanup reached a gang of thirty whores, who were heading north to Michipicoten, and they redirected themselves to Port Arthur.

The Toronto police seized a boat and a prisoner and left. As soon as they were out of town, Wallace and his band returned, with Wallace packing a Winchester rifle, four pistols, and a Bowie knife.

Soon, he moved on to Sault Ste. Marie, Michigan, where he bragged of personally firing a hundred shots at the lawmen's building, and it wasn't long before he was arrested and deported to Canada. When someone raised the argument that this deportation wasn't legal, the Michigan sheriff simply shrugged and said he didn't want Wallace in his town.

When Wallace and his gang were on trial in Sault Ste. Marie, Ontario, that November, Asselin and Goldsberry listed their occupations as bartender and waiter. All of the gang got a year in custody for rioting, except for Wallace, who was inexplicably acquitted.

Unrepentant, he returned to Michipicoten aboard a dogsled full of booze. He was arrested about seven miles from town on January 28, 1885. He had ambushed police and wounded one officer in the leg, but when more police arrived, he surrendered on the order "Throw up your thumbs."

This time, his sentence was quashed for mysterious reasons just ten days after he was brought to Central Prison in Toronto to serve eighteen months in jail for selling liquor to Natives. In the end, it was progress on the railway, and not law enforcement, that dried up the activities of his gang. The rail crews moved west, and the once-notorious port of Michipicoten grew quiet again. *See also:* **Black Hand.**

Mickle, Michael Edward "Zeke": Vanished Biker – In early May 1993, the white late-model GMC Suburban belonging to the president of the Nanaimo, B.C., chapter of the Hells Angels was found in the Harwood area south of Nanaimo, not far from his home. Mickle was nowhere to be seen.

At the time of his disappearance, Mickle listed his occupation as a prospector. His Angels owned a good deal of property and businesses on Vancouver Island, including a former nudist colony – known as Angel Acres – where they held rock concerts.

His body was never found, but rumours surfaced that he was beheaded by a Vietnamese gang that had increasing strength on Vancouver Island. When a reporter asked the Angels what they thought happened, the newsman's thumb was snapped. *See also:* **Hells Angels.**

Miller, Larry: High Flyer – In his prime, in the early to mid-1990s, he cut quite a dashing figure, as co-owner of the Beverly Hills, a fifty-four-thousand-square-foot casino, nightclub, and restaurant complex in Moscow's Red Square. Fellow investors included Hollywood action-film star Chuck Norris, and Miller jetted around in a U.S.$2.5 million Lear jet he bought in Tijuana, Mexico, which cost $66,000 a month to maintain and fly.

He maintained his primary residence was in Massena, an upstate New York town of 11,700, across the St. Lawrence River from Cornwall, Ontario. When in the Massena area, he hung out at the bar of Club 37, a roadhouse on Highway 37 on the outskirts of town, where he sometimes had two cellphones simultaneously on the go. At other times, for particularly intense meetings, Miller would retreat to a private room in the back of the premises.

When not in Moscow or Massena, there was a good chance Miller was at his Las Vegas home, where his fishing buddies including the city's mayor and where he was known as a big player at a casino called Arizona Charlie's.

Miller took his fishing, gambling, and business seriously, and shelled out U.S.$350,000 on a fishing trip at the exclusive Sonora Island Lodge near Campbell River, British Columbia. Approximately forty people were on the trip, including the mayor of Las Vegas and various tobacco and alcohol suppliers, dealers and executives.

This lifestyle was all quite a step up for Miller, who arrived in the Massena area in the late 1980s as a truck driver, hauling gambling equipment from Las Vegas to the Akwesasne Mohawk reservation.

Reportedly born in Oshkosh, Wisconsin, Miller had his first serious brush with the law in Chicago, where he was convicted in 1967 for armed robbery and sentenced to five years. Lesser charges and convictions followed during the 1970s and early 1980s, including possession of explosives, forgery, criminal contempt of court, and tax evasion.

It was in the Massena area that things finally seemed to get on track for him. Soon, he began a smuggling operation with businessman Anthony Laughing, who ran an illegal casino on the Akwesasne reservation in the late 1980s and who was later imprisoned for leading an armed standoff against state troopers. In 1996, Laughing would be convicted again in federal court of assaulting a federal customs agent.

In fact, Miller masterminded a brazen smuggling ring that operated from the St. Regis Mohawk reservation, which straddled the Canada-U.S. border and overlapped the Ontario-Quebec border, and which prosecutors said smuggled $687 million worth of tobacco and alcohol into Canada between 1991 and 1997.

Eventually, Miller brought his mistress, a son, a daughter, and an assortment of others into the operation.

Timing as well as geography made things ripe for big profits. When Canada enacted a nearly $2-a-pack tobacco tax in the early 1990s, it opened up an enormous black market for smuggling cigarettes. Miller's organization bought untaxed Canadian export cigarettes and hauled them to St. Regis on the U.S. side of the St. Lawrence. The tax-free cigarettes were purchased by Mohawk fitness-club owner Fabian Hart.

Hart distributed the contraband cigarettes to individual smugglers, who brought them back across the border into Canada, where they were resold at a profit. Each week, Miller later told authorities, he moved about 1.4 million packs of cigarettes across the St. Lawrence. Soon Hart had enough money to line the outside of his home in marble.

After the goods were sold in Canada, the Canadian money was transferred to U.S. currency with the help of a retired state trooper who ran currency exchange businesses in the nearby towns of Hogansburg and Malone. That officer later pleaded guilty to moving $557 million through his currency-exchange and armoured-car businesses.

According to authorities, Miller later formed a partnership with Lewis C. Tavano, fifty-seven, a reputed organized-crime figure, and his brother Robert J. Tavano, Sr., sixty-one, an ex-Niagara Falls GOP chairman. The Tavano brothers later pleaded guilty to using their importing company to launder $50 million they made through smuggling untaxed cigarettes and liquor into Canada. The Tavanos' plea bargain brought them a sentence of five years in prison and fines totalling $1 million.

When the federal government cut its cigarette taxes to combat smuggling, Miller responded by expanding his operations and reducing costs. He became heavily involved in smuggling to Russia, including schemes to sneak chemicals used in fireworks from Russia into Canada and plans to smuggle container-loads of vodka from Finland into Russia.

Meanwhile, undercover RCMP officers posing as truckers had infiltrated Miller's group. The undercover Mounties delivered thousands of cases of liquor supplied by the Miller organization to a black-market network in the Hamilton area, as well as repatriated Canadian cigarettes to Vancouver.

Undercover agents in Canada and the United States infiltrated some of the smuggling rings, and in June 1997, Larry Miller and twenty others were arrested and charged in Syracuse, New York, with numerous smuggling-related crimes. All twenty-one defendants would eventually plead guilty to reduced charges.

For Miller, the undercover police operation brought a seventeen-and-a-half-year prison sentence, and the loss of his properties, and his gold Rolex watch, boats, snowmobiles, and $25,000 in pocket money. In November 2000, Club 37, the New York State bar that was Miller's former headquarters, was turned into a U.S. Border Patrol office.

Miner, Bill: Holdup Pioneer – When a reporter asked a B.C. resident at the turn of the twentieth century about Bill Miner, the resident

Bill Miner, train robber (1906, Glenbow Archives, NA-837-1r)

The posse that captured Bill Miner near Kamloops, B.C., 1906 (Glenbow Archives, NA-654-5)

replied, "Hell, old Bill Miner ain't so bad. He only robs the CPR once every two years. The CPR robs us all every day."

The silver-haired, moustachioed B.C. man with the gentlemanly demeanour was known to apologize after stickups of trains and banks and wave politely while making his getaway. He's also credited, rightly or wrongly, with being the first cowboy to utter the phrase, "Hands up!"

He wasn't the first bandit to rob a Canadian train, but he was the first criminal to hit the mighty CPR line. Another group, known as the KKK, robbed trains near Toronto.

Average people loved to hear of his exploits. In the eyes of many pioneers, the railways grabbed up land and gouged prices while the banks were considered even more greedy. When Miner robbed trains and banks, people preferred to think of him as a Robin Hood rather than as a real criminal. There were stories about how he was gentle with orphans and the disadvantaged. According to one yarn, as popular as it was unsubstantiated, he paid off the mortgage

for an old widow who was faced with foreclosure, then stole back the money from the bank as soon as he was sure her deed was secure.

By the time Miner arrived in Canada in the early years of the twentieth century, he was already a veteran of the American prison system. On April 3, 1866, he was sent to San Quentin for four years, three months, and three days for his part in a robbery that netted $75,000. On February 9, 1872, he was again convicted of robbery, and sent back to San Quentin for nine years and twenty-one days.

On December 15, 1881, Miner was convicted again of robbery and this time received a sentence of twenty-five years at San Quentin due to his prior convictions. He got out early again for good behaviour, despite briefly escaping from custody, after serving nineteen years, five months, and twenty-seven days. He was then fifty-four, and had served more than thirty-two years behind bars.

In 1904, he had planned to go straight and give up train robbing, and had settled quietly into life in Merritt, British Columbia, under the name of George Edwards, but then he heard of a train loaded with money for San Francisco earthquake relief, and he decided to pull one last, big haul. He teamed up with a sometime-prospector named Shorty Dunn and a former teacher named Louis Colquhou, and together they boarded the westbound CPR train seventeen miles east of Kamloops, British Columbia.

Unfortunately for Miner, Dunn and Colquhou weren't of his criminal calibre. When the heist was over, they fled on a single horse with about a hundred dollars. It was a considerable step down from two years earlier, when Miner robbed another CPR train single-handedly.

There was now a $12,000 reward for his capture, and the B.C. Provincial Police called for the Royal North-West Mounted Police in Calgary to help out. They were told they could identify Miner by a distinctive tattoo on his forearm of a ballet dancer. The officers found three men who matched the robbers' description eating lunch in the Douglas Lake area. Shorty Dunn tried to run for freedom and was stopped with a bullet to the leg.

Miner realized there was no point putting up a fight. Later in court, he bragged to a Canadian judge, "No jail can hold me, sir." At this point, he had managed three jail breaks, so the words were no idle boast. He lasted about a year in the B.C. Penitentiary before escaping in broad daylight. He made his way to Georgia, where he became the first person in that state's history to pull a train robbery.

That pioneering effort brought him a twenty-five-year prison sentence. He escaped from the Milledgeville State Prison, Georgia, on October 18, 1911, but was recaptured. He died in the Georgia State Prison in 1913, at the age of seventy, having spent half of his life behind bars, including in the horrific confines of San Quentin.

See also: **Pearl Hart.**

Moose Jaw Capone Tunnels: Criminal Underground – Chicago mobster Al Capone once quipped, "I don't even know what street Canada is on." However, Capone apparently did know what was under the streets of Moose Jaw, Saskatchewan.

His men were said to hide out during Prohibition in a network of tunnels located under this southern Saskatchewan city, once one of the wildest frontier towns in the Canadian West.

The tunnels were first dug as hideouts in about 1908 by Chinese railway workers after several of them were savagely beaten at the CPR railyards by whites who believed the Chinese were taking their jobs.

This was a time when Western Canada was gripped by hysteria about the "yellow peril," and Ottawa imposed its infamous head tax on Chinese would-be immigrants. Terrified and unable to pay the head tax, which no other immigrants were required to pay, the Chinese workers literally went underground, digging secret tunnels where they could hide until the situation improved. The railway workers managed to bring women to live with them and even raised children in the rat-infested darkness.

These tunnels acquired a whole new purpose in the 1920s, when the United States and much of Canada embarked on Prohibition. As a major CPR terminus, linked to the United States by the Soo Line, Moose Jaw was ideally situated to become a bootlegging hub. The city's relatively remote location also made it a good place to escape U.S. police.

Moose Jaw became something of a gangsters' resort, with regular visits from the Chicago Mob. "They came to lay in the sun," Laurence "Moon" Mullin, an eighty-nine-year-old Moose Jaw resident who worked as a messenger in the tunnels as an eleven-year-old boy, told a reporter.

It didn't hurt that much of the local police force was in cahoots with the bootleggers. Word had it that Chief Walter Johnson let the gangsters hide out in Moose Jaw, in exchange for a

Al Capone mugshot

Right: Moose Jaw Police Chief Walter P. Johnson
(Courtesy Moose Jaw Public Library)

Moose Jaw train station (Peter Edwards)

promise that they wouldn't commit crimes in the city.

The tunnels were apparently as active as anything going on above ground, being used for gambling, prostitution, and warehousing illegal booze. Mullin said one tunnel went right under the CPR station and opened into a shed in the railway yards. It was possible to load and unload rail cars without any risk of being seen by unfriendly eyes.

Mullin says that Chief Johnson would occasionally stop by his newspaper stand. As Johnson paid his nickel, he would whisper into Mullin's ear, "There's going to be a big storm tonight." Young Mullin knew what those words meant: an imminent raid by Allen Hawkes of the Saskatchewan Liquor Commission, who did not share Johnson's lenient attitudes.

The boy would rush to a hidden door under the Exchange Café, give a secret knock, run down a tunnel to a second door, and knock again. There he would be admitted to a room full of gamblers. "The smoke was so thick you could have cut it with a sharp knife and brought it out in squares," he joked to a reporter. "But everyone seemed quite comfortable."

Mullin said he and the other messenger boys got twenty cents for every errand. The gangsters didn't allow them to touch the booze, but did instruct the boys on how to play poker.

As recently as the 1970s, local officials denied the existence of the tunnels, but the denials became difficult to maintain when part of Main Street collapsed, leaving an unsuspecting motorist planted in a deep hole. "I always said some day a truck is going to break through, and it did," Mullin said when knowledge of the tunnels finally became public.

Now you can take a guided tour of the tunnel, which lasts forty-five minutes, beginning at a souvenir shop on Main Street North in downtown Moose Jaw.

See also: **Sam Bronfman, Rocco Perri, Antonio Papalia, Quadeville, Sainte-Pierre and Miquelon.**

Mora, Enio: Frightful Limp – Perhaps the most fearsome thing about 260-pound Enio Mora was his limp. There were whispers that the Toronto mobster had lost his lower left leg in a shotgun blast in 1979 when someone tried to rob a Harbord Street gambling club near the University of Toronto that was frequented by Mora and Mob associates.

The prime suspect in that case was a small-time thug named Anthony Carnevale, but he was never taken to court for the crime. Someone – and many thought it was Mora – killed Carnevale with a shotgun blast in the Keele Street basement apartment of his parents' home in January 1980, shortly after Mora was fitted for an artificial leg.

Mora was born in 1949 in Sora, Italy, and grew up in southern France, immigrating to Canada in 1968. His criminal enterprises included illegal gambling, loansharking, scams involving Toronto-area homebuilding, and laundering money in the Caribbean. Legitimate activities of the North Park Drive resident included selling

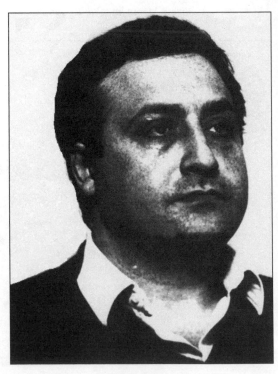

Enio Mora

life insurance, operating a snack bar on St. Clair Avenue West, working as a building contractor, and running a drywalling firm.

In the early 1970s, he had been particularly close to Toronto mobster Rocco Zito, and by the early 1980s, he had a working relationship with Toronto Mob leader Paul Volpe and a crooked member of the Carpenters' Union. He was also moving in Hamilton Mob circles, and on February 5, 1984, he visited Hamilton mobster Antonio "Tony" Musitano at Millhaven Penitentiary with Musitano's brother, Domenic Musitano, and son Pasquale "Pat" Musitano.

In December 1985, Mora was charged with extorting money from Greek gambling houses in Toronto's Pape-Danforth area along with members of the Niagara Mob, including Carmen Barillaro.

There was something curious about his body that was unusual for a Mob hit – his pants were pulled down. That was a sign that he had offended someone on a sexual level. Such killings were considered points of honour in the Mob, and a boss didn't have to gain consent from other bosses before ordering such an execution on a high-level mobster like Mora.

Those who knew Mora best realized they had to take him seriously. When one businessman was too slow repaying a debt, Mora doused him with gasoline and drove him to Hamilton for a meeting with Mob boss "Johnny Pops" Papalia. Papalia lit his cigarette lighter near the man, then asked, "When am I going to get my money?" The man paid up.

In the 1990s, Mora and Papalia drew heat themselves from a new group of Sicilian mobsters who moved into Toronto from Montreal, setting up a ritzy restaurant on Avenue Road and a splashy west-end nightclub. Mora and Papalia were supposed to invest money in real estate for the newcomers, but instead millions of dollars disappeared and Mora and Johnny Pops had a new set of enemies.

The shooting that cost Mora his leg had apparently been the last time anybody got tough

with him – until September 11, 1996, when someone shot him in the head four times at close range and stuffed his large, lifeless body into the trunk of his gold Cadillac near the intersection of Teston and Weston Roads just off Highway 400 in Vaughan, north of Toronto.

The fact that Mora met a violent end in his forty-eighth year wasn't a shock to anyone who knew him. "It [Mora's murder] sure wasn't a surprise," said Ron Sandelli, former head of Metro police intelligence, who worked on cases involving Mora for more than a decade. "He had his hand into so many things."

Those who knew Mora also found it ironic that his body was found in the trunk of a luxury car. Some veteran police officers suspected Mora played a role in luring Paul Volpe to his death in 1983. Volpe, who was also active in skimming money from the housebuilding industry and in gambling, was also found in the trunk of a luxury auto. It was obvious that both the Volpe and Mora hits were not carried out by street criminals, who usually find cheaper, more permanent, hiding place for bodies than the trunks of expensive automobiles.

Not long before his death, Mora won a court fight against Canadian authorities, who sought to deport him to Italy after he was convicted in Canada for drug trafficking and weapons possession. Mora successfully argued that his deportation could cause undue hardship to his wife and three young sons.

The search for clues into the Mora murder led York Region detectives to a farmhouse in Vaughan. Forensic testing established that the farm, which Mora often visited, was the site where he was murdered before he was put in the trunk of his Cadillac.

Police credit Mora for inadvertently leading to the downfall of international Sicilian money launderer Alfonso Caruana. In 1995, while monitoring Mora's telephone conversations, police heard of an upcoming wedding, and set up surveillance at Toronto's posh Sutton Place Hotel. The father of the bride was identified as Caruana, who was wanted by Italian authorities for money laundering and Mafia associations. Caruana had fled from Italy, but police didn't know where he had settled until the wedding.

The investigation that followed involved several countries and a dozen law agencies, and by the time it was over, Mora was dead and several Caruana family members were charged and convicted.

See also: **Giacinto Arcuri, Alfonso Caruana, Anthony Musitano, John "Johnny Pops" Papalia, Paul Volpe.**

Shue Moy: Gambling King – He was known in Vancouver's Chinatown as the "king of the gamblers," and in 1928, he was the focus of a special provincial police inquiry into the corruption of that city's police chief and mayor. Embarrassing stories out of that inquiry about payoffs to police and politicians pushed the city's police chief, H.W. Long, to resign.

This was during a time when scores of opium-smuggling syndicates were broken up by police in Vancouver, Toronto, Montreal, New York City, and the Maritimes. The drugs were often smuggled in luxury ocean liners and the criminals caught for the operations were often deported to China after serving their jail terms.

See also: **Triads.**

Murdock, Ken: Three-Time Killer – He was allowed to plead guilty and was sentenced to life imprisonment with no hope of parole for thirteen years for the three underworld slayings for the Domenic Musitano crime family of Hamilton.

Murdock was the hit man who killed Hamilton Mob boss "Johnny Pops" Papalia and his lieutenant Carmen Barillaro of Niagara Falls in 1997. Murdock also machine-gunned Hamilton janitor Salvatore Alaimo to death in 1985. Alaimo was an honest man, but the Musitanos wanted to use his death to pressure his family.

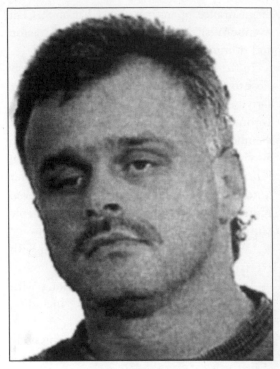

Ken Murdock

Domenic Musitano met Murdock in 1984 in Collins Bay Penitentiary and asked him to protect his sons when Murdock got out of jail. "It proved to be an extremely unhealthy relationship," Angelo Musitano's lawyer, John Rosen, later understated in court. "Murdock was a vicious career criminal."

Murdock managed to sound annoyed when a *Maclean's* magazine reporter told him that Pasquale "Pat" and Angelo Musitano each received a ten-year sentence for the three murders, even though many members of the public thought Murdock also got off lightly. "They're trying to make it look like I decided on my own to kill John Papalia," Murdock told the magazine. "I had no reason to kill Papalia. They ordered the killing, and they get just 10 years. They'll be back on the streets in less than four. It doesn't make sense to me."

See also: **Carmen Barillaro, Angelo Musitano, Domenic Musitano, Pasquale "Pat" Musitano, John "Johnny Pops" Papalia.**

Musitano, Angelo: Angry Brother – He had just finished serving seven years in prison in Calabria in southern Italy for shooting a man to death in 1929 when he heard that his widowed sister was pregnant.

In an apparent attempt to restore family honour, he shot her dead, according to evidence given in Italian court, and then dragged her body by her hair to her lover's home. He shot the lover twice, but the man survived. After Musitano fled, an Italian court sentenced him to thirty years prison *in absentia*.

Musitano escaped to France, then stowed away on a ship to Canada. He jumped ship in Halifax, and made his way west to Hamilton, Ontario, where his brother Pasquale was raising a family of eight children. There, Musitano lived under the name Angelo D'Augustino, working as a bleach salesman and a machinist at a steel plant. Neighbours called him friendly and a regular churchgoer. He never married, and to his many nephews, he was Uncle Angie.

Authorities kept him under surveillance for twenty-two months before finally making the arrest in 1965, and at first he wouldn't admit his true identity. Shown a thirty-five-year-old photograph of himself on an Italian police circular, he finally relented, saying, "Yes, it's me. Was I like that?"

He was deported from Hamilton on March 2, 1965, for illegally entering Canada, and was flown back to Rome to serve his prison term, thirty-six years after the murder of his sister. *See also:* **Angelo, Antonio, Domenic, and Pasquale "Pat" Musitano.**

Musitano, Angelo: Killer Drive – He drove with hit man Ken Murdock to Niagara Falls on July 23, 1997, and waited in the car as Murdock shot mobster Carmen Barillaro dead. The son of Hamilton Mob boss Domenic Musitano, younger brother of Pasquale "Pat" Musitano, and great-nephew of Angelo Musitano, he was sentenced to ten years in prison for his part in the slaying. *See also:* **Carmen Barillaro; Ken Murdock; Angelo, Antonio, Domenic, and Pasquale "Pat" Musitano; John "Johnny Pops" Papalia.**

Musitano, Antonio "Tony" Charles: Bombing Baker – Ten years younger than his brother, crime boss Domenic, he owned the Calabria Pasticceria on James Street North in Hamilton. His uncle was Angelo Musitano, who fled to Hamilton after murdering his sister in Calabria.

While Tony's rich pastries were a veritable taste explosion, he was perhaps most notable for helping turn Hamilton into Canada's leading city for bombings throughout the late 1970s.

A 1983 trial found Musitano guilty of six bombings, one attempted bombing, and two cases of arson, all of which followed extortion demands, as well as attempts to persuade the victims "to join the family."

Musitano, whom a police officer testified was a member of the Calabrian Mafia ('Ndrangheta), was originally sentenced to life imprisonment. In passing sentence, District Court Judge Hugh O'Connell said, "This crime does not, in my view,

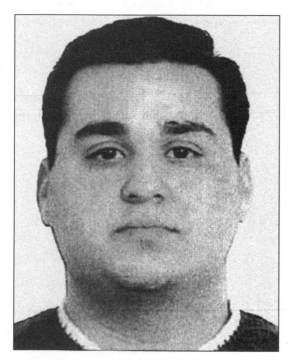

Angelo Musitano, 1997

attract any feeling of mercy or compassion. Nor am I attracted to the idea of tempering justice with mercy."

However, the Ontario Court of Appeal reduced the life sentence to fifteen years. The brush with a life term didn't scare Tony straight; while behind bars in Millhaven Penitentiary in 1983, he plotted the contract killing of Toronto mobster Domenic Racco.

He was eventually convicted of setting up the Racco killing, but this didn't really hurt him, since his new twelve-year sentence was to be served concurrently with his earlier arson sentence.

A year after being sentenced for plotting the Racco murder, Musitano was transferred to a medium-security penitentiary. In 1987, he was transferred to Beaver Creek Institution, a minimum-security prison near Gravenhurst, Ontario, which was sometimes called the "Muskoka Hilton," because of its relaxed rules and comfortable facilities, including a golf course and swimming pool for convicts. Inside prison, Musitano was an untouchable, who quietly served his time and avoided trouble, which helped him when he came before the parole board. The fact that he had arranged a gangland hit while behind bars somehow didn't factor into the decision.

By 1988, he was granted early parole in recognition of his "good behaviour" as a convict, despite setting up the Racco murder. There were howls of protests from police, who said it highlighted their seeming inability to deal with organized criminals. While he had been a model inmate, on the streets, he had recruited motorcycle gang members to enforce his demands around the community, and it cost police more than $1 million to investigate the bombings his gang carried out.

See also: **Domenic Musitano, Domenic Racco.**

Musitano, Domenic: Illegal Tire Dump – He lived in a modest semi-detached home on Colbourne Street in Hamilton, in the city's old north-end Italian district and a ten-minute walk from Railway Street, the epicentre of operations for the Papalia crime family. Ostensibly, he ran a scrapyard where bald automobile tires were dumped. More importantly, he was an old-school 'Ndrangheta leader, enjoying influence over his neighbours more than material trappings.

He was brought up with the exaggerated, odd sense of honour of the Calabrian underworld. His uncle, Angelo Musitano, fled Italy after murdering his pregnant, widowed sister, and Domenic honoured him by naming one of his sons Angelo.

This code of behaviour meant no slights, however minor, could be ignored. He served three years of a seven-year sentence for shooting a Hamilton motorist who irritated him in 1961 by honking his horn at him.

He and his north-end Hamilton neighbour "Johnny Pops" Papalia met regularly in 1982, leading police to believe they were plotting something. In 1983, a Hamilton court cleared Musitano of four counts of conspiracy to commit extortion. Police alleged he was trying to control the dump-truck business there.

Domenic Musitano

In 1985, he was sentenced to six years in prison for his part in the 1983 gangland-style slaying of Toronto mobster Domenic Racco, thirty-two. Murder charges against him were dropped after he pleaded guilty to being an accessory after the fact. Musitano was released on parole after serving the mandatory minimum two years for providing the gun in the slaying.

Racco, who owed him a cocaine debt, was released from prison for that crime in February 1987, after serving the minimum two years of his six-year sentence. His release was strongly opposed at the time by the Hamilton-Wentworth Police. "He was involved in an organized crime murder and he represents a threat to the citizens of this region," said the force's chief, Robert Hamilton.

In the 1990s, the province took control of the illegal 800,000-tire dump that he ran, and sent him and his family a tab for $1.8 million in cleanup costs, but he protested that he had no money to pay the bill. He had earlier applied to the provincial government for $3.5 million to upgrade the dump – in effect trying to use government money to make an illegal operation more advanced than his legal competitors.

He had heart surgery at age fifty-one and died six years later after suffering a heart attack in his home.

See also: **Angelo, Domenic, and Pasquale "Pat" Musitano, 'Ndrangheta, John "Johnny Pops" Papalia, Domenic Racco.**

Musitano, Pasquale "Pat": Funeral Greetings – The son of old Hamilton Mob boss Domenic Musitano, he was front and centre on Barton Street East in Hamilton at the funeral of murdered Mafia boss "Johnny Pops" Papalia.

Papalia had been shot to death the Saturday afternoon of May 31, 1997, in the parking lot of his business, Galaxy Vending, on Hamilton's dead-end Railway Street, in the city's old Italian district.

At Papalia's funeral, Pat Musitano exchanged kisses and strutted about outside the funeral home. It was as if the event was about him, not Papalia. In a sense it was, since the hit man Ken Murdock was working for Musitano.

Musitano ran the Gathering Spot restaurant on James Street North, about a ten-minute walk from Papalia's office. Diners knew the Gathering Spot for its tasty thin-crust pizza, while mobsters thought of it as a place to meet with Musitano, whose father, 'Ndrangheta leader Domenic Musitano, had died a couple years earlier of a heart attack.

Pat Musitano had a long association with Murdock through Domenic. Murdock had been the trigger man for Domenic Musitano in the drive-by machine-gun slaying of Salvatore Alaimo, a janitor at the Stelco steel plan. Later, Murdock learned that Alaimo had done nothing wrong, but simply had the misfortune of being related to someone who angered the elder Musitano.

Murdock considered Pat and his brother Angelo friends, and he liked to think they were showing their trust and respect when they presented him with an expensive gold ring bearing his initials. As Murdock understood it, the hit on Johnny Pops was about money. Pat owed money to the old gangster and, Murdock later said, "there was some pressure. And he went from that to, you know, that he didn't feel too comfortable owing John money is what it boiled down to. I don't feel he had the money to pay John back and from the tone of the voice from him asking me to do basically John, that he was scared."

There were others who thought that Pat Musitano had more far-reaching plans. He was considered friendly with Montreal Sicilians who had recently arrived in Ontario, and they considered Johnny Pops a bothersome obstacle to their expansion and a relic from the old American La Cosa Nostra. Naturally, the Musitanos would not feel the need to share this information with a street-level criminal like Murdock.

Murdock expected money as well as thanks for the murder. He said he was supposed to get

Pasquale "Pat" Musitano in sunglasses (centre) at John "Johnny Pops" Papalia funeral, 1997
Inset: Musitano walking at Papalia funeral

$10,000 and fifteen ounces of cocaine, but declared he would have done it for nothing, because it was "for the family." Ultimately, he got about $2,000 for the hit, and also the cocaine.

It wasn't long before shock waves from the Johnny Pops murder were heard from Buffalo, New York, about an hour's drive from where he was slain. The Musitano brothers heard about a meeting in Buffalo, attended by Carmen Barillaro, Johnny Pops's Niagara Falls, Ontario, lieutenant. What the Musitanos heard about that meeting was both insulting and threatening. "Word came back to Pat more or less that he was next," Murdock later said. "The only details I got was the meeting took place and supposedly through the leader over there, the right-hand man trickled information back and Carmen was stated as saying at the table, at the

meeting, 'I'll take care of that fat piece of s**t [Pat Musitano] myself.'"

That's why Murdock and his friend Angelo Musitano drove down to the Falls on July 23, 1997, on the eve of Barillaro's fifty-third birthday. With Angelo Musitano waiting in a car outside, Murdock knocked on the front door of Barillaro's upscale home. When Barillaro came to the door, Murdock asked him if the red Corvette in the driveway was for sale. Barillaro wasn't one to humour idiots or strangers, and Murdock appeared to be both.

The niceties over, Murdock pushed his way inside. "Barillaro seemed to understand what was about to occur," Murdock said later. Murdock pulled out a 9 mm pistol, as Barillaro ran to another room, then turned and rushed Murdock, who squeezed off two shots, stopping his desperate charge.

Late in 1998, Murdock was arrested for extortion. At first, awaiting trial on that charge, Murdock was stoic in jail, but his mood turned angry when police played him a tape that suggested his life was in danger from the very gangsters he tried so hard to impress, the Musitanos. On October 22, 1998, Murdock signed an agreement to co-operate with police. He pleaded guilty to three counts of second-degree murder, getting life in prison with no chance of parole for thirteen years for the slayings of the janitor Salvatore Alaimo, Papalia, and Barillaro.

When Murdock took the witness stand on June 16, 1999, to testify at the preliminary hearing of his former friends, the Musitano brothers looked at him from the prisoner's dock with expressions of disdain. Pat and Angelo were each charged with one count of first-degree murder, and Angelo was also charged with the murder of Barillaro.

"I've known Ang since he was yay high," Murdock testified in cross-examination by defence lawyer Dean Paquette. "You know, like this is the hardest thing for me to do right here. It's tearing me apart inside because I do love these guys, in a sense."

Then Murdock turned toward Pat and Angelo Musitano and asked, "Do you understand? Even though you don't believe it. I know you're hurt. I'm . . . hurt."

Pat, thirty-two, shrugged and rolled his eyes while Angelo, twenty-two, shot a look to his mother, sister, brother, and several family supporters. The brothers might be disgusted at Murdock, but they knew they were caught, and pleaded guilty to conspiracy to murder Barillaro. They were both sentenced to ten years in jail.

See also: **Carmen Barillaro; Angelo, Domenic, and Antonio Musitano; John "Johnny Pops" Papalia.**

Musolino, Giuseppe "Joe": Nasty Hairstyle – It was the tuft of hair standing up on his head that made him look just a little different as he held

court in the Ward district of downtown Toronto, along York Street, near the courts of Osgoode Hall on Queen Street West.

The Joe Musolino of York Street was initiated into the Picciotteria crime group in November 1896 in a barracks on the outskirts of Santo Stefano d'Aspromonte in southern Italy, and the distinctive bouffant was the style preferred by criminals there.

Musolino's family crime group was considered the forerunner of modern Calabrian organized crime, and was hit with massive police raids on May 12 and 13, 1901, in Santo Stefano d'Aspromonte. The crackdown meant that he would sooner or later end up in jail if he remained there, and so instead, Musolino chose to travel to North America in the hold of a ship.

Many of the Musolino group also fled Calabria for North America, and expanded the enterprises of the Picciotteria. First, Musolino ran a restaurant at 125 Eleventh Street in Niagara Falls, New York, and, not long after he arrived there, Italian immigrants in the Niagara Peninsula were hit with a flood of extortion letters.

Giuseppe "Joe" Musolino

Within a year, Musolino moved north to Toronto and the Italian district then on York Street, near modern-day Nathan Phillips Square. He remained an unknown figure outside the Italian immigrant community until his name surfaced when police in Toronto were investigating the murder of Francesco Scarrone (a.k.a. Tarro) on Front Street near Church Street in 1911. The man who killed Scarrone, Frank Griro, told police that he killed him because he was tired of having to pay Black Hand extortion demands.

"I decided that I would rather be hanged than shot to pieces," Griro later said. On the body of the dead man, police found what they considered to be coded extortion letters from other Italian immigrants, one of which was from a young man in Cobalt named Rocco Perri. At the time, Rocco Perri's name didn't mean much, but within a decade he would be a public figure of sorts as Canada's bootlegging king, based in Hamilton, Ontario.

Police were soon looking at Musolino, Scarrone's boss, who held court in a restaurant–boarding house at 160 York Street, in the heart of the downtown district known as the Ward. There were no Italian officers on the Toronto police force then, and officers could not have been expected to know that significance of his distinctive, upward-curving hairstyle.

After the heat brought on by the Griro trial, Musolino told police he was willing to leave town and go to the United States, if he was given thirty days to clean up his business affairs and collect monies owed him. Told he was no longer welcome in the United States either, Musolino then said he would return to Italy. That was the last he was seen in Toronto.

See also: **Black Hand, 'Ndrangheta, Rocco Perri, Picciotteria.**

N

National Hockey League (NHL): Major Misconduct – Russian immigrant Sergei Fomitchev had fallen on hard times in New York City. Kicked out of two apartments where he'd been staying with friends, Fomitchev drove through the night on March 24, 1994, to Buffalo to look for his old acquaintance Alexander Mogilny. Mogilny was doing considerably better than Fomitchev, starring with the NHL Buffalo Sabres. He'd recently signed a contract worth $3 million a year.

The first time Mogilny and Fomitchev had met was during the world hockey championships in Stockholm, Sweden. Mogilny was then twenty and was impressed by the stereo in Fomitchev's car, which was parked outside the Dalaro Hotel, where he was staying. First they talked about stereos and then, eventually, about how Mogilny could play hockey in the West. Soon, they were plotting how Mogilny could defect from the Red Army. A couple of days later, Fomitchev had hidden Mogilny in a hotel, while his wife, fluent in English, called the Buffalo Sabres, who had drafted his rights.

Things started off well enough in America for both of them. Mogilny gave Fomitchev half of his $150,000 signing bonus and the Sabres hired Fomitchev to live, travel, and translate for the young star. Fomitchev kept hanging around, trying to trade on their association to meet other hockey players.

However, Fomitchev had never been able to build from that, while Mogilny had gone on to become a star, wearing number 89 to celebrate the year of his freedom. When they had lunch in March 1994, as Mogilny later testified in court: "He blamed me for ruining his life . . . and asked for money."

The sum Fomitchev wanted was $150,000. The hockey star refused and then Fomitchev later admitted saying: "In your sport, your legs are very important." Mogilny recalled him asking: "How would you feel if someone stabbed you in your legs or shot you in the back?"

Mogilny, the first Russian player to defect to play in the NHL, now became the first Soviet player in the NHL reportedly to be hit with extortion demands.

Mogilny turned to police, who staked out his house and the Buffalo Auditorium while the smooth-skating forward stayed away. The official reason given was the flu. Fomitchev and another Russian were unarmed when they were arrested outside the Buffalo locker room after a game.

Charged with extortion, Fomitchev eventually pleaded guilty to the misdemeanour of menacing. At the time of his arrest, it was revealed that Fomitchev had returned to the Soviet Union briefly and was now in the United States illegally under the name "Sergey Pavlosky."

The Mogilny case was considered by police to be an isolated incident, and not part of a larger scheme. However, by the time it reached court, there were already rumblings of far more organized efforts to threaten players with injuries of violence to their families back in the former Soviet Union if they didn't hand over money to thugs.

An early mention of Russian criminals muscling in on hockey players came in December 1993, when Réjean Tremblay, a columnist at *La Presse* newspaper in Montreal, wrote that, in the 1990s, a number of Russian players in the NHL were forced to pay the Moscow underworld protection money for their families back home.

Tremblay wrote that New Jersey Devils defenceman Viacheslav Fetisov was among those targeted by the "new Russian mafia." Fetisov strongly denied the story, saying, "I don't know where this came from. There are [44] Russian players in the NHL. All would be paying [if it were true]. No one is paying."

The newspaper wrote that some Russian players, such as Oleg Petrov of the Montreal Canadiens, feared extortionists in their homeland, while others had brought their families with them to North America.

Players who didn't pay up were threatened with having their legs broken or having their families harmed, *La Presse* repeated. One unidentified Russian player was quoted: "Russian players aren't safe anywhere in the world. The Russian Mafia leaders are in league with the former directors of the Communist party. They have all the contacts and control all the channels."

It also said the underworld controlled the Russian hockey league, which received large transfer payments in hard currency for its players who sign with clubs in the NHL or in leagues in Switzerland or Germany.

Other respected newspapers picked up Tremblay's story, including the *New York Times*, which cited an unnamed NHL executive as saying the league was aware of the situation and the Los Angeles Police Department was investigating at least one suspected case of intimidation. The

Vancouver Province said the FBI tipped off Vancouver police about a Russian underworld figure who tried to take over player contracts.

At first, the allegations were roundly denied by players.

In December 1993, the *Vancouver Province* quoted city police sources as saying Canuck winger Pavel Bure was a target of organized-crime groups and had made two payments to a man who had befriended Russian players. Bure was then the NHL's highest-paid Russian player at a salary of $930,000. His father, Vladimir, and the Canucks' general manager, Pat Quinn, denied any money had changed hands.

(Seven years later, Bure would tell *Sports Illustrated* magazine that he was a long-time friend of Anzor Kikalishvili, who has been identified by the FBI and Russian law-enforcement officials as one of the heads of the Russian *mafiya* involved in extortion and racketeering in the United States and Russia. However, Bure said he wasn't linked to Kikalishvili's businesses. Kikalishvili hadn't been charged with a crime, and denied the allegations.)

After the extortion reports, the NHL investigated possible links between players and Russian organized-crime figures, then reported that no evidence existed of any attempts to fix a game or of any player's involvement with organized crime.

For his part, Bure insisted he has done nothing wrong. "I can't control what people say," he told the *Los Angeles Times* in 1999. "I don't feel any guilt. I feel innocent. This is getting old. [Reporters] have nothing to say and they just write it over and over. I was really mad when it happened in 1995 and 1996. It's the same thing now."

Meanwhile, the *Vancouver Province* cited an unconfirmed report that Kings defenceman Alexei Zhitnik had been physically harmed by gang members.

For his part, Mogilny only sat out one game before returning to the ice on March 27, 1994, scoring a goal and an assist in helping Buffalo beat the New York Islanders 4–1. Then he said the threat was already behind him.

"The thing happened a few days ago," he said. "I don't know where the guy is. I don't even want to know. It's just a normal day, a normal, human day. What can I tell you?"

In court in Buffalo in April 1994, Fomitchev's lawyer told a federal judge that Fomitchev was on a KGB "hit list" because he had helped Mogilny defect from the Russian army and join the Buffalo Sabres. For that reason, Fomitchev, thirty-one, used a false name and documents to obtain a visa to leave Russia in January, said attorney Robert J. Riordan.

Mogilny's name surfaced again in May 1996, when a Senate Governmental Affairs Committee in Washington heard that at least three Russian players in the NHL had been targets of extortion and threats of violence from members of Russian gangs. The testimony came from a Russian criminal who was in a U.S. prison and who testified behind a screen to protect his identity. He said he believed he and his family would be killed if his name was made public.

The witness named Mogilny, then with the Vancouver Canucks, Vladimir Malakhov of the Montreal Canadians, and Alexei Zhitnik of the Buffalo Sabres as three of the players who had been threatened if they did not pay extortion money.

"Alexander Mogilny, who plays for the Vancouver Canucks, was threatened by Sergei Fomitchev, a man I know," the Senate committee heard. "Fomitchev has ties to Russian organized-crime groups."

The witness said Zhitnik was threatened when he played in Los Angeles, but did not go to the police. He said Malakhov was approached when he was a New York Islander, but the problem went away after he went to Montreal.

The witness said Russian gangs in the United States were active in extortion, money laundering, drug smuggling, insurance, gas-tax fraud, and murder. "What we have here is a problem that is growing. Just last week I heard that another *vory v zakone*, or Russian godfather, recently arrived in the United States," he said.

In 1996, gangsters in Ukraine kidnapped the mother of Oleg Tverdovsky of the Anaheim Mighty Ducks and held her for eleven days for $200,000 ransom. American and Ukrainian police broke up the plot. "At that time, I couldn't talk to anyone. She was in danger," said Tverdovsky, then just nineteen. "Yeah, it was pretty tough."

The kidnapping was organized by a now-unemployed former coach of the star, who was jealous over his three-year, $4.2-million contract. Later, Tverdovsky said, "I think it is way better now. The country is changing from those times seven, eight years ago when things were out of control. The country is being put back together."

However, his optimistic words seemed empty when, in April 1997, Valentin Sych, the head of the Russian Ice Hockey Federation, died in a hail of automatic-rifle bullets close to his home on the outskirts of Moscow.

His gangland-style slaying came two months after he complained to reporters that Russian criminals were increasingly muscling in on sports, trying to draw stars and officials into illegal activities.

René Fasel, president of the International Ice Hockey Federation, said the murder was a Mob job. "It is 100 per cent Mafia," he stated.
See also: **Introduction, Vyacheslav Sliva.**

'Ndrangheta: Old World Gang, New World Prey – This organization was once derisively called the "lunch-bucket mafia" by some investigators, but police have come to regard it as a significant force in the underworld.

Originally from the province of Calabria in the southern mainland of Italy, it is also known as 'Ndrina. It's a territorial phenomenon, with local 'Ndrangheta groups controlling geographic areas, and their leaders dictate what criminal activities are engaged in within the territories.

In its purest form, the organization has pyramidal structure, made up of twenty-four *camorristas*, or senior members; forty-eight *picciotti* at an intermediate level; and ninety-six honorable youths, or junior members.

In July 1972, the *Toronto Star* reported the police had proof that an Honored Society family was operating in Toronto. But the report created a furor of protest in the Italian community, and Allan Lawrence, then Ontario Attorney General, told a protest meeting that the newspaper's use of the term *Honored Society* was "an unfair and misleading term." He dismissed the group described in the story as "a minor extortion ring."

The joint task force's request for a public inquiry into the Honored Society was rejected and the task force was disbanded.

However, the existence of 'Ndrangheta was officially recognized by the Canadian courts after an RCMP specialist on organized crime testified on July 18, 1982, in a Hamilton courtroom that a three-year investigation by a police task force proved conclusively that the 'Ndrangheta, or Honored Society of Calabria, was operating in Canada.

Insp. Dino Chiarot made the statement while testifying as an expert witness during a pre-sentencing hearing in Hamilton in August 1982 for three men who were convicted of using fraud to take over a family pasta business in that city's north end in 1977.

Chiarot, fluent in several Italian dialects, became an expert on the organization while spending several years in Italy as a criminal liaison officer at the Canadian Embassy in Rome and working as an investigator in Montreal and Toronto. In court, he filed a series of transcripts and summaries of conversations secretly recorded by the police between 1966 and 1972.

A new member is accepted into the group as a "youth of honour," before advancing to the rank of *picciotto* and, ultimately, *camorrista*, Chiarot said. The inspector noted conversations in which members talked of how they were going to "bring forward" the sons of members for membership themselves.

Chiarot said the society has a built-in welfare-assistance program, by which members must contribute to other members in difficulties, such as when the head of a family is in jail or someone has been killed in gang warfare. He said one of the transcripts records an account of a collection for a widow of a person described as a *capo* (captain).

During the pre-sentencing hearing at which Chiarot testified, the owner of the pasta business testified the men warned him that members of his family might disappear if they questioned what was happening. The owner and his family had since been relocated outside Ontario by the police. That was a classic Mafia crime, Chiarot testified.

In the early 1950s, the 'Ndrangheta came to Canada with men like Toronto baker Michele "Mike" Racco, who left small, poor, and unsophisticated communities in which criminal pickings were usually meagre.

In Calabria, membership tended to be restricted to relatives by blood or marriage. For many Calabrian mobsters, the respect accorded them by their fellow members and by the people within their communities was often as important to them as any spoils from criminal activities.

When the first members arrived in Ontario and Quebec, they tended to prey on their fellow immigrants, who, following Old World ways, often would not complain or co-operate with police. During the late 1960s and early 1970s, Italian communities in such cities as Montreal, Toronto, Ottawa, London, and Hamilton were subjected to bombings, arson, and shootings, as the transplanted 'Ndrangheta members continued their traditional extortion and protection rackets and other activities.

In the process, many of the older members established comfortable business positions, since they eliminated much of the competition in the production and marketing of such food products as cheese, baked goods, meat, vegetables, and soft drinks.

In 1969, a joint task force of the RCMP, the Ontario Provincial Police, and the Metro Toronto Police was formed to investigate the organization in Toronto. They zeroed in on a group of Italian immigrants, many of whom, like Racco, had come to Canada from the Siderno Marina area of Calabria. They tapped their phones, followed them, and gradually identified about fifty men who made up a Toronto family of the Honored Society. They found its members were involved with extortion, loansharking, arson, bombings, murder, narcotics, counterfeiting, illegal firearms (including guns with silencers), and stolen bonds and securities.

The Toronto group had links with other members in several Canadian cities, such as Montreal, Ottawa, Hamilton, London, and Vancouver, as well as contacts with other 'Ndrangheta groups in Italy, the United States, and even Australia. It governed itself with what it called La Camera di Controllo, a control board that settled internal disputes and maintained discipline among members. The board consisted of seven senior 'Ndrina members, one of whom was Racco.

In the trial, Chariot noted a document that was found in Woodbridge, north of Toronto, that contained society rules and was full of references to blood, punishment, and violent death. It also contained an oath required of new Honored Society members: "It is better to die than betray the Honored Society." In the initiation ceremony, according to the document, a new member recited phrases in which he talked about taking "a bloody dagger" in his hand and having "a serpent in my mouth."

See also: **Francesco Caccamo, Rocco Remo and Cosimo Commisso, Cecil Kirby, Giacomo Luppino, Domenic Musitano, Michele "Mike" Racco, Paolo Violi.**

'Ndrina – *See* **'Ndrangheta.**

Nelson, Charles "Red" – *See* **Sam Kelly.**

Nelson, Samuel: Homegrown Pirate – The son of a prosperous landowner in Prince Edward Island (then called the Island of St. John) around the time of the American Revolution, Nelson received a farm as a wedding present in 1805 and was also granted a commission in the militia. This wasn't enough for him, and instead he bought a square-rigged brigantine ship and set up a trading business in Halifax.

What followed was some sort of sex scandal. He lost his commission, left his wife and their many children, and was able to secure a new commission as a lieutenant in the Nova Scotia Fencibles.

In Halifax, he met a retired privateer named Morrison, who suggested to him that they would make a good smuggling team, running goods into New England. Nelson had the financial backing and Morrison had the contacts and experience.

Nelson bought an American sloop with ten mounted guns and recruited a crew of ninety men from the Nova Scotia fishing fleet. They set sail for the West Indies, where they began raiding shipping vessels and plantations, and left tales of torture and murder in their wake. Off the coast of Newfoundland, they captured twenty fishing boats and took on more crew and supplies.

Nelson's ship ran aground off Prince Edward Island and Morrison and most of the crew drowned, while Nelson survived to rejoin his family. At that point, he decided it was time to retire from piracy, with a fortune equivalent to that of a modern-day millionaire. He went into legitimate merchant trading in New York, ending his career as the most successful native-born Canadian pirate.

See also: **Charles Bellamy, Eric Cobham, Cupids, Peter Easton, High Island, Captain Kidd, Henry Mainwaring, Sheila Na Geira, Gilbert Pike, Pirates, Bartholomew "Black Bart" Roberts, John Williams.**

Newman, Annie – *See* **Bessie Perri, Rocco Perri.**

Nicolucci, Sabatino: Money Exchange – No free calendars or toasters were offered at the chic, ground-floor Centre International Monetaire de Montréal currency exchange at the busy corner of Peel Street and de Maisonneuve Boulevard in downtown Montreal.

That didn't matter to customers in the underworld. Centre workers didn't ask prying questions when brought funds to the foreign-exchange house in hockey bags, grocery bags, shoeboxes, and suitcases, and converted it to U.S. currency. The money was then shipped through the centre to various countries.

The exchange was a magnet for some twenty-five organized-crime groups including the Hells Angels, Sicilian mobsters, Colombian cartels, the West End Gang, and the old Cotroni group. But all that attention put the business's owners in a fluster, for they definitely weren't in the business of making money – especially for criminals. The exchange's secret owners were the Mounties, and undercover officers were running a police-sting operation there alternately called Operation 90-26C or Operation Contract.

Unfortunately, the Mounties' lack of resources between 1990 and 1994 meant the force could investigate only two of the twenty-five crime groups that used its services to launder money. The Mounties didn't even have the budget and manpower to identify all of the crime groups doing business, let alone crack down on them. They were so inundated with dirty money that, by the time the RCMP pulled the plug on the sting in 1994, it had laundered $135 million.

Sabatino Nicolucci had been a frequent customer, making some 168 transactions over a two-year period and appearing on some 405 RCMP wiretap conversations. Nicolucci was seen as an important member of the Montreal Sicilian Mafia, who was scheming with David Rouleau, leader of the Hells Angels' Sherbrooke chapter, to smuggle cocaine to Angels in England and to help Chinese gangs import heroin into New York State.

Nicolucci's illegal activities were conducted while he was on parole after serving prison time for another drug scheme. In the end, it was criminals and not police who put a halt to Nicolucci's multitiered activities. He was kidnapped from a Jean Talon Street strip club in north-end Montreal after falling behind in payments to his cocaine suppliers from Cali, Colombia. First, he was held north of Montreal and, before police could locate him, he was taken to Miami and then Cali. There, he was allowed to try to work off his debt helping with drug deals while the cartel placed him under house arrest.

At this point, his future was precarious, to put it mildly. Canadian authorities wanted him on some 233 money-laundering and drug-trafficking charges, including the Hells Angels plot to ship 500 kilograms of cocaine into Britain, while the Cali cartel wanted the $1.7 million they said they were owed.

The American Drug Enforcement Agency liberated Nicolucci ninja-style from his Colombian capture, only to turn him over to American authorities in Bogota, who extradited him back to Quebec in May 1996. Nicolucci was sentenced to nineteen years in prison in December 1997 for his role in attempting to import more than 400 kilograms of cocaine and launder some $30 million.

See also: **Vincenzo "Vic the Egg" Cotroni, Hells Angels, West End Gang.**

Nigerian Letter Scam: Junk Mail – At first, the letters were intriguing and enticing. Letter-writers identified themselves as officials of a large Nigerian institution, such as the Nigerian National Petroleum Corporation or the Central Bank of Nigeria, or as civil servants. They asked for an urgent and confidential business relationship with the person receiving the letter, in order to transfer funds out of Nigeria.

The letter-writers stressed that they had a legitimate right to the funds, and the person receiving the letter was offered between 10 and 30 per cent of the total contract, then asked to forward personal financial information, including banking information, copies of corporate letterhead, and invoices so that the payment could be made through a contract claim in the victim's name. The victim was also asked to wire a payment of approximately $15,000 for legal fees and administration costs.

The next step came when the person receiving the letters got a call, saying that the funds had cleared Nigeria and were now in an alleged clearing-house or mercantile bank in North America. The money could be claimed, just as soon as further outstanding fees were paid for things like taxes, duties, or environmental levies. Such fees ranged from approximately $75,000 to hundreds of thousands of dollars. If the victim paid these fees, he was later informed that there were further fees to be settled. This continued for as long as the victim kept paying, and he never received the money promised him.

If payments weren't made, the letters could get nasty. A handwritten fax was sent to a Hamilton, Ontario, man from a man who claimed to be a lawyer for the Central Bank of Nigeria. The letter threatened: "You have just 48 hours to act according to our instructions if you actually do not want to turn your wife into a widow. . . . We are not as simple as you think because we are highly connected the world over. Do not say you were not warned."

Nomads: Angels' "Dream Team" – This elite chapter of the Hells Angels biker gang was set up on December 9, 1994, by Maurice "Mom" Boucher, forming what Quebec biker expert Guy Ouellette called a "dream team" of outlaw bikers.

Their name came from the fact that they had no clubhouse, although the Angels Trois-Rivières chapter was the closest thing they had to a home. They were soon seen as the Angels strongest cell. The idea of this rootless chapter

was to be able to make it tougher for police to monitor them, as other chapters had regular meetings and clubhouses, which police regularly raided.

Only Hells Angels who had proven their mettle were admitted into the Nomads. A key goal was to spearhead expansion into Ontario, where there were about a dozen small gangs, most of them Canadian-based independents.

The original members of the Nomads were: Maurice "Mom" Boucher, head of the Montreal Angels chapter and sponsor of the Rockers puppet club, who became Nomads president; Wolodumyr "Walter" "Nurget" Stadnick, a former Angels national president; Donald "Pup" Stockford, Stadnick's close friend and a stuntman from Ancaster, Ontario, outside Stadnick's hometown of Hamilton; Louis "Melou" Roy, former president of the Trois-Rivières chapter, who was widely considered the richest and most powerful Angel in Quebec in

Wolf Carroll wearing a Filthy Few patch

the early 1990s; Richard "Rick" Vallée, Roy's close associate from Trois-Rivières and an explosives expert; Denis "Pas Faible" Houle; Gilles "Trooper" Mathieu; David "Wolf" Carroll, formerly of the Halifax chapter, who wore a "Filthy Few" patch, which biker experts said signified someone who has killed for the gang; and Normand "Biff" Hamel, who ran the Death Riders puppet club.

Stockford was the only one of the group without a criminal record. Carroll had a strong interest in moving drugs in Northern Ontario, and Hamel moved drugs in Laval and the lower Laurentians. The Nomads became the fifth chapter in Quebec, after Montreal, Sherbrooke, Saint-Nicholas, and Trois-Rivières.

Eight years later, on September 11, 2003, the Nomads were dealt a potentially crippling blow, when nine bikers – including four Nomads – stood up behind bulletproof glass and pleaded guilty in Quebec Superior Court in Montreal to gangsterism, two counts of drug trafficking, and a charge of conspiracy to commit murder. The others included one Nomad prospect and four Rockers, a gang formed specifically to do the Nomads' dirty work.

In exchange for their pleas, the Crown dropped first-degree murder charges against the nine men for thirteen slayings. Most of the thirteen victims were rival drug dealers, but one of them, Serge Hervieux, was killed by gunmen who confused him with their intended target.

Evidence presented in another trial said the Angels targeted 134 people to be systematically killed.

At the time of the guilty pleas, two other Nomads were considered missing. David "Wolf" Carroll had fled the country after being hit with thirteen murder and murder-conspiracy charges, while Melou either fled police or was killed by fellow Angels. No one was left to attend to the day-to-day functions of the chapter.

The Nomads who pleaded guilty in September 2003 included:

- Denis Houle, fifty, a Grade Eight dropout and founding member of the Nomads, who did prison time for being an accomplice-after-the-fact in the 1985 slaughter of five Hells Angels at the gang's bunker in Lennoxville. When asked by a prison psychologist in 1992 why he wouldn't quit the gang, he replied, "With the Hells, I have found a family."
- Gilles Mathieu, fifty-three, another founding Nomad, who was considered particularly intelligent, and owned advertising sign-boards at the West Edmonton Mall worth $2.3 million. He, Houle, and six other gang members were caught in February 2001 holding a meeting in a downtown Montreal hotel room and looking over photos of their rivals.
- Normand Robitaille, thirty-five, did time for a botched extortion attempt;
- René Charlebois, thirty-eight, earned $12,000 monthly while a member of the Rockers puppet club, moving drugs for the Angels; and
- Jean-Guy Bourgouin, thirty-seven, a member of the Rockers puppet club, who was involved in a 1998 altercation in a trendy downtown bar with players from the Alouettes football team, including linebacker Stephan Reid and quarterback Anthony Calvillo. Reid was clubbed with a metal pole outside the bar.

Evidence offered in the Nomads' trial showed they were both ruthless and organized, as they waged a war with rival bikers for drug turf. One victim was killed in front of his eight-year-old daughter, who was left screaming for her mother, and another was shot dead when leaving a children's birthday party with his wife and toddler.

Killers were paid from $25,000 to $100,000, depending on the ranking of their victims in rival gangs. They made their own 9 mm subma-chine guns – which could fire thirty-two shots in less than two seconds – with parts ordered separately to make a gun harder to trace. Silencers and extra-large trigger guards were added to the guns – so they could be operated while wearing heavy gloves.

They had moles in respectable jobs, who could comb through government automobile-insurance records to track down home addresses of enemies, and an electronics expert who could intercept phone numbers of people who called their enemies' pagers.

The Nomads helped the Angels bring in $100 million yearly in cocaine trafficking, the court heard. During the war with the rival Rock Machine, bystanders were often endangered. Stray bullets tore into children's bedrooms or neighbouring homes, as far as eighty metres from the shooting.

The sentences handed out to the nine accused on September 23, 2003, ranged from fifteen to twenty years, which meant, with time already served, even the worst killers could be out in seven and a half years. They were sentenced according to their rank in the gang, which meant that the four Nomads each got twenty years, while the four Rockers, as well as the Nomad prospect, received fifteen years for gangsterism, drug trafficking, and conspiracy to commit murder. Each had already served two and a half years behind bars, which count as double-time and were deducted from the overall sentence.

See also: **Maurice "Mom" Boucher, Hells Angels, Dany Kane, Paul Porter, Rock Machine, Wolodumyr "Walter" "Nurget" Stadnick, Richard "Rick" Vallée.**

O

Oak Island, Nova Scotia: Digging for Dreams
– There's a hole called the Money Pit in this fifty-six-hectare island, nestled next to the coast south of Halifax. It was first discovered by a teenager in 1795, and since then, it has been the focus of a two-hundred-year search for buried treasure.

Searchers are motivated by the knowledge that privateers once frequented Nova Scotia's shores, and the belief that they might have buried some of their gold and silver in the Oak Island shaft. There has even been a rumour that the Money Pit holds the as-yet-undiscovered, original manuscripts of William Shakespeare.

Diggers have found oak and iron, coconut fibre, stones inscribed with strange, cipher symbols – but no treasure. They've been held by seawater flooding the pit at periodic intervals, and rumours that the shaft's original builders left it booby-trapped.

In December 2003, the Association of Land Surveyors found a surveyor, Frederick Nolan, who deliberately mispositioned markers to protect evidence he believed could help solve the mystery of Oak Island. The association found him guilty of professional misconduct and suspended him for three months.

The association's disciplinary committee ruled that Nolan knowingly altered a property line of his by more than ten metres during a 2001 survey on the island in Mahone Bay, site of what many publications call one of the world's greatest unsolved mysteries.

Nolan told the disciplinary hearing that he altered the position of the line to protect evidence of ancient markers. He argued that Oak Island is built on secrecy, and that when he altered the property line, "It was like a game."
See also: **Charles Bellamy, Henry Cobham, Cupids, Peter Easton, High Island, Bill Johnston, Captain Kidd, Mogul Mackenzie, Henry Mainwaring, Sheila Na Geira, Samuel Nelson, John Phillips, Gilbert Pike, Pirates, Bartholomew "Black Bart" Roberts, John Williams.**

Obront, Willie "Willie Obie": Mob Meat Man
– Former police crusader Pax Plante described Montreal-born Obront and Vic Cotroni as "The Untouchables" of the Montreal underworld, because of their excellent political connections.

Obront was a shareholder in the Hi-Ho Café and the Bal Tabarin nightclub, hangouts for underworld figures like Nicholas Di Iorio and Vic Cotroni. His friends included drug-smuggler Lucien Rivard and Salvatore Giglio of the New York City Bonanno crime family.

He gave the Cotroni family a conduit from the streets to mainstream businesses and also between the Italian gangs of St. Leonard and the Jewish rackets. Carmine Galante had given the Italian Mob ascendancy over the Jewish Mobs in the mid-1950s, and Obront was living proof that the relationship endured.

Willie Obront

money ties to the United States and abroad, Willie Obie also sat at the head of thirty-eight companies, one of which was responsible for feeding diseased horsemeat to tourists from around the world at fast-food booths at Expo 67. Although his annual declared income was $38,000, he somehow moved at least $83 million through his bank accounts, allowing himself the luxury of occasional $50,000 wagers on U.S. football games.

His job was to hide the true ownership of Mob funds raised through gambling, loan-sharking, drug smuggling, and other enterprises, and also to put these funds to work, generating further revenue, some of it through investments in a laundry (ironically), in restaurants, and in home-improvement, meat-packing, and construction industries.
See also: **Vincenzo "Vic the Egg" Cotroni, Salvatore Giglio, Lucien Rivard.**

October Crisis: Terror and the Mob – On October 5, 1970, senior British trade commissioner James Cross was kidnapped from his home on Redpath Crescent in Montreal's

His relationship with an attractive blonde woman named Gerda Munsinger was particularly intriguing. She was a German immigrant who worked her way from waiting on tables at Montreal's Chic 'n' Coop Restaurant to dining, dancing, and bedding members of Prime Minister John Diefenbaker's Cabinet in the early 1960s. Mounties constantly came across Obront's name when they investigated Munsinger's role in a major sex-security scandal, and police reports stated that hidden cameras were used by the Cotroni family – always on the lookout for political influence – to get photos of her well-placed clients.

When the scandal broke in 1966, the high-flying former chicken waitress, located in Germany by the *Toronto Star*, said that she feared a Montreal meat-broker named Obie, who knew about her relationship with a Cabinet minister.

A key underling in the Vic Cotroni group of the 1960s and 1970s, with connections through all strata of Quebec society, in addition to

Frank D'Asti

diplomat row by a cell of the Front de Libération du Québec (FLQ).

The FLQ was little-known then, and the kidnappers demanded publication and broadcast of what they grandly called their manifesto. Its sixth paragraph was particularly troubling to the underworld of Mafia chief Vic Cotroni. "We once believed," the kidnappers declared, "that perhaps it would be worth it to channel our energy and our impatience, as René Lévesque said so well, in the *Parti québécois*, but the Liberal victory showed us clearly that that which we call democracy in Quebec is nothing more than the democracy of the rich. The Liberal party's victory was nothing more but the victory of the election riggers, Simard-Cotroni."

The "Cotroni" of the phrase was obviously Vic, who had been involved in election misdeeds for the past five decades. The "Simard" was the wealthy Simard shipbuilding family, Premier Robert Bourassa's wealthy in-laws.

Five days after the kidnapping, Pierre Laporte, a member of the National Assembly, was kidnapped from in front of his Chambly home. Laporte's family and friends were frantic. At about 9:30 that night, René Gagnon, Laporte's aide, said he was visited by mobster Frank D'Asti of the Cotroni group, who "said he could help us find Pierre Laporte. . . . I said, 'Fine. Make the necessary arrangements.'"

The efforts by police and the underworld failed, however, and Laporte's lifeless body was found stuffed into the trunk of a Chevrolet that had been left at a nearby air base.

See also: **Vincenzo "Vic the Egg" Cotroni, Paolo Violi.**

Outlaw Trail – *See* **Big Muddy Badlands, Dutch Henry, Sam Kelly, Sundance Kid.**

Outlaws: Angels' Enemies – Ironically, the American-based Outlaws biker gang came to Canada after tough police work temporarily put Canada's toughest homegrown gang, the Satan's

Outlaws motorcycle gang in police raid

Choice, into a metaphorical ditch. The weakened status of the Satan's Choice gave the Outlaws an opening to move north from the United States.

The Outlaws entered Ontario in March 1977, absorbing half of the chapters of the Satan's Choice. The Hells Angels didn't want to be upstaged by their traditional rivals, the Outlaws, and responded by roaring into Quebec themselves in December 1977, building from a local gang called the Popeyes. What followed was an extended, sometimes bloody, power struggle between the Angels and the Outlaws.

See also: **Hells Angels, Popeyes, Satan's Choice.**

P

Panepinto, Gaetano "Guy": Discount Death –
He was known as the "Discount Coffin Guy"
and sold his product with the slogan "Do not
make an emotional loss a financial loss." At
Casket Royale, his cut-rate coffin shop on St.
Clair Avenue West in Toronto, prices ran from
$295 for decorated pressboard to a bronze
luxury model for $4,900. Children's coffins were
given away free, including a denim-covered
model with cowboy decorations.

There were rumours that he didn't just sell
coffins, but also helped put people in them, and
that he was the Toronto representative of the top
Sicilian gangsters of Montreal.

Panepinto was often sought by mobsters to
carry out rough jobs. In 1994, he pleaded guilty
in a Newmarket court to possessing explosives
found in a vacant warehouse in York Region.
The explosives were linked by police to a foiled
1989 murder conspiracy against former professional boxer Eddie Melo.

On October 3, 2000, Panepinto, then forty-
one, was killed in what appeared to be a carefully planned ambush, just blocks from his
home on Smithwood Drive in an upscale west
Toronto neighbourhood. Officers found him
slumped behind the wheel of his Cadillac with
multiple gunshot wounds. His assailants apparently fired from a passing van. The murder
remains unsolved.

Almost two years after the murder, in
September 2002, the remnants of what police
described as Panepinto's former crew were
arrested in a large police sweep. York Regional
Police arrested thirty-two people from Ontario,
New Brunswick, and New York State, accusing
them of forming a major criminal organization
involved in drugs, credit-card fraud, stolen
goods, and violence. Unstable explosives,
firearms, and cash were also uncovered in the
sixteen-month investigation, which was named
in Panepinto's honour – Project RIP.
See also: **Eddie Melo.**

**Papalia, Antonio "Tony": Prohibition Boot-
legger** – He was born in 1900 in Plati, the same
area of the southern Italian province of Calabria
where Rocco Perri was born in 1887. When the
two men each later settled in Hamilton,
Ontario, Papalia became a lieutenant in Perri's
massive liquor-smuggling operations.

During the Second World War, he was taken
from his home at 19 Railway Street, in the heart
of Hamilton's Little Italy, to be locked up as
enemy aliens and an alleged threat to national
security. Also rounded up were his bootlegging
associates Rocco Perri and Charlie Bordonaro.
When Perri disappeared a few years later, suspicious people looked in Papalia's direction. In a
few years, police would also be looking suspiciously at Papalia's son, John, regarding other
crimes.
See also: **Bessie and Rocco Perri, John "Johnny
Pops" Papalia.**

Papalia, John Joseph "Johnny Pops": The Enforcer – In 1924, the year Papalia was born, there was a string of slayings connected to bootlegging on tiny Railway Street in downtown Hamilton, where his family lived. Seventy-three years later, his life would end on that same street, when he, too, became a murder victim.

He was known in the media at the time of his death as The Enforcer, but on the streets of Hamilton's north end, he was always Johnny Pops or Paps.

In his only full interview, he told Peter Moon of the *Globe and Mail* that he was a product of his time, and spoke with pride of the fact that his father, Antonio, was a bootlegger. "I grew up in the thirties and you'd see a guy who couldn't read or write but who had a car and was putting food on the table. He was a bootlegger and you looked up to him."

Johnny Pops attended St. Augustine's Roman Catholic school on Mulberry Street, but quit school in Grade Eight after a serious bout of tuberculosis placed him in the sanitorium for several months. His biggest disappointment, he later said, was that he never graduated from high school. With a better education, perhaps his life would have taken a different turn. "It's been an interesting one. But maybe I'd have liked it to be different."

When the Second World War began in 1939, he said, he had to defend himself because of his Italian origins. His father was one of the Italians locked up without a trial on claims of national security, and anti-Italian taunts were common.

In the 1940s, Johnny Pops did some breaking and entering, operating out of an old icehouse at the corner of Railway and Mulberry Streets, before Railway Street was made a dead end.

In 1949, at age twenty-five, he was caught in front of Union Station in Toronto with heroin capsules. Tears streamed down his face in court as Johnny Pops talked his way out of penitentiary, saying his ill health meant he couldn't survive a prison term. The judge was sympathetic, and he got two years less a day in the Guelph Reformatory.

Upon his release in 1951, Johnny Pops began his big-time Mob apprenticeship, moving to Montreal to work for Luigi Greco and Carmine Galante. Soon, he was considered a full member of La Cosa Nostra (the American Mob).

Back in Hamilton, Johnny Pops ran a taxi company on James Street North, which attracted police attention when one of its drivers, Tony Coposodi, was killed in gangland fashion in 1954. There were justifiable suspicions that the cab company was a front for a gambling, drug selling, and an enforcement operation.

In 1955, at age thirty-one, Johnny Pops was known as a bachelor with expensive tastes in clothes and women, and a habit of always

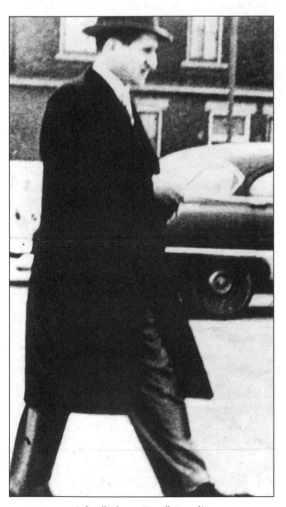

John "Johnny Pops" Papalia

carrying $1,000 in walkaround money. He had ties to the underworlds of Buffalo, New York City, and Montreal, and was helping Galante tap in to Toronto extortion rackets.

Johnny Pops made regular trips to Montreal to collect protection money from restaurant and bar owners and stock racketeers and, in June 1955, he and boxer Norm Yakubowitz were shot at while collecting money in Montreal. Yakubowitz was hit in the leg, while Johnny Pops escaped unhurt.

In the late 1950s, Johnny Pops moved into the vending-machine business with mobster Alberto Agueci of Toronto. At the same time, he loansharked money to business people who couldn't get credit at conventional banks, requiring them to repay $6 for every $5 borrowed, with interest compounded weekly. Business people who couldn't handle their debts got vending machines to operate for Papalia, and those who didn't accept the machines got threats or worse. He was also suspected of hijacking trucks carrying cigarettes, which he used to fill his cigarette machines.

By 1959, Johnny Pops visited New York City, helping set up what would become known as the French Connection heroin ring. Around this time, New York mobster Joe Valachi considered him a member of La Cosa Nostra, under control of Buffalo boss Stefano Magaddino.

Johnny Pops also caught the attention of *Toronto Star Weekly* magazine writer Peter Sypnowich, who wrote an article on him entitled, "HE WANTED TO BE CANADA'S AL CAPONE." In it, Sypnowich called him a "compulsive womanizer," writing, "His relationships with women provide the best clue to his character. Papalia has an inbred need to steal other men's women. They serve as trophies. The women themselves were attracted by his money, but it was his muscle that won them (his last girlfriend was the wife of a major Toronto crook, who got beaten up when he tried to do something about it). And although Papalia had a succession of girlfriends, he was no lover. He used his women only as sounding boards, talking to them by the hour – about Johnny Papalia and his plans to become a big shot."

Johnny Pops didn't just talk about becoming more of a big shot. In 1961, he moved in on the Jewish gamblers of Toronto, demanding control of their operations. As he shoved his way into Toronto, people flocked to the Town Tavern in Toronto's downtown, a block east of the current Eaton Centre, to watch what was billed in the underworld grapevine as "the semi-execution of Max Bluestein."

Bluestein refused to buckle under to Papalia and, for this act of independence, he was almost beaten to death, which brought a stinging *Toronto Star* column by Pierre Berton. Police used it as an excuse to hit the Mob hard, and after a series of police raids, Johnny Pops turned himself in to take the heat off the rest of the underworld.

He was sentenced in April 1961 to eighteen months in prison for the pipe beating of

"Johnny Pops" Papalia, 1950s

Bluestein, but soon had far bigger worries on his mind. In March 1962, he was whisked out of Millbrook Reformatory to be flown to the United States to stand trial for his part in the French Connection. The heroin-smuggling ring was later depicted in the Robin Moore book and film called – what else? – *The French Connection*.

As Johnny Pops was being led to the plane, he screamed in a distinctly un-Mafioso-like way: "I'm being kidnapped! . . . Help me! . . . They're taking me somewhere I don't want to go!"

No one stepped forward to help, and he and fifty-eight-year-old Benedetto Zizzo of Toronto were eventually indicted with New York–based Bonnano family members, including Carmine Galante, for importing seventy-six kilograms of heroin to New York City. The transaction had been partly financed by a Burlington developer he had met in the Guelph Correctional Centre years before.

Papalia was sentenced to ten years in prison, while his mentor, Carmine Galante, got twenty years. His associate Alberto Agueci had it even worse, as he was tortured for three days by underworld figures in upstate New York and then murdered for threatening to talk to authorities about Buffalo boss Stefano "The Undertaker" Magaddino.

The French Connection case was considered so big that U.S. attorney General Robert Kennedy reported it to be "the deepest penetration . . . ever made in the illegal international traffick of drugs."

Johnny Pops served fewer than five years of his ten-year sentence, getting a release in January 1968 on humanitarian grounds, because he supposedly had tuberculosis. When he got out of prison in Lewisburg, Pennsylvania, he told reporters, "Look, fellows, I'm a sick man. I'm not even a spit in the ocean. I'm a nothing."

However, the week he returned to Hamilton, dingy Railway Street was lined with Cadillacs and Lincolns, as an assortment of strong-arms, bookies, extortionists, and heroin peddlers dropped by to pay their respects.

Not everyone in his old milieu welcomed him back, however. In 1966, while Papalia was still in prison, Magaddino had instructed southern Ontario boss Giacomo Luppino to meet with Paul Volpe of Toronto, Papalia's southern Ontario Mob rival. In Papalia's absence, Volpe was promoted to become the Mob's contact with members of the Toronto building industry.

In November 1968, Papalia met Luppino in his home, and talked about Montreal and whether the Cotroni-Violi organization was answerable to the Bonannos or the Magaddinos. Luppino indicated the commission should decide. "We are still under the commission," Luppino said.

Police noted that murders often took place shortly before or after Papalia's meetings with Luppino. On June 28, 1969, Filippo Vendemini visited Luppino in Hamilton, and Vendemini was murdered the next day. Later on the morning of June 29, Papalia met Luppino, leading police to wonder if he killed Vendemini on the direction of Luppino. In late June 1969, Papalia met with Luppino, and a few hours later, Montreal organized-crime member Vincenzo Sicari was murdered in Toronto.

Upon his release from prison, Papalia had assumed he would regain his influence with construction trade unions in Toronto. However, in August 1971, a meeting was set in Toronto that included Paul Volpe and Giacomo Luppino. In that meeting, police suspected, there was a shift in control of construction trade unions in Toronto. It had been felt that Papalia was not exerting enough control over them. Now, Volpe was given more power.

At that time, Papalia expanded his legitimate businesses to include an auto-body shop in Hamilton.

In 1976, Papalia was convicted and sentenced to six years for extorting $300,000 from a Toronto loan shark. The key witness in this trial was Stanley Bader, whose 1982 murder remains unsolved.

Papalia married a hostess at the Gold Key Club, in 1981, but they separated within two years later and had no children. Their marriage contract, one of the few documents Papalia ever signed, stipulated that he had no claim on her property in the event of a marriage breakdown.

In July 1982, Papalia declared bankruptcy but continued to be chauffeured about and flash a sizable "walkaround" (a roll of bills thick with "browns and reds" – $100 and $50 bills).

From the time of his release from prison, there were rumblings that he was looking to oust Volpe from the top spot in the southern Ontario Mob. In November 1983, Volpe was murdered, and some police experts considered Papalia to be the prime suspect. Whatever the case, Volpe's murder meant Papalia's position as the southern Ontario representative for the Buffalo Magaddino family was secured.

Throughout the 1980s, Johnny Pops pushed to increase his loansharking activity in Toronto, and he often lent money to loan sharks for a percentage of their profits. In December 1985, police frustrated a major attempt by him to seize control of illegal Greek gaming clubs on Toronto's Danforth Avenue, in Hamilton, and in Niagara Falls, Ontario.

"Johnny Pops" Papalia

Although Metro Toronto Police succeeded in arresting ten men – including two key figures in Papalia's organization – and charging them with extortion, they were unable to get any evidence that implicated Papalia.

"Yeah, I know the people they charged. They're friends of mine," he told reporter Moon in 1986. "But that doesn't mean I was involved. I wasn't, because I wouldn't have anything to do with Greeks. I don't like them. I don't like their restaurants. I don't like their food."

He went on to tell Moon how upset he was about the murder of Domenic Racco, thirty-two, the son of Michele "Mike" Racco, a long-time fixture at the top of the Calabrian underworld. "I gave my word to his father that, when Domenic got out of jail, I would look after him. [In 1972, Domenic was sentenced to ten years in jail for attempted murder; Mike Racco died of cancer in 1980]," Moon recalls him saying. "All they had to do was come to me and I'd have paid the money. What was it? Twenty, thirty thousand dollars? I would have stood good for Domenic. His father was dead, and I was honour-bound to look after him."

By the time he spoke with Moon, Johnny Pops was sixty-two and enjoying the kind of life he could only have dreamt about as a boy. There were winter holidays in the sun, although he had given up on Acapulco ("too much crime") and now preferred the Caribbean.

Despite his lung troubles, he chain-smoked cigarettes and told Moon he enjoyed the odd cigar, as well as J&B Scotch on the rocks ("but not as much as I used to") and a good meal ("but I don't eat as much as I used to"). There was also boxing, baseball, and football ("American, not Canadian") on television. Old movies ("none of this porno stuff") and jazz piano were other entertainments.

His family business leased out more than two thousand pinball and vending machines and were the largest lessor of beer and liquor dispensers in Ontario. These businesses included extensive real-estate holdings, including almost a complete city block on which the brothers tried unsuccessfully to win planning approval for a new hotel in 1984.

Asked exactly what he did for a living, Johnny Pops smiled at Moon and said, "I go into a bar and I tell them my name and I intimidate people into taking our equipment. That's what the police tell you, isn't it? Listen, I'm lucky to have a couple of good brothers who look after me."

He scoffed at the suggestion that he was trying to take control of Toronto's underworld, with the approval of top organized-crime figures in Buffalo and New York City. "What's organized crime?" he asked Moon. "Listen, I'm sixty-two and I'm tired and I have to crawl out of bed every morning."

At that time, Papalia lived alone in a rented penthouse on the fourteenth floor of an apartment building on Market Street, a few blocks from the Papalia family's offices. He didn't own a car, but had his pick of several expensive cars owned by family businesses.

Then he smiled at Moon and continued, "I did shylocking and bookmaking, but that was back in the fifties. For a guy who's been doing so much in this country, [the police] haven't been able to come up with anything on me. Something stinks. They've got nothing better to do than run around following me all the time at the taxpayers' expense."

He agreed that he had "a short fuse," then added, "Hey, we all lose our temper sometime, don't we?"

Asked why he was seen with so many mobsters, he shrugged and said, "You go to Italian weddings, you meet people. I go to a lot of Italian weddings."

His joking aside, police said he had become a hermit in his penthouse, worried about young mobsters in the Italian gaming clubs of Toronto. By the 1990s, he had chronic gallstones and breathing troubles and spent much of his time sleeping on the black leather couch at Monarch Vending on Railway Street.

He was murdered in April 1997 by Ken Murdock, a thug acting for Pat Musitano, son of the old Hamilton don Domenic Musitano.

See also: **Alberto Agueci, Stanley Bader, Carmen Barillaro, Max Bluestein, French Connection, Frank "Santos" and Vincenzo "Vic the Egg" Cotroni, Carmine Galante, Gold Key Club, Louis Iannuzzelli, Giacomo Luppino, Ken Murdock, Pat and Angelo Musitano, Antonio "Tony" Papalia, Réal Simard, Paul Volpe.**

Payette, François: Deadly Discovery – In February 1966, lawyer François Payette, thirty-six, was discovered dead in his Thunderbird by a motorcycle police officer on a quiet northend Montreal street.

The father of two was a threat to the Quebec underworld at the time, since he had communicated details of an alleged new bankruptcy ring to the provincial Justice Department a short time before his death.

Payette was an honest man – a lawyer who specialized in civil cases, including bankruptcies and construction loans, and the collection of outstanding accounts. Payette was reportedly nervous as he readied himself to talk with police about the bogus bankruptcy scheme he discovered in the homebuilding industry. By the time police called him to arrange a meeting, he was already dead.

Perri, Bessie: Queen of Bootleggers – Born Besha Starkman in Poland, she seemed like countless other new arrivals to Canada in 1912 when she and her husband, a bakery driver, took a boarder into their home on Chestnut Street in Toronto's downtown Ward area.

Their boarder was a good-looking Italian labourer, Rocco Perri, and soon he and Bessie were lovers.

Bessie would never be considered ordinary again.

She ditched her husband, Harry, and two daughters for a life of crime with Rocco in Hamilton.

She was no gangster's moll who sat on the sidelines. It was believed that her word had bootlegging rivals killed. Many thought she was the brains behind Rocco's bootlegging empire, and she certainly handled his money with a tight fist.

In a 1924 interview with the *Toronto Daily Star*, Bessie laughed dismissively when asked about two recent gangland murders.

"Bootleg war, that is funny!" Bessie laughed. "You tell them, Rocco," she said, patting her husband on the back, "that there is no war. You are the king of the bootleggers. That is what they say. You should know."

"There is no bootleg war," said Rocco obediently.

To give the event a touch of class, Bessie had a symphony playing on the radio. "It is New York," she explained, gesturing toward a modern radio cabinet. "You would like something else, perhaps? But no, you are here to talk, and you must not be interrupted."

When Prohibition ended, the underworld had to redefine itself, and many looked toward drug trafficking. It was a particularly dangerous business, as Bessie found out when she and Rocco returned to their posh Hamilton home on the night of August 13, 1930.

Rocco parked their two-seater Marmon roadster in the garage. Bessie got out to unlock the kitchen door, as Rocco closed the garage doors. There were several shotgun blasts and, when they ended, Bessie was lying on the garage floor, face up and dead.

"She died as she deserved to die," said Harry Tobin, still legally her husband and never willing to forgive her.

Her funeral was the largest in Canadian underworld history, as a crowd estimated at ten thousand watched as her $3,000 bronze casket was driven to a small Jewish cemetery on the brow of Hamilton Mountain.

Motives for Bessie's murder are legion, and some even claim that Rocco himself staged it. Among those questioned by police was Antonio Papalia, founder of the Papalia crime family of Hamilton. The likeliest explanation is that Bessie was killed because she refused to pay for a shipment of drugs.

See also: **Antonio "Tony" Papalia, Rocco Perri.**

Perri, Rocco: King of the Bootleggers – The Hamilton, Ontario–based Mob boss was known as "Canada's Al Capone," running a bootleg empire that linked Ontario to New York State, Chicago, and the Maritimes. He was quite possibly Canada's first big-time Mafia leader, and his influence was felt by American and Canadian Customs officials, senior politicians, and police.

Perri was born in Plati, Calabria, in 1887, and arrived in Boston in 1903. He moved to Massena in upstate New York, and by 1908, he was working as a labourer in the Ward, Toronto's downtown neighbourhood of poor immigrants. There, he boarded with a family named Starkman and fell in love with his landlady, Bessie, a mother of two. They ran off together and settled in Hamilton in 1916, just as the Ontario Temperance Act – Prohibition – went into effect. The couple operated a grocery store on Hess Street North, but their real money came from bootlegging.

Rocco also said he was a macaroni salesman – a convenient cover that allowed him to travel the province making deals as a bootlegger.

In Ontario, Prohibition meant that breweries and distilleries were working flat out to supply the illicit U.S. market – although ostensibly they could only ship "offshore" – and vast fortunes were made. Canadian bootleggers like the Perris would place orders, ostensibly legal orders for out of the country. However, when shipments had cleared customs for export, they would often mysteriously find their way back into Canada, and then be smuggled into the thirsty United States. Once, a ship, supposedly bound for Cuba with liquor, left the dock four times the same day.

Perri, who was soon ensconced with Bessie in a grand brick home at 166 Bay Street South in

Hamilton, seemed always to be in the vicinity when there was a big liquor bust, but he was never caught red-handed.

In October 1923, for example, Toronto police discovered men unloading liquor from a boat at the foot of Leslie Street. When the boat sped off, the officers opened fire, killing one of the bootleggers. Among those arrested at the scene was Rocco. He told the court that he had been showing a friend the way to Woodbine racetrack when he had run across the people unloading the boat. "When I seen they were going to unload whisky, I wanted to go home," he protested. The charges were dismissed.

In 1924, he granted an interview to the *Toronto Daily Star* to argue that he wasn't behind a rash of underworld slayings. That's when he gained the nickname King of the Bootleggers.

"While I admit I am king of the bootleggers, I can assure you I had nothing to do with these deaths," he told the newspaper. "I only give my men fast cars and I sell only the best liquor, so I don't see why anyone should complain, for no one wants prohibition. . . .

"I was disappointed when the last plebiscite went dry, for I thought I'd go back to Italy and retire. But when money is this easy and prohibition continues, why should I? Some days I handle 1,000 cases for my customers, and the very best families are among my customers."

Bessie was an active – perhaps even controlling – partner in his operations, and in 1930, someone shot her outside their seventeen-room mansion. Rocco sobbed hysterically and collapsed during the funeral, but soon found a second love and partner-in-crime in Annie Newman. She was not as colourful as Bessie, but she was as sharp in business affairs.

Clearly, Perri was under siege in the late 1930s, as the Mob moved from bootlegging to other ventures, like drug trafficking. In March 1938, there was an attempt to dynamite the Perri home on Bay Street South, but Rocco was out with the maid, and the bomb went off in front of the building.

Eight months later, Rocco was playing cards at the home of a friend at 499 Hughson Street North in Hamilton's north end. He went outside to talk with friends, and turned on the ignition to get the car lighter working, so he could light a cigar. The explosion that followed was so strong that it knocked out power lines, but Rocco wasn't hurt, and even collected insurance for the new sedan.

In 1940, the Mounties made one final effort to put Rocco and Annie behind bars for their part in corrupting customs officials in Windsor, but charges fell apart after key witnesses mysteriously disappeared.

Mussolini had declared war on the Allies, and the RCMP used this to round up not just those Italians whom they considered sympathetic to Fascism but mobsters too. Rocco was interned under the War Measures Act at Petawawa until 1943.

By the time Rocco got out, the underworld had reinvented itself. The Buffalo Mob was in control of what had been his fiefdom. Rocco moved to Toronto, but was back in Hamilton on Sunday morning, April 20, 1944, visiting his cousin Joe Serge at 49 Murray Street West, near the old CN station.

Complaining of a headache, he swallowed two Aspirins, drank a cup of coffee, and walked out the door. Serge and his wife kept lunch waiting, but when he wasn't back by midnight, they called police.

A police bulletin stated: "The missing man is 55 years of age, five feet, four inches in height, 170 pounds, dark complexion, and an Italian. He was last seen wearing a blue striped suit, black oxfords, light brown spring overcoat, light brown fedora." Shortly afterwards, Toronto police said they had underworld information that Perri "is in a barrel of cement at the bottom of Hamilton Bay."

However, there were also reports that Rocco spent his final years sunning himself in Mexico. Italian-born crime journalist Antonio Nicaso of Toronto reported in 2003 that Rocco may have headed to upstate New York. Nicaso said he had found a letter apparently written by Perri years after he vanished.

The letter was dated June 10, 1949, and Nicaso said it was in the possession of a Perri relative in Italy. Perri's Italian relatives said he died in 1953 in Massena, New York, the same city where he had originally settled after moving to North America in 1903.

The letter suggested that he may have orchestrated his own disappearance.

"Dear cousin," it said, "With this letter, I will tell you I am in good health. Let them know I'm fine if you've heard the news."

It was signed "Rocco Perri."

See also: **Antonio "Tony" Papalia, Bessie Perri.**

Petrossov, Vatchagan: Banned at Border – When the Denver restaurant owner tried to cross into Canada from the United States on August 12, 1996, Canadian authorities stopped him and held him for questioning. He was released the next day, with the warning that he was permanently barred from Canada.

Police later said several factors entered into that decision, among them Petrossov's relationships with notorious Russian mobsters, the number of Russians in Canada who claimed Petrossov was an organized-crime leader, and Petrossov's own reluctance to give details about his planned visit.

Petrossov, who was a black-market trader in Moscow and did hard time in a Russian prison, originally entered the United States via Toronto in 1992. He won when American authorities tried to deport him in 1994 for failing to mention then that he had a criminal record in the former Soviet Union.

Canadian authorities also noted that Petrossov spoke regularly with the man who would be deported in 1997 as the alleged leader of the Russian Mob in Canada: Vyacheslav Sliva, Ivankov's brother-in-law.

See also: **Vyacheslav Ivankov, Vyacheslav Sliva.**

Petrula, Frank – *See* **Carmine Galante, Luigi Greco.**

Phillips, John: Short, Nasty Career – His pirate career lasted about a year, and ended abruptly when someone swung an axe into his head.

He began life in an English family of shipwrights, and moved to Newfoundland in 1720, because of what seemed to be the promise of plenty of work in his trade, as the English had taken island shipyards from the French at Placentia under the Treaty of 1713.

Things immediately started to go badly. The ship he was sailing upon to Newfoundland was captured by pirates on the Grand Banks, and he was pressed into service as a ship's carpenter. The pirate who captured him, whose name was Anstis, was considered truly horrific, even by pirate standards. Anstis's raids generally meant the murder of men and the gang rape of women.

Like many pirates of the time, Anstis secured a pardon from Great Britain and Phillips got to work on a trading ship bound for England. Finally, in the spring of 1723, Phillips landed in Placentia, Newfoundland, three years after he set out on his original voyage.

He wasn't able to find work as a shipwright there, however, and travelled to the island of Sainte-Pierre (then called St. Peter's Harbour), but had no luck there either. He settled for work on a Newfoundland fishing crew, which he didn't enjoy. It meant eighteen-hour workdays, for little more than room, board, and rum. The pirate life he had recently escaped looked good in comparison, so with some fellow fishermen, Phillips went back to Sainte-Pierre, where they signed a set of pirate articles and took an oath on the blade of an axe.

Their code decreed that deserters would be marooned on an uninhabited island, and that anyone who stole from their communal loot would be shot or marooned. Anyone who endangered the ship or picked a fight with the crew would be flogged. Pirates who lost limbs in battle would be compensated. Carrying an uncovered candle or smoking an uncovered ship would bring "Moses's law on the bare back" – thirty-nine lashes on the back.

Their ship had a good pirate name, *Revenge*, and it captured at least thirty-three ships over the next few months. One of Phillips's crew was John Rose Archer, who had been a pirate with the notorious Blackbeard, who had been killed five years earlier. Another crew member was John Fillmore, whose great-grandson, Millard Fillmore, would one day become the thirteenth president of the United States.

One of the original crew who signed the pirate articles, Thomas Fern, tried to leave, and they tied him to a tree and executed him, as their laws decreed. A carpenter they had captured plotted a new mutiny, and when it broke out on April 17, 1724, on the Grand Banks, Phillips was struck dead with an axe to the back of the head. His body was thrown overboard and his severed head was left hanging from a yardarm.

Pirates John Rose Archer and William White were publicly hanged for piracy in Massachusetts Bay, Boston, with the black flag of the *Revenge*, with its white skeleton, fluttering in the wind behind him. Reverend Cotton Mather, the hanging parson of Boston, officiated, as he often did at the executions of witches and pirates. Phillips's head was taken from the *Revenge* and displayed on the Boston waterfront as a warning to potential pirates.

See also: Charles Bellamy, Eric Cobham, Cupids, Peter Easton, High Island, Captain Kidd, Henry Mainwaring, Sheila Na Geira, Samuel Nelson, Gilbert Pike, Pirates, Bartholomew "Black Bart" Roberts, John Williams.

Picariello, Emilio: Emperor Pic – He was nicknamed Emperor Pic, and his castle was the Alberta Hotel in Blairmore, Alberta. There was supposedly a maze of underground tunnels leading out from the basement of the hotel, as well as a specially built room adjoining the hotel's basement for storing bootleg liquor. This allowed vehicles to drive inside for loading and unloading.

At appropriate times, a player piano upstairs in the barroom would pound the keys at full volume to drown out any noise from the clandestine business activities below.

Picariello and his wife, Marianino Maria, had seven children: Stephano "Steve," Angelina Rose "Julie," Carmine, Luigi "Louie," Charles "Chuck," Albert, and Florence Eleanor "Helen" (later Matson). The Picariellos had moved from Italy to Fernie, British Columbia, in 1911, and subsequently to Blairmore.

Picariello saw unbounded opportunities when Prohibition became law in Alberta in 1916. The hotel keeper became a bootlegger, running illegal alcohol from Sweetgrass, Montana, across the foothills, through the Crowsnest Pass, across the B.C. border, and into Alberta.

He sped about in a fleet of powerful McLaughlin "Whisky Special" cars that made many trips to British Columbia and Montana to carry the illegal liquor back to Alberta.

On September 21, 1922, a stool pigeon tipped off the Alberta Provincial Police that a large amount of booze would be coming into Picariello's hotel, and two officers were waiting when the hotelier and his son Steve wheeled up in their McLaughlin Buicks. Picariello spotted the officers and hit his horn, signalling for his son to flee back to safety on the other side of the Alberta-B.C. border, but the police phoned ahead, and Const. Steve Lawson was ready to intercept them on the narrow road west toward Coleman.

Lawson fired a volley at the fleeing McLaughlin on Coleman's main street, which was also the highway, and young Steve Picariello took a bullet to the hand but kept on driving until he reached the provincial boundary.

The elder Picariello assumed the worst when he heard that his son had been shot. He went to the Coleman police detachment, accompanied by his friend/housekeeper/mistress Florence Lassandro. There was a scuffle between Picariello

Emilio "Emperor Pic" Picariello and family, 1915 (Glenbow Archives, NA-1136-1)

Const. Steve Lawson, Alberta Provincial Police

and Lawson and, when it was over, the constable was dying from a gunshot to his back.

The following day, Picariello, Lassandro, and the murder weapon were recovered near Blairmore. The two were hanged on May 2, 1923, at the Fort Saskatchewan jail, and the intense public sympathy for them and disgust at the executions were reasons why Prohibition ended shortly afterwards in Alberta.

See also: **Florence Lassandro.**

Picciotteria: Mafia Forerunner – The first recorded case of a member of this criminal society in Canada was Giuseppe "Joe" Musolino, who fled to New York State and then to Toronto's downtown Ward district after massive raids in May 1901 in Santo Stefano d'Aspromonte, Italy, against his family's crime group.

The Picciotteria were considered the forerunner of modern Calabrian organized gang, the 'Ndrangheta. Italian archival records studied by journalist Antonio Nicaso noted this description of members: "He swears to be faithful to everyone connected to the Society of the Picciotteria, to help them unto his last drop of blood, to assist the other members in robberies, to present exactly all stolen goods to be divided equally with all other members cent for cent; to slash or to murder, when it is necessary, or because the boss tells him to, spies and all people who try to get in the way of the society, including the police."

Like the early Birbevis criminal society of Spain, the Picciotteria had a pyramidal structure, with two distinct levels: *camorrista* and *picciotti*. Both levels were dominated by a *saggio capo* or *capo bastone*, who co-ordinated robberies or extortions.

Nicaso notes the *camorrista* was at a higher level than the *picciotti*. To enter the society, a potential *picciotto* had to be introduced by a member of the *camorrista*, then pay a tax.

Their mannerisms were described by a judge of the town of Palmi in Reggio Calabria province court, when he passed sentence on June 11, 1892, in the first maxi-trial against the Picciotteria: "These people had used signs and slang to communicate, and upon entering in a cantina to eat, drink without paying the bill of the owner of the cantina. Most of them were tattooed."

In another trial in Italy, Vincenzo Mangione, chief of police in Santo Stefano d'Aspromonte, wrote in a report to the judge that all of the aims of this group were illegal. "But the principle of this association is to receive respect, in the sense the Picciotteria gives to this expression, imposing oneself . . . like a man of honour with intimidation, with arrogance and with threats."

Even in its early stages, there was a clear distinction between the Picciotteria and common bandits, the documents found by Nicaso state. Police in the small village of Gioia Tauro Plan could do little to stop daily and public showcases of violence, such as the *tirata*, the trademark duel of the *camorrista*, in which they would face each other, holding in one hand a knife and in the other a mirror, which they would use to shine sunlight in their enemy's eyes. Duels were fought at midday, when the sun was highest. Losers were slashed in the face and left with a *sfregio*, or cut face. In the early years of the twentieth century, slashed faces were still seen on some Mafiosi on the streets of Canada, a permanent reminder of a past defeat.

Members of the Picciotteria wore long, wide sideburns, and strutted about with rolling gaits, proud of doing little, because others tended to their needs. They sported *cammuffi*, or brightly coloured scarves with ornate fringes. The front of their hair was styled in a bouffant, described in archives as "like a butterfly" – like the hairstyle sported by Joe Musolino.
See also: **Black Hand, Giuseppe "Joe" Musolino.**

Pike, Gilbert: "The Pirate and the Princess" – Pike's pirate tale was truly romantic.

He sailed under Peter "The Pirate Admiral" Easton and settled near what is now Carbonear, Newfoundland, shortly after 1600, with the Irish Princess Sheila Na Geira, whose last name comes from the old Gaelic word that means "the beautiful."

Pike had rescued her from a Dutch privateer, and Newfoundland legend has it that the couple had the first white baby born on the island, although the Vikings may have beaten them to that distinction. The area where they lived is now a national park, where re-enactments of "the landing of the Pirate and the Princess" became a mainstay for folk festivals.
See also: **Charles Bellamy, Eric Cobham, Cupids, Peter Easton, High Island, Captain Kidd, Henry Mainwaring, Sheila Na Geira, Samuel Nelson, John Phillips, Pirates, Bartholomew "Black Bart" Roberts, John Williams.**

Pirates: Salty Stories – Newfoundland's pirate past lives on in place names, family names, and folklore. The *Heart's Desire* ravaged both sides of the Atlantic for years until 1620, when the ship was finally captured by a Newfoundland skipper and brought back to the island as a prize, and now the name survives as the moniker of a community. Happy Adventure, Heart's Content, Heart's Desire, and Black Joke Cove are other Newfoundland spots named after pirate ships. Turk's Gut was a favoured Newfoundland harbour for pirate ships, which got its name because settlers called pirates "Turks."

In the seventeenth century, it was common for seamen to take on the surnames of their captains, which helps explain why there are so many Pikes and Eastons in Newfoundland. Between wars, the seas teamed with pirates who might overwise had been employed in the British navy.

There's a widely circulated story that, during the eighteenth century, privateer Captain Kidd frequently visited the region of Oak Island off the shore of Nova Scotia to rest, relax, and to repair his ships. According to the folklore, Kidd's treasure pit there was almost two hundred feet deep and exceedingly tough to get at. It has been the subject of numerous excavations since 1795, costing millions of dollars, and has caused the death of at least ten treasure hunters. Fortune-seekers have included corporations and individuals, such as former American president Franklin D. Roosevelt, swashbuckling actor Errol Flynn, and westerns star John Wayne.

There are plenty of families on Canada's East Coast with personal pirate stories, like the Moore family of Prince Edward Island. In 1808, Dr. David Moore, with his wife and family – excepting their daughter, Mary – emigrated from Devonshire, England, to Massachusetts. They were loyal Britishers and, soon after their arrival in North America, decided they would be more comfortable in Charlottetown, Prince Edward Island.

After getting the family settled in Charlottetown, Moore went back to England and returned with his daughter, Mary, and a young man named Molyneaux. While crossing the ocean, they were attacked by pirates. Having some guns and ammunition on board, they tried to defend themselves. Mary's task was to hand the men gunpowder. However, they were finally captured and, but for the fact that Moore was a Freemason high up in the order, they would have, to use the piratical term, been obliged "to walk the plank." Instead the pirates placed them in an open boat, with a defective compass and Mary's feather bed. They took from them all their other possessions but some sterling silver teaspoons that Mary concealed in the front of her bodice. These are still owned by some of their descendants. After drifting for some time they landed at Newfoundland and later on succeeded in making their way back to Charlottetown, greatly to the relief of all the family. They afterwards moved out to Milton some seven miles from the town and there several of their descendants still reside.

See also: **Charles Bellamy, Henry Cobham, Cupids, Peter Easton, High Island, Bill Johnston, Edward Jordan, Captain Kidd, Mogul Mackenzie, Henry Mainwaring, Sheila Na Geira, Samuel Nelson, Oak Island, John Phillips, Gilbert Pike, Bartholomew "Black Bart" Roberts, John Williams.**

Plante, Pacifique "Pax" – *See* **Harry Davis.**

Popeyes: Hells Angels' Forerunners – This outlaw biker gang first appeared in Quebec in the early 1950s, around the same time the Satan's Choice popped up in Ontario.

Both clubs were loosely structured groups and attracted police attention by their manufacture of drugs like methamphetamine. Although the Satan's Choice were based in Oshawa, Ontario, they had a Montreal chapter, while the Montreal-based Popeyes had chapters in major Quebec urban centres.

The Popeyes packed a punch on the streets, collecting debts for the Dubois brothers and the Mafia. In December 1977, the American-based Hells Angels roared into Canada by absorbing the Popeyes, months after their rivals, the

Outlaws, absorbed half of Ontario's Satan's Choice members.

See also: **Yves "Le Boss" Buteau, Dubois Brothers, Hells Angels, Outlaws, Satan's Choice.**

Porter, Paul "Sasquatch": Biker Heavyweight – He has stature both figuratively and literally in the biker underworld, standing at least six-foot-four and weighing something upwards of four hundred pounds.

A founding member of the Rock Machine gang in Montreal, he survived a couple of murder attempts in the six-year war with the Hells Angels that began in 1994. Once, his life was saved only because he was wearing a tent-sized bulletproof vest.

Despite his massive size, he had a reputation for being able to keep a low profile, and also as an intelligent and even-tempered negotiator. His verbal skills were put to the test in 2000, which began with him working to establish the upstart Rock Machine as a national gang. He sponsored its Kingston, Ontario, chapter and became its inaugural president.

By October 2000, he was a key negotiator for the Rock Machine as they announced a truce

Paul "Sasquatch" Porter and Maurice "Mom" Boucher

with the Hells Angels. Porter and other members of the Rock Machine sat across a Montreal restaurant table from Hells Angels, making champagne toasts over seafood and pasta.

By December 2000, the U.S. Bandidos gang – with some five thousand members in more than ten countries – absorbed the Rock Machine. The dream of expansion seemed to be coming true, although under a different name, as Porter was the Rock Machine representative at Luxembourg for talks with Bandidos from around the world.

However, later that month, Porter shocked police and the outlaw biker world as well when he defected to the rival Hells Angels and was installed as president of the Ontario Nomads. He was perhaps the most surprising – and significant – of the 168 bikers who patched over to the Hells Angels in December 2000. Up until that point, Ontario had no Hells Angels chapters.

Before leaving for his new gang, Porter wrote an Internet note to his old Rock Machine comrades: "Hello to all the RMMC [Rock Machine Motorcycle Club]. I wish you all the best with your new colours. 'Bye my brothers."

See also: **Maurice "Mom" Boucher, Hells Angels, Dany Kane, Nomads, Rock Machine, Thanksgiving Summit.**

Pozza, Michel: Mob Money-man – There are plenty of people willing to do violence for the Mob, but Pozza brought something much more rare and valuable – brains.

More specifically, Pozza was extremely bright with money.

Pozza was born in the non-Mob city of Trento, north Italy, on August 22, 1925, and attended university. His specialty was finances, and he was considered like a son to old Montreal Sicilian boss Luigi Greco back in the 1950s when Montreal's Sicilian and Calabrian mobsters were able to work together.

He moved freely about the Montreal Mob's inner circle, and attended the marriage of Paolo Violi and Grazia Luppino in Hamilton on July 10, 1965, when Montreal bosses Vic Cotroni and Greco both played a part in the ceremonies. After Greco's death, Pozza's advice was sought after and respected by the Calabrian-born Cotroni. The Quebec organized-crime probe of 1974 said that Pozza was one of Cotroni's three financial men, along with Willie Obront and Irving Ellis. By 1976, Pozza had risen to be the family's financial *consigliere*, or trusted adviser.

Pozza's skills were by now recognized internationally. Salvatore Catalano of the Bonanno family introduced him to Vito Ciancimino, the former mayor of Palermo, Sicily, in 1979. They met in Mondello, near Palermo, where the two allegedly discussed drug trafficking.

On November 16, 1980, Pozza was photographed at the posh Hotel Pierre in New York City, in the middle of high-ranking Mafiosi guests at the wedding of Giuseppe "Pino" Bono. Other guests included high-ranking members of the Ciaculli Mafia family of Palermo, who had strong connections to organized-crime groups in Italy, including the Cammorra of Naples.

When the Cotroni family split into Sicilian and Calabrian factions in the early 1980s, no one felt the heat more than Pozza. He was from

Michel Pozza

neither group, and chose to go with the Sicilians. It was the smart, percentage move, as befitted a money-man, since the Sicilians were moving most of the money, and they seemed best set for the future.

Naturally, this angered the Calabrians around Cotroni, who tried to pull Pozza over to their side. Pozza sensed something was wrong in the fall of 1982. He would drive his grey Audi past his house on rue Desjardins in Mt. Rolland, a town fifty kilometres north of Montreal, then pull a U-turn and circle back. It was as if he was looking for someone hiding in the shrubs or bushes outside his home, ready to jump out and attack him.

He seemed to spend a lot of time then with union people, especially in the garment industry. In the late summer of 1982, intense police surveillance of Pozza was halted because of tight manpower. Perhaps Pozza was nervous that fall because he realized he would have to be protected by his wits, not by police officers.

The Cotronis kept pushing him to deal with them exclusively, but Pozza didn't seem to be budging. As he left one meeting, Cotroni's younger brother Frank muttered to his hit man, Réal Simard, that, "Something has to be done about him." Simard, who was eager to score points with his boss, interpreted this to mean "kill him."

Pozza hadn't realized things had gone so wrong when, on the night of September 27, 1982, he shared a meal with Frank Cotroni and Simard. His wife, France, was in Florida, and he was free for the evening. When the dining was done, Simard drove immediately to Pozza's home and hid in the bushes. When Pozza wheeled home around 2.30 a.m., Simard fired a .22 into his head, killing him at age fifty-seven.

Police naturally searched Pozza's files in the credit-union office on Papineau Avenue in Montreal, where he was secretary-treasurer. There, they turned up documents linking Pozza to Palermo's corrupt former mayor, Vito Ciancimino. In Pozza's house, police found bank reports showing Ciancimino's sons had transferred millions of dollars in illicit funds from Italy to Canada. The Ciancimino boys, Giovanni and Sergio, had flown to Canada to handle his father's affairs, since their father was afraid to fly. Vito Ciancimino had invested $2.6 million into Montreal real estate, including a south-suburban shopping centre and a Maisonneuve Street apartment building.

Also in Pozza's papers was a copy of a secret Quebec government study on the possibility of legalized gambling casinos in Quebec.
See also: **Frank "Santos" Cotroni, Vincenzo "Vic the Egg" Cotroni, Willie Obront, Réal Simard.**

Project Gyakuzuki: No Cold Comfort – *Gyakuzuki* means knockout punch in Japanese, which is the optimistic name police gave one of their projects in the late 1990s. Police in Nunavut in the late 1990s found the Hells Angels' Sherbrooke chapter had penetrated the Far North marijuana market. In the end, it was the authorities who took it on the chin, as the case fell apart due to lack of evidence.
See also: **Hells Angels.**

Purple Gang: Worst of the Worst – Their control over the Detroit underworld began in 1918 when the State Prohibition Referendum banned alcohol in Michigan. With that law, Detroit held the dubious honour of being the first major American city to test the dry waters, and the Purple Gang were poised to tap its potential.

Brothers Abe, Ray, Joe, and Izzy Bernstein grew up in a poor section on Detroit's east side, and formed a street gang who terrorized local merchants. Legend has it that one of these shopkeepers complained, "These boys are not like other children of their age. They're tainted, off-colour."

"Yes," a second shopkeeper supposedly agreed. "They're rotten, purple like the colour of bad meat. They're a purple gang."

They graduated to hijacking, extortion, armed robbery, and rum-running, after Michigan passed its dry law in 1918. Driving cars with false floorboards and second gas tanks, they headed south of the Michigan border to Toledo, Ohio, where booze was not only plentiful but legal.

When Prohibition spread across the United States in 1920, Windsor, Ontario, found itself an underworld funnel, as it was separated from Detroit only by the slow-moving Detroit River. By some estimates, three-quarters of all liquor smuggled throughout the United States during Prohibition first passed through Windsor.

The Purple Gang was so known for violence that even Chicago boss Al Capone gave them a wide berth, reasoning it was better business to buy Canadian whisky from the Purple Gang than risk their rage.

Their careers were finally ended when the brothers were given life sentences without parole for murder, to be served in Marquette prison in Michigan's upper peninsula.

Quadeville, Ontario: Caponeville – Local legend has it that members of the Al Capone Chicago Mob used to hide out in a cabin on a hill just outside this secluded community, about 150 kilometres west of Ottawa.

The cars that pulled up to the cabin in the 1940s were particularly fancy in a hamlet where a pickup truck was considered just fine. Visitors to the cabin often wore smart suits instead of the standard garb of plaid shirts and jeans.

The well-dressed men in the cabin kept to themselves, and one day in 1952, they were suddenly gone, leaving behind a bill for lumber at Quadeville's only store. A local merchant drove to Toledo, Ohio, where he had heard that one of the former cabin resident had relatives.

When he got there, a state trooper advised him to forget about collecting the money he was owed, and to get out of town quickly instead. "That guy is a gangster, and if you hang around, you might as well consider yourself dead," the police officer warned.

If there had been gangsters hiding out in the cabin in the early 1950s, it certainly wasn't Capone, who died in 1947 of a heart attack brought on by syphilis. Back in Quadeville, local kids explored the abandoned cabin, and reported finding an underground tunnel, located behind a bogus fireplace.
See also: **Moose Jaw Capone Tunnels, Rocco Perri, Sainte-Pierre and Miquelon.**

Quesnel, Serge: Sold Out Angels – In 1989, when he was nineteen, he requested that he be allowed to serve a two-year theft charge in a federal institution rather than a provincial facility. A big reason for his decision was education, which Quesnel craved. Quesnel wanted access to the "teachers" in the Donnaconna Penitentiary outside Quebec City – big-time criminals who could speed up his progress in the underworld.

Quesnel, who had teardrops tattooed under his eyes, ingratiated himself with the Hells Angels while behind bars, and when he was released, he killed five people for *les hells* in Quebec, although he liked to note that all of his victims were involved in the underworld. He then sold out the Angels for a payment of $500 a week for fifteen years, tax-free.

Le Soleil newspaper shocked its readers in 1995 with provocative photos of his stripper girlfriend visiting him in a police station after he turned informer. The Canadian Press wire service gasped, "A police station has turned into a pleasure palace for a key witness in a Hells Angels trial who has taken drugs and had sex with his girlfriend while under police protection."
See also: **L'Association des témoins spéciaux du Québec, Hells Angels, Nomads, Richard "Rick" Vallée.**

Al Capone's suspected cabin, Quadeville, Ontario

Interior of the cabin at Quadeville

R

Racco, Domenic: Fallen Son – On the last day of his life, December 9, 1983, the son of respected Toronto 'Ndrangheta boss Mike Racco was frantic. The panicky, nervous tone to his voice was a far cry from the normal, cocky demeanour of the man who had once been touted as the future leader of the Toronto 'Ndrangheta, or Calabrian Mafia. Domenic was certainly no stranger to police, and the man they knew was confident and aggressive, not afraid of police or attention.

Anyone close to old Mike Racco would be noted by police, but Domenic brought enormous unwanted attention to himself – and his father's operations – through his own actions. His history was one of privilege and rashness. In 1971, he had opened fire with a pistol on three youths at a suburban Toronto plaza in a dispute over a cigarette. He then fled to the United States, and returned in a chartered aircraft only after police launched a relentless series of raids in Toronto's Italian community. He was

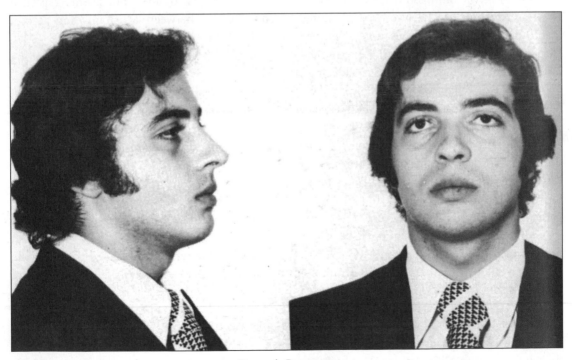

Domenic Racco, 1971

twenty-one then, and his future now included a ten-year sentence for three counts of attempted murder.

While behind bars, he enjoyed the status and protection that came with being Mike Racco's only son. He habitually sat at the head of any table in the prison, because he regarded himself a leader, and others obviously felt the same way. The Metro Toronto Police intelligence squad wrote in 1975 that he was "being groomed to become a major Mafia leader."

In 1976, a report by the federal Solicitor-General's Department said considerable influence had been brought to bear by politicians and prominent members of Toronto's Italian community to try to obtain Racco's release from prison. Meanwhile, his father arranged for mobsters to visit him each week while he was in prison.

In November 1976, two U.S. citizens from Albany, New York, were given penitentiary terms after they were found guilty of conspiring with Domenic Racco – while he was a convict in Collins Bay Penitentiary near Kingston, Ontario – to wound Tony Commisso, his brother-in-law, by shooting him in the legs. Racco wanted Commisso shot in the legs because he believed Commisso had co-operated with police in their investigation of the shopping plaza shootings. Police said Racco had warned that anyone who tried to testify against him would not make it to the courtroom.

During his final days in prison, at the minimum-security Frontenac Institution, he was sometimes seen driving a late-model Lincoln Continental in the Kingston area, practising for his driver's-licence test.

Upon his release from prison, he became both a cocaine dealer and a frequent user, and was often seen in the bars and restaurants of Toronto's trendy Yorkville area, where some of the clientele were heavy cocaine users. He wore his hair long, drove a white Cadillac, and split his nights between the family's home above their bakery on St. Clair Avenue West and that of his girlfriend in the west end of Toronto.

He was proud of the muscles he developed lifting weights in prison, and maintained his reputation as a hot-tempered individual who would retaliate violently against what he considered to be the smallest slight.

However, with the death of his father to cancer in 1980, Domenic's charmed status in the underworld evaporated. That explained the nervous tone to his voice in conversations intercepted by police during the late months of 1983. Those tapes showed that he was desperately trying to raise more than $500,000 by mortgaging his family's business to pay his drug tab. A trust company told him that the money could not be advanced for several months, and so Racco proceeded to mortgage a vacant lot for $21,000 and borrowed an additional $20,000 from two of his brothers-in-law.

The wiretaps indicated Racco was on edge as he was pressed for money by Domenic Musitano, Hamilton scrap-dealer and mobster, who made it clear to Racco that he had run out of patience over an outstanding debt.

On October 31, 1983, police intercepted a conversation between Musitano and Racco, which included this conversation;

Racco: Listen, we're trying to get that thing cashed.

Musitano: How long is it going to take?

Racco: It's just a matter of them at the bank. . . . You got to have a little patience. . . . I would have lost my patience already. . . . You got more patience than I got.

Later in the conversation, Musitano said, "It's gone real beyond patience now."

Racco replied, "I know. I can feel the heat. You're steaming."

On November 11, they talked again on the telephone, and Musitano asked Racco, "How are you coming with that thing, then?"

"I got it," Racco replied. "It needs to be changed. It's a matter of $550,000."

As Racco pleaded for more time, small-time hood William Rankin was being released on mandatory supervision from Millhaven Penitentiary in Kingston, Ontario. While serving a three-year prison term for robbery and being unlawfully at large, Rankin had met Musitano's brother, Anthony, who had begun a life sentence in January 1983, for a series of bombing incidents in Hamilton between 1976 and 1980.

Rankin got out of prison on December 7, 1983, and was met by Peter Majeste, twenty-three, a friend who later testified in court that he and Rankin planned a life of crime together trafficking in drugs. They drove to a motel about three kilometres from the prison, celebrating Rankin's release with two women and a generous supply of hashish oil and liquor.

That night, Domenic Musitano and Racco met in the coffee shop of the Holiday Inn in Oakville, Ontario. Unknown to both men, they were followed into the hotel by a plainclothes officer from Hamilton-Wentworth Regional Police, who had heard about two murder contracts, but didn't know who the targets were or when the killings were supposed to take place.

On the morning of December 9, 1983, Racco picked up a cheque for $21,506.97, the proceeds of a mortgage on a vacant lot the family owned near the bakery. After leaving the lawyer's office, Racco went to a nearby branch of the National Bank of Canada and cashed the cheque. He also obtained a certified cheque in his own name for $8,000.

That night, he signed in at RCMP headquarters in Toronto at 8:48 p.m. as part of the conditions for bail on a charge he was facing of conspiring to traffic in cocaine.

At 10 a.m. the next day, Racco's body was spotted by a passenger on a GO commuter bus en route to Milton from Toronto, in a field north of Derry Road, two kilometres east of Trafalgar Road in the town of Milton.

Racco was dressed in well-cut and expensive brown slacks and a sports jacket. He had on two gold necklaces, a ring on the little finger of his left hand. There was $111.76 in his pockets, and

three bullets in his head and two in his heart. He was thirty-two years old.

One theory for his murder was that he was "poaching" on drug-trafficking territory claimed by Domenic Musitano in Hamilton.

The Musitanos weren't about to explain. Anthony Musitano, thirty-eight, and William Rankin, thirty-three, each pleaded guilty to murder conspiracy and were each given twelve-year prison terms. Musitano's nephew, Giuseppe Avignone, twenty-three, was sentenced to five years after pleading guilty to playing a role in the conspiracy, while Domenic Musitano, forty-eight, pleaded guilty to being an accessory after the fact and received a six-year term.

Graham Court and Dennis Monaghan, both of Hamilton, were each convicted of first-degree murder, but their convictions were overturned on appeal. Their new trial was derailed when Justice Stephen Glithero of Ontario Court (General Division) accused police and prosecutors of tampering, negligence, and "flagrant and intentional misconduct."

The Ontario Provincial Police investigated the accusations, and issued a press release on April 3, 1998, which stated the force couldn't find any evidence of police misconduct, and also could find no evidence of any attempt by prosecutors to obstruct justice.

See also: Michele "Mike" Racco, Domenic Musitano, 'Ndranghcta, John "Johnny Pops" Papalia.

Racco, Michele "Mike": Respected Baker – The 1980 funeral for the baker who ran a shop on St. Clair Avenue West in Toronto was one of the largest in the history of the city's underworld. When he died at age sixty-six after surgery for cancer, thousands turned out to pay their respects.

Aside from fluffy bread rolls and to-die-for bread, Racco was considered *capo crimini*, or "boss of bosses," in Toronto's Calabrian Mafia. His influence extended well into the United States, according to informer Cecil Kirby, a biker who did dirty work for the Calabrian Mob.

Racco sat atop a fifty-member Mob family in Metro Toronto, which was part of the Siderno group from southern Italy. American intelligence officers said the Siderno mobsters were recruited by the traditional Sicilian Mob for manpower when some of their own sons refused to become involved with criminal activity. Police speculated that, once the Siderno Mob saw there was big money available for illicit activities, they began branching out for themselves. Racco's crime group became known by police as the Siderno Group, because most of its members came to Canada in the 1950s from the Siderno area.

Racco was born on December 12, 1913, in Siderno Marina, a small town in the southern Italian province of Calabria. Italian police said he was already a member of the Calabrian Mafia when he migrated to Canada in 1952.

After a short period at Thunder Bay, he moved to Toronto and started his bakery store on St. Clair Avenue West at Nairn Avenue. The business prospered, and the bakery became a landmark in the predominantly Italian district. In the late 1970s, he added on a coffee shop and an ice-cream parlour.

Racco was installed in Toronto as part of the Stefano Magaddino clan, but after the Buffalo don's death in 1974, he established ties with the Violi brothers of Montreal. He also had connections with Toronto mobster Paul Volpe, but the two had a falling out for some reason in the mid-1960s. Things around Racco were always a little fuzzy to police, which was the way he wanted them. When Racco-associated bakeries were hit in the 1960s with a string of bombings, police first thought there was a fight underway for underworld control in Toronto. Later, police adjusted their theories and concluded that Racco was bombing his own stores for insurance money to help finance underworld operations.

Late one night, he was almost caught with counterfeit money when police went to his bakery. They found a bundle of $25,000 in counterfeit bills on the sidewalk beneath the window of his bedroom over the bakery, and could only report the incident as found money.

In 1962, La Camera di Controllo (board of control) of the Ontario 'Ndrangheta included Michele Racco, Rocco Zito, Salvatore Triumbari, a Downsview soft-drink bottler, and Filippo Vendemini, a shoe-store owner.

Racco was never convicted of a crime in Canada, although he had convictions for a number of minor offences in Italy as a young man. He simply laughed when a *Globe and Mail* reporter told him the police regarded him as a leader of the Toronto Mafia. He volunteered to let the reporter spend a day working with him in the bakery and coffee shop and then decide for himself. "That would be a day in the life of this so-called Mafia leader," Racco scoffed.

"What is this Mafia?" Racco asked the reporter. "You really believe it exists?" His comments seem to be standard issue for mobsters of his generation. When "Johnny Pops" Papalia of Hamilton was asked a similar question, he had

Michele "Mike" Racco

Michele "Mike" Racco (right) and
Cosimo Stalteri (left) on Nairn Street

member, and there could easily have been another victim, but police said Racco was so disturbed about the massive police investigations that followed the Triumbari and Vendemini killings that he spared the life of a third person involved in the disfiguring, so that the police attention would cool down. Police also saw Racco's hand in the murder of Salvatore Palermiti, a visitor to Toronto from Siderno, killed in 1976 in an attempt to settle a dispute between two feuding underworld figures. Despite the strong police suspicions, no one was ever charged in any of the murders.

During his life, Racco turned up at all the right Mafia weddings, baptisms, and funerals, and was always seated in a place of honour. In death, his pallbearers included Rocco Zito and Racco's nephew Rocco Remo Commisso.

See also: Rocco Remo and Cosimo Commisso, Cecil Kirby, Giacomo Luppino, 'Ndrangheta, Domenic Racco.

replied, "What's organized crime?" while Vic Cotroni of Montreal had queried someone bold enough to question him, "What is the Mafia? I made my money in clubs and in gambling. All the rest is nothing but talk."

Police certainly believed the Mafia existed, seeing Racco as a planner, arranger, and adviser who was frequently consulted by immigrant members of the Calabrian Mafia and other Mafia organizations across Canada and the United States. He was also in frequent contact with senior members of the Calabrian Mafia in Italy.

They say he often sought the advice of Mafia leaders in Calabria, who regarded the Toronto organization as an overseas branch and who authorized him to sanction organized-crime murders in the Toronto Italian community.

Racco sanctioned three such murders, according to the police. These were the shooting deaths of his co-leaders of the Ontario 'Ndrangheta, Salvatore Triumbari, killed in 1967, and Filippo Vendemini, killed in 1969. Both Triumbari and Vendemini were slain because of their involvement in the ritual disfigurement of a fellow Calabrian Mafia

Radisson, Pierre-Esprit: Fur-Trading Double-Crosser – In the seventeenth century he was considered an outlaw with a price on his head by the government of New France, although he was considerably more popular with the English government.

The English were happy to deal with him and his partner, Sieur des Groseilliers, because of their access to rich fur-trading routes. He and Groseilliers founded the Hudson's Bay Company to further English interests.

He was about thirteen or fourteen when he arrived in Canada in May 1651 with his family and settled in Trois-Rivières on the north shore of the St. Lawrence, upriver from Quebec. About a year after his arrival, he was captured by the Iroquois while duck hunting, and treated like an adopted member of the Iroquois tribe. Eventually, he escaped to the Dutch trading post in New Amsterdam, now New York.

When he made his way back to New France, he found the colony's rules stifling. He knew he was forbidden to go upriver without the

Radisson meets the Indians in a Winter Camp (C.W. Jefferys, National Archives of Canada)

supervision of one of the government's men and a priest, but he balked at this and went into the woods anyway. "We were Cesars, being nobody to contradict us," he wrote in his journal.

He travelled through the area that is now the states of Wisconsin and Minnesota, despite strict laws against trading without a licence. He acted as a spy against the English, then double-crossed the French and arrived in England with furs in 1684, where he was entertained by the King and Duke of York.

Within three years, in 1687, his fortunes suffered yet another reversal, as he was brought back from Fort York (later York Factory), at the mouth of the Hayes River, to England as a prisoner amidst accusations of illegal trading. This turned out to be a lucky break, as Pierre Lemoyne d'Iberville of New France had just

been raiding Hudson Bay, and had captured the English posts at Fort York. If he had captured Radisson, he almost certainly would have sent him to the gallows for previous double-crosses.

Instead, Radisson was acquitted of the charges against him in England. He lived out his life there, although he no longer had any support in court after the fall of James II.
See also: **Coureurs de Bois, Sieur des Groseilliers.**

Rat Portage: Political Rat's Nest – The north-western Ontario rail town of Kenora was known as Rat Portage back in the 1880s, when it had a reported thirty-six saloons and forty-eight residences, and was home to characters like Boston O'Brien the Slugger, Patsy Roach, Al Mulligan the Bad Man, Charlie Bull-Pup, and Black Jim Reddy of Montana.

Not surprisingly, Rat Portage had a rough-and-ready reputation as a bootleggers' paradise, whose prime trade was helping rail workers forget their thirst and boredom.

What was surprising was that it also had three sets of police (Manitoba, Ontario, and federal) and dual Ontario and Manitoba jails, magistrates, justices of the peace, constables, and courthouses.

The heavy police presence – and dramatically low police efficiency – came because both Ontario and Manitoba claimed Rat Portage to be in their territory. Manitoba granted liquor licences to several hotel and wholesale outlets, and Ontario magistrates refused to recognize the legality of these licences.

Soon, constables from both provinces were busy arresting each other while criminals involved in gambling and bootlegging went about their illegal business. A newspaper reporter at the time wrote: "Dominion Commissioner McCabe with two policemen, Ontario Magistrate Burdon with twenty-five policemen and Stipendiary Magistrate Brereton with fifteen policemen acting on behalf of Manitoba have been arresting each other all day."

Things only got worse when the Ontario government lured some of the local gamblers and bootleggers, including the character known as Boston O'Brien the Slugger, into the fray with the lure of free whisky and pay as special constables. Prisoners arrested on the order of one magistrate were sprung free by men who claimed they were upholding the rights of the rival province. Meanwhile, police on both sides worried that the telegraph wires were tapped, and everyone but the criminals had to shudder when a gang descended on one of the Rat River jails and set it on fire, after releasing the prisoners.

Finally, the governments of Ontario and Manitoba worked out a joint agreement for the administration of the hamlet, leaving the final decision to the Privy Council of England, which ruled in 1884 that Rat Portage and the criminals inside it fell under Ontario's jurisdiction.

Red Deer: Biker Bash – This central Alberta city advertises itself as "Alberta's trading and distribution centre," and for good reason. There are more than a million people living within a 160-kilometre radius and local merchants have no business tax and the lowest overall taxes in the country.

It's just a ninety-minute drive to either Calgary or Edmonton, which helps explain why the Hells Angels were attracted to set up shop in the city of 60,000 on July 23, 1997, absorbing the local Grim Reapers club. The bikers celebrated with bear hugs, kisses, and whacks on the back, while Det. Greg Park of the Calgary police force's intelligence unit moaned, "It's the first day of the rest of our lives."

Community leaders called for businesses to boycott the Angels, but some, like one liquor-store owner, put up a sign saying, "Welcome Hells Angel! Who is causing trouble?"

There were some three hundred Angels and associates at the patch-over ceremony, which included a bar and a band in the hotel and plenty of roast beef, shrimp, crab, beer, and wine. Some Grim Reapers were so excited to get the death's-head patches of the winged skull that they sewed them on by hand in the Waskasoo ballroom at 1 a.m., rather than waiting for daylight and a professional tailor.

The patches were from a tailor in Voralbergh, Austria, and after he got his, Kevin "Critter" Press, formerly of the Calgary Grim Reapers, gushed to a reporter, "I feel like I'm walking three inches off the ground."

The previous Sunday, many of the city's churchgoers said special prayers about the arrival of the Angels. "Some pastors were contacted by the RCMP and asked to cover them in prayer and just pray for the whole situation," said Pastor Matt Kitchener of the First Baptist Church. There would be more to pray about in November 1999, when the Angels set up a chapter of the elite Nomads in Red Deer.
See also: **Calgary Hells Angels, Diefenbunker.**

Redliners: Wally's Private Army – Police dubbed this biker gang the Redliners when an officer noticed a member wearing a Redliner Racing jacket.

Exactly what the gang called themselves was never that clear.

They were formed in the spring of 1995 by disgruntled members of the Spartans gang in Winnipeg and had eighteen members and twenty associates or possible prospects.

They were so close to Walter Stadnick, then the Hells Angels national president, during his time in Winnipeg that the entire gang was considered Hells Angels' associates. Because this group was formed under the direction of tight-lipped Stadnick, virtually every action was shrouded in secrecy.

The group adopted colours consisting of a deaths'-head skull encircled in flames, but these colours were not worn publicly. However, club members routinely wore a similar insignia on sweatshirts.

Their strength by the end of 1995 was twenty-four members and sixty more associates. By June 1997, the gang was on its last legs, as members were increasingly disorganized, and several of them were fettered by clauses by the courts that forbid association with criminals, as well as by curfews.

See also: **Los Brovos, Spartans, Wolodumyr "Walter" "Nurget" Stadnick.**

Red Zone: Slaughter in the Streets – Outlaw bikers in the 1990s and early 2000s called Quebec "the red zone" because the violence was so hot there. A study by Montreal criminologist Pierre Tremblay concluded that the nickname was as apt as it was colourful. Tremblay found that, of 859 murders in Quebec between 1970 and 1986, 118 were biker-related. That worked out to 13.7 per cent of the provincial murder rate. Ironically, that was during the bikers' "peace time," before the war began in 1994 with the Rock Machine that killed some 165 people – including an eleven-year-old boy and two

prison guards – and caused three hundred serious injuries.

See also: **Michel Auger, Daniel Desrochers, Diane Lavigne, Nomads, Rock Machine.**

Rivard, Lucien: Political Poison – The story about how the heroin trafficker Rivard escaped from Bordeaux Jail in 1965 wasn't true, but it was so good that people loved to tell it anyway. As the story went, the mobster persuaded guards into allowing him to water the prison ice rink, even though it was a spring day when the temperature outside was 4°C.

What was true was that Rivard was helped out of jail by a Bordeaux worker, and that he scaled the prison wall with a garden hose. It was also true that Rivard destroyed the career of a federal justice minister and nearly sank Lester Pearson's Liberal government in one of the great scandals of Canadian political history.

Rivard, a squat, strongly built man, was convicted in 1933, at age seventeen, of breaking into a storage shed. By the early 1950s, he had fallen into the heroin business, after setting up a casino in Cuba, and he also ran guns for Fidel Castro's rebels before being imprisoned, then expelled.

Back in Quebec in the late 1950s, Rivard opened the Domaine Ideal, a beach resort in Laval, which the *Globe and Mail* described as an ideal spot for those "with strong appetites for wenching and drinking." When not tending to those appetites, some patrons were involved in Rivard's drug-smuggling and arms-trafficking operations.

Rivard was a major figure in the Montreal underworld, and looked the part in expensive suits and pointy shoes, often rubbing shoulders with Giuseppe "Pep" Cotroni, brother of the city's leading Mafiosi, Vic Cotroni.

Rivard's fortunes changed in October 1963, when U.S. agents in Laredo, Texas, nabbed drug-runner Michel Caron as he tried to enter from Mexico with thirty-five kilograms of heroin. Caron opened up to police, implicating

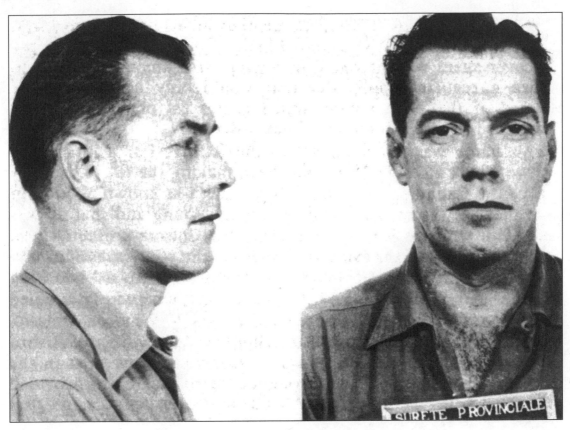

Lucien Rivard, 1952

Rivard and a mobster from New York's Gambino crime family.

Word of Caron's confession reached all the way to U.S. Attorney General Robert Kennedy, who called his Canadian counterpart to make sure Caron's family would be taken to a safe house.

Meanwhile, Rivard was arrested, and his efforts to get bail by contacting Liberal contacts entangled the Pearson government. Pierre Lamontagne, the lawyer hired by the U.S. government, was offered $20,000 by an assistant to Immigration Minister René Tremblay to secure Rivard's release on bail. Lamontagne was also pushed by an aide to federal Justice Minister Guy Favreau, and by Guy Rouleau, a Member of Parliament and Pearson's parliamentary secretary.

The RCMP looked into it, but concluded there wasn't enough evidence to lay charges. Through it all, Rivard remained in prison.

However, in November 1964, the opposition Conservatives learned of the affair and MP Erik Nielsen led a ruthless campaign against Favreau, who had been considered a rising star in the Pearson cabinet.

Things only got worse for the Liberals when Rivard escaped the Bordeaux jail with another inmate in March 1965. Outside, they hijacked a car. Rivard gave the driver money to take a cab home, and later called him to tell him where to find his car. While Rivard was on the lam, he annoyed authorities with a series of letters. In one, mailed on March 30 to Prime Minister Pearson, he philosophized, "Life is short, you know. I don't intend to be in jail for the rest of my life." In a missive to his prison warden, he boasted, "I've never taken a penny from someone poorer than me."

His time on the run lasted just four months, but the scandal was enough to push Favreau to resign. Pearson regrouped by recruiting three new leading Quebec candidates – Jean Marchand, Gérard Pelletier, and Pierre Trudeau.

The escapade made Rivard something of a folk hero, celebrated in a song titled "The Gallic Pimpernel."

Favreau would die in 1967, and many who knew him said his health collapsed at the strain of being made a scapegoat. "Guy Favreau was the most brilliant Quebec MP of the time," said Judge Jules Deschênes, who was Favreau's lawyer during the affair. "I'm certain the scandal killed him."

"The harshness of politics has destroyed no better man," mourned Tom Kent, then an adviser to Pearson.

The Dorion Inquiry was held to investigate how Rivard managed to escape from prison. It didn't tell of how he was aided in his escape by a prison worker. However, it did find that he had many backers among federal Liberal organizers in Quebec, although Rivard never divulged names of his alleged political pals.

He served nine years of a twenty-year sentence in the United States, and his wife, Marie, wrote him daily. He lived quietly in Laval until his death February 3, 2002, at Montreal's Sacré Coeur Hospital. He was nearly blind at the time of his death at age eighty-six.
See also: **Giuseppe "Pep" Cotroni.**

Rizzuto, Nicolo "Nick": War Survivor – It was impossible to talk about the murder of Montreal Mafia boss Paolo Violi without mentioning Nick Rizzuto.

Rizzuto was likely out of the country when gunmen went into Violi's coffee bar on Jean Talon East on January 22, 1978, and shot him dead, using a traditional Italian *lupara* shotgun, with one barrel on top of the other. All of the men convicted of the contract killing had a connection to Rizzuto, but none mentioned his name to police.

It had been clear as things ever are in the Mafia that, since the early 1970s, either Rizzuto

or his Mob family rival, Violi, would be murdered. Violi had tried to get approval from the top level of the Bonnano family to kill Rizzuto, but was denied. Now it was Rizzuto's turn, and he was nothing if not patient. Both men wanted to head Montreal's underworld after Vic Cotroni, and neither would step aside gracefully.

From 1978 through 1981, more than twenty reputed mobsters and associates tied to Rizzuto and Violi were killed in Montreal and Italy. By 1982, all of the Violi brothers were dead, Vic Cotroni was dying of cancer, and Rizzuto was recognized as Montreal's new boss.

Rizzuto watched the gang war from afar – in a compound in Venezuela to be specific – where he had fled in the early 1970s.

Even if Rizzuto and Violi had liked each other – and there was no hint that they did – geography kept them from mixing well. Rizzuto was a traditional Sicilian Mafiosi, while Violi was a Calabrian 'Ndrangheta criminal, and neither man was flexible enough to coexist with his rival.

Nicolo "Nick" Rizzuto

Rizzuto was born on February 18, 1924, in Cattolica Eraclea, Agrigento, Sicily, the same dusty town as Giuseppe "Joe" LoPresti, who would move onto the same exclusive block as Rizzuto in Montreal. Nick's brother-in-law, Dominico Renda, was in turn the brother-in-law of LoPresti, meaning they married into the same family.

Around 1971, the Cuntreras, Caruanas, and Rizzutos began to set up a base in Venezuela, and they graduated into the ranks of the world's most sophisticated drug shippers and financiers, authorities believed.

After Violi's murder, Rizzuto was freer to come and go as he pleased in Montreal, and still maintained the compound in Caracas, which he saw as a safe haven. He had ties there with the Cuntrera-Caruana Sicilian Mafia family, which also had a Montreal base. His freedom was curbed when he was arrested in early 1988 by Venezuelan police on drug charges, and he was held in custody until February 1992.

When finally released, he began spending more time on exclusive Antoine-Berthelet Avenue in the posh Cartierville section of Montreal, where there were just four houses. Nick Rizzuto and his son Vito lived side by side, along with Vito's sister Maria and her husband, Paolo Renda, who had some gambling arrests on his record. The fourth house belonged to Giuseppe "Joe" LoPresti, a lieutenant in the Rizzuto family, whose role was to act as a "bridge" between the Sicilian and American Mafia families running drugs from Venezuela to Montreal to New York.

Nick Rizzuto's name was mentioned in the halls of Parliament in March 2001, as Anne McLellan, the Justice Minister, told the Commons that confidentiality rules prevented her from explaining why the Justice Department did not tell Immigration officials that an alleged Mafia hit man was living in Montreal.

The hit man, Gaetano Amodeo, was described by Italian prosecutors as a member of Sicily's Cattolica Eraclea Mafia clan, and was alleged to have murdered a German underworld figure in 1981 and played a role in the 1992 murder of a police investigator. Italian authorities had requested his arrest on January 10, 1999, but Canadian authorities did not move to scoop him up.

Stockwell Day, the Canadian Alliance party leader, asked why the RCMP ignored the request, when they had photographed him in April 1999 talking to Rizzuto. "The RCMP monitored his motions and even photographed him in the company of the head of the Montreal Mafia," Day said in Parliament. "How could the RCMP just take pictures of him rather than put handcuffs on him?" (In August 2001, a little over two years after he was photographed with Nick Rizzuto, Amodeo was sentenced to life in prison in Italy.)

See also: Giuseppe "Joe" LoPresti, Vito Rizzuto, Gerlando Sciascia, Paolo Violi.

Rizzuto, Vito: "Mediator" – Vito Rizzuto speaks French, English, Italian, and Spanish and rarely gives interviews in any of them.

However, the dapper Montrealer was in an uncharacteristically chatty mood with the press in December 2003, during a break from an impaired-driving case he was fighting in municipal court.

Speaking in English, he dismissed past statements by the RCMP, prosecutors, and the federal government that he was the head of an organized crime family as "nothing more than allegations."

He also told the *Montreal Gazette* that Revenue Canada got things wrong when he was described in a document presented in tax court that alleged he was "the godfather of the Italian Mafia in Montreal."

"I deny everything they say," he said.

He smiled when asked to describe himself professionally, then replied, "I'm the jack of all trades."

He put it another way while speaking in French to crime reporter Michel Auger, saying, "I'm a mediator. People come to me to solve disputes because they believe in me. They have respect in me."

Until his arrest in January 2004 for three gangland hits in New York in 1981, Rizzuto could be found on an almost daily basis at the Consenza Social Club, a grungy north-end Montreal coffee shop between a cheese shop and a tanning salon on Jarry Street, where he sipped coffee under a fading picture of the main square in Cattolica Eraclea, in Agrigento, Sicily, where he was born on February 21, 1946. One wall is also full of photographs of golf tournaments, a favourite past-time of Rizzuto.

His family, headed by father Nicolo "Nick" Rizzuto, reportedly moved to Canada when he was eight. Rizzuto said he travelled back to Sicily to work in construction when he was a young man.

Although the Cosenza was a decidedly modest venue, there were often $100,000 Mercedeses parked outside and Rizzuto often arrived at the wheel of his late-model white Jaguar. He was known as the "Dapper Don" in reference to his expensively tailored, form-fitting suits.

In arrest documents filed in January 2004, the FBI, U.S. Justice Department, and the New York Police Department didn't call him a "jack of all trades" or a "mediator," but rather a top-level Canadian mobster and sometime hit man, as they filed charges that threatened him with twenty years behind bars.

Others charged in a crackdown of the New York–based Bonanno crime family – described in the New York Post as a "Bonanno Bonanza" – included such colourfully named goodfellas in the United States as Patty Muscles, Mickey Boots, Mickey Bats, Baldo, and some two dozen others, who had been charged with everything from fixing baccarat games to murder for the Mob. One of the alleged informants was known in Mob circles as Good Looking Sal, who was born Salvatore Vitale, and who was underboss and brother-in-law to Bonanno leader, Joseph Massino.

Good Looking Sal told authorities that on May 5, 1981, he was a member of an elite, four-person hit team, along with Rizzuto, Gerlando "George from Montreal" Sciascia of Montreal, and a Canadian known to him only as Emanuel.

In a scene that was recreated in the film Donnie Brasco, starring Johnny Depp, Vitale said three members of the hit team hid in a closet of a social club, then burst out firing a hail of bullets that brought down Alphonse "Sonny Red" Indelicato, Philip "Lucky" Gicaonne, and Dominick "Big Trin" Trinchera.

Court documents also state Vitale was expected to testify that the triple homicide was allegedly ordered to resolve a Bonanno family conflict.

The next day, Rizzuto was photographed by investigators leaving his room at the Capri Motor Lodge in the Bronx, heading for a black sedan with Sciascia and Joseph Massino, who would emerge as the new godfather of the Bonanno family. Rizzuto and Sciascia returned to Montreal.

As the son of Montreal Mafia don Nicolo "Nick" Rizzuto, Vito was known to police well before the 1981 triple murders.

In 1972, he was convicted of attempting to set fire to a Montreal shopping plaza, and in 1986, he was acquitted on a drunk-driving charge.

On December 18, 1989, he was acquitted in Sept-Îles, Quebec, on charges of conspiring to import 32 tons of hashish and he was acquitted again on November 8, 1990, in Newfoundland of conspiring to traffic in 16 tons of hashish. Those charges were dropped after it was revealed that the RCMP had illegally wiretapped discussions between his lawyer and other defence lawyers involved in the case. After his 1990 acquittal, Rizzuto was uncharacteristically talkative, and quipped to a reporter, "One word can mean so much, especially when that word is acquittal."

In 1994, the RCMP arrested fifty-seven people in connection with a money-laundering scheme that included a plot to ship cocaine to Britain. Rizzuto was mentioned as a co-conspirator, but wasn't charged.

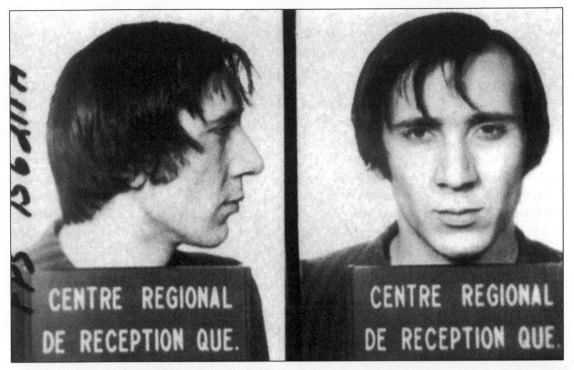

Vito Rizzuto

Vito Rizzuto (left) sits with Juan Ramond Fernandez

Vito Rizzuto

Vito Rizzuto walking

Also in 1994, Canadian police suspected him of trying to get his hands on some of the multi-billion-dollar fortune that was stashed away in Swiss bank accounts by the late Philippine president Ferdinand Marcos.

Canadian police suspected he had a mandate from members of the family of a now-deceased Filipino general – Severino Garcia Santa Romana, a close associate of the late dictator – to try to find some of Marcos's fortune on their behalf. Some estimates pegged the fortune that Marcos stashed overseas at as much as $40 billion.

Things were particularly hectic for him in 2001. That year, Revenue Canada described him as "the godfather of the Italian Mafia in Montreal," but he managed to avoid the potentially embarrassing media scrutiny of a trial when his lawyer, Paul Ryan, reached an out-of-court settlement in August 2001.

Revenue Canada had accused him of using middlemen to purchase penny stocks on the Alberta Stock Exchange and said he didn't report revenues – more than $1.5 million between 1986 and 1988 – from the investment. The government was seeking unpaid taxes plus interest, as well as more than $127,000 in penalties.

In civil court documents, Vito Rizzuto described himself as a businessman and provided his spacious home on Antoine-Berthelet Avenue, in the north end of the city, as a business address. His legal counsel said they had a strong case, but wanted to avoid a media circus.

A trial certainly would have been interesting. Federal documents indicated the government intended to focus heavily on Rizzuto's alleged ties to organized crime, including Maurice "Mom" Boucher of the Hells Angels biker gang.

According to Canadian investigators, Rizzuto created an organized-crime group called "the Consortium," which included the Hells Angels, West End Gang, Colombian cocaine cartels, and Mafiosi. The Consortium sought to put their energies into making money together rather than infighting.

Also in 2001, Rizzuto managed to avoid two murder plots to kill him at the Cosenza Social Club. While foiling the hits, police said that they found Rizzuto's enemies had armed themselves with an AK-47 automatic rifle, a .357 calibre magnum revolver, two 9-mm pistols, two bullet-proof vests, walkie-talkies, piles of ammunition clips, a .350 Magnum, and sticks of dynamite.

Despite all of the tensions on the streets and in the courtroom – or perhaps because of them – Rizzuto was an avid golfer, and often played in Montreal-area charity fundraisers. He lost a couple of golfing partners in the 1990s to a police sting into the laundering of drug money. His friend and schoolmate Valentino Morielli was convicted of conspiring to bring cocaine into Canada via Miami and the Cayman Islands, and another golf buddy, lawyer Joseph Lagana, was found guilty of money laundering.

The 1999 murder of his friend Sciascia made Rizzuto leery of New York, police say. That hit was ordered by the top level of the Bonanno family. Sciascia was considered the top Canadian in the Bonannos at the time of his murder.

After Sciascia's murder, Rizzuto started to appear in Ontario more frequently, and was in the Toronto area about four times a month, visiting relatives and planning business, as he frequented the area's finer restaurants and golf courses.

"He was looking in Ontario to explore opportunities for investment – any kind of investment," said author Antonion Nicaso, who has written several books on organized crime. "He has lots of money to invest."

His investments were made in Quebec, Ontario, Alberta, and even the former Northwest Territories, where he was interested in diamond mining.

Police said his Ontario interests ranged from a discount coffin business to an illegal multimillion-dollar bookmaking operation in Ottawa, Montreal, Toronto, Woodbridge, Mississauga, Bolton, and Hamilton, in which gamblers bet on major league baseball, the

NHL, and NBA games using the Internet, cellphones, Palm Pilots, Blackberry wireless devices, and storefronts.

In recent years, Rizzuto has gone to great pains to avoid setting foot in the United States, said Andrew Cedilot, a veteran organized crime reporter for *La Presse* newspaper in Montreal.

"He doesn't like the States," Cedilot said. "He doesn't know what they have on him. He goes to Mexico, Cuba, and the Dominican Republic to play golf, but never to the United States, even in transit. He'd pass through Toronto when going out of the country instead of going through the United States. He doesn't want to see a (U.S.) customs officer coming onto the plane and saying, 'We want you.'"

"His mentality is to think bigger – not to think locally," said Nicaso. "I don't think that there is anyone on the police radar (in Canada) like him."

See also: Maurice "Mom" Boucher, Alfonso Caruana, Giuseppe "Joe" LoPresti, Sabatino Nicolucci, Nicolo "Nick" Rizzuto, Gerlando Sciascia.

Roberts, Bartholomew "Black Bart": Eye for Talent – The Welsh pirate hit hard at the hamlet of Trepassy on the southern shore of Newfoundland in 1720, looting the community of provisions, then torching it.

Despite his hostility, there were many sailors in Newfoundland who welcomed him, and who warmed to his call of "Lads, who'll come with me and be a free man?" For pirates like Black Bart, captain of the *Royal Rover*, Newfoundland offered both a convenient stopover point and a deep talent pool for recruiting crewmen. Sailors knew they could make their fortunes with him, as he was extremely accurate in navigation, and prowled from West Africa to Brazil, from the Spanish Main of the Caribbean to Newfoundland's fishing grounds.

Much is known about life on his ships through articles recorded by Captain Charles Johnson, who noted that he liked democracy

(one sailor, one vote) and health insurance ($800 for arms or legs lost in service), and was a patron of the arts of a sort (fiddlers got Sundays off). Roberts cut a dashing figure in his white plumed hats and tailored clothes, flaming red-damask waistcoats and breeches. His pistols hung from silk sashes and, about his neck, he sported a conspicuous gold chain on which hung a diamond-inlaid gold cross. While his crews drank heavily, he was a teetotaller, who discouraged profanity and observed the Sabbath with regular services. His crews were also expected to say nightly prayers. Robbery of a crewmate meant a sailor's nose and ears would be split and he would be put ashore. Defrauding the crew of any money at all also meant a sailor would be put ashore. Sailors on the *Royal Rover* who persisted in swearing could expect a whipping.

He would not allow his crew to bring women or young boys aboard, feeling that this would create jealousy and thus disunity amongst his crew. However, the *Royal Rover*'s mate was John Walden, twenty-two, who shared Roberts's bed,

Bartholomew "Black Bart" Roberts

and was known by the rest of the crew as "Miss Nanny," slang at the time for a gay man.

Bart's motto was "A merry life and a short one," but he made it to about age forty, which was considerable longevity for a pirate of the time. Most were in their twenties. He died onboard ship in December 1721, when his *Royal Fortune* was caught off guard by the British navy off the Guinea coast. His mate, Walden, honoured his last wishes by throwing his body overboard, so that it would not be publicly hanged in a gibbet onshore, as was the custom with slain pirates. Walden lost a leg in the battle, but survived to be hanged onshore. The British navy captain who won the battle, Chaloner Ogle, looted the *Royal Fortune* of gold, then turned the rest of her cargo over to British authorities. He was knighted for his sea victory and later promoted to the rank of admiral.

See also: **Charles Bellamy, Henry Cobham, Cupids, Peter Easton, High Island, Bill Johnston, Edward Jordan, Captain Kidd, Mogul Mackenzie, Henry Mainwaring, Sheila Na Geira, Samuel Nelson, Oak Island, John Phillips, Gilbert Pike, John Williams.**

Rock Machine: Drug Wars – In the mid-1990s, the Hells Angels and the Rock Machine began fighting for control of Montreal's lucrative drug trade. For seven years, the gangs ambushed each other, set off bombs, and torched bars affiliated with the other gang. More than 160 people died, including innocent victims.

Weakened by the battle, the gang joined the larger U.S.-based Bandidos in December 2000.

See also: **Bandidos, Maurice "Mom" Boucher, Cazzetta Brothers, Dark Circle, Stéphane "Godasse" Gagné, Hells Angels, Dany Kane, Nomads, Paul Porter, Red Zone.**

Rondeau, Pierre: Murdered Prison Guard – On Monday September 8, 1997, the prison guard, along with fellow guard Robert Corriveau, pulled up in an empty prisoners' van for a coffee at a Tim Hortons doughnut shop near Bordeaux Jail in Montreal.

Hells Angels hit men Paul "Fon Fon" Fontaine and Stéphane "Godasse" Gagné had been waiting in a nearby bus shelter for someone from the jail to drop by. It didn't matter who that person was, as long as he or she

Rock Machine Canada

was a jail guard. Rondeau was simply the next convenient target, and when Fontaine saw him, he pumped several shots from his .357 revolver into the stranger. Gagné's semi-automatic 9 mm pistol jammed as he stood at the passenger door and, even when it did work, he was able only to wound and not kill Corriveau.

The Hells Angels followed up that attack with the murder of fellow Bordeaux guard Diane Lavigne, a mother of two. More than two thousand prison guards walked off their jobs in protest. Within two days, the province announced that guards could wear bulletproof vests and carry guns when they transported prisoners.

See also: **Michel Auger, Maurice "Mom" Boucher, Stéphane "Godasse" Gagné, Diane Lavigne, Nomads.**

Ross, Allan "The Weasel": West End Gang Leader – His ties weren't just to outlaw bikers, the Medellín cocaine cartel, the Montreal Mafia, or the Irish Mobs of Boston, although that was scary enough.

He also had a pipeline directly into the top ranks of the Royal Canadian Mounted Police (RCMP).

That became clear the week before December 1992, when Insp. Claude Savoie, forty-nine, took out his service revolver at RCMP headquarters in Ottawa, wrapped it in his jacket sleeve to muffle the noise, pressed the barrel to his head, and squeezed the trigger. The twenty-seven-year police veteran left no note.

The suicide came just before RCMP officers were about to confront the former RCMP drug-squad chief about his links to Ross, who headed the city's West End Gang. Savoie had headed the force's drug squad from 1989 to 1991, and was assistant director of the force's Criminal Intelligence Service.

Earlier that week, Savoie had heard he was going to be questioned by internal-affairs officers about allegations that he funnelled information through Mob lawyer Sydney

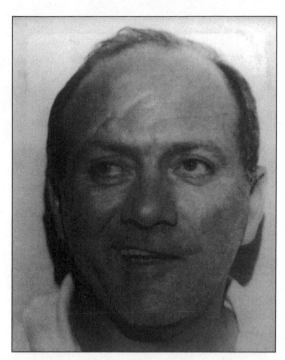

Allan "The Weasel" Ross

Leithman to Ross. Montreal detectives investigating the 1991 murder of Leithman questioned Savoie about three meetings he had with Leithman and Ross at Leithman's office building.

At the time, Ross was in a Florida prison after being convicted in the spring of 1992 for importing more than 22,000 pounds of cocaine and 300 tons of marijuana. He had been sentenced to three life terms, with no chance of parole.

His path to the Florida prison began in the 1960s, when he was in his twenties, and little more than an errand boy in Montreal's loosely knit West End Gang. He rose up to become a lieutenant to the gang's leader, Frank Peter "Dunie" Ryan, and his loyalty to Ryan was heartfelt. When Ryan was murdered on November 13, 1984, it took Ross just two weeks to track down and kill two of the men responsible for the hit.

He suspected that West End Gang member Edward Phillips also played a part in the Ryan murder. In March 1985, Phillips was about to get into his car when a hit man pumped several shots into his back, and a final shot into his skull. The gunman climbed onto the back of a motorcycle, driven by David Singer, another member of the West End Gang.

Singer moved to Florida to escape the police attention, but Ross had his doubts whether he could handle the pressure. Two West End Gang members were dispatched to silence him permanently.

Meanwhile, Ross had picked up Ryan's network and contacts, which included sending large shipments of cocaine to Europe, for distribution by the Sicilian Mafia.

When Ross was arrested in October 1991 in Fort Lauderdale, police said he offered an agent a $200,000 bribe, which was refused.

American law enforcement officials were troubled that Ross seemed to have a pipeline to police intelligence, including who was under investigation and the locations of investigating officers.

At the end of his drug-trafficking trial, Ross sucked on a candy as he heard himself sentenced to life imprisonment and a $10-million fine.

Next, he was put on trial for the Singer murder and conspiracy to traffic in cocaine. One government witness said Ross agreed to pay members of the Hells Angels $13,000 if they killed John Quitoni, a corrupt former New Jersey detective and Ross associate, who was now the prosecution's star witness.

He was acquitted of first-degree murder, sparing him the electric chair. However, he had two thirty-year-terms tacked on to the three life terms he was already serving.

See also: **Sydney Leithman, Gerald Matticks, Frank Peter "Dunie" Ryan, West End Gang.**

Ryan, Frank Peter "Dunie": West End Gang Founder – Things started rough for Dunie Ryan, and seemed to go downhill from there.

His father and namesake abandoned the family when Ryan was just three, and, by the age of sixteen, Ryan was a school dropout who regularly stole racks of garments from trucks and grabbed coats from the Montreal fur district.

By his early twenties, he had served two years in St. Vincent de Paul Penitentiary for theft with violence and, shortly after he got out, he was convicted of burglary and possession of stolen goods. The next year, 1965, he was free, but accidently killed a drunk with his Pontiac Bonneville convertible. The year 1966 saw no improvement. Ryan was convicted, along with four other Montrealers and a Boston gangster, for a bank robbery in Massachusetts.

He was paroled in December 1972 and married a beautiful redhead from the Gaspé named Evelyn Lemieux.

Ryan was now making a living robbing jewellery stores and loansharking, and exploring the narcotics business with a few friends. First he imported hashish, then he moved on to heroin and cocaine. By the late 1970s, his mostly Irish crew was called the West End Gang, and they made most of their money through hashish.

Anglophone sons of poor Irish families, the gang members used to inhabit the ramshackle

Frank Peter "Dunie" Ryan

streets of Pointe St. Charles and Griffintown, and were at the top level of Montreal organized crime in the 1970s, along with the Dubois brothers and the Italian Mafia.

Their strength was controlling the city's waterfront, which allowed them to smuggle large quantities of hashish and cocaine into the city. They were content to be wholesalers, supplying outlaw bikers and street gangs, and staying out of the battles for distribution turf.

It wasn't long before Dunie was rumoured to be worth $20 million. Perhaps the figure was inflated, but he was clearly rich. He was also disrespectful, both to the criminal and non-criminal worlds. When told that one of his group had offended the Mafia in the United States, Ryan reportedly said, "Mafia, pafia. If there's a war, we've got the IRA."

He was considerably more sensitive about insults directed toward him. Hughie McGurnaghan, a member of his own gang, suggested that Ryan had cheated him out of drug profits. Ryan hired Hells Angels hit man Yves "Apache" Trudeau to make an example of him, and McGurnaghan was blown up while stepping into his Mercedes in Westmount.

Ryan clearly didn't want to share his wealth with the Cotroni family or the Hells Angels, reportedly saying, "If your tap was flowing $100 bills, would you turn it off? I've got three hundred guys working for me. What are they gonna do?"

On November 13, 1984, Dunie was in his Montreal office at Nittolo's Jardin Motel, in St. Jacques Street West, which he owned, when he was approached by Paul April, a French-Canadian mobster. April told Ryan that he had an attractive young woman waiting for him in one of the hotel rooms. Ryan let his guard down and followed him into the room.

Inside was Robert Lelievre, another French-Canadian gangster, who waited with a shotgun. The plan was to tape Ryan to a chair and force him to say where he kept his money. Ryan swung a chair at them and Lelievre responded with a shotgun blast.

The killers bragged about the murder for about two weeks. Then on November 25 – twelve days after Ryan's murder – April, Lelievre, and two other men were blown up in a downtown apartment.

Ryan was forty-two when he died. He had once boasted to a girlfriend that he planned to "live fast, love hard, and die young." Considering his philosophy, it was a wonder he lasted as long as he did.

See also: **Gerald Matticks, Sydney Leithman, Allan "The Weasel" Ross, West End Gang.**

Ryan, Norman "Red": Captured in Literature – Red Ryan always had a hard time keeping his hands off of other people's things. He began his criminal career in 1907 at age twelve by stealing bicycles, and a year later, he found himself in reform school for stealing chickens. By 1914, Ryan was on his second prison term at Kingston Penitentiary when he was released to become a soldier. Wartime didn't change his stealing ways, and he spent much of his time overseas in lockup for robbing stores.

So it was really no great surprise to those who knew him when, in 1923, Ryan was in prison serving twenty-five years for a string of bank robberies in Hamilton. He impaled a jailor with a pitchfork when he and other inmates broke out of prison, and a young writer for the *Toronto Daily Star* was sent out to cover the story. The reporter, Ernest Hemingway, had been stripped of his byline because editors feared he was getting too big for his britches and considered himself too much of a writer.

The story offered a foreshadowing of what would become Hemingway's lean vivid prose, as well as introducing readers to Ryan, and includes this passage:

It was at ten o'clock yesterday morning that a great cloud of thick, yellow-white smoke began to pour from the barn just inside the east wall of the penitentiary. It was the thick dense smoke of a burning straw stack and as it rose it cut off the view of the guard standing with his rifle in the watchtower overlooking the burning barn.

Five men, in the grey prison clothes, ran out of the barn toward the twenty-foot, steep wall. One of them carried a long two-by-four in which spikes had been driven at intervals. The fat man carrying the long scantling leaned it against the wall and a slim kid, his prison cap pulled down over his eyes, swarmed up it to the top of the wall. He carried a length of rope, which he fastened to the end of the scantling. He made the rope fast and then slid down the other side of the wall.

A big husky with a heavy undershot jaw followed him over. On his heels came a little runt who scrambled up the scantling like a monkey. He was followed by a thick-set, ham-faced man who scrambled awkwardly over the wall.

Standing at the foot of the scantling, while they all went up was a thick, freckle-faced man whose prison cap could not hide his flaming head. It was "Red" Ryan.

Ryan and his accomplices were finally caught in Minneapolis. Not surprisingly, they had been robbing banks there. If not for his charm and acting abilities, the story would have ended with Ryan in Kingston Penitentiary serving out a life term for bank robbery. However, Red impressed a Catholic prison chaplain, and invented what he called a pick-proof lock for post-office mail bags.

Reporters were drawn to him, and soon the Toronto Daily Star was hailing him as a poster boy for prison reform. He told reporters he was using his stash of hot money to help his sister, dying of tuberculosis. In 1929, a story headlined, "FAMOUS BANDIT PROVES TENDER NURSE IN PRISON" described Red working in the prison hospital, sweeping floors, feeding prisoners, taking their temperatures, and even scrubbing

them. When not helping prisoners, he was an altar boy, and soon the prison chaplain was joining the Daily Star in campaigning for his release.

On July 23, 1934, Prime Minister R.B. Bennett showed up for a surprise inspection of the Kingston Penitentiary, and he made a point of spending forty-five minutes in private with Ryan. Bennett was clearly impressed, stating, "I was greatly impressed by what he said to me . . . I can only say that his demeanour, his clothes, his sleeping cot and surroundings were calculated to stimulate him to renewed efforts for usefulness. The minister charged with responsibility in such matters is at the moment absent. When he returns I will speak to him about this matter."

The prime minister pushed for his release, and within the year, Ryan was free. The Toronto Daily Star loved the story. Hemingway was long gone by now, and so they hired Ryan himself to write stories about being the author of his own misfortune. When not scribbling for the newspaper, Ryan made a living as a greeter for a Toronto hotel and car dealership.

That should have been the happy ending to the story, but one night early in 1935, a Sarnia police officer was shot dead trying to stop two armed men from robbing a crowded liquor store. The officer managed several shots, and hit both robbers. When the shooting stopped, near the bodies of the police officer and a petty criminal lay Red Ryan, celebrity do-gooder by day and killer and their by night.

The prison chaplain who advocated his release went into a deep depression and lived the rest of his life in a seminary, while Daily Star reporter Athol Gow, who had written passionately that Ryan was reformed, burst into tears when he heard the news. Then he went and got drunk. Two years after his death, in 1937, Ryan appeared in print again, this time as the fictionalized character Kip Caley in Morley Callaghan's novel More Joy in Heaven.

S

Sainte-Pierre and Miquelon: Capone Stronghold – The day Al Capone arrived in this tiny French outpost off the Newfoundland coast, sporting his trademark straw boater, a local gendarme was reportedly so nervous all he could do was stare.

Perhaps what scared him was the famous long, deep scar a few inches below the straw hat, running across Capone's cheek. However, he limited his comments to the straw hat.

"Bonjour," the gendarme said sheepishly. "That ees a nice 'at."

Capone, who was heading toward l'Hôtel Robert in Sainte-Pierre, flipped him the hat and kept on walking.

This was during the 1920s, which was a heady time on the islands of Sainte-Pierre and Miquelon, just twenty kilometres off the southern coast of Newfoundland. The passage of the Volstead Act on January 16, 1920, brought Prohibition to the United States and big business to the rocky island – which explained Capone's visit.

Sainte-Pierre and Miquelon remained French territory, ceded to France under the 1763 Treaty of Paris, and French law made it legal to import alcohol into the islands during Prohibition. It became illegal only when it was placed on high-speed smuggling boats bound for the United States.

That helped explain why John "Legs" Diamond, who ran the Hotsy Totsy Club in New York City, was another underworld visitor, since Sainte-Pierre became the headquarters for a smuggling fleet estimated at around eighty vessels.

Basements throughout the island became warehouses for wooden crates of contraband West Indian rum, British gin, French champagne, and Canadian whisky with names like Babbling Brook Old Bourbon Whiskey and Goodwill Pure Rye Whiskey, much of which was destined to be unloaded off Fire Island, New York. To prevent the bottles from clanging against each other in the boats, which might both damage the product and alert authorities, bottles were wrapped in burlap covers sewn by local women.

Capone alone smuggled the contents of up to three hundred thousand cases of contraband liquor into the United States each month, and the wooden liquor crates left on the tiny French islands stimulated a housing boom. One cabin made completely of crates became known as Cutty Sark Villa. Decades later, a couple Sainte-Pierre houses still had shingles and walls made from the sides of old Cutty Sark crates.

The first Sainte-Pierre smuggler during Prohibition was likely American Bill McCoy, whose wares were of such high quality that authentic liquor became known as the "the real McCoy."

When Prohibition was finally repealed in 1933, flags on Sainte-Pierre were lowered to half-mast. Long after the trade ended, tourists were served a cocktail called a "Volstead on the rocks," after the Volstead Act.

See also: **Moose Jaw Capone Tunnels,** *Nellie J. Banks,* **Quadeville.**

Satan's Choice: Decades of Rumbling – One of the first times the Satan's Choice Motorcycle Club was introduced to readers of the *Toronto Star* was on August 29, 1966, in a story headlined, "FIVE ARRESTED IN MOTORCYCLE RUMBLE," which began: "A policeman had a guitar smashed over his head during a brawl in a local hotel cocktail lounge Saturday after two motorcycle clubs ganged up on a musician.

"Police said about 12 members of the Golden Hawks and Satan's Choice were out to get even with a musician after he fought with a Golden Hawk Friday and kicked over his motorcycle."

The guitar-bashing incident pretty much set the tone for Satan's Choice interactions with mainstream society in the first few years of the club. Further stories around the time of Canada's centennial chronicle how a Toronto police officer had his finger pinched when a Choice member kicked the licence plates the officer was trying to remove from his defective car, how Ottawa members stole lawn sculptures, how four Choice members used a knife to cut the club patch from the jacket of a London Road Runners motorcycle club member at a motorcycle hill climb near Heidelberg, on the outskirts of Kitchener, and how the Choice rumbled with gangs with names like the Chain Men, Henchmen, and Fourth Reich.

There were also stomach-turning photos from an August 1968 field-day near Wasaga Beach, north of Toronto, in which Choice members competed to run down a live chicken and then tear it to bits. The biker with the largest chicken chunk won. There were no takers when the Humane Society of Ontario offered a $200 reward for information leading to the conviction of the chicken-killers.

Some of the stories were darker, like how a Kitchener-area man was beaten to death in a brawl with the Choice; how an eighteen-year-old girlfriend of a gang member was found semiconscious and seminaked in a Markham ditch with severe internal injuries; or how a businessman was beaten to death in a Vancouver clubhouse.

The gang then had eleven chapters – Vancouver, Montreal, Windsor, Preston, Kingston, Ottawa, Peterborough, Hamilton, St. Catharines, Guelph, Oshawa – all of which fell under the leadership of "supreme commander," or national president, Bernie Guindon.

Choice members were no one's first choice for babysitters, but then they weren't serious mobsters either. Police raids generally uncovered guns and brass knuckles and a little marijuana, but the gang was more into using drugs than selling them.

By 1973, Guindon was thirty, with two divorces behind him, three children, and an inmate's residence at maximum-security Millhaven Penitentiary, where he was serving five years for indecent assault. He then dreamed of representing Canada in boxing in the 1976 Olympics, but prison life was making that tough, he told Arnie Keller of the *Toronto Star*: "All I can do up there is hit the heavy bag, do lots of leg exercises, work with the weights and do exercises to strengthen my stomach. There are no ropes which I can use to skip or mirrors to look into to check my style. Nothing resembling a weapon is allowed."

Guindon, Choice president since 1965, noted that he was Canadian amateur light middleweight boxing champion. He complained that it was tough for him to get parole, since authorities wanted him to refrain from associating with criminals, which often included bikers. "They're the only friends I have. I'm not going to give them up."

He told Keller he would like to coach kids, but added that he needed some guidance of his own. "I'm a sort of Jekyll-and-Hyde character. I try to set them on the right path. I tell them not to go the way I did. Then, when I get the chance, I go and do the same things I did before."

In Quebec in the late 1970s, the Hells Angels sat back patiently and watched as the Satan's Choice, Popeyes, and Devil's Disciples fought a bloody war for control of Montreal's booming drug market. When the smoke cleared, the Angels took over the largest surviving group, the mainly French-speaking Popeyes.

Meanwhile in Toronto, the Satan's Choice formed an alliance with the Chicago-based Outlaws, Vagabonds, and Para-Dice Riders to keep the Hells Angels from expanding there from Quebec.

Despite the tensions with the Angels, the gang was healthy, even cocky, despite continual police surveillance. They had a particularly strong presence in Kitchener, where the club was indignant in 1987 when the Kitchener-Waterloo *Record* refused to run an advertisement bearing its Christmas greetings. The previous year, the Choice had taken out an eight-centimetre-square advertisement declaring: "Satan's Choice Motorcycle Club would like to take this opportunity to wish everyone in Waterloo Region a very Merry Christmas and to let you know that we are still here and will always be here. Choice Forever Forever Choice."

There were rumblings in the early 1990s that violence would flare up between the Choice and the Hells Angels. In 1991, about 150 Hells Angels from Europe, Eastern Canada, and the West booked into a suburban Winnipeg hotel. That meeting was taken as a challenge to the local Los Brovos gang, who were friendly with the Satan's Choice.

In June 1993, the Satan's Choice weren't invited to a party at Wasaga Beach, Ontario, hosted by the Quebec-based Hells Angels, who brought along a farm team of gang members from affiliated clubs. The Angels spent much of the time meeting with members of the Loners, a breakaway club from the Choice. The talks were to discuss the expansion of the Angels into Ontario, police said.

In the summer of 1995, Guindon's old gang was brawling with the Loners in Toronto, who were founded by disgruntled former Choice members. In August 1995, less than two hours after Toronto Mayor Barbara Hall announced a crackdown on biker violence, the clubhouse of the Loners on Denison Road West, in the Weston area of Toronto, was rocked by a massive explosion. One of the Loners found humour in the incident, saying, "The mayor has stolen our rocket launcher." (Two weeks before the bombing, the steel door on the Satan's Choice clubhouse in the South Riverdale section of Toronto had been rocked by a blast from what police believed was a rocket launcher.)

The gang seemed to be expanding in December 1996, when a half-dozen members were involved in the bombing of the Sudbury Police Station. Naturally, the police didn't take well to this, and an investigation led to charges against six Choice members from the Hamilton and Sudbury areas, including John Croitoru, the president of the Hamilton chapter, who was known in the pro-wrestling ring as Johnny K-9.

The arrests were the result of Project Dismantle, a police team that had been targeting the residences and clubhouses of Satan's Choice members and associates across Ontario. Since May 1996, members of the police team had charged 161 people with 1,192 offences, most of them drug-related. During the same period, weapons and about $1.05 million in drugs were seized and two marijuana labs with a potential annual yield of about $13.8 million were shut down.

However, in September 2003, an Ontario Provincial Police officer involved in Operation Dismantle was accused by a judge of repeatedly lying to five Toronto judges, and destroying evidence, allegedly to ensure a task force probing the Satan's Choice biker gang could get permission to secretly wiretap the gang's phone conversations.

The judge's sharp words meant drug charges against four alleged traffickers were tossed out of court following a hearing on the legality of the wiretaps. The four men were alleged to be associates, though not members, of the Satan's Choice motorcycle gang.

For his part, Guindon never did make the Olympics, but he did retain his leadership of the Choice until December 2000, when the gang patched over to the Hells Angels. He went along with the change, donning a vest with the Angels' winged death-head logo.

See also: **Gary Comeau, Hells Angels, Cecil Kirby, Outlaws, Rock Machine.**

Savoie, Claude: Threat from Within – He was assistant director of the RCMP's intelligence service when he shot himself to death in his Ottawa headquarters in 1992, just before he was to meet with internal-affairs investigators to answer charges of corruption. The force suspected Savoie had taken $200,000 from Allan "The Weasel" Ross, head of Montreal's West End Gang, in exchange for information.

The week of his suicide, Savoie learned he was going to be questioned by internal-affairs officers about allegations he funnelled information through Mob lawyer Sydney Leithman to Montreal drug king Allan Ross. Montreal detectives investigating the 1991 murder of Leithman questioned Savoie about three meetings he had with Leithman and Ross at Leithman's office building.

Ross had avoided prosecution in Canada for a decade, but U.S. enforcement officials were closing in on him. Savoie had claimed he met Ross because he hoped to persuade him to co-operate with the RCMP.

However, Savoie hadn't alerted his superiors or followed any standard procedures during the meetings.

Police believe Leithman's killer was a Colombian hit man, and he was murdered because Ross and his Colombian cocaine suppliers feared Leithman would inform on them.

Savoie took his life a day before CBC-TV's *the 5th estate* broadcast a documentary on Ross. Asked about his relationship with Ross, Savoie was quoted as saying, "He wasn't an informant, nor was I an informant for him. But I knew him. Put it that way. I met him."

See also: **Sydney Leithman, Allan "The Weasel" Ross, West End Gang.**

Scarcella, Pietro Paolo: Volpe Driver – When he first arrived in Toronto in the late 1960s, from his birthplace of Castellammare del Golfo on the Sicilian coast, Scarcella worked as a downtown parking-lot attendant at Dundas Square. Within a decade, he rose to become an organizer in the Carpenters' Union, and then an international organizer, before he quit in 1984 because of bad publicity over his Mob connections.

Those connections became publicized after he and his associate Paul Volpe were the target of a murder plot by brothers Rocco Remo and Cosimo Commisso, which was to be carried out by biker Cecil Kirby in 1981. Instead, Kirby turned informer.

Eddie Melo and Pietro Scarcella (left)

Two years later, there was another murder attempt on Volpe, and this time it succeeded. Scarcella was believed to be the last person – besides his killer – to see Volpe alive.

See also: **Rocco Remo Commisso, Cecil Kirby, Paul Volpe.**

Sciascia, Gerlando: Canadian Dreams – The shooting started when Sciascia ran a hand through his greying hair at a Brooklyn social club.

That was the signal for three hooded gunmen hiding in a closet to charge out and open fire on soldiers in the Bonanno crime family who were believed to be disloyal to Joseph Massino.

Authorities were given details of the triple murder by one of the participants, Salvator "Good Looking Sal" Vitale, an underboss in the Bonanno family and a confessed member of the hit team.

The hits took place on May 5, 1981, as the Bonanno family caught wind of a plot by three captains, each heading a crew of foot soldiers and associates, to depose imprisoned family boss Phil Rastelli.

The three rebellious captains were lured to a meeting in a Brooklyn social club, where three killers, armed with a machine-gun, shotgun, and a pistol, were hiding in a closet.

"Everyone in the closet wore a ski mask and was told that Sciascia would give them the signal to shoot by running his hands through his hair," said the witness, referred to by authorities as CW#1 – the first "confidential witness."

The three rebellious captains were dead within minutes. Dominick "Big Trin" Trinchera was dropped almost instantly, while Philip "Phil Lucky" Giaccone stood in front of a wall, apparently trying to surrender. Alphonse "Sonny Red" Indelicato bolted for the door, but Sciascia, armed with a pistol, shot him in the head.

A cleanup crew wrapped the bodies in painter dropcloths and placed them in a van that was driven to Howard Beach. Weeks later, children playing in a park smelled something foul in the dirt, and when they kicked at the soil,

Gerlando Sciascia (far left) leaves the Capri Motor Lodge in the Bronx with Vito Rizzuto, Giovanni Liggamari, and Joseph Massino, New York, May 6, 1981

they uncovered an arm. Sonny Red, still wearing a Cartier watch worth U.S.$1,500, was found by authorities in the shallow grave while the other bodies have not been found.

Authorities said the Mafia Commission – the Mob's ultimate authority – authorized the slayings of the upstart *capos* when it was learned that they planned to seize control of the Bonanno family from boss Philip "Rusty" Rastelli.

Sciascia was one of the Bonanno Sicilian faction known as the "Zips" for the rapid-fire way they spoke. Born in Cattolica Eraclea, Sicily, on February 15, 1934, Sciascia immigrated to the United States in 1955, running California Pizzeria on Long Island, New York. and living in a small home in the Bronx.

In 1983, he was under indictment for heroin trafficking. His co-accuseds in the heroin case included Gene Gotti, the younger brother of imprisoned Mob boss John Gotti, and John Carneglia, who were each sentenced to fifty years.

Sciascia's role in the drug pipeline was to act as the liaison between major New York City and Montreal mobsters, co-ordinating the importation of tons of heroin into the United States through Canada and laundering the illicit proceeds around the world.

For a couple of years, Sciascia lived in Montreal under an alias. The RCMP picked him up, and he was detained in Canada for two years until 1988, then shipped back to the United States.

Sciascia, Gambino *capo* (captain) Edward Lino, and Bonanno soldier Giuseppe "Joe" LoPresti of Montreal were acquitted after a juror received a $10,000 payoff, according to turncoat Gambino underboss Salvatore "Sammy the Bull" Gravano.

During the 1980s, Sciascia was recognized as the top member of the Bonanno family in Montreal, but he was not able to achieve his dream of becoming a Canadian citizen.

Canadian authorities noted that a 1988 U.S. Senate subcommittee report on organized crime listed him as a member of the La Cosa Nostra Bonanno organized crime family in New York. He must have worried about fellow family members during this time, as his former co-accused Lino was executed in 1990 in Brooklyn and LoPresti was murdered in 1992 in Montreal.

After his acquittal, Sciascia and his wife, Mary, a native of Scotland, tried to settle in Canada. He told Canadian authorities that he spoke both French and English, owned and operated two restaurants and a car wash, and would bring U.S.$200,000 in cash assets to Canada.

In a "Danger to the Public Ministerial Opinion Report" about Sciascia, an immigration officer argued that Sciascia was tightly linked to the Mob, even if he denied it. "Indications received from different sources lead [me] to believe there are reasonable grounds to believe Gerlando Sciascia is a member of a criminal organization."

The officer continued: "I am concerned that Mr. Sciascia's close relationship to figures of the Mafia in New York, Sicily and Montreal would strengthen the Mafia situation in Montreal. Mr. Sciascia is a danger to the Canadian public because of his involvement with the Mafia and that the nature of the activities carried by these organizations."

Again, his attempt to settle in Canada had failed, and in 1997, he moved back to New York, where he lived in a luxurious home in upstate Harrison and owned a house on Stadium Avenue in the Bronx. He ran a construction company and conducted his Mob business out of a small jewellery store in the East Tremont section of the Bronx. More importantly to police, he was a member of the Bonanno family's ruling panel, with a crew of soldiers located in Canada.

In March 1999, he complained about the cocaine use of another Bonanno family member. Shortly afterwards, his body was found dumped outside the Baptist Chapel Church on dead-end Bollner Avenue in the Bronx in 1999, with four shots to the left side of his head. He was sixty-five.

When police checked his wallet, they found a business card for a Montreal jewellery shop that caught their eye. It was run by the wife of Gaetano Amodeo, a Sicilian Mafia hit man found hiding in Canada in 2001.

Charged with Sciascia's murder was Bonanno boss Joseph Massino, who was one of Sciascia's accomplices in the 1981 triple murders. Massino, who faces a possible death penalty sentence for the Sciascia murder, was originally charged with the 1981 murder of the Bonanno family member who allowed FBI agent Joseph Pistone to infiltrate the clan. Pistone was known to the Mob as Donnie Brasco and his undercover work was later depicted in the film of the same name.

According to informants within the Bonnano family, Sciascia's fate was apparently sealed when he complained that a fellow Mafia member had a cocaine problem.

"It served him right for telling me how to run the family," Massino allegedly told an underling. *See also:* **Alfonso Caruana, Giuseppe "Joe" LoPresti, Nicolo "Nick" Rizzuto, Vito Rizzuto.**

Scibetta, Santo: Steel City *Consigliere* – His specialty was extortion with finesse, and the Hamilton man would take payments from grateful business people for getting thugs off their backs.

What Scibetta didn't disclose was that he was the one who brought the thugs into the deal in the first place.

He was a *consigliere* (adviser) to Giacomo Luppino of Hamilton, the old don of the Calabrian Mafia, and he had business ties to Joe Todaro, Sr., and Sam Pieri of the Buffalo Mob, as well as to bikers.

He died of natural causes in 1985, at age sixty-five.

See also: **Giacomo Luppino, 'Ndrangheta.**

Seagal, Steven: Under Seige – In movies like *Out for Justice*, this tough-guy actor used his fists, feet, and sometimes a pool cue to put bad guys in their place. Real life wasn't so easy when, in October 2000, while he was filming *Exit Wounds* in Toronto, mobsters tried to extort hundreds of thousands of dollars from him.

The shakedown continued, he told a New York City court in 2003, when he met in a private dining room in a Brooklyn restaurant with a Mob captain. Seagal packed a gun himself, and had a bodyguard waiting nearby. In that meeting, the New York mobster sounded like a character in *Goodfellas* as he barked at Seagal, "Look at me when you're talking."

Prosecutors said the fifty-year-old actor was targeted for extortion after a falling out with his one-time manager Jule Nasso, an alleged associate of the Gambino crime family. The trouble began after Seagal allegedly backed out of making four motion pictures, on the advice of his Buddhist spiritual adviser.

Wiretaps caught Nasso being instructed to demand money from Seagal. Anthony "Sonny" Ciccone told Nasso he should be tougher on the action star, saying, "You really gotta get down on him . . . 'cause I know this animal, I know this beast."

According to the court papers, Ciccone became concerned about Seagal talking about the alleged extortion attempt, and ordered an underling to "smooth this guy over – he's going around saying stupid things."

Some of the evidence in the alleged extortion bid surfaced in a trial in 2003 of Peter Gotti, the brother of late New York City Mob boss John "The Dapper Don" Gotti, and six co-defendants, whom prosecutors said were members of the crime family. They were all convicted for the Seagal shakedown.

Authorities allege Nasso turned to the crime family to help him settle the score after his falling out with Seagal. Defence attorneys denied any threats were made, calling Seagal a "pathological liar" who owed Nasso $500,000.

Investigators said that Seagal, whose other films include *Marked for Death*, was so shaken that he paid $700,000 to the Mob. In a bugged VIP room in a Brooklyn restaurant, suspects chuckled over how "petrified" Seagal looked at a meeting. "I wish we had a gun with us," one said. "That would have been funny."

Seagal was a reluctant star witness in Peter Gotti's racketeering trial, only venturing forward after federal agents hit him with a subpoena and granted him immunity. "I'm a movie star," Seagal said. "If you want to keep making movies, you don't want to start a war with these people. I can't go into the witness-protection program."

Settecase, Giuseppe – *See* **Alfonso Caruana.**

Sheila Na Geira: "Carbonear Princess" – There are plenty of people with the name Pike in the Carbonear Island area of Newfoundland who love to tell the story of the beautiful Celtic princess who fell into the hands of privateers.

She was called Sheila Na Geira, which translates in Celtic to "Sheila the Beautiful," and her real surname was likely O'Connor. Her story began in 1602, when she was captured by Dutch privateers while sailing between Ireland and France. One story says she was escaping the English invasions of Ireland, while another was that she was dispatched to France to escape Irish freedom fighters.

Legend has it that she was captured in the English Channel by the privateers, who had a letter of marque from the English Queen, giving them legitimacy to fight for the Crown and raid enemy ships.

The Dutch ship that captured her was itself attacked by English privateer Captain Peter Easton, who was en route to Newfoundland. After a short sea battle, Sheila Na Geira was in English hands. Somewhere in the mid-Atlantic, she and Easton's navigating officer, Gilbert Pike, fell in love. They were married at sea and set foot in Newfoundland as husband and wife.

A year later, Easton shifted from being a privateer to a pirate, after England made peace with Spain. Easton didn't plan to quit his buccaneer ways, and the newlyweds didn't want a life of crime, so they settled down in Mosquito Valley, near Harbour Grace. Their newborn child was said to be the first European child born in Newfoundland since the departure of the Vikings.

In 1610 and again in 1612, Easton ravaged the coast, including tiny Mosquito. A local story says that Sheila led the women and children into the hills to hide and, when they returned, they found some forty men had been taken captive, including her husband, Gilbert.

The community was reduced to just forty-two women, twenty-seven children, and six men, and Sheila assumed the role of leader. She helped construct a stone wall to safeguard against further attack. Although she had no medical training, she also treated the sick and planted crops.

Some fifteen years later, according to the legend, Gilbert and other men from the community escaped from the pirates and returned home to Newfoundland. The Pikes moved to fortified Carbonear Island, where they lived for the rest of their lives, founding one of the largest clans in Newfoundland. A headstone in Carbonear reads, "Here lies the body of John Pike who departed this life July 14th, 1756, also Julian his wife. Also Sheiah Nageria, wife of Gilbert Pike and daughter of John Nageria, King of County Down, Ireland, died August 14th, 1753, at the age of 105 years." The dates on the headstones only add to the mystery, since if they're correct, she was at least 170 years old at the time of her death.

See also: **Charles Bellamy, Eric Cobham, Cupids, Peter Easton, High Island, Captain Kidd, Mogul Mackenzie, Henry Mainwaring, John Phillips, Gilbert Pike, Pirates, Bartholomew "Black Bart" Roberts.**

Shoofey, Frank: Little Guy's Champion – A man called the *Montreal Gazette* newspaper shortly before midnight on Tuesday, October 15, 1985, and said he was a member of the Red Army Liberation Front.

"I and my colleagues have just assassinated Frank Shoofey," the *Gazette* quoted the caller as saying. "Good riddance."

The call came shortly after the murder of the popular and flamboyant Montreal lawyer. It was likely that mobsters, not some unknown political group, were the killers of Shoofey, a lawyer to the underworld, as well as a champion of the disadvantaged.

Shoofey, forty-four, a father of two, had spent three hours of the final evening of his life at the offices of the Montreal Athletic Commission, trying to keep American boxing promoter Don King from being allowed to co-promote a Matthew Hilton–Vito Antuofermo bout.

At 11:30 p.m., Shoofey's life ended in the hall outside his Cherrier Street law office in downtown Montreal, when several bullets were fired into his head.

Shoofey had a blunt, flashy style and loved to grandstand, but he also had a genuine empathy for the poor and the nerve to stand up to the underworld – as well as to represent its most frightening figures. High-profile underworld clients included Richard Blass, who was killed when police raided his chalet in the Laurentians in 1975, and Sicilian mobsters accused of murdering Montreal's Cotroni family leader Paolo Violi in 1978.

Another client included a paraplegic pencil peddler who was sentenced to eleven months in jail for begging. Shoofey won his freedom on the condition that he not return to begging, saying, "It's very humiliating for them to have to beg, but the humiliation should belong to a society which forces them to do something like this."

He was born in a working-class section of downtown Montreal to parents of Lebanese descent, and his mother wanted to name him Franklin Delano after Franklin Delano Roosevelt. However, a Greek Orthodox priest pointed out that a saint's name was obligatory, and so she made his middle name Dimitrios.

Shoofey's father died when he was seventeen, and Shoofey worked to pay for his

Frank Shoofey

education at McGill University and to support his mother, selling real estate, insurance, furnaces, and encyclopedias. He also worked in nightclubs. All the jobs involved hype, something he was very good at.

He failed civil law when he sat for his bar examinations, perhaps because he had spread himself too thin, or perhaps because it bored him. Whatever the case, he began to focus on criminal law and, three months out of law school, he was defending a man accused of rape.

Shoofey had little time to prepare to defend his client, so he chose to put his client through a withering interrogation. The man didn't snap, and Shoofey's case was won.

Shoofey would use that technique often after that. He estimated that 90 per cent of his clients were guilty, but he wasn't bothered by this, saying a defence counsel was essential to the judicial system.

There were some people he would not defend. "Some crimes revolt me," he once said. "I won't take it if it's a senseless offence, like the murder or rape of a little child. No one forces us to take a case. But if you take it, you must do your best. . . . Many lawyers don't. Some take a client's money and don't even show up in court. Any lawyer who gets threats from the underworld usually deserves them."

Shoofey often worked sixteen- to eighteen-hour days, but looked after his health by not drinking, eating health foods, and exercising every morning.

He was often called upon by police to negotiate between them and the underworld, and was also called upon when Brother André's heart was stolen from St. Joseph's Oratory in Montreal. André had been beatified in 1982 by Pope John Paul, and Montrealers were horror-struck when his heart was stolen. Shoofey negotiated its return.

After Shoofey's shooting, Kirk Makin of the *Globe and Mail* wrote: "Mr. Shoofey was a shameless publicity hound but also a social benefactor of the highest order." Makin continued: "His presence was a must on radio talk shows. He played Santa Claus at Christmas parties for urchins and bought sports equipment for inner-city children."

Three times he had tried to get the Liberal nomination in the working-class Saint-Jacques riding, where he worked tirelessly for the provincial party, and three times he was derailed by party brass who feared a public association with someone who represented notorious underworld figures.

His final fight was to protect the Hiltons from what he considered the dangerous influence of Frank "Santos" Cotroni. Shoofey sent a telegram to Quebec Sports Minister Guy Chevrette, seeking an investigation to clear the air and asking him to accelerate the startup of a provincial agency to control boxing, wrestling, and kick-boxing.

"When Willie Mays or Mickey Mantle wanted to accept jobs with casinos, they were told they had to quit their association with baseball," Shoofey told James Christie of the *Globe and Mail*. "But Cotroni had been accepted like a fixture around boxing and it seemed to be tol-erated, not only by the Hiltons, but by the Montreal Athletic Commission and by the police. Nobody came up and warned them. If everyone accepted this situation, why blame the Hiltons?"

His murder remains unsolved.

See also: **Richard "The Cat" Blass, Boxing, Frank "Santos" Cotroni, Sydney Leithman, François Payette.**

Shufelt, Ed – *See* **Big Muddy Badlands, Dutch Henry, Sam Kelly, Sundance Kid.**

Sigalov, Joseph: Last Laugh for Tomato Head – What do you do if you're a politician and you learn that one of the unsolicited donors to your campaign is a senior member of the Russian *mafiya*? Worse yet, that the donor is now a dead member of the Russian *mafiya*, with an extremely murky private life, including an undetermined number of wives? That was the ticklish situation faced by federal Cabinet ministers Paul Martin and Art Eggleton in 2000, when they tried to give back $33,000 in unspent donations that came from Toronto businessman Yosif "Joseph" Sigalov.

The MPs placed the money in trust in 1997 after learning that the donor, Sigalov, a hard-drinking bon vivant who described himself as an import-export entrepreneur, was a suspected Russian organized-crime figure. Complicating things further, Sigalov died of brain cancer in September 1996, at the age of forty-six.

Things only got more tangled when a Toronto woman, who said she married Sigalov in October 1995, filed suit against the politicians, claiming to be the trustee of Sigalov's estate and his sole beneficiary.

David Hill, a Liberal party lawyer in Ottawa, said the MPs had been planning on giving it to charity, because of its questionable source. He added that it was unclear who should receive the money if it was returned, since Sigalov, whose will wasn't probated, left behind multiple wives, children, creditors, and confusion.

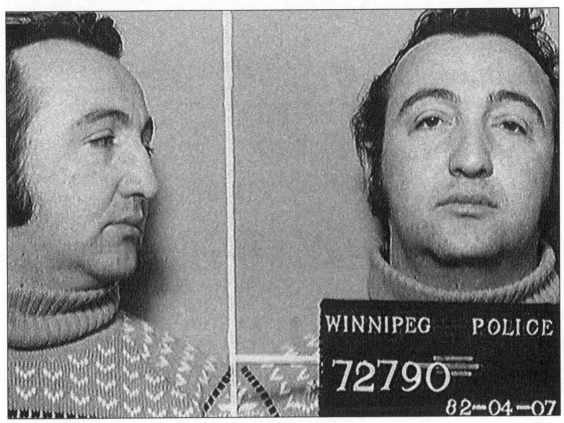

Joseph Sigalov, 1982

"It was a very confused family situation," said Hill, noting that Sigalov got a tax deduction for the donation.

Court documents filed by the "Mrs. Sigalov" who was suing, stated that Martin, then the federal finance minister, received a $10,000 campaign donation from Sigalov or companies he controlled; Eggleton, the minister of national defence, was given $5,000; Toronto-area Liberal MP Maurizio Bevilacqua received $10,000; and Toronto-area Liberal MP Jean Augustine was given $8,000. In all, the suit demanded $33,000, plus accrued interest.

Sigalov's alleged organized-crime connections were first made public in March 1996, when Vyacheslav Ivankov, then reputed to be the most powerful Russian organized-crime boss in the United States, was about to be convicted on extortion charges in New York City. Ivankov, dubbed the "Red Godfather," was

reportedly Sigalov's brother-in-law.

Wiretaps by the RCMP of telephone conversations between Ivankov and Toronto-based Russian crime boss Vyacheslav Sliva allowed the FBI to uncover a plot by Ivankov to extort $3.5 million from two New York investment bankers.

Ivankov ended up in a U.S. federal penitentiary, while Sliva was deported from Canada in 1997.

Sigalov died in Toronto. However, with the absence of his birth date, Hill's office also couldn't be sure of when he died or where he was buried.

Sigalov was nothing if not a complicated man, professionally and privately. He was a Russian Jew who used the name Joseph instead of Leonid to sound less Jewish — yet donated tens of thousands of dollars to Jewish charities. Even his unflattering nickname of Tomato Head was tough to get a handle on. Friends would say

Joseph Sigalov, at car trunk

it was because he was a hard worker who got his start selling fruit and vegetables. People who were less kind said it was a nasty joke about how his complexion took on a reddish colour after radiation treatments.

Apparently, his first job in Canada was as a Winnipeg cab driver, and he moved on to become a baker and a commodities trader before billing himself as an "import-exporter."

According to affidavits filed with the federal court in Brooklyn, New York, Sigalov was recorded discussing murder, extortion, and protection rackets and bragging that he made $40 million yearly running a vast business empire that included brick kilns, clothing factories, and the importation of frozen bagels to Russia. Sigalov was named in a series of FBI wiretap affidavits, which describe him as a drug dealer, an extortionist, and a gunrunner.

In January 1995, Sigalov had attended a Russian crime summit in Puerto Rico, as FBI agents spied on them in the El San Juan Hotel and Casino. According to an FBI affidavit,

Sigalov was heard telling a relative that he was at the crime summit to "discuss whom we will kill." Police said they also overheard him discussing how to extort a casino in the Ukraine and how to get false travel documents, so that another crime boss could attend the summit.

Meanwhile, Liberal lawyer Hill said in 2003 that the donated money was still sitting in trust until it could be determined where it should go. "It's just a pain in the butt to hold it," Hill said. "It's not as if the party wants the money. It's trying to get rid of it."
See also: **Vyacheslav Ivankov, Vyacheslav Marakulovich Sliva.**

Silent Riders: Riding into Oblivion – This biker club was made up of former members of the Spartans of Manitoba, and their new colours were first noticed at the B.C. Hells Angels anniversary party in July 1984. The members of the new gang were signalling that they had left the Spartans, and gang members had hopes of soon being absorbed into the Hells Angels.

The celebration didn't last long. Soon, they were at war with the Los Brovos from Winnipeg. Two members were murdered and the Silent Riders ran up a debt of more than $200,000 to the Hells Angels of British Columbia.

There were mass defections after a leader raped another biker's common-law wife and, in March 1988, the remaining four members of the Silent Riders surrendered their colours to four members of the rival Los Brovos, who burned them. The now-defunct Silent Riders were granted amnesty by the Los Brovos in return for surrendering their colours.
See also: **Los Brovos, Redliners, Spartans, Wolodumyr "Walter" "Nurget" Stadnick.**

Simard, Aimé: Lovesick Hit Man – The small-time crook was born April 10, 1968, in Quebec City, and grew up to become a member of the Rockers, a Hells Angels affiliate. The Angels in Quebec had a "football team" that murdered people and a "baseball team" that beat them up

Aimé Simard

and threatened them. Simard made the football team, killing three men for the Angels.

Privately, Simard lived a secret bisexual lifestyle. He took out a personal ad in a newspaper, looking for another man. When he met Dany Kane in November 1996, each man thought the other was a businessman. Then, when they were sitting together in a hot tub, Simard saw tattoos on his new lover showing that he was a Hells Angels associate, like himself.

The lovers felt they had no future in the homophobic biker world, and police were able to flip Simard into becoming an informer in 1997. They declined his request to pay $3,200 for his liposuction, but the prosecution did agree to recommend that he be eligible for parole after serving twelve years.

Not surprisingly, Angels leader Maurice "Mom" Boucher was infuriated by the defection. To prevent it from happening again, he decided to push key members of the gang to kill prison guards, prosecutors, or judges. After such a crime, they would have no hope of cutting a deal with authorities, Boucher reasoned, and so they would have to remain loyal. Ironically, the

plan ended with Boucher sentenced to life in prison for the murder of two guards.

Simard thought he had found love behind bars with another inmate, and they were married via telephone by a member of a Montreal religious sect in 2001. However, Simard felt the need to challenge authorities constantly, and was often placed in solitary confinement. Eventually, he was transferred from the maximum-security Kent Penitentiary in Agassiz, British Columbia, to the Saskatchewan Penitentiary in Prince Albert, home to several of Boucher's associates.

Simard had once bragged to Quebec crime reporter Michel Auger, saying he wasn't worried about the Angels. "They will not get me," he boasted. Now, however, he feared that he might not get out of Saskatchewan alive. Five weeks after his transfer, in July 2003, his body was found in his maximum-security cell, with 106 stab wounds.

See also: **Maurice "Mom" Boucher, Dany Kane, Diane Lavigne.**

Simard, Réal: *Gentleman's Quarterly* **Killer –** As Simard told it, he didn't murder people out of anger or for money or power; it was because he craved approval. He needed to feel important. He needed some kind of security. He got that from Montreal Mob boss Santos "Frank" Cotroni, who gave him the "love, attention, and friendship" that he never found in his early home life.

"I have to take care of him," he later recalled. "I was with him every day. I was protecting him."

On January 18, 1980, Simard proved his loyalty by stalking Michel Marion, one of Cotroni's enemies, and shooting him dead while he ate breakfast in a restaurant. Then he returned proudly to Cotroni. "We kissed each other on the side of the cheek," he later recalled. "It's an old tradition in Italian families when you do something for the godfather, the family." Once asked what it was like to murder for the

Réal Simard

frequently seen in the city's best steakhouses and behind the wheel of his four-door Lincoln Continental, smoking fine cigars. Simard was impressed.

As Simard told the story, he was raised by a brutal father. He recounted cowering under a bed as his enraged father flailed away at him with a belt. His childhood was one of poverty, abuse, and alcoholism, and he was kicked out of the house at thirteen.

By the time Simard met Cotroni, he had served a stint in the army and prison time for extortion, and then bank robbery.

Cotroni installed him in Toronto in July 1983, to open the drug market for the Cotroni family. "We figured in Toronto we can make $750,000 a year," he later recalled.

Simard lived in a posh thirtieth-floor apartment in downtown Toronto's Sutton Place and toured about the city in a new Mercedes-Benz. In the summer of 1983, Simard set up a meeting with "Johnny Pops" Papalia at Hanrahan's strip club on Barton Street East in Hamilton.

The Hamilton gangster arrived with three bodyguards. A phone call to Frank Cotroni's Montreal home confirmed that Simard enjoyed his blessing. Unknown to the mobsters, a police surveillance team caught the meeting on film, including the scene when Simard, Papalia, and Simard's associate Frank Majeau stood together while Simard called Cotroni's home in Montreal to prove he was acting on his behalf.

Simard racked up a murder toll of five – and it would have been six if his gun hadn't jammed in a Toronto hotel. When police arrested him in 1983, Simard found a new way to be feared and gain attention. He became a police informer, cutting a deal with the Montreal Organized Crime Squad and the Quebec and Ontario Crowns to provide evidence against a number of underworld figures, including his old mentor, Cotroni. For this, Simard pleaded guilty to one charge of second-degree murder and four charges of manslaughter, and served relatively comfortable prison time with a microwave, a

first time, Simard said he was nervous, but proud to pass the ultimate Mafia test.

He was never paid for the murder, because that's generally not the way it's done in an Italian mob or biker gang.

"It's part of your job. . . . I do what I have to do. People start giving me respect for that." The Cotroni gang coached him carefully at his new trade. He was taught to destroy his clothes afterwards to get rid of powder burns and to always make sure his victim was dead. "You never leave a body without giving it a bullet in the head," Cotroni instructed him.

Simard and Cotroni met by chance in 1979, and it didn't hurt that Simard's uncle was Armand Courville, a long-time underworld friend of Frank's older brother Vic.

With Cotroni, Simard was happy to become a driver and errand boy, since the mobster offered him a sense of escape from an impoverished, anonymous youth. Frank Cotroni was telephone, an exercise bicycle, and a television. Then he received early parole and was relocated in a witness-protection program.

Because of Simard's testimony, Cotroni and his son, Francesco, were put behind bars for the 1981 slaying of suspected police informer Joseph "Giuseppi" Montegano, at a private St. Leonard, Quebec, club managed by Francesco Cotroni.

Simard told his biographer, Michel Vastel, who wrote *The Nephew*, that he was profoundly moved by Shirley MacLaine's book *Out on a Limb*. That book convinced him that he has a soul, as Simard told the story, and that: "Whatever action one takes will ultimately return to that person – good and bad – maybe not in this life embodiment, but sometime in the future. And no one is exempt."
See also: **Frank "Santos" Cotroni, Eddie Melo, Michel Pozza.**

Skating: Nasty Edge – The sport of Olympic figure skating had just weathered the unseemly scandal in which American star Tonya Harding ordered the clubbing of her rival Nancy Kerrigan, when along came Alimzan "Alik" Tokhtakhounov.

The dark-haired, stocky Russian wasn't well known in the world of Lutzes and Salchows, but organized-crime investigators certainly knew his name. They knew him as Taivanchik, or Little Taiwanese, a nickname given him because of the Asian cast to his features.

Police believed he was involved in illegal arms sales, drug distribution, and the sale of stolen cars, and so the phones at his resort home in Forte dei Marmi, Italy, were bugged. Organized-crime investigators, expecting to hear evidence of these other activities, were therefore startled to hear about the Russian mobster fixing skating results at the 2002 Salt Lake City Winter Games.

More specifically, they heard Tokhtakhounov talk about how the Canadian Olympic figure-skating pairs team of Jamie Salé and David Pelletier had been cheated out of gold medals.

Millions of people watching television had thought there was something strange about the judging, even for the sport of figure skating, after the Canadians placed second, despite a brilliant skate in the long program. Many observers assumed they had won the gold, and were shocked when they ended up with silver behind Russians Elena Berezhnaya and Anton Sikharulidze in a 5–4 judging split.

According to American prosecutors, Tokhtakhounov used his influence with Russian and French skating officials to guarantee that, in exchange for the vote of French judge Marie-Reine Le Gougne for the Russian pairs team, the Russians would ensure the French team won the gold medal in ice-dancing.

It was a classic *quid pro quo*.

The day after the Russians were awarded gold in a controversial decision, Le Gougne said she'd been pressured by French skating officials to vote for the Russians. Then she flipped her story yet again.

By this time, the pressure on the International Skating Union from the public, the media, and the International Olympic Committee was so intense that duplicate gold medals were awarded to the Canadian pair.

Tokhtakhounov, who had lived in France but was forced to leave the country, engineered the scheme in part to earn an extension of his French visa from French officials, according to the American criminal complaint, which identified Tokhtakhounov as a "major figure in international Eurasian organized crime" and claimed he "has been involved in drug distribution, illegal arms sales and trafficking in stolen vehicles." He reportedly had French, Swiss, Israeli, and German passports when he was arrested at his Italian home, where he lived with his third wife.

The FBI was also told by a confidential source that, during the early 1990s in Moscow, he had also fixed beauty pageants.
See also: **National Hockey League.**

Sliva, Vyacheslav: Kicked Back to Moscow –
The Russian immigrant wasn't kicked out of Canada because police considered him a major gangster. Sliva was expelled because he admitted that he lied on his immigration form.

Sliva, who lived from 1995 to 1997 in a luxury high-rise condominium on Finch Avenue at Bayview Avenue in Toronto, admitted in an immigration detention hearing that he put "false information about my marriage situation" on his visa application form. He said that he had been told by acquaintances in Moscow that he'd be more likely to gain entry to Canada if he was married, so he put down the name of his brother's wife – Anzhela Sliva – on the form.

More damaging, Sliva answered "no" when asked on the form whether he had ever been convicted of a crime. The Immigration Department argued that he had several criminal convictions in Russia, dating back to 1961, including a robbery conviction for which he received a ten-year prison sentence in 1982. An Immigration Department lawyer also submitted an affidavit from the New York trial of Vyacheslav Ivankov, who was convicted in January 1997 of extortion, which he said suggested Sliva's involvement in organized crime.

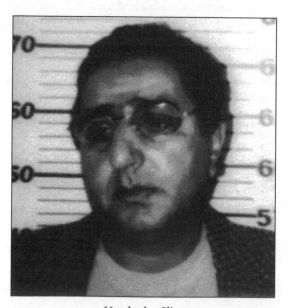
Vyacheslav Sliva

The government argued at Sliva's bail hearing that he had gone to great lengths to conceal his past and that his involvement in organized crime made him both a danger to the community and likely to flee.

For his part, Sliva told the review he was a close friend of Ivankov's and a relative by marriage, but not his business partner. "We grew up together. . . . we went to the same school." He said he had spoken with Ivankov on the phone only a couple of times. "He once told me this is a good country, stay in this country . . . and if you need anything, you can come to the States."

Sliva added that he claimed on his immigration form that he hadn't been convicted of a crime because the Gorbachev government pardoned him in 1990 of his robbery conviction after he had spent more than nine years in jail. He said his other offences were the theft of a watch when he was a teenager and a four-year prison term served when he refused to join the army in the 1960s.

The government noted that Sliva also claimed on his visitor's visa that he had been invited to the country to visit hockey player Valeri Kamensky of the Quebec Nordiques, which had since become the Colorado Avalanche. However, when the Department of Immigration contacted Kamensky, the government lawyer said, "He indicated that he did not invite Mr. Sliva and he hardly knows Mr. Sliva."

For his part, Kamensky told the *Denver Post* that he was not connected with the Russian Mob in any way. "If you need some information, call the NHL. The NHL knows everything about this. . . . I'm upset because I never hear about Russian *mafiya*. [They] never bothered me and I have never contacted them."

Canadian authorities said that Sliva had been sent by the Russian Mob to co-ordinate its activities in Toronto in conjunction with Brooklyn's Brighton Beach branch run by Sliva's brother-in-law Vyacheslav Ivankov.

Meanwhile, in Toronto, Canada's East European organized-crime squad heard Sliva on an international telephone line, conducting what sounded like a takeover of Russian crime activities in Canada. Over a wiretapped telephone, Canadian investigators said, they also heard Sliva extorting business people, making death threats, and discussing the division of payments with his brother-in-law Ivankov in New York.

Sliva "was here to obtain permanent status in Canada and then assume control of Russian-based organized crime activities here," said Glenn Hanna, an investigator who testified at Sliva's deportation hearing. Among other things, police heard Sliva discussing strategies for helping Ivankov and talking about several other organized-crime figures in Eastern and Western Europe.

Looking haggard and unshaven, Sliva was deported back to Moscow in 1997.

"I think the deportation of Mr. Sliva will disrupt the expansion of Eastern European crime in Canada," said RCMP Insp. Ben Soave. "He was one of the biggest Russian organized-crime figures we know of in Canada."

However, the RCMP suspected there were about a dozen Russian mobsters in Canada trying to set up cells and ready to fill the underworld void left by his absence. "As soon as he's gone, other key players that were underlings will try to take over," Soave said.

The Sliva operation was called Project Osada by police, using the Russian word for "siege," and police said it demonstrated that Sliva had established a criminal network in Toronto with ties to top Russian mobsters in New York, Tel Aviv, and Moscow.

In December 1999, the RCMP would show the fruits of Project Osada II. Dozens of alleged mobsters in the Greater Toronto Area, Montreal, Ottawa, Windsor, and Seattle were arrested in pre-dawn raids in one of the biggest assaults on East European organized crime in Canadian history. They included members of an Ukrainian tae kwon do team in the country for a competition. Suspects were charged with

offences ranging from conspiracy to drug importation, contravening the Immigration Act, and the new charge of contributing to the operation of a criminal organization.

Perhaps most interestingly, Osada II showed a new twist on debit-card fraud that police believed was the first of its kind uncovered anywhere in the world. Police said the group had devised a system that allowed electronic data contained on debit cards, including encrypted personal identification numbers, to be downloaded, copied, and used without the owners' knowledge.

This meant that the coded information could be intercepted when transmitted from a customer at a store to a bank, so that banks and credit-card companies could be defrauded of millions of dollars.

Police said the alleged activities were Sliva's legacy, and that the alleged conspiracy was directed from the Toronto area, not from abroad. While almost all of the people arrested were emigrés from the former Soviet Union, police said they had links to tradition Mafia and Asian crime groups.

"This is a fallout of what Sliva came here to do," Soave said. "He has left a legacy of organized crime in place."

See also: **Vyacheslav Kirillovich Ivankov, National Hockey League, Vatchagan Petrossov, Joseph Sigalov.**

Smith, Jefferson "Soapy": Dirty Money – There's a bistro named Soapy Smith's in a gentrified part of Denver, named after the criminal who preyed on gold miners coming into Canada's Yukon in the gold rush of the late nineteenth century.

It was here in Denver, at 17th and Larimer Streets, where Jefferson Smith set up a stand in the 1880s, selling to gullible folks cakes of soap he claimed contained $5, $10, $20, and $100 bills. The only soap that contained the bills were those he "sold" to cohorts who were planted in crowds watching his presentations.

Jefferson "Soapy" Smith

He certainly had moxie, and when Theodore Roosevelt, the future American president, caught his act, he exclaimed, "Damn, that man has style."

Smith didn't have scruples, however. Among his scams in Skagway, Alaska, was a fake telegraph office. The telegrams actually went no farther than an alley behind the bar. Finally, someone shot him dead, and was immediately hailed as a hero by fellow gold miners.

In Soapy Smith's bistro in Denver, they remember him with the song:

From each bottle break the neck,
Fill each glass with Pomeroy Sec.
And let each true friend drink this toast:
Here is to old Soapy's ghost.

Spartans Motorcycle Gang: Winnipeg Bikers – When they first appeared in 1967, the club's original eight members from the Elmwood area of Winnipeg wore a crest with a Trojan helmet and a shield.

They enthusiastically sold illegal drugs while associating with the Vagabonds of Toronto, the Satan's Choice of Ontario, the Wild Ones of Hamilton, and the Grim Reapers of Calgary.

By 1978, members of the Spartans were travelling extensively and associating with the Apollos of Regina. In addition, they kept an uneasy peace with the local Los Brovos, as they supported each other in various drug transactions.

Other criminal activities included prostitution, multiple assaults, collections, and property and weapons offences. By the early 1980s, the club had forty-three full members and controlled a portion of the city's drug and prostitution trade.

In April 1982, the Spartans and Los Brovos merged into one club, with a total of 141 colour-wearing members. This unity didn't last too long, as a group of dissident Los Brovoses formed a revived rival club in the winter of 1983–84. Eventually, they all faded into oblivion when the Hells Angels set up shop for good in July 2000.

See also: **Hells Angels, Los Brovos, Silent Riders, Redliners, Darwyn and Kevin Sylvester, Wolodumyr "Walter" "Nurget" Stadnick.**

Spitzee Cavalry – *See* **Whisky Runners, Wolfers, Fort Whoop-Up.**

Stadnick (sometimes spelled Stadnik), Wolodumyr "Walter" "Nurget" : Wally World – A police officer once asked him what his nickname Nurget meant, and the biker simply grinned.

Stadnick wasn't one to give away information, especially to police, which helped explain why he had risen so far in the biker world. He certainly wasn't going to explain what plenty of police and bikers wanted to know: how an anglophone from Hamilton's working-class north end could become national president of the Hells Angels, when the gang was largely Quebec-based and francophone.

Stadnick, the son of a Hamilton, Ontario, tree cutter, was an undistinguished student in high school, except for a pronounced interest in auto shop. As a teen, he was connected with the biker club the Cossacks, who stood out because of a signature odd tuft of hair on the back of their heads. Later on, he ran a roadhouse bar on Hamilton Mountain, and managed to be enough of an irritant to the Outlaws gang that they plotted to attack the bar with a rocket launcher. Police foiled the plot and Stadnick kept on irritating the Outlaws.

In many respects, much of his life was quiet, even after he joined the Angels. When in Hamilton, he could be seen taking his elderly parents to church. But there was also a constantly bizarre streak to Walter. He ran the biggest, toughest biker gang in Canada, but stood only about five-foot-four and wasn't particularly imposing physically. On the occasion when he brawled with police in Winnipeg, the

Wolodumyr "Walter" Stadnick (1st row, 3rd from left) and "Mom" Boucher (back row, left)

court ruled with him and decided that police officers were out of line. For much of his adult life, the only blots on his rap sheet were for driving offences.

All that changed in March 2001 when he and all of the members of the Quebec Nomads chapter of the Hells Angels were hit with thirteen charges of murder and attempted murder.

Police watching him – and there were many – were struck by the deference he was shown by others, including the junior bikers who would stand on the street acting as guards while he dined in swank Toronto restaurants. "You look at him walking down the street and you think, 'What's he got?'" said a Toronto-area police officer who often shadowed Stadnick.

Stadnick was a driving force behind the Angels expansion into both Ontario and Manitoba. What Stadnick offered the Angels was an eye for underworld talent. In the increasingly corporate world of outlaw bikers, Stadnick was viewed as the ultimate talent scout.

He often presented himself in downtown Winnipeg in a full-length wolf coat, and also

Walter Stadnick

sported a snakeskin belt, with a solid-gold belt buckle shaped in an Angels' death-head, which he got to mark his tenth anniversary in the club. The natty belt didn't just look expensive; it was found to conceal $15,000 in thousand-dollar bills when confiscated by Winnipeg police.

Ironically Stadnick was a peacemaker of sorts on Winnipeg streets, ordering the warring Spartans and Los Brovos gangs to ease up on their in-fighting and work together.

During the early and mid-1990s, Stadnick seemed to be in the middle of everything, and often on the move, preparing things for an Angels expansion. Although he was constantly surrounded by violence and death, the only time he was seriously injured was in a freak accident. The person who almost killed him was a priest, rushing to see the papal visit in 1984. The Angels were having a procession of their own at the same time as the papal parade, since they were commemorating the first anniversary of the murder of their national president, Yves "The Boss" Buteau. The priest ran a Stop sign and crashed into a group of Angels.

Walter Stadnick getting out of car

Some say Stadnick had got to the national presidency of *les hells* in 1988 by default, taking over a club gutted by prison terms after the testimony of former member Yves "The Mad Bumper" or "Apache" Trudeau, who told authorities of having a bloody hand in forty-three underworld slayings.

The Angels were then at rock bottom. Of fifty members in Quebec, Trudeau's testimony meant nineteen were in jail on murder charges, thirteen were hiding from murder charges, and five were in jail awaiting trial on murder charges. Another half-dozen were dead, murdered and dumped in the St. Lawrence River by fellow Angels.

Soon, Stadnick had his biker brothers dreaming of expansion, rather than dwelling on the recent bloody past. Winnipeg was a key to his expansion, and his second home for about six years during the 1990s, as he put together a network of bikers and businessmen to expand the Quebec drug pipeline westwards and stave off expansion of rival outlaw motorcycle gangs – the Outlaws, the Rock Machine, and the Bandidos. That network would eventually call itself the Redliners, a short-lived third motorcycle gang to compete with Los Brovos and Spartans for membership in the new Hells Angels Manitoba chapter.

Stadnick would eventually serve eight years as the club's national president and, toward the end of this time, he helped found the elite Nomads chapter. The Nomads, led by Maurice "Mom" Boucher, had the ultimate goal of winning the drug war in downtown Montreal with the Rock Machine and establishing Hells Angels chapters in the Golden Horseshoe region of Ontario.

Stadnick's dream of expansion came true in December 2000, when some 180 members of existing Ontario clubs – the Satan's Choice, Para-Dice Riders, Lobos, and the Last Chance – suddenly joined the Angels. Stadnick and his friend Donald "Pup" Stockford of Ancaster, on the fringes of Hamilton, had once been the only resident Hells Angels in Ontario. Suddenly, the Toronto area had the highest concentration of Hells Angels in the world.

They didn't have long to celebrate. Stockford was arrested at his comfortable home on a tree-lined street in March 2001 and hit with thirteen counts of murder and attempted murder. Stadnick was charged with similar offences while holidaying with his wife at a five-star resort in Montego Bay, Jamaica.

He was sent to the Remand Centre, a foreboding razor-wire-enclosed compound in Kingston's west end, where prisoners share a communal toilet bucket in the middle of a crowded, hot concrete cell.

He had spent a few days there when a police escort arrived to take him back to Canada. A Canadian officer jokingly asked if he would like to spend a few more weeks in the jail.

"Couple more weeks, I'd be running the place," Stadnick replied.

He was found guilty of conspiracy to commit murder and traffick drugs in June 2004.

See also: **Los Brovos, Donald Magnussen, Nomads, Redliners, Spartans.**

Steinert, Scott: Short-Lived Success – In 1996, Steinert had clearly arrived in the underworld. In 1997, he was brutally dispatched from it.

The Wisconsin-born biker moved to Quebec with his family in 1970 at the age of eight. He grew up to become a feared member of the Hells Angels Montreal chapter, and was a member of the gang's bomb-making team, with plenty of plastic explosives at his disposal. He also owned three stripper agencies and an escort service, and acted as godfather to the Death Riders gang, supervising the gang's activities in Laval and in the lower Laurentians.

All that activity meant that, in 1996, Steinert could afford to move into an extravagant Lavigueur mansion in Île-Jésus suburb. He ringed his new digs with an eight-foot-high fence and installed security cameras. His bodyguard, Donald Magnussen, who had once provided muscle for Angels national president

Scott Steinert at 1997 wedding
(*Jacques Bourdon,* Le Journal de Montréal)

Walter Stadnick, moved into one of the homes on the compound.

The estate wasn't just a home. It was also the base of Steinert's operations, and other members of the Hells Angels and the Death Riders puppet club often did business there. His business included directing and starring in several porno movies filmed on the property, the most famous of which was *Babe's Angel.*

By late August 1997, the war between the Hells Angels and the Rock Machine was in full gear, and Steinert's escort service was torched, but he didn't let the hostilities spoil his plans to marry that October.

Steinert called Magnussen on the evening of November 4, 1997, and told the bodyguard they had a meeting to attend. The two men were never seen alive again. At first, the Sûreté du Québec thought that Steinert had gone into hiding to escape deportation, and they issued a warrant for his arrest on January 22, 1998, charging him with possessing goods obtained with the proceeds of crime. The Lavigueur estate, two houses in Sorel, and a garage were seized.

On May 23, 1998, Magnussen's body was found in the St. Lawrence Seaway, wrapped in plastic. Steinert's corpse surfaced almost a year later. There was a strong suspicion that both men had been beaten to death by the Angels, but no arrest was ever made.

Word eventually filtered out to police that Steinert was killed by the Hells Angels because Magnussen killed a criminal who was friendly with the bikers, and Steinert was killed because Magnussen was his responsibility. He likely was killed by André "Toots" Tousignant, who himself was later killed by the gang.

Steinert's old mansion was put on the market by authorities under the proceeds-of-crime legislation. Someone from Vancouver bought it, but it was burned to the ground before the new owner could move in. The Angels might have killed Steinert, but they were still possessive of his property. The message over the mansion's resale was blunt: You might be able to seize Angels' property, but you'll never be allowed to use it.
See also: **Donald Magnussen.**

Sun Yee On: Expanding Triad – In December 2000, a White House report complained that Chinese gangs, including Sun Yee On, were using Canada as a gateway to enter the United States illegally. The International Crime Threat Assessment report by key American security agencies pointed at Canada as a prime venue for Triads engaged in credit-card fraud, heroin trafficking, illegal migration, and software piracy.

The two largest Hong Kong Triads, 14K Association and Sun Yee On, made substantial property investments in Canada during the 1990s, according to the report. The 14K, which maintained a base in Toronto, was reportedly the fastest-growing Triad in Canada. It has been linked to Asian criminal activities in New York and other American cities.

"Sun Yee On members are involved in trafficking heroin and methamphetamine, as well as alien smuggling, to the United States, where the Triad has ties to New York's Tung On gang," the report said, adding that prominent 14K members from Hong Kong and Macau have emigrated to Canada, and Sun Yee On members have settled in Toronto, Edmonton, and Vancouver.

See also: **14K Association, Triads.**

The Sundance Kid: Alberta Ranch Hand – His real name was Harry Alonzo Longabaugh and he also answered to Harry Place and Frank Boyd, but he's best known as the character played by Robert Redford in the 1969 movie *Butch Cassidy and the Sundance Kid.*

What's not so well known are his Canadian roots, and that he often hid out in southern Saskatchewan and lived in Alberta from 1890 to 1892, when he was in his early to mid-twenties. Longabaugh didn't advertise his nickname – The Sundance Kid – and certainly no one asked about it when he showed up to work as a cowboy for the North-West Cattle Company – known as the "Bar U" – west of High River, Alberta.

He got the nickname when, as a youth, he served an eighteen-month jail term in Sundance, Wyoming, for stealing a horse, a saddle, and a gun from a ranch worker in Crook County, Wyoming, when he was either sixteen or seventeen years old. Upon his release from jail on February 8, 1889, the Sundance *Gazette* noted that, "The term of 'kid' Longabaugh has expired." From then on, he was known as the Sundance Kid.

Longabaugh returned to Colorado, where he had lived with a distant cousin, and joined Robert Leroy Parker (a.k.a. Butch Cassidy), Tom McCarty, and Matt Warner in holding up the San Miguel Valley Bank in Telluride on June 24, 1889. After that, he needed a new safe haven, and fled north to Canada in time for the 1890 cattle season.

There he looked up an old friend from Wyoming, Cyril Everett "Ebb" Johnson, who lived in the Cochrane, Alberta, area. They had worked together earlier in Wyoming at the Power River Ranch, which expanded into Canada in 1886, leasing land on Mosquito Creek, near where the town of Nanton is today. It had the brand of "76" and that was its local nickname.

The Sundance Kid (seated, first on left) beside Bill Kilpatrick

Johnson was foreman of the "Bar U," which had 10,410 cattle and 832 horses in 1890. Sundance quickly proved to be a valuable employee, as well as a popular one. Fred Ings of the nearby Midway Ranch noted that "a thoroughly likeable fellow was Harry, a general favorite with everyone, a splendid rider and a top notch cow hand." Ings also said that the Kid was law-abiding and "no one could have been better behaved or more decent."

Ings had reason to say nice things about him, since he believed the Sundance Kid saved his life during a fall roundup. "One . . . night on Mosquito Creek was one of the worst times I ever went through. A blizzard was coming from the north with blinding snow. I was given the ten o'clock shift, and with me was Harry Longdebough [sic], a good-looking young American cow puncher who feared neither man nor devil."

The herd was large, made up mostly of heavy beef cattle. Sundance drove ahead to direct them while Ings stayed at the back to hold them together.

Ings continued: "I was riding a sure-footed, thick-set, little grey horse, but I had a dozen falls that stormy night. In spite of being warmly dressed, we found it desperately cold and in the thickly falling snow lost all sense of locality."

The Sundance Kid rode back to find Ings lost at the rear of the herd, and helped guide him back to camp, likely saving his life.

Rancher Bert Sheppard also had a high opinion of Sundance, describing him as "a good rider, roper and all-round top hand." Most of his acquaintances seemed to know he had been in trouble in the United States, but he was fully accepted because of his ability and his friendly attitude.

He also worked for the McHugh Brothers at the H2 Ranch, on the Bow River near Carseland, Alberta, where they had a contract to supply beef to the nearby Blackfoot reserve. Also while in Alberta, he was believed to have worked breaking horses for contractors who were laying the railroad from Calgary to Fort MacLeod.

He appeared in the spring 1891 Dominion Census, District No. 197. The Bar U Ranch was enumerated on April 6, 1891, with eighteen residents, including "Henry Longabough [sic], age 25, birthplace U.S.A., occupation horse breaker."

Not everyone liked him. A cowboy at the Bar U, Herbert Millar, claimed that he saw a small hacksaw hidden between Sundance's saddle and his horse blanket. This may be tied to his arrest by the North-West Mounted Police for "cruelty to animals" on August 7, 1891. Sundance hired a lawyer, J.A. Bangs, and the charges were immediately dismissed the same day by Superintendent J.H. McIllree and Inspector A.R. Cuthbert. No explanation was given for their immediate dismissal. He was kept on at Bar U, suggesting the ranch's owners did not believe the charges of animal cruelty had any factual foundation.

On November 18, 1891, Sundance signed as the witness and best man at the wedding of his friend Ebb Johnson and his bride, Mary Eleanor Bigland, at The Grange, a Calgary-area ranch owned by her uncle, with Rev. J.C. Herdman of Knox Presbyterian Church in Calgary presiding.

Some time after the wedding, Sundance left the Bar U, perhaps because Millar, who had pushed the cruelty to animals charges, had become the foreman there. He went into partnership with Frank Hamilton at the Grand Central Hotel saloon on Atlantic Avenue in Calgary, across the street from the railway depot. There are unverified reports that Butch Cassidy visited Calgary during that time, and that he even may have worked at a Calgary livery stable.

The partnership between Sundance and Hamilton didn't last long, and ended in gunplay. Hamilton had a reputation for taking in partners and then choosing to fight them rather than hand over their share of the profits.

Sundance wouldn't be intimidated. Author Vicky Kelly said that he vaulted over the bar and "before his feet hit the floor his gun was jammed in his partner's middle." The debt was paid, but

The Sundance Kid's Grand Central Hotel, Calgary (Glenbow Archives, NA-5)

the partnership was over, and early in 1892, Sundance returned to the United States.

There, he soon hooked up with rustlers Dutch Henry Ieach and Frank Jones, and together they ran stolen horses from the Culbertson and Plentywood area of Montana across into the Big Muddy Badlands of southern Saskatchewan, near the community of Big Beaver. It was the first stop on the Outlaw Trail, a string of safe havens stretching down to Mexico. This one was particularly safe, because American authorities could not cross the border into Canada.

Sundance joined a band of about ten outlaws called the Wild Bunch, who thrived from 1896 through 1901, and whose ranks included Robert Leroy Parker (Butch Cassidy). Sometimes the gang included Bill Curry, an outlaw originally from Prince Edward Island.

The Wild Bunch robbed banks and slow-moving, cash-carrying trains, but perhaps their proudest moment came on September 19, 1900, after they held up the First National Bank in Winnemucca, Nevada. They made off with $30,000, and legend has it they headed for Fort

Worth, Texas, where they posed for a group photograph, then mailed it to the bank, with a note of thanks for the "withdrawal."

Often, in times of stress, Sundance retreated to the Big Beaver area of southern Saskatchewan. He had fled there after the November 29, 1892, robbery of a Great Northern Railway train at Malta, Montana, and a police report from the time speculated he may have also gone to Calgary to visit Ebb Johnson.

However, times changed. Trains got faster and private security companies got more efficient, and ultimately Butch Cassidy and the Sundance Kid ended up in Bolivia. A 1909 report said that Sundance and Butch were killed there by a posse after a payroll robbery. News of his robberies filtered up to the Calgary area, where he had many friends. Fred Ings wrote, "We all felt sorry when he left and got in bad again across the line."

Another story, promoted by Cassidy's sister, was that the Sundance Kid lived under an alias and died in Casper, Wyoming, in 1957. But the account can't really be trusted. Folklore about

his partner Butch Cassidy's death has him alternately dying in Vernal, Utah, in the late 1920s; on an island off the coast of Mexico in 1932; in Tombstone, Arizona, in 1937; and twice in Spokane, Washington, the same year.
See also: **Big Muddy Badlands, Dutch Henry, Sam Kelly.**

Sylvester, Darwin: Dreams of Glory – There was a time when the biker from rural Carberry, Manitoba, dreamed of bringing the Hells Angels to Winnipeg. Sylvester was leader of the Spartans motorcycle gang there, and in the late 1980s and early 1990s, he loved the idea of teaming up with the mighty Angels against his bitter local rival, the Los Brovos.

In the end, Sylvester achieved only half his dream. The Hells Angels moved into Winnipeg in the early 1990s, but they didn't back him against the Los Brovos. In fact, they likely murdered him.

Not long after the Angels arrived in Winnipeg, they had identified Sylvester as an impediment to their expansion, with his hot-and-cold, unstable personality and dictatorial ruling style.

Sylvester vanished after a meeting with the Hells Angels in the Spartans clubhouse on Chalmers Avenue in Winnipeg in June 1998, and was never seen again.

Police suspect his body was buried somewhere outside the city limits.

The body of his driver, Robert Glen Rosmus, was found on February 8, 1999, in a ditch on snow-packed Transport Road east of the Perimeter Highway, just outside the city. He had been shot dead.

Police suspect Rosmus's body was deliberately dumped outside the city limits in RCMP jurisdiction – like the bodies of four other bikers murdered in the mid-1990s – in hopes that jurisdictional wranglings between the city police and RCMP would slow investigations.

See also: **Los Brovos, Redliners, Kevin Sylvester, Spartans.**

Sylvester, Kevin: Grieving Brother – In the summer of 2001, Kevin's brother, Darwin, had been missing for three years and was presumed murdered.

That summer, he was both the intended target or the gunman in a flurry of tit-for-tat drive-by shootings. Four were on residential streets while the other, which Sylvester carried out himself, was in broad daylight near the busy downtown intersection of Portage Avenue and Broadway.

That attack sent pedestrians fleeing for cover and was considered low, even by subterranean gang standards. His Hells Angels rival was sitting in a truck beside his two-year-old son when Sylvester opened fired. The boy and his father survived and, soon afterwards, Kevin Sylvester began co-operating with police.
See also: **Los Brovos, Redliners, Spartans, Darwin Sylvester.**

Sylvestro, Antonio "Tony" and Frank "Chich": Battling Brothers – The Hamilton brothers were core Mafia members for southern Ontario in the 1940s and 1950s, along with Matteo "Big Joe" Cipolla in Guelph and Nicholas Cicchini in Windsor.

Frank, who sometimes travelled under the name Frank Ross, was a bootlegger and a lieutenant of Rocco Perri and was interned in the Second World War for his Mafia associations and as an enemy alien. He often reminded friends that he was frequently searched by police and advised them they should not carry embarrassing addresses or phone numbers in case they were also searched.
See also: **Antonio Papalia, Rocco Perri.**

T

Tews, Robert Blaine – *See* **Russell Krowetz.**

Thanksgiving Summit: Talking Turkey – In October 2000, there was an unprecedented biker dinner party in a downtown Montreal restaurant, as top Rock Machine members and Hells Angels members sat down together, toasting each other with champagne and dining on seafood and pasta.

It was an attempt to calm the public and the politicians, amidst calls for tougher anti-gang legislation in the face of escalating biker wars, and the deaths of innocent civilians. The most memorable moment was when the Angels' Quebec boss, Maurice "Mom" Boucher, and Rock Machine boss, Fred Faucher, shook hands for the camera and called for peace – not blood.

That peace lasted for just a few months, but considering the biker climate of Montreal, even that was enough to make Montrealers feel thankful.

See also: **Maurice "Mom" Boucher, Paul Porter, Rock Machine.**

Thanksgiving Peace Summit, 2000

239

Tian Li: Hot Plastic – A member of the Big Circle Boys gang, he moved in the early 1990s from Vancouver to California. There he was convicted of a scheme to sell hundreds of counterfeit credit cards to undercover agents in a sting investigation run by the U.S. Secret Service, the San Francisco police, and the California Department of Justice.

Assistant district attorney George Butterworth said Tian's counterfeiting scheme was "not some street-level, nickel-and-dime situation. This is a very sophisticated operation. It involved the use of a runner. . . . It involved the use of lookouts. It involved the use of cellphones that were in other people's names."
See also: **Big Circle Boys.**

Todaro, Joe: Hot Wings – When Todaro became Buffalo Mob boss in October 1984, "Johnny Pops" Papalia assumed the role of his southern Ontario representative. Todaro's family was involved in racketeering with the Laborers Union and the cheese and the pizza business.

His pizzeria on West Ferry Street was perhaps the most popular in the city, and that's where he retired when he said he left the Mob. He had supplied pizzas and wings to the Clintons and Gores and to soldiers serving in the Persian Gulf War.
See also: **John "Johnny Pops" Papalia.**

Town Tavern – *See* **Max Bluestein, John "Johnny Pops" Papalia.**

Tousignant, André "Touts" "Peanuts": Tough Nut – He was a member of the Hells Angels' puppet gang, the Rockers, which was formed on March 26, 1992, by Luc "Bordello" Bordeleau and André "Marine Boy" Gagnon. The Rockers were often used as shock troops in the biker

André "Touts" Tousignant (no beard) and friend from the Rockers bike gang

wars, carrying out bloody tasks for the Angels.

Tousignant impressed fellow bikers in March 1995 when he yanked the detonator out of a remote-controlled bomb that had been placed at the Rockers clubhouse and threw it across the street, where it exploded. He was trusted enough to be bodyguard for the head of the Hells Angels Nomads chapter, Maurice "Mom" Boucher, and he killed prison guard Diane Lavigne for Boucher.

Tousignant was told to lay low after the Lavigne murder, but word reached Boucher that he had been involved in a drunken argument in a bar. Boucher worried that Tousignant was a loose cannon, and called him on December 6, 1997, for a visit. Tousignant's fingerless, burned body was found near Bromont, northeast of Montreal, on February 27, 1998. He had been shot several times and then set on fire, and the damage was so extensive that it wasn't until March 28 that the body was finally identified through dental records and tattoos left on his partly burned skin.

Ironically, that was on the eve of Boucher's preliminary hearing for ordering the murder of two prison guards, including Lavigne.
See also: **Maurice "Mom" Boucher, Diane Lavigne, Donald Magnussen, Scott Steinert.**

Asau Tran: Final Victim – Peace came to Toronto's Chinatown when gang leader Asau Tran was shot more than thirty times in his face and knees outside a downtown Toronto restaurant in 1991. That marked the end of a bloody war between rival gangs that claimed ten lives and injured more than a dozen other victims.

Before the killers fled the scene, they placed a white glove – the same type worn by police officers at funerals – under Tran's body. Scribbled on the palm was the badge number of a Toronto police officer who was active against the gangs.

The message to police was clear and chilling: Back off.

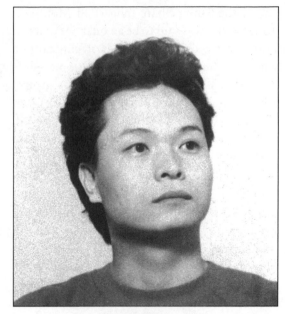

Asau Tran

Police cited Tran's presence in Canada as an example of lax immigration standards. A convicted extortionist, Tran arrived in Canada in the early 1980s as a refugee, then moved on to the United States. He was later deported to Toronto from Los Angeles, but Canadian immigration law wouldn't allow him to be sent back to Vietnam, where he would face death.

In a rare television interview just a week before his killing, Tran told reporter-host Isabel Bassett that he wasn't such a bad guy. However, he predicted that he could get shot nonetheless. Vietnamese gang leaders seldom reach forty and Tran seemed to know he would be no exception, telling Bassett, "These guys – one of these groups may not let me stay alive."
See also: **Trung Chi Truong, Vietnamese Gangs.**

Trepassy, Newfoundland – *See* **Bartholomew "Black Bart" Roberts.**

Triads: Pre-Confederation Roots – The first known case of a Canadian Triad society was in 1863 in the gold-mining community of Barkerville, British Columbia. The group was called the Hung Shan Tong (Red Mountain Tong) and it was said to be an offshoot of a San Franciscan tong (a tong is technically a Chinese businessmen's association, while a Triad is strictly an organized crime group) whose members travelled north to avoid racial abuse in California. Other societies followed, many of them legally constituted as Freemason societies.

In 1908, opium was declared illegal in Canada, and Triad members smuggled it into Canada from Hong Kong, where it was still legal. One of the leading smugglers in Vancouver between 1905 and the late 1930s was Shu Moy, who used cabin-crew workers on the *Empress* and *Blue Funnel* passenger liners to move the drug between China and Canada.

Triads moved in the 1880s to Toronto, brought by railroad workers migrating east after the railway was completed. They were active in bordellos, bakeries, and laundries and, during the Second World War, they helped smuggle Chinese immigrants, as well as Jews fleeing Nazi Germany.

Agencies contributing to the report included the Central Intelligence Agency, the Federal Bureau of Investigation, the Secret Service, and the Customs Service, and they jointly concluded that the rapid spread of international crime since the end of the Cold War posed a significant threat to democratic governments and free-market economies.

It pointed at what it considered Canada's lax rules for newcomers, particularly a plan aimed at attracting foreign investors: "Members of ethnic Chinese criminal groups from China, Hong Kong, Taiwan and Macau have exploited Ottawa's immigration policies and entrepreneur program to enter the country and become Canadian residents, which makes it easier for them to cross into the United States."

The report described the Triads, which collectively have an estimated global membership exceeding 100,000, as fluid associations of ethnic Chinese criminals and quasi-legitimate businessmen involved in an array of criminal enterprises.

See also: **Big Circle Boys, 14K Association, Ghost Shadows, Lau Wing Kui, Kung Lok, Sun Yee On.**

Triumbari, Salvatore "Sammy": Fatal Meeting – On January 5, 1967, this member of Toronto's 'Ndrangheta met with five other men – including two New York City extortionists – in a Little Italy restaurant in Toronto. The next day, Triumbari was murdered. The killing was never solved.

See also: **Giacomo Luppino, 'Ndrangheta, John "Johnny Pops" Papalia, Michele "Mike" Racco, Filippo Vendemini.**

Trudeau, Yves "Apache" "The Mad Bumper": Countless Killings – He murdered so many people for the Hells Angels and their friends that he lost count of his victims.

Trudeau had once been leader of the Hells Angels chapter in Laval, Quebec, and he earned the disapproval of his biker brothers by trying to extort $250,000 from the gang's Halifax chapter.

News of his collection efforts against fellow bikers and enthusiastic pill-popping wasn't well received among fellow Quebec Hells Angels. Hells Angels from Halifax, Sorel, Quebec, Sherbrooke, and the United States all agreed that Trudeau and his Laval comrades were attracting too much attention and that their drug use was out of control, so a contract was put out on the entire chapter. The killers missed Trudeau, however, because he was in a drug treatment centre at Oka at the time.

Hearing his chapter had been rubbed out, he gave himself up to authorities, which meant he would be able to survive, unless his former biker brothers found him. Trudeau received $40,000 and agreed to plead guilty to forty-three charges of involuntary manslaughter in exchange for testimony against his former Hells Angels colleagues. He was given a life sentence

Yves "Apache" Trudeau (Yves Malette)

when he was sent to prison in 1986, but became eligible for parole after just seven years.

Word was that his old Angels cohorts put a $300,000 price on his head.

On April 29, 2004, Trudeau pleaded guilty to four sex charges involving a boy under the age of fourteen. He was acting as his own legal counsel when he made the plea.

See also: **Hells Angels, Red Zone.**

Trung Chi Truong: Trademark Anger – The glass counter shattered easily in the New Phnom Penh jewellery store in Lowell, Massachusetts, when Truong crashed a hammer onto it October 16, 1986. He and two other two men screamed some threats and left quickly, with $100,000 in jewellery.

It was such an easy haul that they decided to

come back three months later. This time, their hammers bounced off new unbreakable plastic counters, and they turned their frustration – and weapons – on the owner's wife, Mon Ly. When they left, the Cambodian immigrant's skull had been cracked open with the butt of a pistol and she lay in a pool of blood.

"It was probably one of the most violent robberies the area had seen," a Boston detective said. "It was typical of Ah Sing's style."

Ah Sing was better known in Toronto and Montreal as Trung Chi Truong. The brutal attack on the shopkeeper bore the bloody trademark of the *dai lo*, or gang boss: intense anger.

"I would say he is the most dangerous Vietnamese gangbanger in North America," one Toronto investigator told the *Boston Globe*.

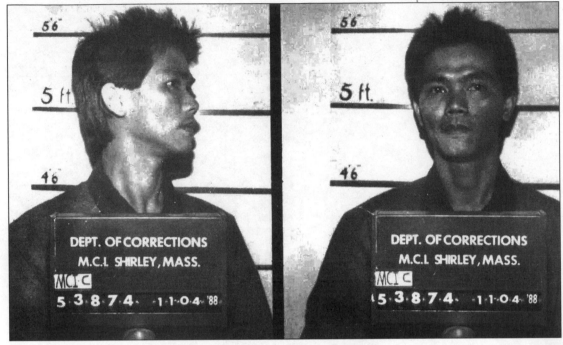

Trung Chi Truong

"You just mention his name, and everybody runs."

Truong's Vietnamese gang was known as Ah Sing's Boys, and their crimes bore the imprint of Truong's fury. In 1991 in Toronto, Truong's gang gunned down three strangers, because one had glanced at a woman in a nightclub.

The roots of his anger can be traced back to his childhood in Saigon in the early 1960s, according to his Boston attorney, Norman Zalkind. Wartime destruction was the norm for this son of Chinese-born merchants as he grew into his late teens in Vietnam.

A perilous four-day ride on a rickety boat took Truong and his brother from Vietnam to a refugee camp in Malaysia in 1978. They lived there for eleven months, then moved on to Texas. By 1980, they were in Boston, where Truong's brother earned his citizenship and opened a barber shop, while Truong hooked up with Chinatown gangs, extorting money from other small-business people.

Truong tried to impress Stephen "Sky Dragon" Tse, then leader of Boston's Chinese

Ping On gang, with his violence and mobility. Six weeks after the first Lowell robbery, Truong organized the execution of Boston gambler Son Van Vu, twenty-eight. Shortly after Vu's body was discovered with a bullet in his head in a Hollywood Boulevard motel, Truong was in Toronto, organizing two more robberies.

Then he bounced back to New Phnom Penh jewellery store in Lowell for the raid that almost killed Mon Ly.

As Truong rose in the underworld, Tse's grasp slipped, and in 1989, Tse fled to his native Hong Kong. Six years later he was arrested there on racketeering charges. However, before he left Boston, Tse kicked Truong out of the Ping On for committing unsanctioned jewellery-store heists.

This didn't matter much to Truong, who had forged ties with the powerful New York–based Vietnamese gang BTK, or Born to Kill gang.

In 1990, Truong was in Montreal, directing a Calgary robbery by cellphone. When his gang started to get nervous, he ordered them back into a store for the heist, which netted $500,000.

By 1991, his extortion ring was collecting $10,000 a week in Montreal alone.

Truong was scooped up by Massachusetts police, but escaped custody and fled to Canada. He was known in Toronto in the early 1990s as the *dai lo* of an intensely loyal Vietnamese street gang, which was involved in an unprecedented wave of Chinatown murders and extortions. By late summer of 1991, ten people in Toronto were dead, all associates of Truong's main rival, Asau Tran, the dapper self-proclaimed King of Chinatown. Tran himself was machine-gunned to death as he left the Pot of Gold Restaurant on Dundas Street West near Beverly Street. Truong was in jail in Boston at the time, but police said he was suspected of ordering the hit from there.

His gang was also behind a triple-murder on March 3, 1991, at the A Don restaurant on College Street.

His most blatant crime was the one that triggered his downfall. He publicly assassinated Phong Ly, a rival gang member, on August 27, 1994, in a gambling den in Boston's Chinatown. He organized the killing for weeks, and obsessively planned the escape route along Tyler Street.

Two suspects in that case were arrested in Toronto in 1995, and things were now falling fast for Truong. His gang's loyalty had waned as he grew greedy and shared less with them. "It was Truong's failure to look after his followers that ultimately led to his downfall," Const. John Glenn of the RCMP's criminal intelligence section told John Duncanson of the *Toronto Star*.

In 1998 in Boston, Truong pleaded guilty to Ly's murder, as well as heroin trafficking, extortion, and the jewellery-store robberies, ensuring he would spend at least twenty-two years in prison, unless he could again escape custody. At that point, he had been on the run from police in Canada and the United States for more than a decade. When he finally went behind bars, Mon Ly, his victim from the Phnom Penh jewellery store attack, still suffered from memory loss.

See also: **Born to Kill, Asau Tran.**

V

Vallée, Richard: Wrong Turn – A group of Quebecers were bowling in tiny Rouses Point, in northern New York State, at an alley where Lee Carter, Jr., thirty-one, worked as a bartender, when one of the men made him an interesting offer.

Would Carter be interested in driving a car up from New York City to the border? The trip would involve transporting a large package in the trunk of his car and, if Carter agreed, his fee would be hefty.

Carter, a prison guard's son, was naturally suspicious, and reported the offer to a state police investigator in northern New York. Soon he agreed to work with police in an undercover sting operation to learn the identity of the stranger. "In essence, he was just an ordinary person who reported the possibility of criminal activity and helped the authorities," said Don Kinsella, a former assistant U.S. attorney in Albany.

On June 8, 1992, a few months after the initial approach, Carter drove south to New York City, with a state police investigator accompanying him part of the way. He made

Richard Vallée

the return trip with fifty-four kilograms of cocaine in the trunk.

Two Montreal men arrived to pick up the cocaine from Carter in Rouses Point, but they could fit only about half of it in their trunk. They were nabbed by customs inspectors on their drive back into Canada, in what authorities tried to make appear a random search, so that Carter's cover wouldn't be blown.

Eventually, Carter was contacted by other Montrealers, who invited him to Quebec and convinced him to bring the rest of their cocaine. With federal and Canadian authorities looking over his shoulder, Carter went to Montreal and made contact with various Hells Angels members, including Richard Vallée, a demolitions expert and a founding member of the Angels' elite Nomads chapter. Vallée was considered by police to be one of the most dangerous criminals in the world, and was a suspect in several killings and murder plots, although Quebec authorities were never able to convict him.

Carter was the only witness who could tie Vallée to the cocaine-smuggling plot when, on July 26, 1993, a man in a U.S. Postal Service uniform asked one of Carter's neighbours where he lived.

Two days later, Carter climbed behind the wheel of his older-model Porsche, turned the key, and ignited a blast that threw pieces of his car on top of the bowling alley next door to his trailer.

When authorities raided a Montreal residence tied to Vallée, they found blasting caps, explosives, and a U.S. Postal Service uniform.

In December 1996, a federal grand jury in Albany indicted Vallée *in absentia* on murder charges. In June 1997, two days before Vallée was scheduled to be extradited to Albany, he was in downtown Montreal's St-Luc Hospital, awaiting surgery for a broken jaw. There he got a telephone call from someone who the guards thought was his wife and, also around this time, nurses saw a man in sunglasses walk toward the shower in Vallée's room.

Vallée asked to go to the shower, and one of the two unarmed security guards in his room accompanied him. A Hells Angel accomplice, who had been hiding in a closet, pulled a twelve-gauge shotgun on the guard and, within minutes, the guards were gagged and bound and Vallée and three accomplices were fleeing on stolen motorcycles.

His story appeared on the television show *America's Most Wanted*, and a wanted poster issued by the U.S. Marshals Service was posted in American federal buildings, which read: "Armed and dangerous. . . . Vallée is a member of a large-scale international cocaine-smuggling organization and a demolition expert with a violent criminal history."

Vallée had been on the run for six years when, at 1:30 a.m. on Friday, April 11, 2003, a motorist turned right on a red light at the corner of Sherbrooke Street West and Décarie Boulevard in west-end Montreal. Anywhere else in North America – except for Montreal and New York City – and that right turn on a red light would have been legal. However, this was Montreal, and a police officer pulled him over.

The bearded, bespectacled man behind the wheel looked a bit drunk and, when police searched his car, they found a loaded pistol and $3,500 cash. The driver was taken into custody, where he was fingerprinted and failed a breathalyzer test. He said his name was Guy Turner, and he had credit cards, a Quebec driver's licence, and a Canadian passport under that name. He sounded like a businessman and told officers that he was the owner of a scuba-diving school in Costa Rica, and that the $3,500 cash was to buy diving equipment. Then he was set free, on a promise to appear in court for the failed breathalyzer and illegal-firearms charge.

When police later checked his fingerprints, they realized they had just freed Richard Vallée, whom they had been hunting for almost six years.

Police won't say exactly how, but shortly afterwards, they had tracked him to an address in

U.S. Department of Justice
United States Marshals Service

MOST WANTED

Name: Richard VALLEE
Alias: Rick Vallee, Rich Vallee, Rick Valley, Rich Vallee

Description:

Sex: . . . . MALE
Race: . . . . WHITE
Date of Birth: . . . . NOVEMBER 10, 1957
Place of Birth: . . . . QUEBEC
Height: . . . . 5' 10"
Weight: . . . . 195 POUNDS
Eyes: . . . . BLUE
Hair: . . . . BROWN
Skintone: . . . . MEDIUM
Scars/Tattoos: . . . . SCAR ON LEFT THIGH

Wanted For: . . . . Murder of a Government Witness
Warrant Issued: . . . . . . Northern District of New York, Albany
Warrant Number: W007294002
Date of Warrant: . . . . . . August 28, 1996

ARMED AND DANGEROUS

VALLEE is a member of the Hells Angels Three Rivers, Quebec Chapter. VALLEE is charged with using a car bomb to murder a government witness in Plattsburg, New York. VALLEE escaped from Canadian authorities while awaiting extradition to the United States. His escape was effected with the assistance of armed associates. VALLEE is a member of a large scale international cocaine smuggling organization and a demolition expert with a violent criminal history.

NOTICE: Before arrest, verify warrant through the National Crime Information Center (NCIC). If arrested or whereabouts known contact the nearest United States Marshals Service office or call the United States Marshals Service Headquarters at 1 (800) 336-0102.

For more information see the U.S. Marshals Service website www.usmarshals.gov

Richard Vallée

Laval and began trailing him through Montreal. Heavily armed tactical officers arrested Vallée at 7 p.m. on April 17, 2003, as he walked out of a downtown Montreal convenience store on St. Mathieu Street. No shots were fired.

Canadian police believe Vallée, now forty-five, had slipped back into Montreal on March 25, 2003, with the forged identity papers and his features altered by plastic surgery. On the American side of the border, prosecutors noted, if they hoped to get him extradited, that they would not be able to seek the death penalty. Canadian authorities only extradite criminals if they are convinced they will not face execution.

"He's lucky he got caught in Canada," said Don Kinsella, the former assistant U.S. attorney who handled the original Carter murder case. *See also:* **Nomads.**

Vancouver Stock Exchange: Lead Trading – There was a time when brokers here might have been forgiven if they wore bulletproof vests under their suspenders.

Between 1969 and 1997, more than a dozen promoters and brokers were shot, beaten, murdered, or had simply vanished, and most of these cases were never solved.

The Vancouver Exchange acted as a magnet for millions of dollars of high-risk capital every year, and criminals have been drawn to "junior stocks," which are far easier to manipulate than blue-chip giants.

Police have nervously watched as criminals connected to the Hells Angels biker gang, the Italian and Russian Mobs, and various other organizations have played the market. Among those criminals was Martin Chambers, who obtained a master of laws degree from Oxford University and who was known by police and underworld figures alike as "Lex Luther." Chambers was sentenced in December 2003 in Florida to a fifteen-year term for money-laundering there. Another active player on the Vancouver Exchange was Ernie Ozolins, former leader of the Hells Angels Haney, B.C., chapter,

who was involved in what's known on the market as a "pump-and-dump scheme." Ozolins and two associates pumped up the price of a bogus mining company, then bailed out and pocketed the profits. Ozolins was shot dead with his girlfriend on June 2, 1997, in a murder that remains unsolved.

The British Columbia Securities Commission countered with a five-member securities-fraud office, while the RCMP's local commercial-crime unit boosted its staff count.

Among the Vancouver Exchange's low points:

- On March 9, 1987, Vancouver Stock Exchange promoter and fraud artist Guy LaMarche, fifty, was shot to death in Toronto's Royal York Hotel.
- On July 23, 1988, Robert White, president of VSE-listed Duck Book Communications Inc., was shot and killed by robbers in Central America.
- On August 11, 1994, Vancouver Stock Exchange director Nick Masee, fifty-five, and his wife, Lisa, thirty-nine, vanished without a trace.
- On October 7, 1995, Howe Street financier Assa Manhas, forty-four, fell from the twentieth floor of a San Francisco hotel. He had been a key figure in several Vancouver Exchange stock plays.

See also: **David Ward, Ray Ginnetti.**

Vendemini, Filippo: Popped – He worked as a soft-drink salesman in the 1960s at Cynar Beverages in Toronto, where his boss was Salvatore Triumbari. Then he moved on to set up a shoe store at Bloor Street West and Gladstone Avenue.

Vendemini had been a suspect himself in an extortion racket that bombed and burned bakeries owned by Italian-born businessmen, and he was also known to smuggle bootleg whisky and handle European counterfeit money. The father of five lived in a bungalow on Sherman Court in North York, where suspicious police observed a meeting of about thirty men on January 3, 1967.

It was at the shoe store that Vendemini was murdered on June 6, 1969, at thirty-four. The killing was never solved, but the reason was believed to be a power struggle in the 'Ndrangheta.

See also: **Giacomo Luppino, 'Ndrangheta, Michele "Mike" Racco, Salvatore Triumbari, Paolo Violi, Rocco Zito.**

Vietnamese Gangs – They were first noticed on the streets of major Canadian cities in the early 1980s, and what they lacked in finesse, they made up for in violence.

Many of the gang members lost their families during the Vietnam War and grew up in grim, overcrowded, refugee camps, where they learned about narcotics, weapons, and extortion. Others arrived as boat people after terrible journeys.

They formed tight bonds with other young criminals, who they often call "brother," "uncle," and "father." When refugee camp members eventually were allowed entry into Canada and the United States, many of them retained their old ties and values. That means that criminals in Toronto had bonds to cells in Calgary, Windsor, Kitchener, Montreal, and Ottawa, as well as in New York, Boston, and San Francisco.

Many of their original members grew up not expecting to live long, and they didn't invest money or aim for respectability like earlier crimes groups such as the Asian Triad secret societies or the Mafia.

See also: **Lotus Gang, Asau Tran, Trung Chi Truong.**

Violi, Domenico: Grieving Grandfather – Italian police had called him a boss of the 'Ndrangheta (Calabrian Mafia), and he was twice deported from Canada as an undesirable alien. Settling in Parma, Ohio, near Cleveland,

he made three trips north to bury his sons, Paolo, Francesco, and Rocco, after they were murdered in Montreal underworld struggles of the 1970s and 1980s. He outlived them all, dying March 5, 1990, in a Cleveland-area hospital of a liver ailment.

See also: **'Ndrangheta; Francesco "Frank," Paolo, and Rocco Violi.**

Violi, Francesco "Frank": Logical Victim – He was murdered February 8, 1977, at age thirty-nine in the office of the Violi family importing business in Rivières-des-Prairies, Quebec. He was known as his older brother Paolo's chief enforcer, and was the logical first person to attack in an assault on the family. Attacks on the other brothers followed, as the Sicilian Mob shoved rival Calabrians to the side in the Montreal underworld.

See also: **'Ndrangheta; Domenico, Paolo, and Rocco Violi.**

Violi, Paolo: Lord of Jean Talon East – Pegged for the leadership of the Cotroni Mafia family of Montreal, he was murdered shortly after he came to power. It was a short trip to death after a long move up the underworld ladder.

Violi immigrated to southern Ontario from Calabria in 1951 at age twenty, and was arrested five years later, after he fatally shot an immigrant named Natale Brigante in Toronto. The charge was reduced to manslaughter, as police witnesses proved uncooperative. Violi, who had been stabbed in the dispute, pleaded self-defence and was acquitted.

In April 1961, he was charged with a bootlegging offence, when alcohol was found in a rear garage on Ossington Avenue in Toronto. The car was registered to Filippo Vendemini, who was later killed by the Mob. At the time, Violi was suspected of arranging bootlegging between Toronto and Montreal.

By 1962, he was meeting with Rocco Zito at a bakery in Hamilton, with about thirty well-known bootleggers from Montreal, Toronto,

Paolo Violi outside his Reggio Bar coffee shop in North Montreal

Paolo Violi (standing, right, in bright shirt) in custody in the Bordeaux Jail in Montreal in the mid-1970s

Paolo Violi

At Giuseppe Violi's funeral, Paolo Violi (far left) in front

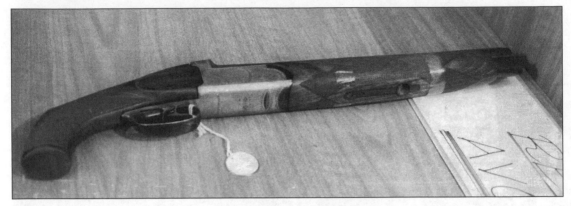

Gun used to murder Paolo Violi

and Hamilton, including Antonio Papalia, the father of mobster "Johnny Pops" Papalia. The purpose of the meeting, chaired by Violi, was to put two large stills in the Toronto-Hamilton area and to make sure Ontario distributors would deal only with him.

By 1965, his stature was high enough for him to marry Grazia Luppino, daughter of Hamilton don Giacomo Luppino, at a wedding attended by Vic Cotroni and Luigi Greco of Montreal. Cotroni was his best man and later godfather to his first-born son. "Johnny Pops" Papalia was godfather to his second son, and Joe Gentile of Vancouver was godfather to one of his daughters.

In 1970, with his brother Francesco and Vic and Frank Cotroni, he went on a "holiday" in Acapulco, where he met with U.S. Mob money-man Meyer Lansky to discuss what to do if Quebec legalized gambling.

By now, he was playing the role of Mob boss with a smile and a warm handshake. Violi was now a key figure in the Mob family of Vic Cotroni, which ran the Canadian branch-plant operations for the Bonanno family of New York City. He sponsored bicycle races from his *gelateria* on Jean Talon East and drove around Montreal in his white Cadillac, often stopping to offer a ride to those he knew. Behind the smiling face, however, was a man who wanted a cut of everything, even the loot taken during break-ins at homes of Italian families attending weddings.

His undoing came in the form of an under-cover police officer, Bob Menard, who, from 1970 to 1976, posed as an electrician and bugged many of Violi's conversations from a room above his ice-cream parlour. The penetration of his ranks by the police officer lowered his respect among mobsters, and made him seem like a petty tyrant to many of the public.

In 1976, he was acquitted in Montreal on the charge of conspiracy to assault a restaurant owner, then jailed for refusing to testify at a Quebec crime inquiry. At that inquiry, things started to fall apart.

Meanwhile, Cecil Kirby, a Toronto biker who did enforcement work for Rocco Remo Commisso and Cosimo Commisso of Toronto, said the Commisso brothers wanted to kill Violi. Others who wanted him dead included sup-porters of the Sicilian wing of the Montreal Mob led by Nicolo "Nick" Rizzuto of Montreal. Violi tried in vain to get permission to have Rizzuto killed in the early 1970s, but senior mobsters in New York City balked. Ultimately, it was the Americans who called the shots for the Canadian Mob.

However, when Rizzuto supporters sought to have Violi killed, the New Yorkers gave the go-ahead.

Violi was gunned down in 1978 during dinner at his ice-cream shop and pool room on Jean Talon Street. His hooded killers used a rare twelve-gauge shotgun made only in a small village in southern Italy. It's widely believed that Violi must have known he would be murdered that night, and that he chose death to running. *See also:* **Natale Brigante, Vincenzo "Vic the Egg" Cotroni, Cecil Kirby, Giacomo Luppino, 'Ndrangheta, Nicolo "Nick" Rizzuto; Domenic, Francesco "Frank," and Rocco Violi.**

Violi, Rocco: Marked for Murder – A sniper ended his life on October 17, 1980, as he sat at the kitchen table of his east-end Montreal home with his wife and two children. One shot had been fired from an office window across the street, hitting Violi in the heart. The killer was never caught but police found the gun, a .308 rifle with telescopic sight.

He was the last of the Violi brothers in Montreal, and he must have known he was marked for death. Two of his brothers had been murdered before him, and killers had tried to kill him months earlier, but the attempt was bungled when a man on a motorcycle hit him with only a few shotgun pellets in the face and neck.

Violi was twenty when he was convicted in 1960 on an assault charge involving a knife attack on another man and sentenced to six months in

Violi brothers (from left): Francesco, Paolo, and Rocco

jail. He had been in Canada only a year, and was ordered deported because of the criminal conviction. Immigration Minister Ellen Fairclough of Hamilton unexpectedly rescinded the order, putting him on probation and allowing him to remain in Canada. His twin brother, Giuseppe, was ordered deported after a criminal conviction for leaving the scene of an accident, but was later also allowed to remain in Canada.

Giuseppe died in 1970, when his sports car crashed into a bus.

See also: **Natale Brigante, Vincenzo "Vic the Egg" Cotroni, Cecil Kirby, Giacomo Luppino, 'Ndrangheta, Nicolo "Nick" Rizzuto; Domenic, Francesco "Frank," and Paolo, Violi.**

VVT: Toronto Gang – This was the original Sri Lankan gang in the Toronto area, operating out of Etobicoke, with members ranging in age from their early teenage years to men in their thirties.

The gang was formed in the early 1990s and named for Valvettithurai, a northern Sri Lankan town. Although federal authorities have claimed that some Toronto gang members are linked to fighting between the Tamil Tigers and the People's Liberation Organization of Tamil Eelam back in Sri Lanka, Toronto detectives who track the local gangs believe the rivalry is Canadian-born.

They soon had a rivalry with another Sri Lankan group named AK Kannan, alluding to the street name of a leader and his love for the AK-47 assault weapon.

There was a brief truce in the gang war in 1998 after community members brokered a peace deal in a Thornhill mosque. But a homicide a year later renewed the fighting.

Gang members targeted investigators as well as other gang members. Gang members were seen in police-division parking lots, videotaping the licence plates of officers' personal vehicles. One officer had his truck stolen and torched.

See also: **AK Kannan.**

Chanh Thong Vo: Fatal Dissing – Gerrard Street East near Broadview Avenue in Toronto's Chinatown East resembled a war zone the night Chanh Thong Vo died. Dozens of early-morning diners witnessed his murder outside the Jun Jun Seafood Restaurant at 3:30 a.m. on December 17, 1995, as Vo was cut down in a hail of bullets and two other men were injured. The killers fled, leaving Vo, twenty-four, lying face down on the street, an abandoned AK-47 assault rifle beside him.

Vo knew this murder weapon well. Easy to clean and rarely jamming, the AK-47 had been the weapon of choice of the Viet Cong and other guerrilla groups, and Vietnamese gang members in Toronto had little difficulty getting them on Native reserves in Ontario and Quebec.

Vo was a minor but violent member of Toronto's Vietnamese gangs, known on Toronto's Chinatown streets as Tommy or No Wang Vo, because, four years before his death, he accidentally shot off part of his penis with the 45-calibre handgun he kept stuffed down the front of his baggy blue jeans.

Vo was born in Vietnam, after his parents fled there from mainland China to escape Communist persecution before his birth. Fluent in both Vietnamese and Chinese, he spent time in an Asian refugee camp before his family finally arrived in Canada as "boat people."

Asian crime specialists say that many North American Vietnamese gang ties were cemented in refugee camps in Hong Kong, Malaysia, and Singapore in the 1970s and 1980s.

Vo became known to police while still in his early teens. First, he delivered drugs and conducted petty robberies, then moved on to more violent crimes such as extortion and assault with a weapon.

He spent much of his time in Toronto as a hired gun for Chinese gangs, heading a small gang of three or four Vietnamese thugs. His group, like most Vietnamese gangs, had no name.

Police arrested twenty-year-old Tien Dung Duong for the murder after hearing that the shooting spree was in retaliation for "a physical altercation" earlier that evening at a karaoke bar. In his first-degree murder trial, witnesses were extremely nervous. Terrified of retaliation, one of the original witnesses who had identified Duong as the gunman was cited for contempt for refusing to answer even questions by defence lawyer Jack Pinkofsky.

Duong unsuccessfully tried to pin the murder on a phantom gunman. Mr. Justice John O'Driscoll sentenced Duong to life for first-degree murder and two counts of attempted murder, with these words: "Mr. Duong, you killed Mr. Vo. You blew him away for dissing you on your own turf. I cannot come to any other conclusion but that you are a very vicious, remorseless killer. It's bad enough that you killed, but then you put forward this phony defence."

Volpe, Paul: Mob Fox – During the summer of 1980, a stranger appeared at the door of an associate of mobster Paul Volpe in Woodbridge north of Toronto. The homeowner was away with Volpe on a trip to New Jersey, so the stranger spoke to his wife. He said he was from the "Philadelphia Church" and looking for donations. "When you come to visit the church, you're expected to make donations," he told her, before she panicked and slammed the door.

The stranger climbed into a black car, where three other strangers sat, then drove off, knowing Volpe would clearly understand the message. Volpe had been aggressively expanding into the new casinos of Atlantic City and this didn't sit well with the Mob in nearby Philadelphia.

The visit and the talk of church donations were Mob-ese for "Philadelphia boss Nicky Scarfo and his associates in Philadelphia expect a cut of any money Paul Volpe makes in Atlantic City."

True to form, Volpe simply ignored the warning. He told his associate, a former Italian police officer, to return to Atlantic City and get back to business.

Volpe was used to outfoxing his rivals. His name means "fox" in Italian and, like a fox, Volpe was clever and a loner by nature. He was born in Toronto, the son of an impoverished tailor with no organized-crime involvement. While details of his life could be collected without too much difficulty, Volpe remained a hard man to figure out. Fellow mobsters considered him troublesome and distant, a man who jealously guarded his secrets and the fortune he had gained through loansharking, gambling, and labour racketeering. They eyed him suspiciously because of his moral position, rare in the Mob. He looked upon lucrative businesses like pornography, prostitution, and narcotics trafficking as dirty and beneath his dignity.

Volpe eschewed Toronto's Mob enclaves in Woodbridge, and on St. Clair Avenue West and College Street. Instead, he lived apart in Schomberg, northwest of Toronto, in a flood-lit Tudor mansion with a turret that he had bought from a judge. A large Canadian flag flew outside the manor that, fittingly, was called Fox Hill.

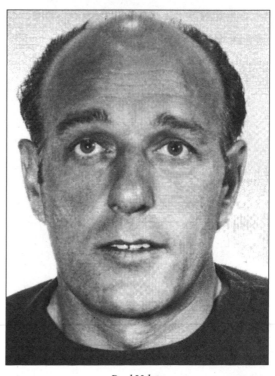

Paul Volpe

He was the youngest of five brothers, but clearly the family's natural leader. His wife, Lisa Dalholt, of Danish background, was a liberated, intelligent woman who built her own career, rising from modelling to become a fashion buyer for the upscale fashion store Creeds. And Volpe did something astounding in the macho world of the Mob, telling stunned associates he had had a homosexual fling as a young man with an actor who had won modest fame in a Shirley Temple movie.

Mobsters carefully mark their territories, like animals of the wild, but Volpe often roamed far afield in search of profit. He was involved in grand casinos in Port-au-Prince, Haiti, in the early 1960s and once met with the prime minister and the minister of tourism for Dominica in the hope of setting up his own casinos there. Volpe himself also pumped money into a failed takeover in Haiti that aligned him with the Ku Klux Klan.

Volpe's travels came to an end on November 13, 1983, when he was found in the trunk of his wife's leased BMW in the parking garage at Terminal 2 of Toronto (now Pearson) International Airport, with his tall body curled in a fetal position. The killer was never found. One theory was that it was "Johnny Pops" Papalia, a rival from within his own group. That move eliminated a rival for Papalia and ensured greater harmony with the Philadelphia Mob. It was Volpe's trusted driver, Pietro Scarcella, who delivered him to his killers after the two enjoyed breakfast together, police said.

"It's not your enemies you have to worry about," Staff Sgt. Ron Sandelli of Toronto police said. "It's your friends that do you in."

See also: **Giacomo Luppino, Stefano Magaddino, Enio Mora, John "Johnny Pops" Papalia, Pietro Scarcella.**

Vor v zakonye – *See* **Vyacheslav Kirillovich Ivankov, National Hockey League, Joseph Sigalov, Vyacheslav Marakulovich Sliva.**

W

Waisberg Commission: "Dark Underbelly" –
The Waisberg Inquiry was established to probe
a wave of violence that had swept the Ontario
construction business between 1968 and 1973,
and the 1974 report of County Court Judge
Harry Waisberg was as thick as a cement foundation block, filling 770 pages in two volumes
entitled, "Report of the Royal Commission on
Certain Sectors of the Building Industry."

Those weighty volumes were jammed with
what the judge called "a sinister array of characters." In the words of Geoffrey Stevens of the
Globe and Mail, Waisberg "laid open the dark
underbelly of the Ontario construction industry," cataloging assaults, shootings (including an
incident where a submachine gun strafed a con-
struction-company office), bombings, theft, and
sudden death, and the recruitment of enforcers
with underworld connections to people like
mobster Paul Volpe.

Waisberg's reports were rife with accounts of
bribery. Union business agents had been bribed
by employers to supply them workers at low
wages. Subcontractors had paid off contractors
for work, and companies had bribed civil servants to throw jobs their way with liquor, gift
certificates, porcelain and crystal, a stereo,
a Bahamas vacation, a silver tea service, and a
colour television.

In the words of plaster-and-drywall contractor Anthony Cesaroni, "The construction business is not a lily-white business, as we all know."

See also: **Giacomo Luppino, John "Johnny
Pops" Papalia, Pietro Scarcella, Paul Volpe.**

Walkley Crew: Mean Street – This Montreal
Jamaican street gang took its name from tree-
lined Walkley Avenue, where it set up eight crack
houses in the early 1990s.

At its peak, the crew had only eighteen
members, but they made a violent impact on the
underworld. The crew ceased operations in June
1994, after its leader Delroy Anthony Hunter
stepped out of a shoe store with a pair of suede
desert boots in hand and was shot dead with a
bullet to the head.

At the time, his crew was fighting for
dominance with three other Montreal
Jamaican–Canadian drug gangs, most of
whom were based in the downtown and
Côte-des-Neiges districts. Two days after
his death, a carload of men fired shots in the air
in the parking lot of a McDonald's restaurant
near Walkley Avenue, signalling that the territory now belonged to the rival gang Grand
Massive.

Violence was a trademark of the gangs, who
were made up largely of illegal immigrants or
permanent residents (formerly called landed
immigrants) or refugee claimants. Most gang
members had lived in Canada less than ten
years. Most of Hunter's crew came to Canada
from Jamaica in their late teens, sponsored by
relatives or on student visas.

Jamaican drug gangs first surfaced in the United States and Canada in the 1970s, as members fled political violence in their island country. By the time of Hunter's murder, a dozen of his fellow gang members had been ordered deported. Three of them had actually been deported, with the rest either serving prison terms or appealing deportation orders. *See also:* **Robert Blackwood, Jamaican Posses.**

Wallace, Charles – *See* **Michipicoten.**

Ward, David: Disgraced Stock Promoter – The Vancouver man left the headlights on and the engine running when he double-parked his Nissan Pathfinder on a quiet suburban street in the east end of Vancouver early on the evening of January 14, 1997.

Whoever he was meeting, he didn't plan on staying long.

Ward was still behind the wheel when someone shot him in the head at close range, execution-style. The killer didn't bother to take the cash or the jewellery Ward was wearing.

Ward had been a key figure in one of the Vancouver Stock Exchange's most notorious scandals. In May 1984, Ward and Toronto promoter Edward Carter cut a lucrative deal with a San Antonio, Texas, mutual-fund manager to trade fifteen different stocks on the Vancouver Stock Exchange controlled by Carter and Ward.

Between them, they had 147 accounts that bought and sold shares from one another at increasingly inflated prices. This gave the investing public a false impression of prosperity and sucked many of them into the market.

Their scam went undetected for twelve months, and exactly how much money Ward made was impossible to determine, as funds were funnelled into overseas bank accounts.

Ward eventually pleaded guilty to stock-manipulation and bribery charges, and was given three years. Less than a year later, he was released and back on the streets of Vancouver, working ties with companies listed on the Alberta Stock Exchange.

Police investigated whether Ward's murder was linked to the 1990 slaying of stock promoter John "Ramon" Ray Ginnetti, but no charges were laid and Ward's death remains a mystery. *See also:* **Vancouver Stock Exchange.**

Warriors – *See* **Manitoba Warriors.**

Watts, Terrance Frederick: Shady Trade – He had a blemished reputation on the Vancouver Stock Exchange even before he tried to buy $731,000 of hashish from an undercover RCMP detective posing as a drug dealer. The case was dismissed on constitutional grounds, but Watts still had to worry about his alleged debts to the Hells Angels. In August 2003, Watts, forty-one, was found shot to death in the trunk of his car in Vancouver's Chinatown. *See also:* **Vancouver Stock Exchange.**

Webmasters: Net Worth – Barrel-chested Frederick Landry-Hétu certainly looked like a biker, with his leather vest and scruffy beard. However, the Hells Angels value him not because of his brawn, but rather for his computer smarts, which made him the Angels' Webmaster for the Canadian East Coast.

It was Landry-Hétu, with a degree in computer engineering, who was credited with building the club's database of information on members of the rival Rock Machine, which has since merged with the American-based Bandidos.

In September 1999, Landry-Hétu was arrested in the Toronto suburb of Mississauga on drug-trafficking and weapons charges. During a search of his home, police found nearly two kilograms of cocaine, $76,000 in cash, a list of drug debts, fake identification, weapons and ammunition, Hells Angels paraphernalia, a credit-card-embossing machine, and a number of computers.

Landry-Hétu was eventually convicted and sentenced in 2000 to close to four and a half years in prison. During his incarceration at a medium-security Ontario prison, sources say he was discovered with what police grimly called his "cellphone." It is not unheard of for guards to discover bikers with phones in their cells. What startled guards was that Landry-Hétu had managed to hook up his computer to a satellite dish, devising a homemade Internet connection.

Sylvain "Sly" Grégoire was Landry-Hétu's Webmaster counterpart in the rival Bandidos. Before the Bandidos gang member was shot to death in August 2001 in his Montreal car dealership, Automobiles Sans Tracas (Automobiles without Trouble), Grégoire had stumbled onto a shocking discovery.

The thirty-three-year-old found a CD-ROM containing the names of 614 people connected to the Rock Machine/Bandidos gang in Quebec and Ontario. Compiled by the Angels, the CD-ROM contained a wealth of information – names, dates of birth, addresses, licence-plate numbers, social-insurance numbers, driver's-licence identifications, addresses of wives and mistresses, favourite haunts, a physical description, photos, and members' status in the Rock/Bandidos organization. In short, it was a *Michelin's Guide* for a Hells Angels' hit man.

The CD-ROM also contained information on more than a dozen businesses friendly with the Bandidos in Ontario and Quebec, in addition to information on other rivals in the criminal underworld, including the Outlaws motorcycle gang and the Sicilian Mafia.

Grégoire was fatally shot shortly after discovering this information, and police have made no arrests in the murder. By the time he was slain, the CD-ROM had already been copied and passed on to other gang members.

He must have known that running an outlaw Web site was a dangerous business, as the previous Bandidos Webmaster, Réal "Tintin" Dupont, was murdered in January 2001. Police found computer files of information on the Hells Angels in the forty-one-year-old's home, but, again, no arrests were made.
See also: **Claude De Serres.**

West End Gang: Irish Mafia – They don't have elaborate rituals like the Mafia and Triads, or coast-to-coast reach, like the Hells Angels biker gang. However, the West End Gang does have considerable clout on the waterfront of Montreal.

In the first half of the twentieth century, they were known simply as the Irish gang. They grew in strength through the 1960s, through truck hijackings, kidnapping, and armed robbery.

However, the gang became a top-level power in the underworld in the 1970s when it got into large-scale importation of hashish and cocaine through the Montreal dockyards. At the same time, the gang nurtured contacts in Colombia, the United States, and Europe.

The gang has about 150 individuals members, many drawn from the bleak streets of the Pointe St. Charles district near the Lachine Canal. They were once known simply as the Irish Gang, and never developed a strict Mafia-like hierarchy. Instead, the gang has a series of captains who run separate crews.

Today, the West End Gang sits alongside the Mafia and Hells Angels on the "Consortium," fixing the price of drugs for the wholesale and retail markets. Often the gangs work together importing drugs through the port, and their work was made easier in 1997 when the federal government disbanded the national ports police, which specialized in waterfront corruption.
See also: **Gerald Matticks, Allan "The Weasel" Ross, Frank Peter "Dunie" Ryan, Claude Savoie.**

Whisky Runners: Prairie Plague – Until the North-West Mounted Police was established in 1873, whisky runners roamed the West at will, trading rotgut booze for furs, robes, and horses.

In his book *Firewater*, author Hugh Dempsey wrote that hundreds of Native peoples died in what is now southern Alberta between 1870 and 1875 as a result of the illegal whisky trade. Deaths came from drunken quarrels, from bullets fired by whisky traders, by freezing while drunk, and from the noxious whisky itself.

Dempsey noted that chiefs lost their authority and families disintegrated, with children suffering abandonment and neglect, while whisky traders John J. Healy, Al Hamilton, I.G. Baker and Company, and T.C. Power and Brother each pulled in some $50,000 a month.

Part of the blame for the sweeping negative effects on the Blackfoot people goes to the fact that the Canadian government didn't bring in any law enforcement after it purchased what is now Alberta from the British government in 1869.

About that time, to the south, there had been rumblings that Washington was about to shut down the whisky trade, and now Montana whisky peddlers needed new markets, which they found across the border in Canada.

When the North-West Mounted Police finally arrived in 1874, at least fifty whisky-trading posts existed north of the border, with names like Fort Standoff, Robber's Roost, and Fort Slideout. Their trade of rotgut liquor caused enormous misery on the Blackfoot reserve, which spanned the modern-day Montana and Alberta border.

They were seen as a politically destabilizing force, and the North-West Mounted Police were formed in large measure to bring them under control. The force assembled at Dufferin, Manitoba, in the summer of 1874, and then some three hundred officers marched out toward the Rocky Mountain Foothills, looking for whisky forts and traders. By 1875, the Mounties had set up Fort Macleod on the banks of the Oldman River, along with outposts in Fort Saskatchewan, Fort Calgary, and Fort Walsh.
See also: **Al Hamilton, Fort Whoop-Up, Wolfers.**

Winterhalder, Edward Warren: Don't Bomb the Messenger – Immigration officials didn't accept his argument that the Canadian government should welcome the American biker as a messenger of peace. Winterhalder, a top member of the U.S.-based Bandidos biker gang, wanted to cross the border freely, despite his criminal

record and reputed ties to organized crime.

Winterhalder argued in 2001 that he should be welcomed into Canada to visit newly created Bandidos chapters, saying the Bandidos actually calmed the Quebec biker war that had killed some 160 people since 1994. The Bandidos absorbed the Rock Machine gang in December 2000, and hostilities with the Angels cooled but were not extinguished.

Winterhalder and a driver were waved through when they crossed on January 5, 2001, at Fort Erie, Ontario. They drove on to Kingston to oversee the induction of about sixty probationary members, mostly former Rock Machine bikers.

Shortly afterwards, police arrested Winterhalder, saying he had entered the country illegally by not identifying himself as a gang member to the border guard. They also argued that he posed a danger to the public because of his alleged links to organized crime. Immigration officers wanted to detain Winterhalder for up to six months, so they could have time to look into criminal allegations against the biker, but an adjudicator quashed the government's motion, saying the forty-six-year-old single father should not be separated for so long from his daughter and his construction business in Oklahoma.
See also: **Bandidos, Hells Angels, Nomads, Rock Machine.**

Wolfers: Poisonous Relationship – Wolf pelts were worth plenty of money in the late nineteenth century, and the wolfers had an easy way of killing their prey. They would simply poison a buffalo and then poison the carcass with strychnine. The wolves would die when they fed on it.

Not surprisingly, the Native peoples of the plains hated this practice, since they respected wolves and were also upset that the poisoned buffalo killed their own dogs.

Meanwhile, the wolfers were upset at the whisky traders, who sold Natives repeating rifles, which made them a far more dangerous enemy.

One of the leading wolfers of the day was a man named Harry Taylor, whose Native name, Kamoose, meant "Squaw Thief." In the summer of 1872, Taylor rode out from his base at Fort Spitzee in what is now southern Alberta with a band of about ten men, who called themselves the Spitzee Cavalry.

The "cavalry" forced whisky traders to sign pledges to end the arms trade, but when they reached Fort Whoop-Up, the biggest arms-trader on the plains, its leader, Johnny Healy, called them mad dogs and refused to promise anything. Then Healy told them he had a cannon trained on the fort, and would have it blown up with them inside. Another version of the story is that Healy held a lit cigar over a powder keg, and threatened to ignite it, if the wolfers didn't come around to his way of thinking. At that point, the wolfers agreed that they were all in the business of making money off of the Indians, and returned to poisoning buffalo.

Business interests in Fort Benton, Montana, backed both the wolfers and whisky traders. That's where American and Canadian wolfers were heading in the spring of 1873, when their horses were stolen by Indians, who considered this sport.

The wolfers were furious that they had to complete the trip on foot. Thirteen of them got horses and chased the Indians to Cypress Hills, in southern Saskatchewan. They lost sight of their quarry, but near Battle Creek they found another band of Assiniboines, led by Chief Little Soldier.

The wolfers started that first Sunday of May with a whisky breakfast. There had been another horse theft, and by the time the liquid meal was over, the wolfers were furious. They went to the Assiniboine camp of Little Soldier, who told them the animal had probably wandered off.

A battle followed shortly afterwards, the Indians using muzzle loaders and bows and arrows, while the wolfers opened fired with high-powered repeating rifles. When the fighting was over, some thirty Natives and one wolfer lay dead, and the head of Little Soldier was mounted on a pole. The wolfers also tore apart the camp and abused Native women and children.

Back in Fort Benton, the slaughter was called a great victory, and the wolfers were hailed in the local press as "thirteen Kit Carsons." Canadian newspapers described the raid as a criminal assault of the Canadian West, and pressured Ottawa to do something.

The North-West Mounted Police were formed, as people around Fort Benton agitated for an outright invasion of Western Canada.
See also: **Fort Whoop-Up, Whisky Runners.**

Wolverine: Crime Biters – This special Quebec anti-gang squad included the RCMP, the Sûreté du Québec, and the Montreal police. It was established after eleven-year-old Daniel Desrochers was killed on August 9, 1995, by a biker's bomb in the peak of the Hells Angels–Rock Machine biker war.

Although racked by serious police in-fighting between the Montreal police and the Sûreté du Québec, the Wolverine squad, with its budget of some $5 million, eventually helped contain the bikers. Some members of the Wolverine squad considered containment the best they could hope for, grumbling that an outright victory was unrealistic.
See also: **Maurice "Mom" Boucher, Daniel Desrochers, Nomads, Red Zone, Rock Machine.**

Woody the Lion: Four-Legged Biker – The residents of a farmhouse just north of Toronto said, in January 2001, that they would like to be thought of as average pet owners.

However, their pet was a declawed, neutered eighty-hundred-pound African lion named Woody. And the pet owners at a compound on Jane Street, about ten minutes north of Canada's Wonderland were members of the Loners motorcycle club, referred to by police as criminal bikers and occasional associates of the Hells Angels.

Woody the Biker Lion (Ken Faught, Toronto Star)

"He's more like a dog or a domesticated cat," a woman who did not wish to be identified said during a visit by the *Toronto Star*. "He wants you to play with him, pet him just like a housepet."

"The only thing is, he's eight hundred pounds," cautioned a Loners member. "You don't want him to jump on you." The bikers didn't normally give tours of their grounds, but they were appealing for public sympathy, as local authorities tried to take away their pet.

The jungle beast had been a club pet since he was a three-week-old cub, the Loner said, adding authorities have known about him since a June 1998 raid by the Ontario Provincial Police on a previous gang clubhouse on Rutherford

Road, near Highway 400. Woody was not put behind bars by police after that raid netted police some $11,000 worth of heroin.

During the reporter's visit, the bikers noted that Woody got regular visits from a veterinarian, dined on at least ten pounds of beef and chicken daily, and had two separate sheds for shelter and privacy. A biker said he could not comprehend why local authorities wanted to take away Woody. "Tell me, what is the big issue?" the biker asked.

He said that Woody was named after a biker who originally owned him, who was killed in a motorcycle accident. "It was given to him as a gift. I don't know exactly how he got him."

Woody had been neutered and had no mane as a result. He had also been declawed, and the bikers have made a point of making sure he has never got the taste of warm blood during feedings. "He's never had anything live given to him and never will," said the biker.

The 0.9-acre biker compound was surrounded by a locked 3.5-metre-tall gate with barbed wire on top and Woody was locked inside a steel-framed cage inside that fence. The Loner dismissed the suggestion that Woody the lion was there for security, pointing to his solidly built cage and asking, "Now, can he do guard duty when he's in a cage?"

Eventually, the bikers lost their court fight and Woody was transferred to a non-biker compound in the Barrie area in Ontario's cottage country. The Loners faded from the landscape with the arrival of the Hells Angels en masse into Ontario in December 2000.

Y

YBM – **Dirty-Money Magnet** – YBM Magnex International Inc., which sold bicycles and industrial magnets, proved attractive for investors until the FBI raided its head office in Pennsylvania in May 1998. Trading of its shares on the Toronto Stock Exchange was halted and never resumed, leaving investors with millions of dollars in losses.

Things only got worse in November 1999, when, in Toronto, the Ontario Securities Commission (OSC) charged YBM with violating Canadian securities laws. By that point, the magnet-maker had been linked by American authorities to a possible Russian money-laundering plot.

The OSC alleged that YBM filed a prospectus in 1997 that "failed to contain full, true, and plain disclosure of all material facts relating to the securities offered." Specifically, the company failed to disclose it was under investigation by the U.S. Attorney General's Office.

That American investigation included a hard look at how billions of dollars moved through several accounts at the Bank of New York. In June 1999, YBM Magnex International Inc. pleaded guilty to conspiracy to commit securities and mail fraud, and the corporation agreed to pay a $3-million fine and make restitution to thousands of defrauded shareholders.

The criminal investigation by the Organized Crime Strike Force of the U.S. Attorney's Office in Philadelphia "may involve or relate to the possible links between YBM and certain alleged organized-crime members," according to the statement. Names weren't provided. A forensic audit also uncovered a version of the company's books that showed "sales to nonexistent U.S. customers."

Among the YBM directors was former Ontario premier David Peterson, but he and the other directors said they were innocent of any wrongdoing. Some of their lawyers argued that, because of the OSC's police contacts, its staff should have known as much, if not more, about the alleged Russian Mob connections as the directors and officers of the firm. Still, the OSC allowed the YBM prospectus to be issued and the share sale to go ahead.

Yuetch, Dutch Henry – *See* **Dutch Henry.**

Z

Zangari, Giovanni and Saverio: Project Oaf – These two brothers from London, Ontario, thought they were setting up their own cell, or 'Ndrina, of the 'Ndrangheta of the Calabrian underworld in 1985, and had grand plans of then approaching the *crimini* (ruling body) in Toronto for recognition.

In fact, they were giving RCMP undercover officer Const. John Persichetti an upclose view of their operations in what police indelicately called Project Oaf. The undercover officer became the first police officer in Canada to take the secret Calabrian Mafia oath when the brothers performed an induction ceremony with him in a tiny plaza, in the back of a greasy spoon in south London.

See also: **'Ndrangheta.**

Zig Zag Crew: "Surfers on Steroids" – On the night of February 12, 2002, a Winnipeg police

Ralph "Junior" Moir, Zig Zag Crew, Stony Mountain Penitentary, Manitoba (Lucas Oleniuk, Toronto Star)

officer was in her home in the North Kildonan district when someone threw a chunk of concrete through her front window. She switched on the lights, and two men ran from her lawn, leaving behind several gas-filled Molotov cocktails. On another occasion, her van was torched.

Police eventually arrested members of the Zig Zag Crew for the attacks. The gang was formed in 1997 in Manitoba's Stony Mountain Penitentiary, taking their name from Zig Zag cigarette rolling papers. Soon many members had tattoos on the product's logo, a sailor, and were working as a junior puppet club of the Hells Angels.

Members tended to be from Winnipeg's middle-class south end, rather than inner-city poor, and looked more like "surfers on steroids" than hard-core bikers, according to a police officer. One Zig Zag member, Ralph "Junior" Moir, twenty-four, was Canadian amateur middleweight boxing champion before being sent to Stony Mountain Penitentiary outside Winnipeg to serve a four-year term for a shooting spree in the fall of 2000, which included shooting a fifteen-year-old in the head. (The youth made a full recovery.)

The gang was confined to Manitoba, and mostly Winnipeg. In 2002, it had between twelve and twenty-two members. In early 2003, Winnipeg police laid a total of sixty-eight charges against Zig Zag members in connection with a series of arsons, drive-by shootings, and assault that started in late 2000, and included the attempted firebombing of the police officer's home.

See also: **Los Brovos, Redliners, Spartans, Wolodumyr "Walter" "Nurget" Stadnick.**

Zito, Rocco: Connected from Birth – His father, Domenico, was a senior member of the Vincenzo Crupi group, which, according to Italian court documents, was a criminal group in southern Italy in 1930, while his uncle was leader of a criminal gang in Calabria.

Rocco Zito, who was born in 1928 in Fiumara in Reggio Calabria, Italy, was a 'Ndrangheta cell leader on La Camera di Controllo, also known as the *crimini* (ruling body).

When up-and-coming mobster Paolo Violi was arrested in 1960, running liquor into Toronto, police found Zito's phone number on him. At that time, Zito was a waiter and part-time strong-arm associate of Alberto Agueci.

When Filippo Vendemini of Toronto was murdered, the first call his family made was to Vendemini's old associate Rocco Zito. Zito's other associates in the 1960s in Toronto included Tommaso Buscetta, who later became one of the biggest turncoats in Mafia history.

Zito's brother Giuseppe was murdered in 1975 in a Mafia power struggle in Calabria. His father, Domenico, had hoped to move permanently to Canada, but was refused landed-immigrant status because he had been convicted years earlier of being a member of 'Ndrangheta in Fiumara, Calabria. He was deported and died in 1977.

Rocco Zito was suspected of supplying documents to Sicilian mobsters fleeing crackdowns in the 1980s. In October 1980, his associate Italo Luci was caught with hundreds of passports in his possession.

Zito had a temper as well as nasty connections. He was sentenced on October 8, 1986, to four and a half years in prison after pleading guilty to manslaughter for killing Rosario Sciarrino, sixty. Sciarrino, a former photographer who was then working as a food salesman, borrowed money from Zito to open a photography studio, but couldn't keep up the payments. Zito appeared insulted and clubbed him to death with a liquor bottle.

See also: **Alberto Agueci, Tommaso Buscetta, 'Ndrangheta, Paolo Violi, Michele "Mike" Racco.**

Zizzo, Benedetto: French Connected – His brother, Salvatore, was considered the undisputed Mafia leader of Salemi, Sicily, and Benedetto, born in 1914 and four years younger, was a major underworld figure on the North American side of the ocean.

Benedetto was indicted in 1961 in what became known as the French Connection heroin-trafficking case with major New York City Bonnano family members, including Carmine Galante, for importing seventy-six kilograms of heroin to New York. He was sent to prison again in 1973 after being found guilty in what was then Ontario's biggest drug case. That case involved the importation and distribution of $32-million worth of heroin.

Zizzo, who ran a marble-importing business in Concord, just north of Toronto, was released from prison on full parole in June 1983.

See also: **French Connection, Carmine Galante, John "Johnny Pops" Papalia.**

Benedetto Zizzo

SELECTED BIBLIOGRAPHY

Books

Albini, Joseph L. *American Mafia: Genesis of a Legend*. Meredith Corporation, New York, 1971.

Auger, Michel. Translated by Jean-Paul Murray. *The Biker Who Shot Me: Recollections of a Crime Reporter*. McClelland & Stewart Ltd., Toronto, 2002.

Big Beaver Historical Society. "Happy Valley Happenings: Big Beaver and District." W.A. Print Works Ltd., Regina, 1983.

Blumenthal, Ralph. *Last Days of the Sicilians; At War with the Mafia; The FBI Assault on the Pizza Connection*. Times Books, New York, 1988.

Bonanno, Joseph, with Sergio Lalli. *A Man of Honor: The Autobiography of Joseph Bonanno*. Simon and Schuster, New York, 1983.

Dempsey, Hugh. *Firewater: The Impact of the Whisky Trade on the Blackfoot Nation."* Fifth House, Calgary, 2003.

Dubro, James. *Mob Rule: Inside the Canadian Mafia*. Macmillan of Canada, Toronto, 1985.

———, and Rowland, Robin F. *King of the Mob: Rocco Perri and the Women Who Ran His Rackets*. Viking, Markham, Ontario, 1987.

Edwards, Peter. *Blood Brothers: How Canada's Most Powerful Mafia Family Runs Its Business*. Key-Porter Books, Toronto, 1990.

———. *The Big Sting: The True Story of the Canadian Who Betrayed Colombia's Drug Barons*. Key-Porter Books, Toronto, 1991.

———, and Nicaso, Antonio. *Deadly Silence: Canadian Mafia Murders*. Macmillan of Canada, Toronto, 1993.

Eisenberg, Dennis; Dan, Uri; Landau, Eli. *Meyer Lansky: Mogul of the Mob*. Paddington Press Ltd., New York & London, 1979.

English, T.J. *Born To Kill: The Rise and Fall of America's Bloodiest Asian Gang*. Avon Books, New York, 1995.

Fairman, Bruce. *Moose Jaw: The Early Years*. HomeTown Press, Moose Jaw, 2001.

Friedman, Robert I. *Red Mafiya: How the Russian Mob Has Invaded America*. Berkley Books, New York, 2002.

Gosch, Martin A., and Hammer, Richard. *The Last Testament of Lucky Luciano*. Little, Brown and Company, Boston, Toronto, 1974.

Gray, James H. *Booze: The Impact of Whiskey on the Prairie West*. Macmillan of Canada, Toronto, 1972.

Handelman, Stephen. *Comrade Criminal: Russia's New* Mafiya." Yale, New York, 1997.

Harris, Michael. *Con Game: The Truth about Canada's Prisons*. McClelland & Stewart Ltd., Toronto, 2002.

Horwood, Harold, and Butts, Ed. *Pirates and Outlaws of Canada, 1610-1932*. Doubleday, Toronto, 1984.

Humphreys, Adrian. *The Enforcer: Johnny Pops Papalia, a Life and Death in the Mafia*. HarperCollins Publishers Ltd., Toronto, 1999.

Lacey, Robert. *Little Man: Meyer Lansky and the Gangster Life*. Little, Brown and Company, Boston, Toronto, London, 1991.

Lavigne, Yves. *Hells Angels at War: The Alarming Story Behind the Headlines*. HarperCollins Publishers Ltd., Toronto, 1999.

———. *Hells Angels: Taking Care of Business*. Deneau & Wayne, Toronto, 1987.

———. *Hells Angels: Into the Abyss*. HarperCollins, Toronto, 1996.

Lowe, Mick. *Conspiracy of Brothers: A True Story of Murders, Bikers and the Law*. Seal Books, McClelland-Bantam, Inc., Toronto, 1989.

Maas, Peter. *The Valachi Papers*. G.P. Putnam's Sons, New York, 1968.

Martineau, Pierre. Translated by Jean-Paul Murray. *I Was a Killer for the Hells Angels: The True Story of Serge Quesnel*. McClelland & Stewart Ltd., Toronto, 2003.

Morton, James. *Gangland International: The Mafia and Other Mobs*. Warner Books, a division of Little, Brown and company (U.K.), London, 1998.

Newsome, Eric. *Pass the Bottle: Rum Tales of the West Coast*. Orca Book Publishers, Victoria, B.C., 1995.

Posner, Gerald L. *Warlords of Crime: Chinese Secret Societies, the New Mafia*. Penguin Books, London, England, 1988.

Sher, Julian, and Marsden, William. *The Road to Hell: How the Biker Gangs Are Conquering Canada*. Alfred A. Knopf Canada, Toronto, 2003.

Simard, Réal, and Vastel, Michel. Translated by David Homel. *The Nephew: The Making of a Mafia Hitman*. Prentice-Hall Canada Inc., Scarborough, Ontario, 1988.

Talese, Gay. *Honor Thy Father*. A Fawcett Crest Book, New York City, 1972.

Vallée, Brian. *Edwin Alonzo Boyd: The Story of the Notorious Boyd Gang*. Doubleday Canada, Toronto, 1998.

Zacks, Richard. *The Pirate Hunter: The True Story of Captain Kidd*. Hodderheadline, New York City, 2003.

Articles

August, Oliver. " 'Big Sister' faces extradition for migrant racket," *The Times*. August 24, 2000. Page 14.

Barnes, Edward. "Two-Faced Woman In Search of the American Dream, Thousands Came to Big Sister Ping. The Feds Think She's a Big Crook," *Time Magazine*. July 31, 2000. Page 48.

Blackburn, Maria. "Town poses as scene of the crime; Bowling alley lures 'America's Most Wanted' downtown," *Baltimore Sun*. November 3, 2000. Page 1B.

Brelis, Matthew, and Sennott, Charles M. "Arrest in Hong Kong leaves Sky Dragon grounded in Boston," *Boston Globe*. January 7, 1994. Page 18.

Brown, Barb. "Secret Report on Mobster Slaying Sought: police cleared in handling of gangland murder," *Hamilton Spectator*. October 11, 2003. Page A14.

Brown, DeNeen L. "China's Most Wanted Sits in Canadian Limbo: Accused Smuggler, Fearing Death, Fights Deportation," *Washington Post*. July 25, 2003. Page A 22.

Burdman, Pamela. "Inside the Chinese Smuggling Rings/'Snakeheads' operating a global crime network," *San Francisco Chronicle*. August 23, 1993. Page A1.

Butts, Ed. "Newfoundland celebrates its piracy past," *Toronto Star*. June 18, 1988. Page E.

———. "They're robbing, and they're hoods; Drug lords, like pirates and petty thieves, are not folk heroes," *Globe and Mail*. March 7, 1990. Page A7.

Capeci, Jerry. "Why the Mob Loves Canada: A civilized place where it's still easy to launder money," *Financial Post*. February 1, 1992. Page 10.

Cernetig, Miro, and Mickleburgh, Rod. "Mister Big's big day," *Globe and Mail*. June 23, 2001. Page F4.

Chapman, Art. "The Last Stand: At Adobe Walls in the Panhandle, a little-known battle marked the beginning of the end for Indians on the Texas plains," *Houston Chronicle*. August 2, 1992. Page 10.

Cherry, Paul. "The bosom of a gang: A look at the 9 who pleaded guilty," *Montreal Gazette*. September 12, 2003. Page A2.

Coppola, Lee. "The Withered Arm: The death of the Buffalo Mafia is all about losing its old-fashioned values and falling behind the times," *Buffalo News*. February 2, 1998. Page M6.

Demont, John. "First rum, now drugs: Atlantic coastal security is a constant challenge," *Maclean's*. May 13, 2002. Page 46.

DeStefano, Anthony M. "Picking Up the Trail," *Newsday*. June 1, 2003. Page A6.

Dickie, Mure, and McGregor, Richard. "Xiamen's Red Mansion lifts the lid on China's underworld," *Financial Times*. November 3, 2001.

Dimmock, Gary. "Ottawa's outlaw biker kingpins: Survivors of Quebec's bloody gang wars, these men are leading the way as the Hells Angels establish their franchise in Ontario," *Ottawa Citizen*. June 8, 2002. Page A1.

Edwards, Peter. "Feuds, alliances fire up biker gangs Violent summer as Hells Angels seek Metro links," *Toronto Star*. August 17, 1995. Page A6.

———, and Millar, Cal. "New Gangs terrorize Chinatown," *Toronto Star*. January 13, 1991. Page A1.

Elliott, Héllène. "Harried by the Mob? Reputed crime boss's alleged attempt to rig Olympic skating may be tip of iceberg for international sports," *Los Angeles Times*. August 11, 2002. Page D1.

———. "The NHL: Old Baggage Doesn't Weigh Down Bure With the Panthers," *Los Angeles Times*. October 7, 1999. Page D6.

Ernst, Donna B. "The Sundance Kid in Alberta," *Alberta History*. Autumn 1994.

Ferguson, Jock. "Convicted bomber spends and parties: Living it up before judge's gavel falls," *Globe and Mail*. July 26, 1986. Page A1.

Fife, Robert. "Italy's request 'confidential,' minister says: Alleged Mafia hit man: McLellan tells House she's bound by state rules," *National Post*. March 14, 2001. Page A4.

Frei, Terry. "Kamensky insists mob story 'not true': Avalanche winger still denies ties," *Denver Post*. April 11, 1998. Page D9.

Gelman, Mitch. "The New New Yorkers: A Life on the Skids; Hockey star's ex-aide jailed in extort case," *Newsday*. May 2, 1994. Page A15.

Gordon, Sean. "West End Gang ran. Supplied bikers, street gangs: Linked to crime families and Colombian drug barons," *Montreal Gazette*. December 5, 2002. Page A3.

Ha, Tu Thanh. "Montreal police arrest most-wanted fugitive," *Globe and Mail*. April 19, 2003. Page A1.

——. "Gang fought well-organized war for turf; Grisly details from a Hells Angels trial: fees for killers, shops to make weapons," *Globe and Mail*. September 12, 2003. Page A6.

——. "Jailbirds of a feather ʀᴏᴄᴋ together; Police informants in Quebec, contending that authorities aren't fulfilling their side of the bargain, have formed an association to see to their rights," *Globe and Mail*. April 14, 2004. Page A3.

——. "Misconduct accusations hit Canadian police on two fronts; Hit man says police ignored drug killing," *Globe and Mail*. May 4, 2004. Page A1.

Hall, Neal. "Ex-lawyer wants video link to B.C.," *Vancouver Sun*. November 29, 2002. Page B3.

Harder, James. "Mother of All Snakeheads," *Insight Magazine*. February 5, 2001. Page 18.

Harney, Robert F. "Toronto's Little Italy, 1885-1945," in *Little Italies in North America*, ed. by Robert F. Harney and J. Vincenzo Scarpaci. (Toronto: The Multicultural History Society of Ontario, 1981).

Herbeck, Dan. "Extortion Suspect was on Hit List of ᴋɢʙ, Judge told," *Buffalo News*. April 22, 1994. Page C4.

Hess, Henry. "Who is Dmitri Iakoubovski?," *Globe and Mail*. August 28, 1993. Page A1.

——. "Toronto sex ring not alone: Slavery racket involving Asian females growing in North America, officials say," *Globe and Mail*. September 12, 1997. Page A10.

Humphreys, Adrian. "Mafia charged in slaying of Montreal mobster: 1999 murder: 'George from Canada' made millions importing heroin," *National Post*. August 22, 2003. Page A3.

Jones, Jack, and Yaro, Boris. "Police Seek Eastern Link to Killing L.A. Detectives Suspect Asian Gang Network Is Involved," *Los Angeles Times*. January 7, 1987. Page 15.

Kalogerakis, George. "Matticks tales go around: Court testimony reveals convicted drug supplier's charitable work for poor," *Montreal Gazette*. August 7, 2002. Page A3.

Kasindorf, Martin. "'*Mafiya*' hoods set out to conquer new world; In chaotic post-Soviet era, crime is a leading export," *USA Today*. July 11, 2000. Page A4.

Kennedy, Sarah. "Ottawa Valley connection: Back in the 1940s, a stranger appeared in tiny Quadeville, built a cabin and disappeared. Residents swear he was the infamous Chicago gangster," *Ottawa Citizen*. August 26, 2003. Page B3.

Kornblut, Anne E. "Guilty Pleas Ends Gang Terror Spree; Vietnamese Boss Hunted Down After Years of Violence," *Boston Globe*. January 13, 1998. Page B1.

Legall, Paul. "Hells Angel in Armani: Walter Stadnick, whose designer wardrobe is more befitting a boardroom than a bunker, expanded the Quebec-based Hells Angels into a national organization," *Hamilton Spectator*. March 1, 2004. Page G11.

Leggett, Karby. "Mr. Lai Is at Center of China's Crusade Against Corruption – Beijing Cracked Down When He Went Too Far – Gold Leaf, Jiang's Mercedes," *Asian Wall Street Journal*. November 26, 2001.

Loten, Angus. "Illegal right turn snags top biker," *Montreal Gazette*. April 18, 2003. Page A1.

Lyons, Brendan. "Flight ends for blast suspect," *Albany Times Union*. April 19, 2003. Page A1.

Makin, Kirk. "Murder splits Montreal legal community; Judges, prosecutors avoid Shoofey rites," *Globe and Mail*. October 26, 1985. Page A1.

Marcus, Dunk. "Captain Kidd – pirate or man of honour?" *The Express*. February 1, 2003. Page 38.

Michael, Peter, and Bradford, Sara. "The end of the road for 'Big Sister' Ping," *South China Evening Post*. June 12, 2003. Page 3.

Michaelson, Mike. "French foothold; Tiny islands belonging to France are one of North America's best-kept vacation secrets," *The Spokesman-Review*. January 14, 2001. Page H3.

Millar, Cal, and Edwards, Peter. "How does a hitman say he's sorry?" *Toronto Star*. September 22, 1991. Page D1.

Mitrovica, Andrew. "We warned you, former agent says Refugee hearing backs up the findings contained in secret report, ex-spy insists," *Globe and Mail*. November 30, 2000. Page A9.

Moon, Peter. "The Enforcer: Is powerful Hamilton mobster Johnny Pops muscling his way into Toronto's underworld?," *Globe and Mail*. November 28, 1986. Page A1.

——. "Son of Hamilton bootlegger enjoys the good life," *Globe and Mail*. November 28, 1986. Page A15.

Mudry, Brent. "B.C. Securities Commission–BCSC concerned about Angels as Smith murder toll rises," *Canada Stockwatch*. October 10, 2001.

——. "B.C. Securities Commission–BCSC Eron figure Chambers gets harsh sentence in Miami," *Canada Stockwatch*. December 5, 2003.

——. "B.C. Securities Commission–Net 1 promoter Dekanich killed by biker, court told," *Canada Stockwatch*. July 28, 2003.

Mycio, Mary, and Norwood, Robyn. "Tverdovsky's Mother Kidnap Victim; Hockey: Ordeal ends with her rescue after 11 days. Former coach of NHL player is arrested in Ukraine for alleged involvement in plot," *Los Angeles Times*. March 3, 1996. Page 5.

Neilson-Bonikowsky, Laura. "Early settler sent to Newfoundland to reform himself: John Guy's Cuper's Cove, now known as Cupids, became England's first colony in Canada," *Edmonton Journal*. July 12, 2002. Page C4.

"NHL stars targeted by Russian gangs, committee told." Reuters News. May 15, 1996.

Nolan, Dan. "Rocco Perri Uncovered?" *Hamilton Spectator*, July 5, 2003. Page A1.

O'Hanlon, Terry, and Henry, Ian. "Exclusive – Storm as Yardie Gangsters Sneak Back into Britain," *Sunday Mirror*. July 21, 1996. Page 6.

Olinger, David, and Finley, Bruce. "Alleged mob ties dog Russian immigrant Denver businessman unable to shake officials' suspicions," *Denver Post*. November 22, 1998. A1.

Plafker, Ted, and Pomfret, John. "'Snakeheads'" at Your Service; Smugglers of People Play Big Part in Chinese Town's Economy," *Washington Post*. June 24, 2000. Page A17.

Platt, Leah. "Regulating the global brothel," *American Prospect*. Volume 12, Issue 12. July 2, 2001. Page S10.

Price, S.L. "Hot Shot: Whether the latest rumors link him to the Russian mob or to Anna Kournikova, Panthers scoring sensation Pavel Bure is at the center of attention in gossip-hungry South Florida – and he's loving every minute of it," *Sports Illustrated*. January 31, 2000. Page 56.

Sanger, Daniel. "The Many Lives and Singular Death of Dany Kane," *Saturday Night*, April 2002.

Scovel, Jim. "The Pirate Who Paid for His Pew," *Newsday*. June 28, 1987. Page 19.

Silvester, Norman. "Revealed – Ranking Dread is Yardie crime boss flooding Scotland with crack cocaine," *Scottish Sunday Mail*. March 9, 2003. Page 29.

——. "Yardie boss is king of crack," *Scottish Sunday Mail*. March 9, 2003.

Simons, Paula. "Evidence simply overwhelmed Crown and police: Edmonton's trial of the century a judicial debacle that wasted millions," *Edmonton Journal*. September 13, 2003. Page B1.

Simpson, Cameron. "Kidd had a licence to lord it over pirates," *The Herald*. March 18, 2003. Page 9.

Skelton, Chad. "Sliva admits lying on visa form in bid to enter Canada, Denies allegations at immigration review of involvement in Russian organized crime," *Globe and Mail*. July 23, 1997. Page A8.

Smyth, Mitchell Smyth. "'Girl Bandit' from Ontario lives on in wild west lore," *Toronto Star*. November 23, 1991.

Spears, Toms. "Informer tells all about life as a mob enforcer Mafia Assassin," *Toronto Star*. October 4, 1986. Page M4.

Symonds, William C., and Wolman, Karen, in Rome, with William Marsden in Montreal, John Sweeney and Pete Engardio in Caracas, and bureau reports. "The Sicilian Mafia is Still Going Strong: The alleged drug dealings of the Cuntrera-Caruana clan suggest the Mafia is as virulent as ever," *Business Week*. April 18, 1988. Page 48.

Taylor, Bill. "Wild West characters linked to Canada, eh?" *Toronto Star*. May 11, 1996.

"The Convict Jas. Browne; Preparations for the Execution," *Globe*, March 10, 1862. Page 2.

"The Execution of Browne; His Last Hours; Five Thousand Persons Present; He Declares His Innocence on the Scaffold," *Globe*, March 11, 1862. Page 1.

"The great escapes," *South China Morning Post*. July 23, 2003. Page 14.

Vallée, Brian. "Toronto slaying riddle solved after 55 years – 'Gentleman' bank robber confessed, Chilling murder shows darker side," *Toronto Star*. November 30, 2002.

Wallace, Bill. "Chinese Crime Ring Muscles In/Violent gang moving into state from Canada," *San Francisco Chronicle*. December 1, 1997. Page 1.

Ward, Olivia. "Russian hockey chief slain in 'mafia' hit," *Toronto Star*. April 23, 1997. Page B1.

"Who's afraid of Captain Kidd? – The question," *Sunday Times*. March 23, 2003.

Wilson, Paul. "He was King of the Bootleggers; Perri's final stroll still haunts street," *Hamilton Spectator*. April 16, 1994.

Yanko, Dave. "Big Muddy Badlands," *Virtual Saskatchewan* online magazine.

Zucchi, John E. "Italian Hometown Settlements and the Development of an Italian Community in Toronto. 1875-1935," in *Polyphony* 7 No. 2, pages 54-59 (Toronto: Multicultural History Society of Ontario, 1985).